Shojo Beat

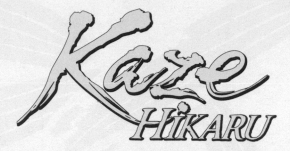

23

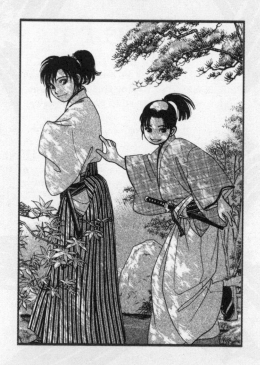

Story & Art by
Taeko Watanabe

Contents

Story Thus Far

It is the end of the Bakufu era, the third year of Bunkyu (1863) in Kyoto. The Shinsengumi is a band of warriors formed to protect the shogun.

Tominaga Sei, the daughter of a former Bakufu *bushi*, joined the Shinsengumi disguised as a boy by the name of Kamiya Seizaburo to avenge her father and brother. She has continued her training under the only person in the Shinsengumi who knows her true identity, Okita Soji, and she aspires to become a true *bushi*.

Saito fell in love with the boy Kamiya, but now he's found out Sei's secret. He tells Okita that he will reveal Sei's identity to the Shinsengumi in order to officially make her his wife. For the first time, Okita and Saito become rivals in love for the girl named Sei.

Sei is gravely wounded while shielding Okita from injury during an intense battle. After witnessing this, Saito realizes the full extent of Sei's feelings for Okita, and at the same time he must acknowledge her achievements as a *bushi*. He decides not to reveal Sei's true gender.

Characters

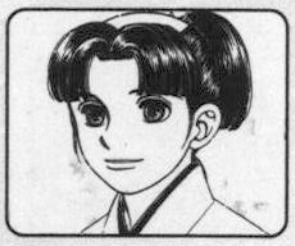

Tominaga Sei
She disguises herself as a boy to enter the Mibu-Roshi. She trains under Soji, aspiring to become a true *bushi*. But secretly, she is in love with Soji.

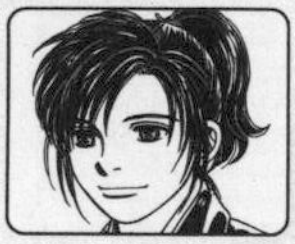

Okita Soji
Assistant vice captain of the Shinsengumi and licensed master of the Ten'nen Rishin-ryu. He supports the troop alongside Kondo and Hijikata and guides Seizaburo with a kind yet firm hand.

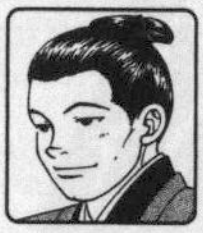

Kondo Isami
Captain of the Shinsengumi and fourth grandmaster of the Ten'nen Rishin-ryu. A passionate, warm and well-respected leader.

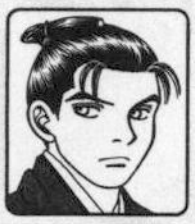

Hijikata Toshizo
Vice captain of the Shinsengumi. He commands both the group and himself with a rigid strictness. He is also known as the "Oni vice captain."

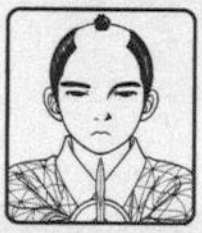

Saito Hajime
Assistant vice captain. He was a friend of Sei's older brother. Sei is attached to him in place of her lost brother.

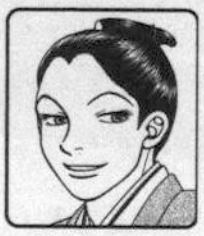

Ito Kashitaro
Councilor of the Shinsengumi. A skilled swordsman and an academic with anti-Bakufu sentiments, he plots to sway the direction of the troop.

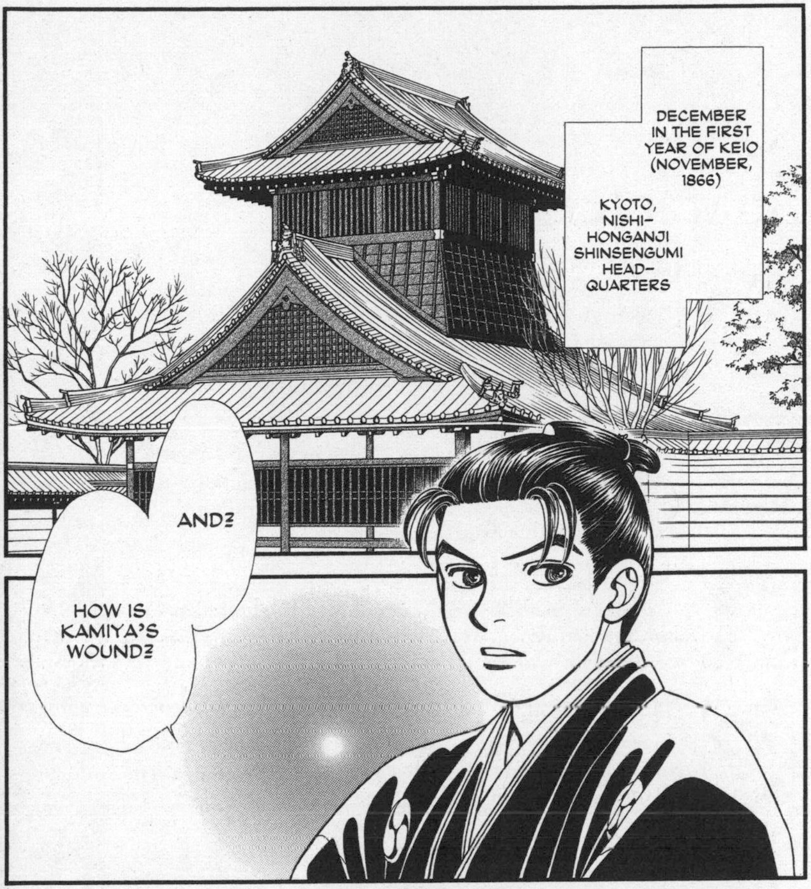
DECEMBER IN THE FIRST YEAR OF KEIO (NOVEMBER, 1866)
KYOTO, NISHI-HONGANJI SHINSENGUMI HEAD-QUARTERS
AND?
HOW IS KAMIYA'S WOUND?

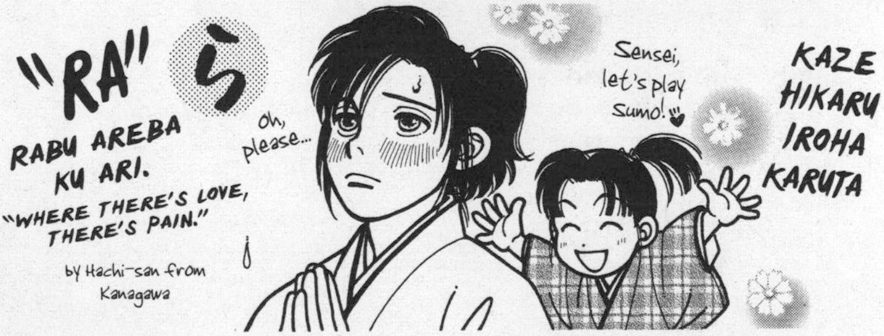
KAZE HIKARU IROHA KARUTA
"RA" ら
RABU AREBA KU ARI.
"WHERE THERE'S LOVE, THERE'S PAIN."
by Hachi-san from Kanagawa
Sensei, let's play sumo!
Oh, please...

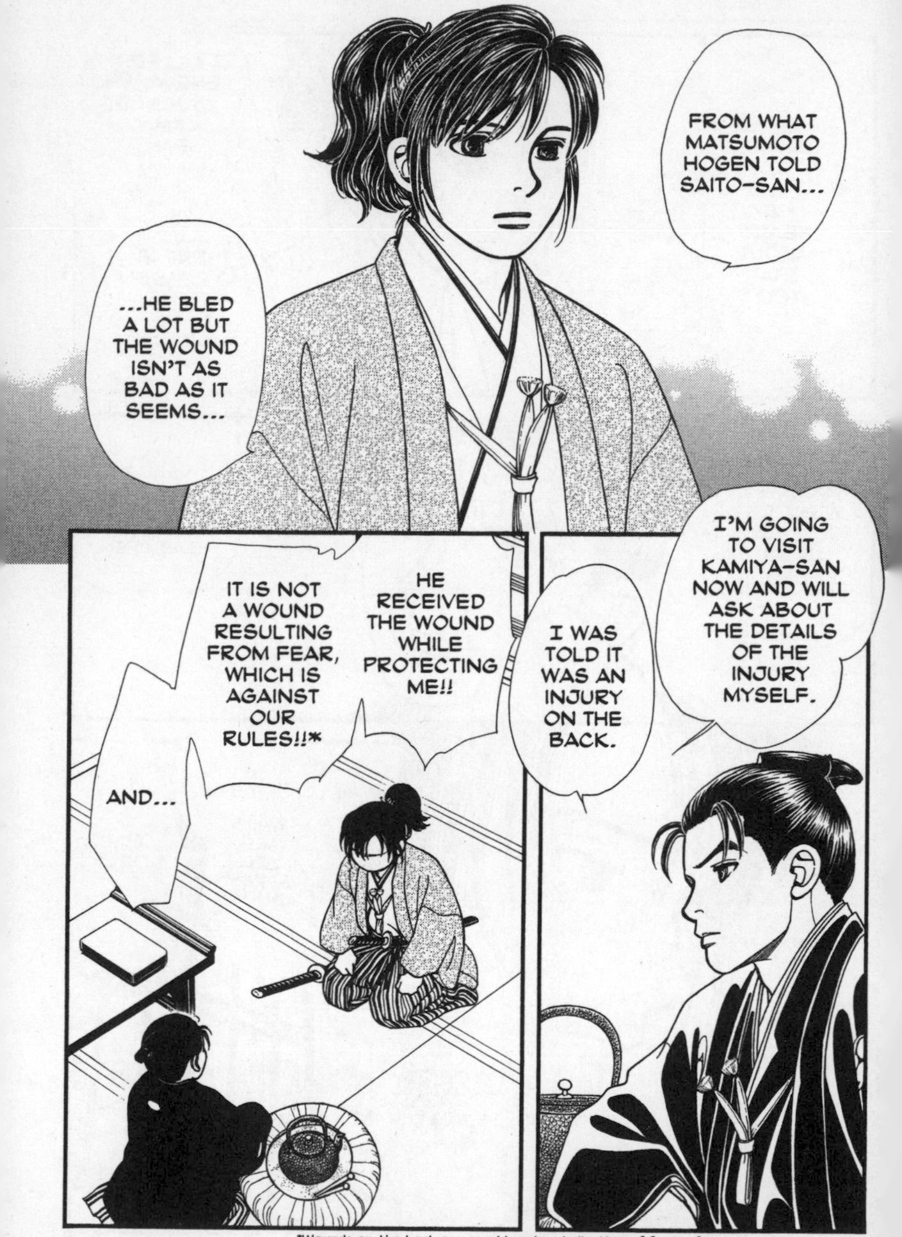
FROM WHAT MATSUMOTO HOGEN TOLD SAITO-SAN...
...HE BLED A LOT BUT THE WOUND ISN'T AS BAD AS IT SEEMS...
I'M GOING TO VISIT KAMIYA-SAN NOW AND WILL ASK ABOUT THE DETAILS OF THE INJURY MYSELF.
I WAS TOLD IT WAS AN INJURY ON THE BACK.
HE RECEIVED THE WOUND WHILE PROTECTING ME!!
IT IS NOT A WOUND RESULTING FROM FEAR, WHICH IS AGAINST OUR RULES!!*
AND...

*Wounds on the back are considered an indication of fleeing from the enemy, and the wounded person will be punished unless they kill their opponent.

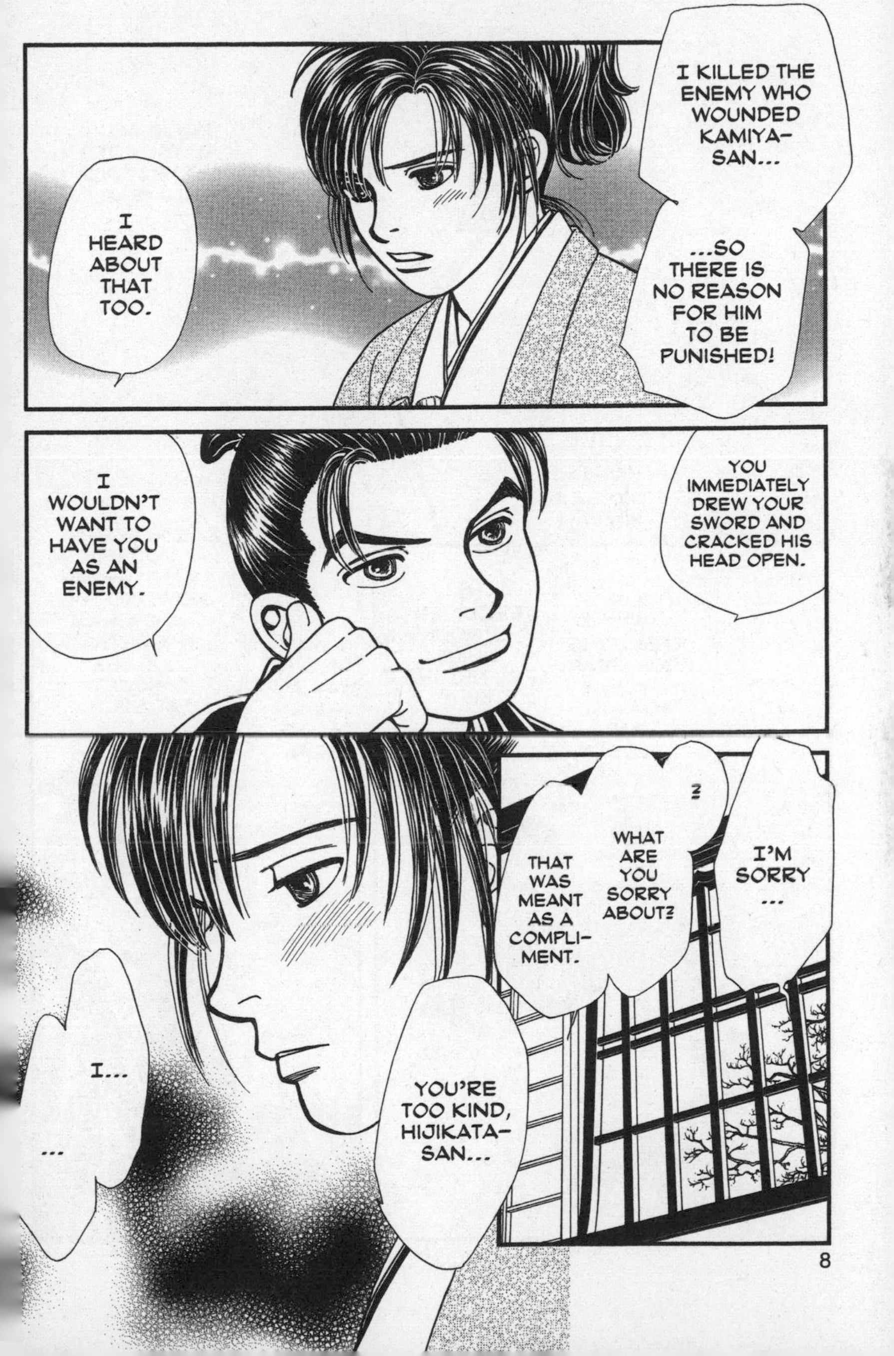
I KILLED THE ENEMY WHO WOUNDED KAMIYA-SAN...
...SO THERE IS NO REASON FOR HIM TO BE PUNISHED!
I HEARD ABOUT THAT TOO.
YOU IMMEDIATELY DREW YOUR SWORD AND CRACKED HIS HEAD OPEN.
I WOULDN'T WANT TO HAVE YOU AS AN ENEMY.
I'M SORRY ...
?
WHAT ARE YOU SORRY ABOUT?
THAT WAS MEANT AS A COMPLIMENT.
YOU'RE TOO KIND, HIJIKATA-SAN...
I... ...

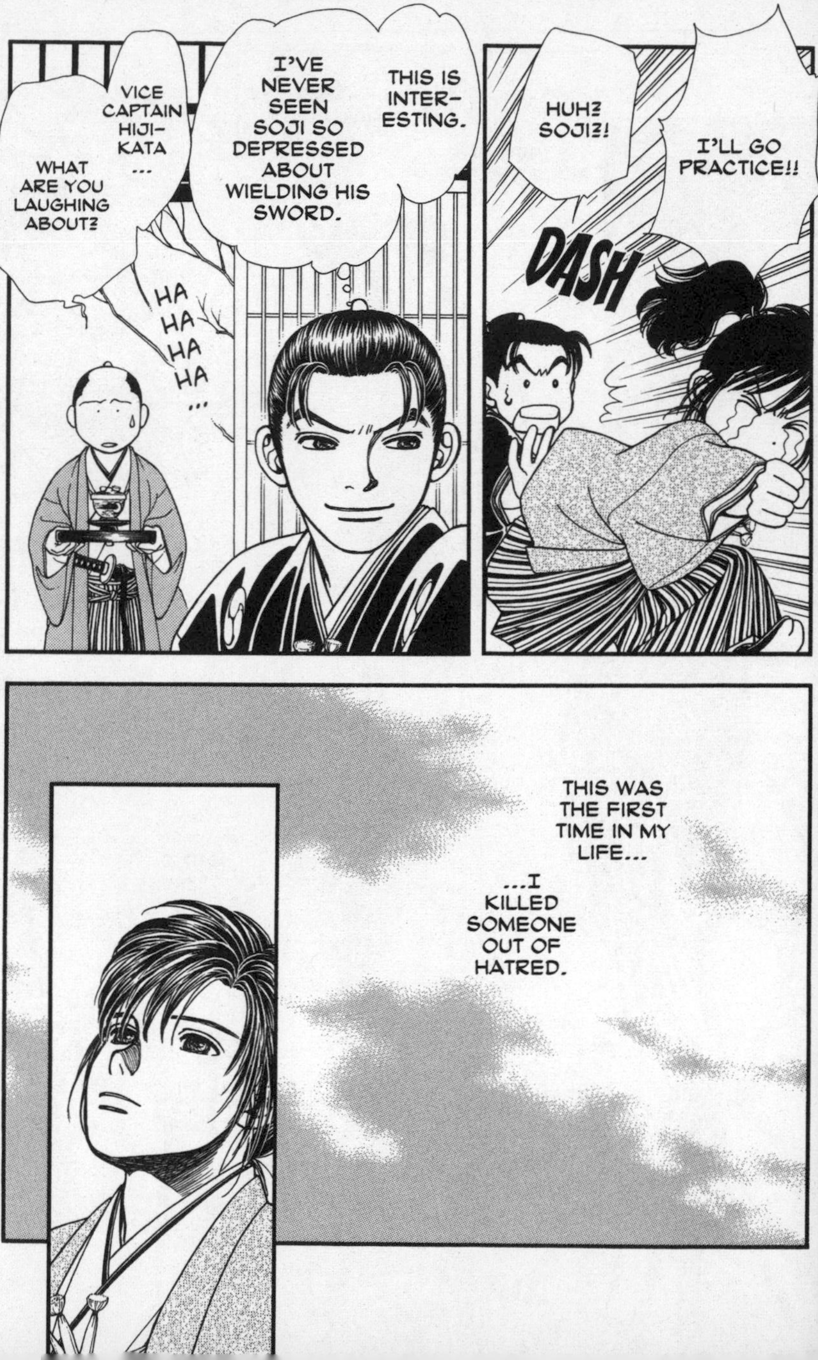
I'LL GO PRACTICE!!
HUH? SOJI?!
DASH
THIS IS INTERESTING.
I'VE NEVER SEEN SOJI SO DEPRESSED ABOUT WIELDING HIS SWORD.
VICE CAPTAIN HIJIKATA...
WHAT ARE YOU LAUGHING ABOUT?
HA HA HA HA...
THIS WAS THE FIRST TIME IN MY LIFE...
...I KILLED SOMEONE OUT OF HATRED.

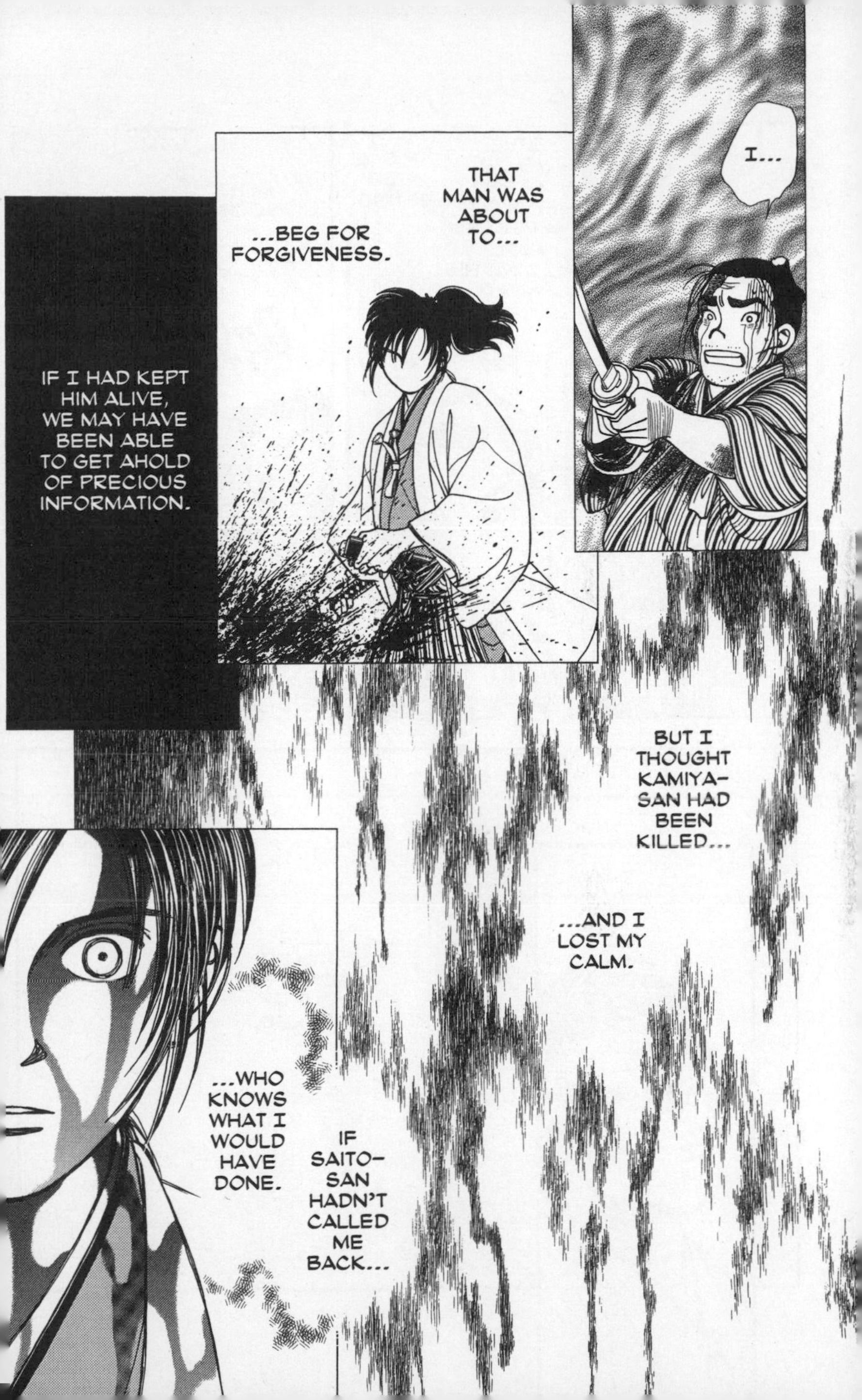
I...
THAT MAN WAS ABOUT TO...
...BEG FOR FORGIVENESS.
IF I HAD KEPT HIM ALIVE, WE MAY HAVE BEEN ABLE TO GET AHOLD OF PRECIOUS INFORMATION.
BUT I THOUGHT KAMIYA-SAN HAD BEEN KILLED...
...AND I LOST MY CALM.
IF SAITO-SAN HADN'T CALLED ME BACK...
...WHO KNOWS WHAT I WOULD HAVE DONE.

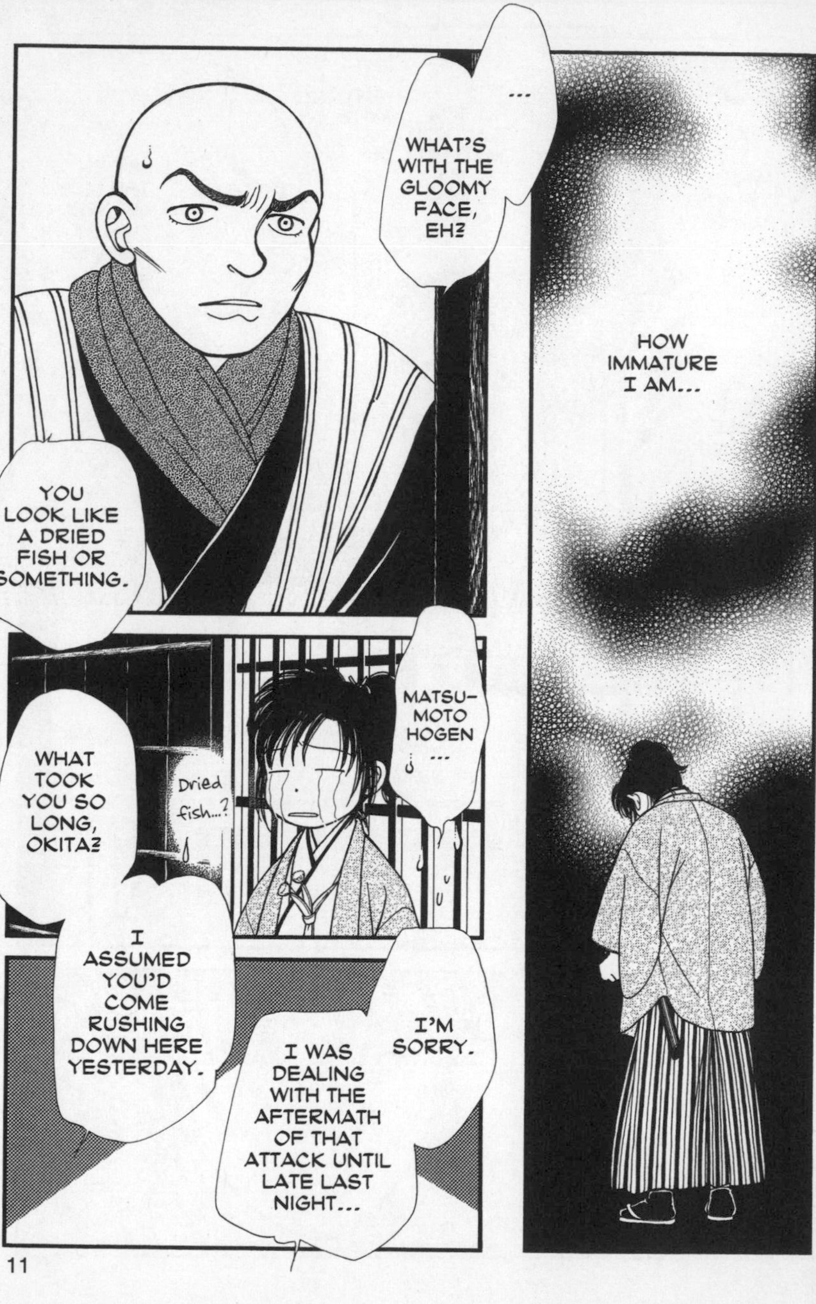
HOW IMMATURE I AM...
...
WHAT'S WITH THE GLOOMY FACE, EH?
YOU LOOK LIKE A DRIED FISH OR SOMETHING.
MATSU-MOTO HOGEN ...
Dried fish...?
WHAT TOOK YOU SO LONG, OKITA?
I ASSUMED YOU'D COME RUSHING DOWN HERE YESTERDAY.
I'M SORRY.
I WAS DEALING WITH THE AFTERMATH OF THAT ATTACK UNTIL LATE LAST NIGHT...

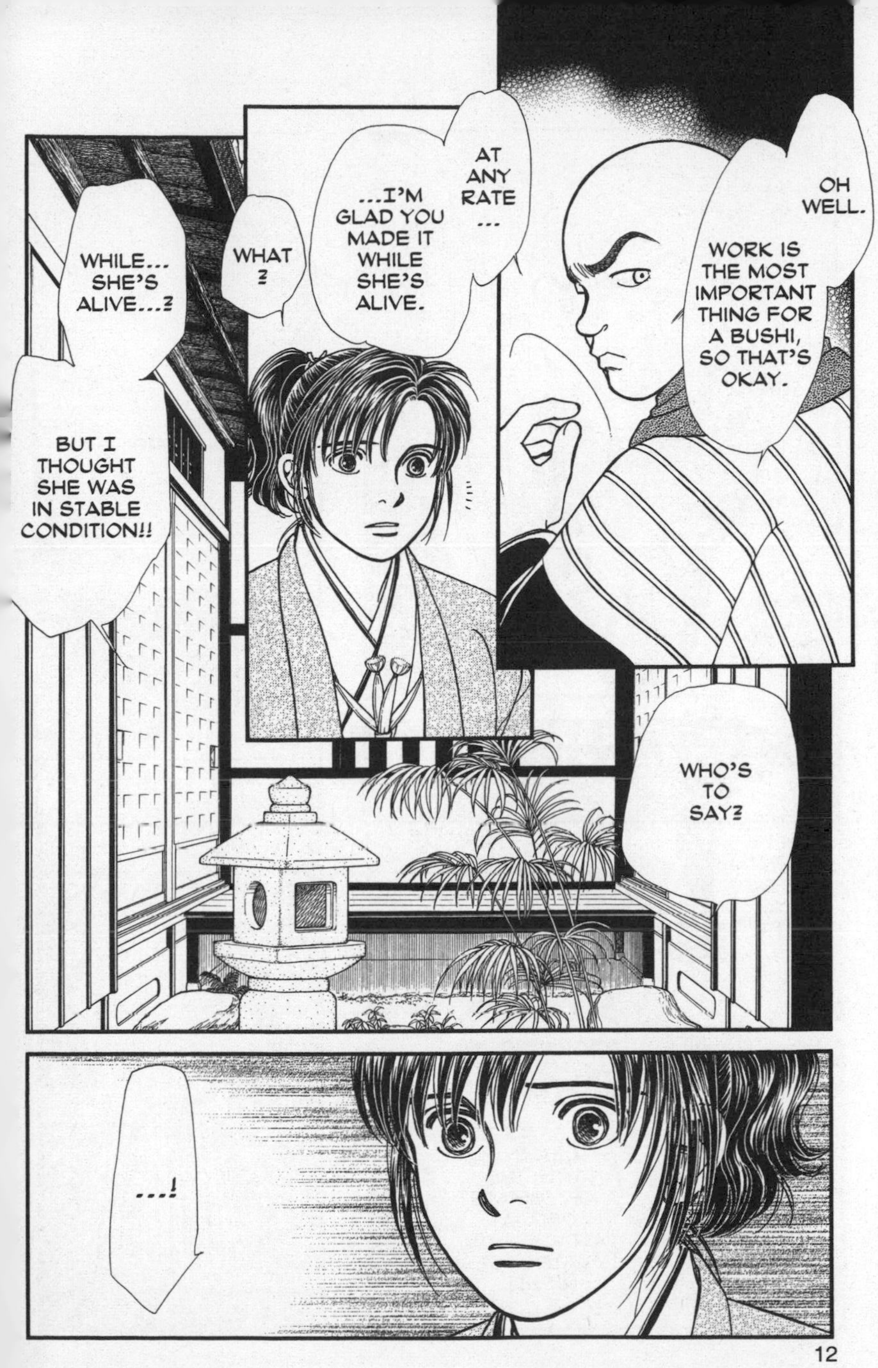
OH WELL.
WORK IS THE MOST IMPORTANT THING FOR A BUSHI, SO THAT'S OKAY.
AT ANY RATE...
...I'M GLAD YOU MADE IT WHILE SHE'S ALIVE.
WHAT?
WHILE... SHE'S ALIVE...?
BUT I THOUGHT SHE WAS IN STABLE CONDITION!!
WHO'S TO SAY?
...!

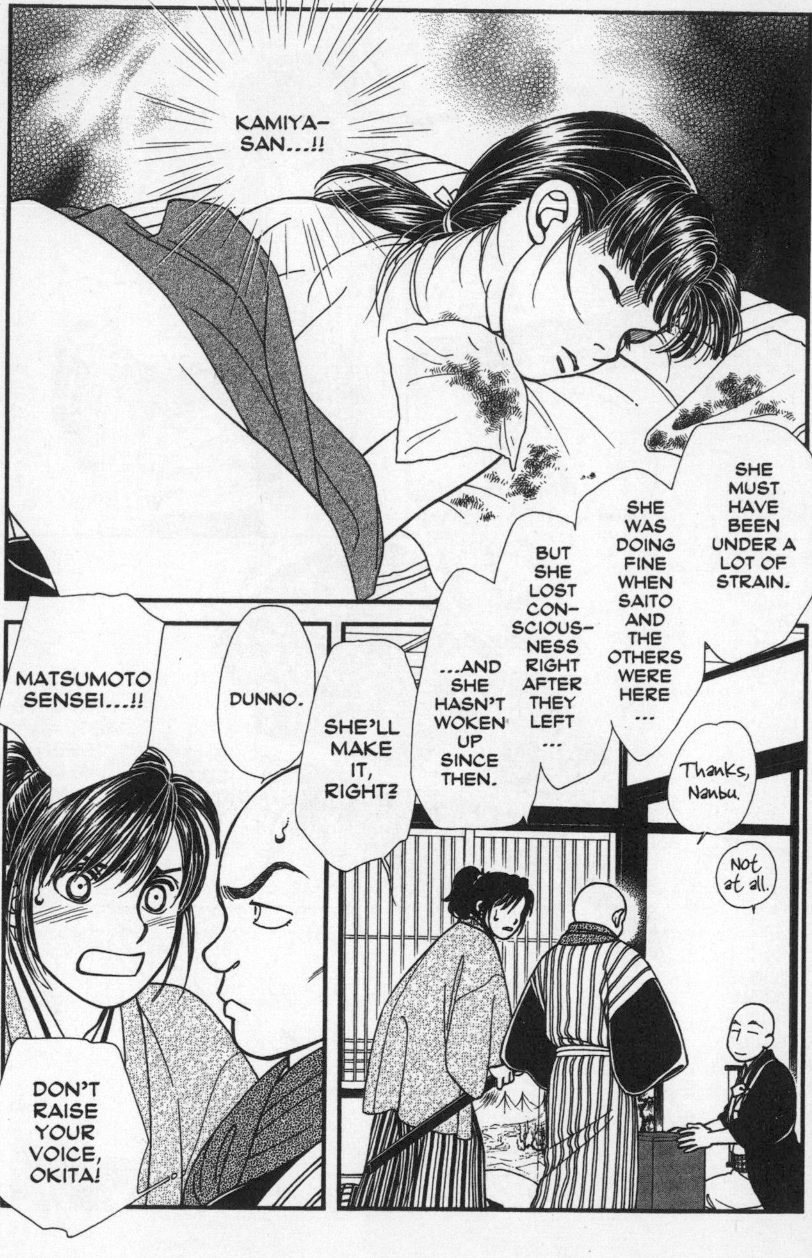

KAMIYA-SAN...!!
SHE MUST HAVE BEEN UNDER A LOT OF STRAIN.
SHE WAS DOING FINE WHEN SAITO AND THE OTHERS WERE HERE...
BUT SHE LOST CONSCIOUSNESS RIGHT AFTER THEY LEFT...
...AND SHE HASN'T WOKEN UP SINCE THEN.
Thanks, Nanbu.
Not at all.
SHE'LL MAKE IT, RIGHT?
DUNNO.
MATSUMOTO SENSEI...!!
DON'T RAISE YOUR VOICE, OKITA!

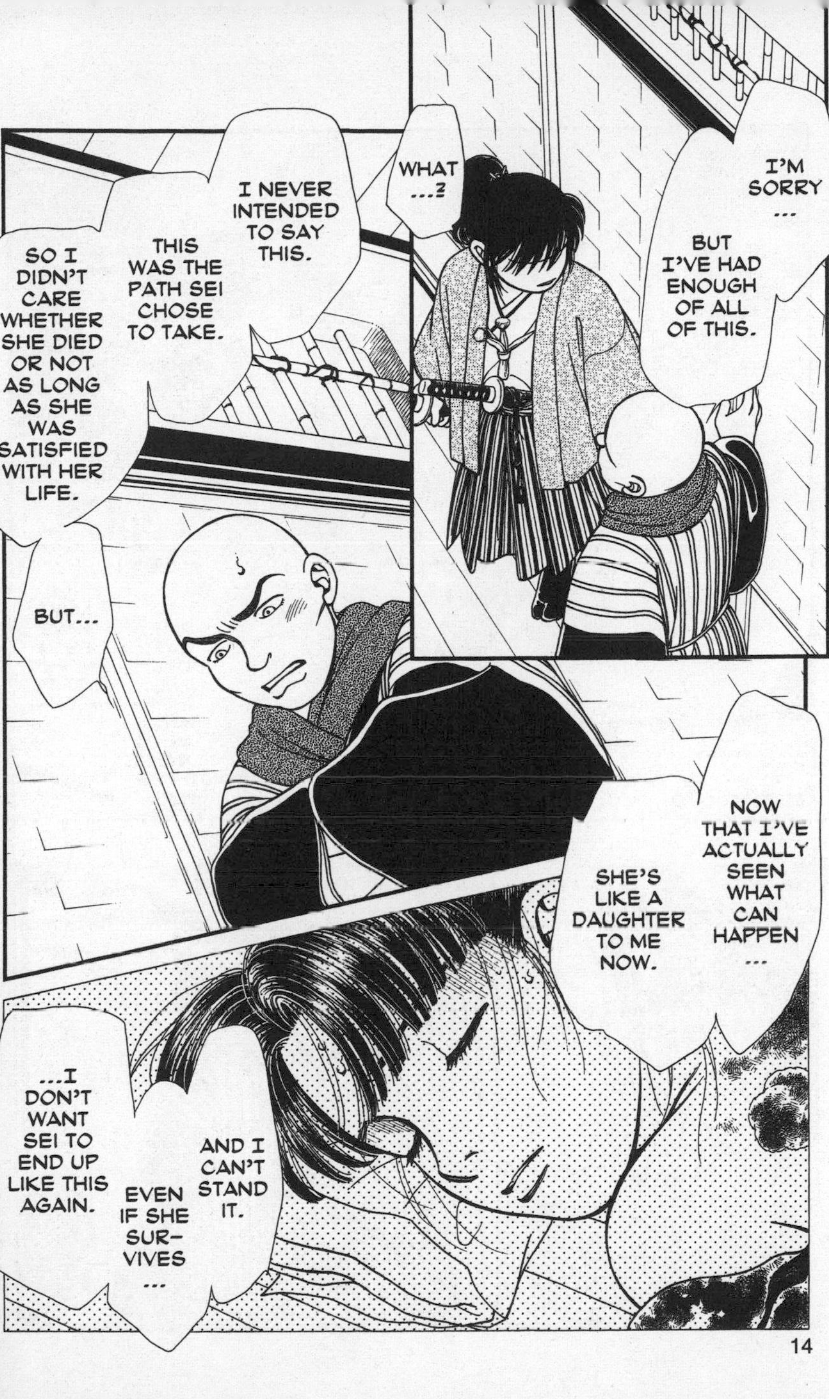
I'M SORRY ...
BUT I'VE HAD ENOUGH OF ALL OF THIS.
WHAT ...?
I NEVER INTENDED TO SAY THIS.
THIS WAS THE PATH SEI CHOSE TO TAKE.
SO I DIDN'T CARE WHETHER SHE DIED OR NOT AS LONG AS SHE WAS SATISFIED WITH HER LIFE.
BUT...
NOW THAT I'VE ACTUALLY SEEN WHAT CAN HAPPEN ...
SHE'S LIKE A DAUGHTER TO ME NOW.
AND I CAN'T STAND IT.
EVEN IF SHE SURVIVES ...
...I DON'T WANT SEI TO END UP LIKE THIS AGAIN.

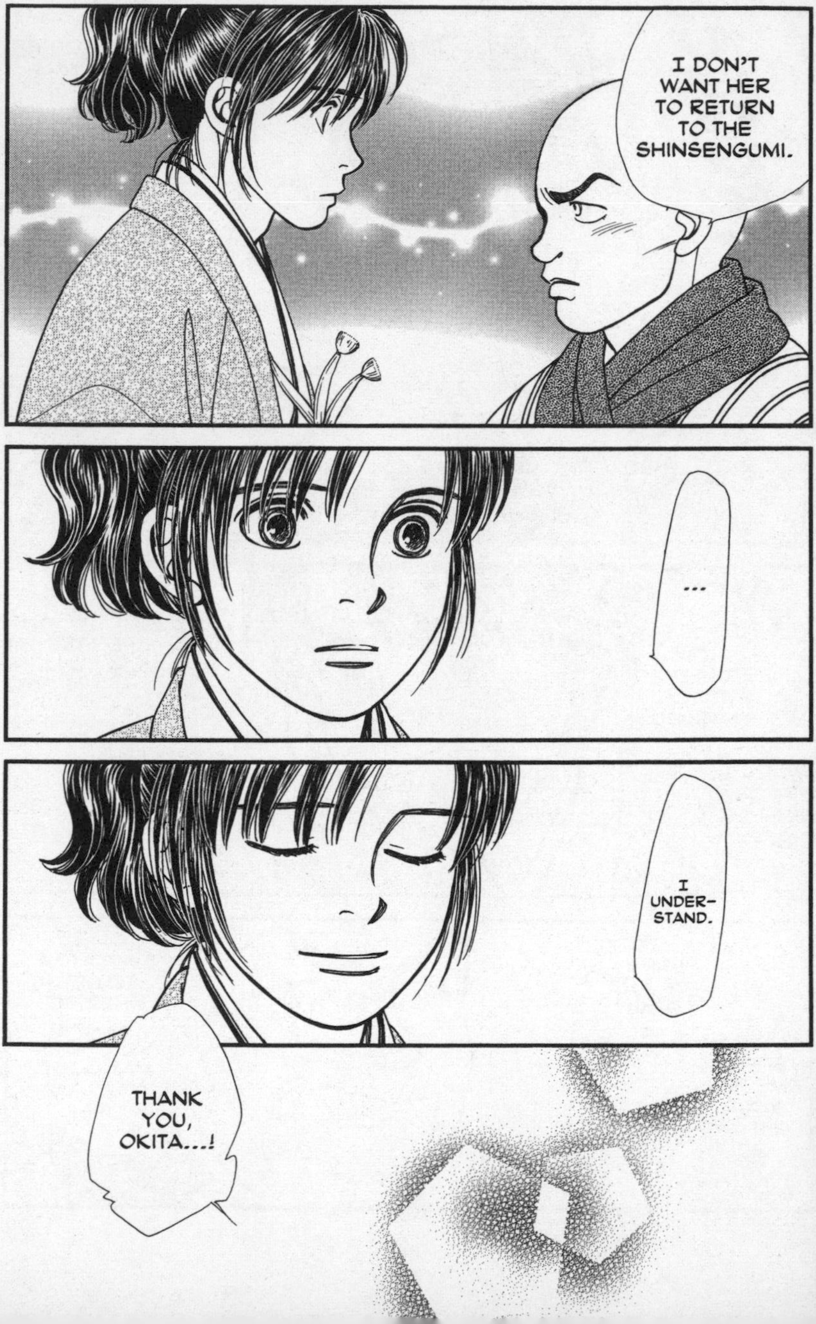
I DON'T WANT HER TO RETURN TO THE SHINSENGUMI.
...
I UNDER-STAND.
THANK YOU, OKITA...!

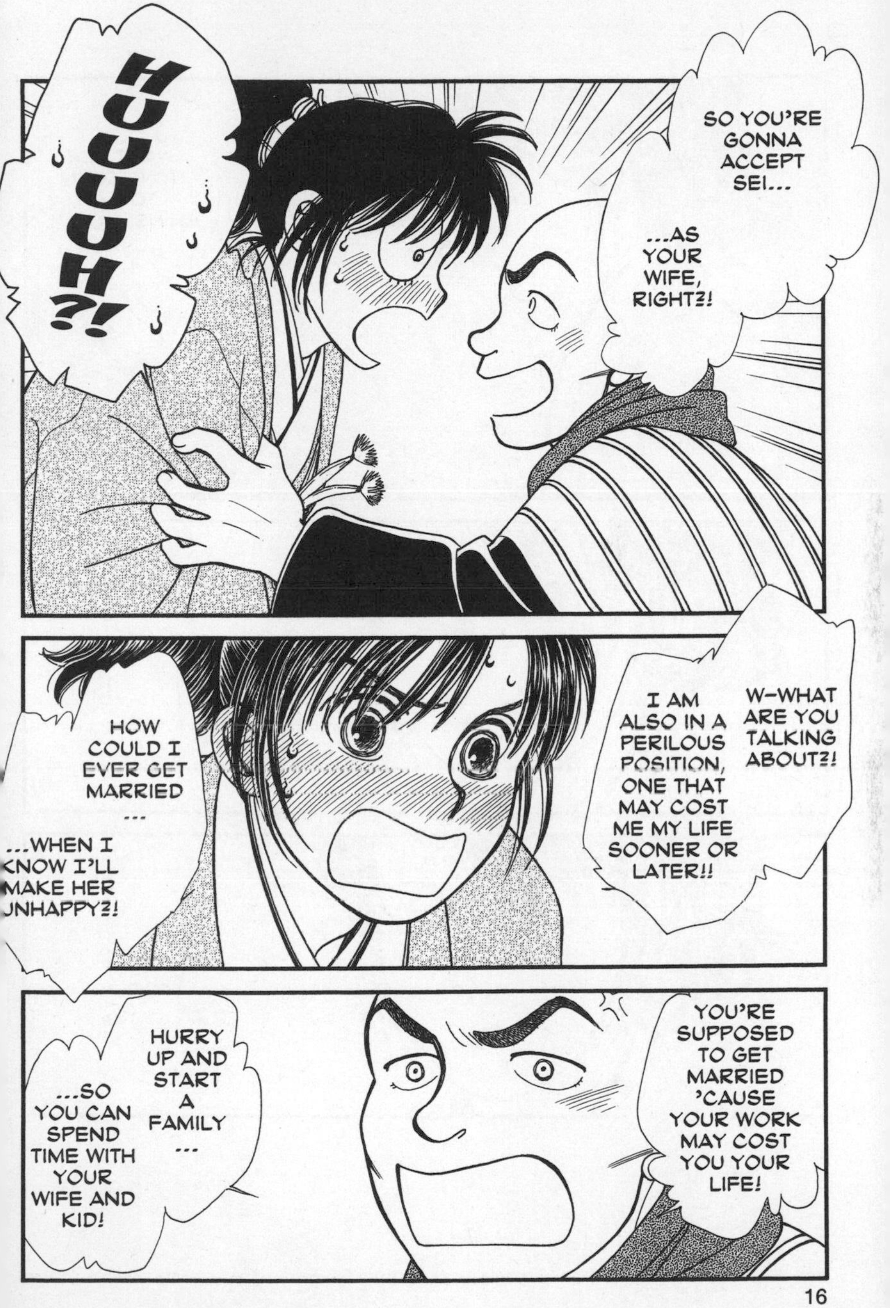
SO YOU'RE GONNA ACCEPT SEI...
...AS YOUR WIFE, RIGHT?!
HUUUUH?!
W-WHAT ARE YOU TALKING ABOUT?!
I AM ALSO IN A PERILOUS POSITION, ONE THAT MAY COST ME MY LIFE SOONER OR LATER!!
HOW COULD I EVER GET MARRIED...
...WHEN I KNOW I'LL MAKE HER UNHAPPY?!
YOU'RE SUPPOSED TO GET MARRIED 'CAUSE YOUR WORK MAY COST YOU YOUR LIFE!
HURRY UP AND START A FAMILY...
...SO YOU CAN SPEND TIME WITH YOUR WIFE AND KID!

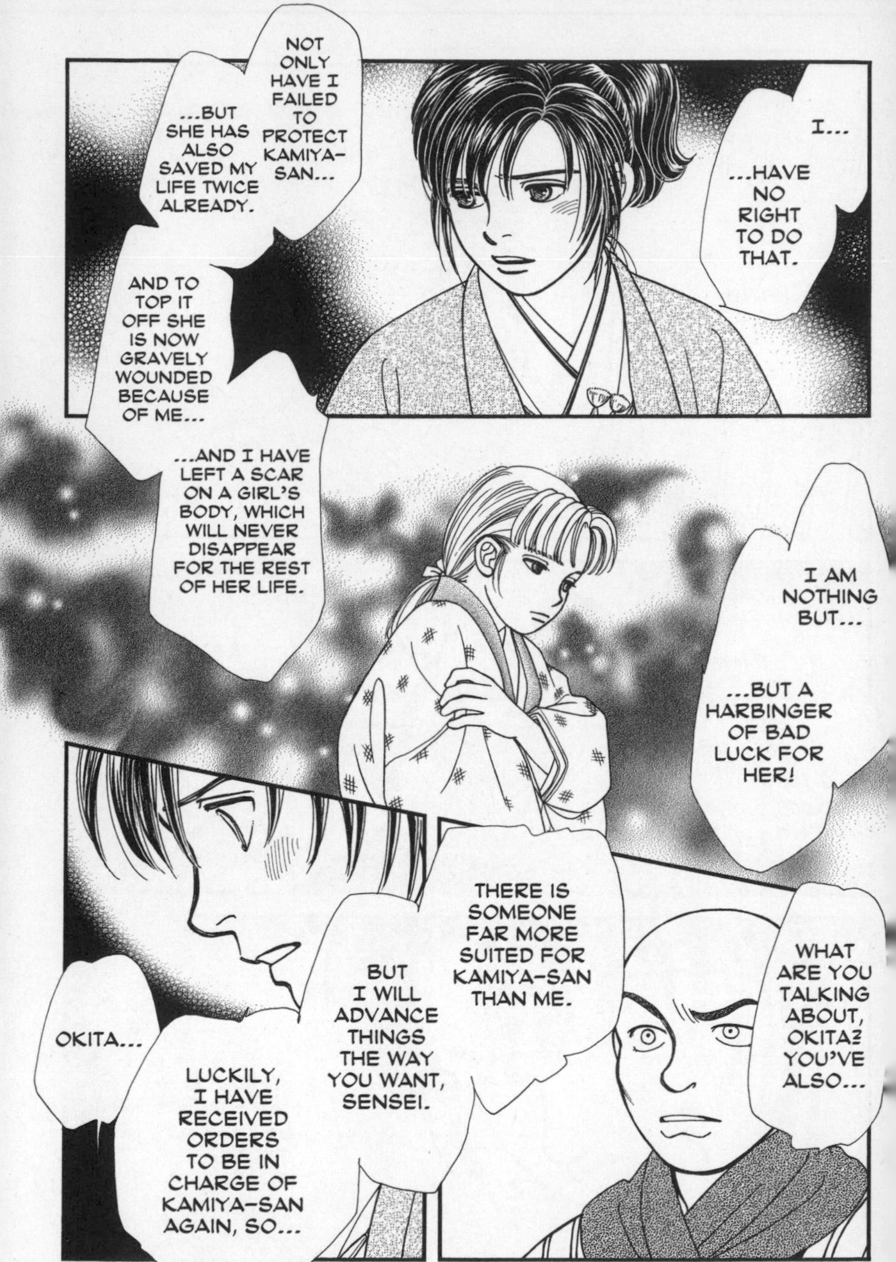
I...
...HAVE NO RIGHT TO DO THAT.
NOT ONLY HAVE I FAILED TO PROTECT KAMIYA-SAN...
...BUT SHE HAS ALSO SAVED MY LIFE TWICE ALREADY.
AND TO TOP IT OFF SHE IS NOW GRAVELY WOUNDED BECAUSE OF ME...
...AND I HAVE LEFT A SCAR ON A GIRL'S BODY, WHICH WILL NEVER DISAPPEAR FOR THE REST OF HER LIFE.
I AM NOTHING BUT...
...BUT A HARBINGER OF BAD LUCK FOR HER!
WHAT ARE YOU TALKING ABOUT, OKITA? YOU'VE ALSO...
THERE IS SOMEONE FAR MORE SUITED FOR KAMIYA-SAN THAN ME.
OKITA...
LUCKILY, I HAVE RECEIVED ORDERS TO BE IN CHARGE OF KAMIYA-SAN AGAIN, SO...
BUT I WILL ADVANCE THINGS THE WAY YOU WANT, SENSEI.

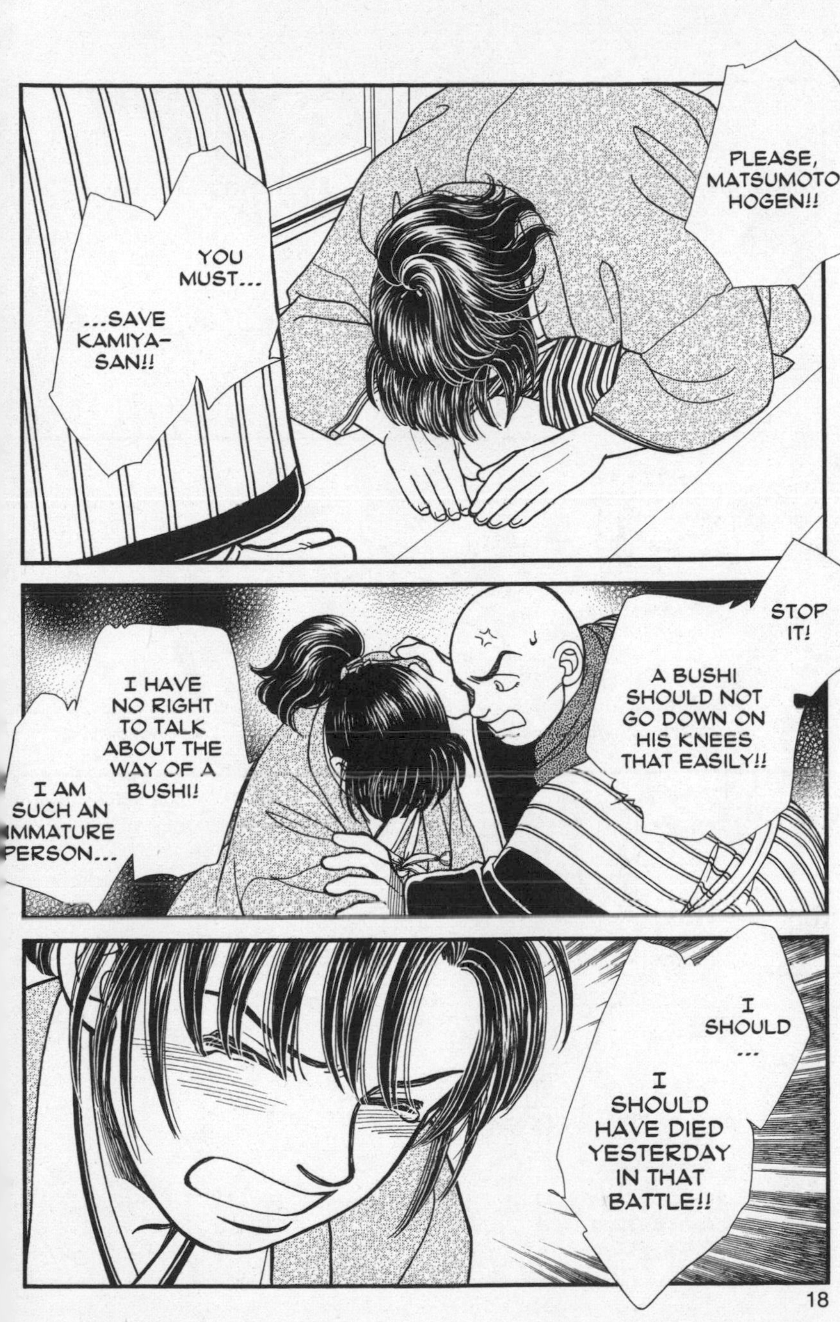
PLEASE, MATSUMOTO HOGEN!!
YOU MUST...
...SAVE KAMIYA-SAN!!
STOP IT!
A BUSHI SHOULD NOT GO DOWN ON HIS KNEES THAT EASILY!!
I HAVE NO RIGHT TO TALK ABOUT THE WAY OF A BUSHI!
I AM SUCH AN IMMATURE PERSON...
I SHOULD ...
I SHOULD HAVE DIED YESTERDAY IN THAT BATTLE!!

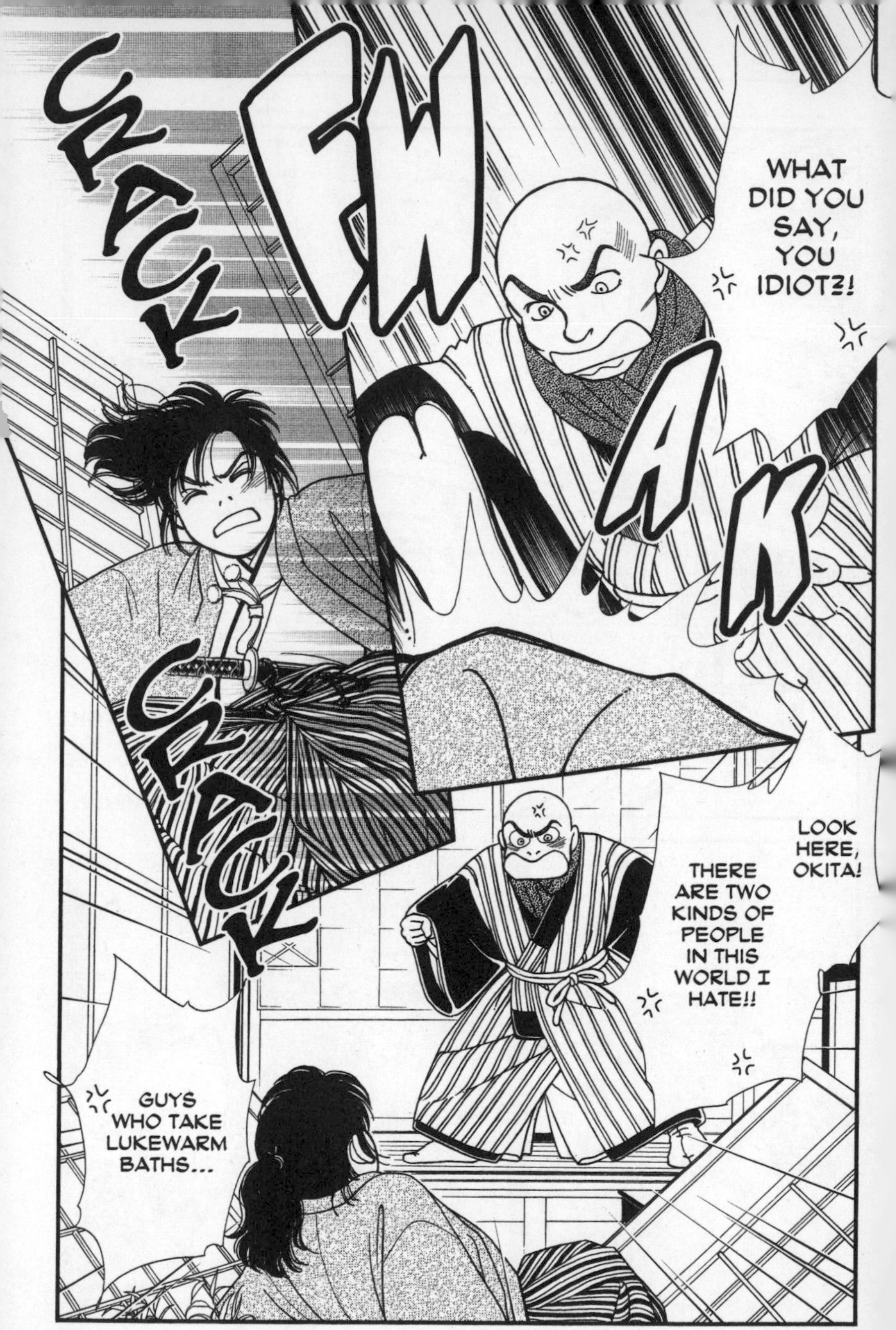
WHAT DID YOU SAY, YOU IDIOTS?!
CRACK
CRACK
LOOK HERE, OKITA!
THERE ARE TWO KINDS OF PEOPLE IN THIS WORLD I HATE!!
GUYS WHO TAKE LUKEWARM BATHS...

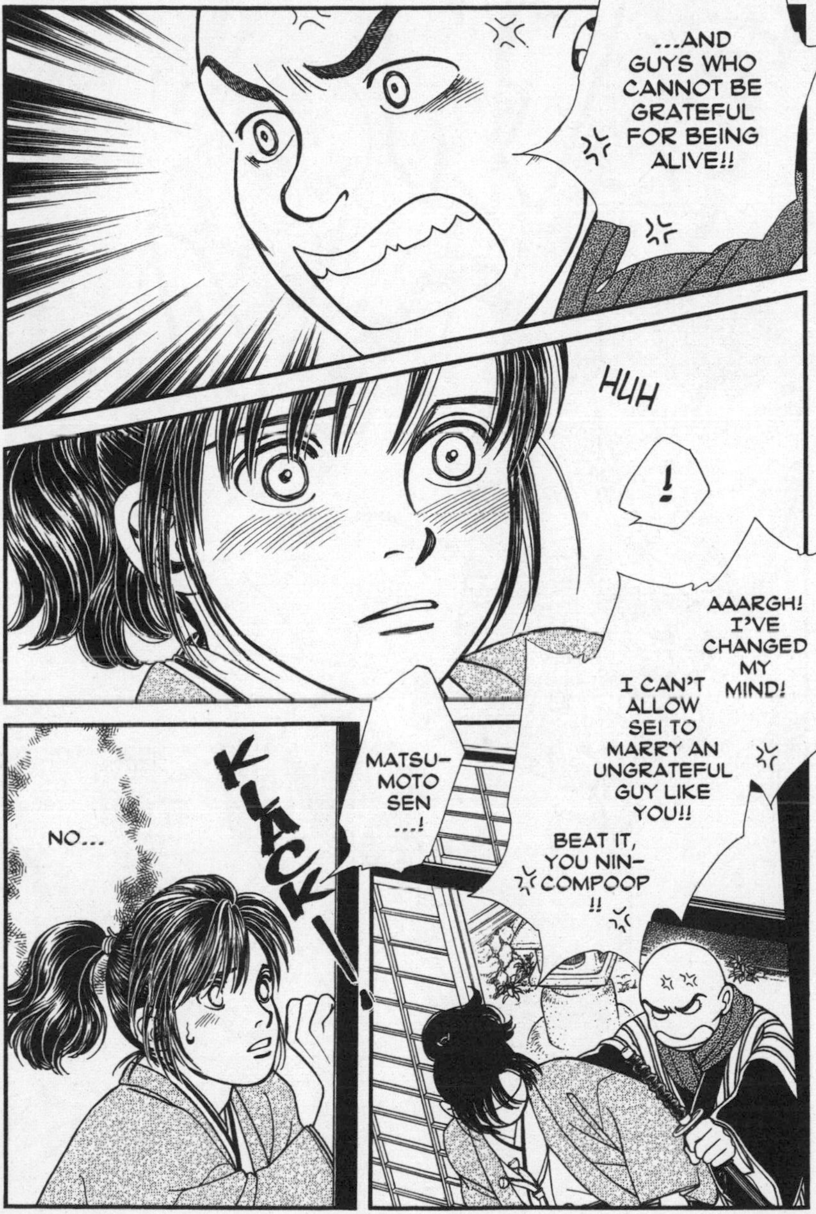
...AND GUYS WHO CANNOT BE GRATEFUL FOR BEING ALIVE!!
HUH
!
AAARGH! I'VE CHANGED MY MIND!
I CAN'T ALLOW SEI TO MARRY AN UNGRATEFUL GUY LIKE YOU!!
BEAT IT, YOU NIN-COMPOOP !!
MATSU-MOTO SEN ...!
KLACK!
NO...

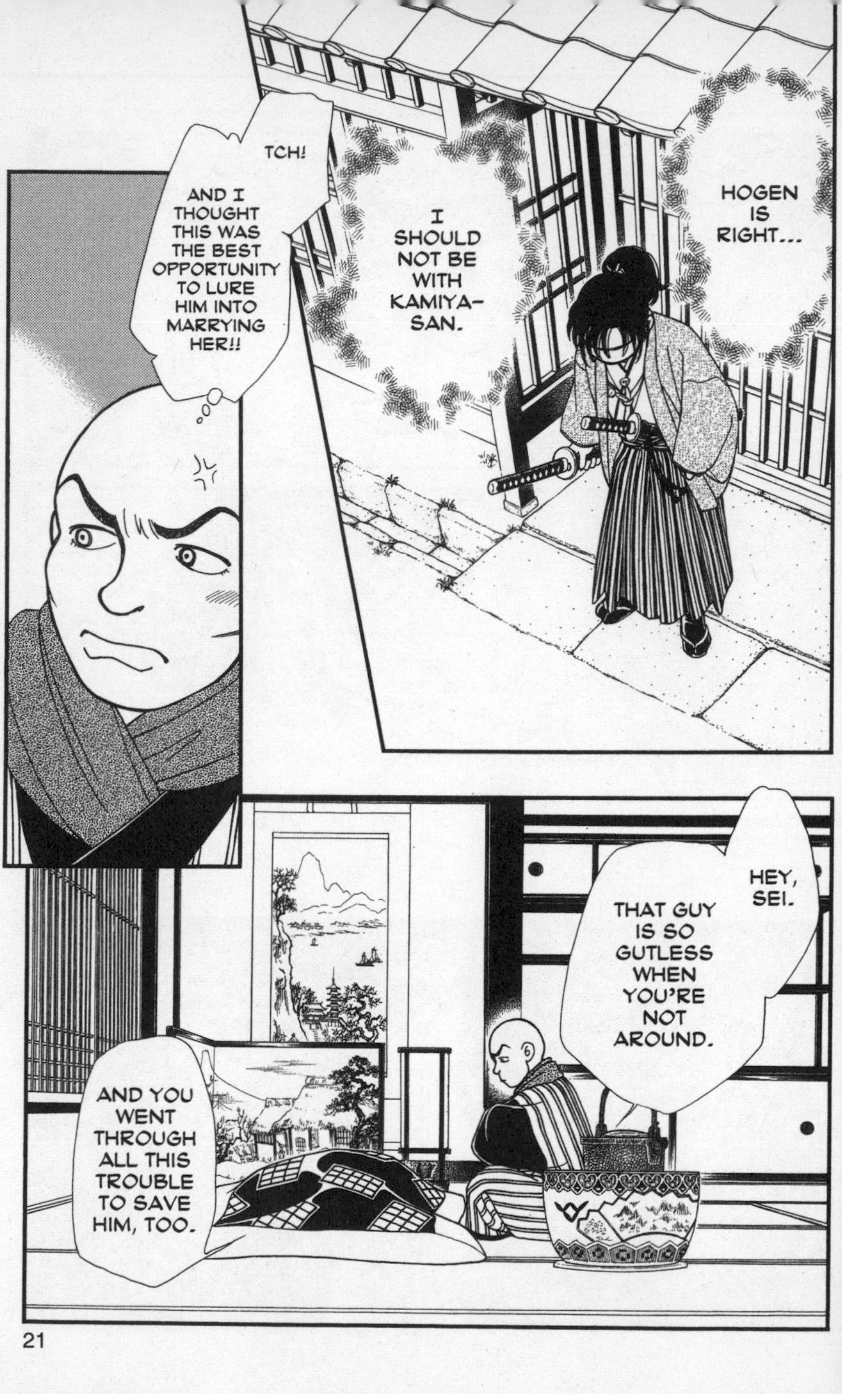
HOGEN IS RIGHT...
I SHOULD NOT BE WITH KAMIYA-SAN.
TCH!
AND I THOUGHT THIS WAS THE BEST OPPORTUNITY TO LURE HIM INTO MARRYING HER!!
HEY, SEI.
THAT GUY IS SO GUTLESS WHEN YOU'RE NOT AROUND.
AND YOU WENT THROUGH ALL THIS TROUBLE TO SAVE HIM, TOO.

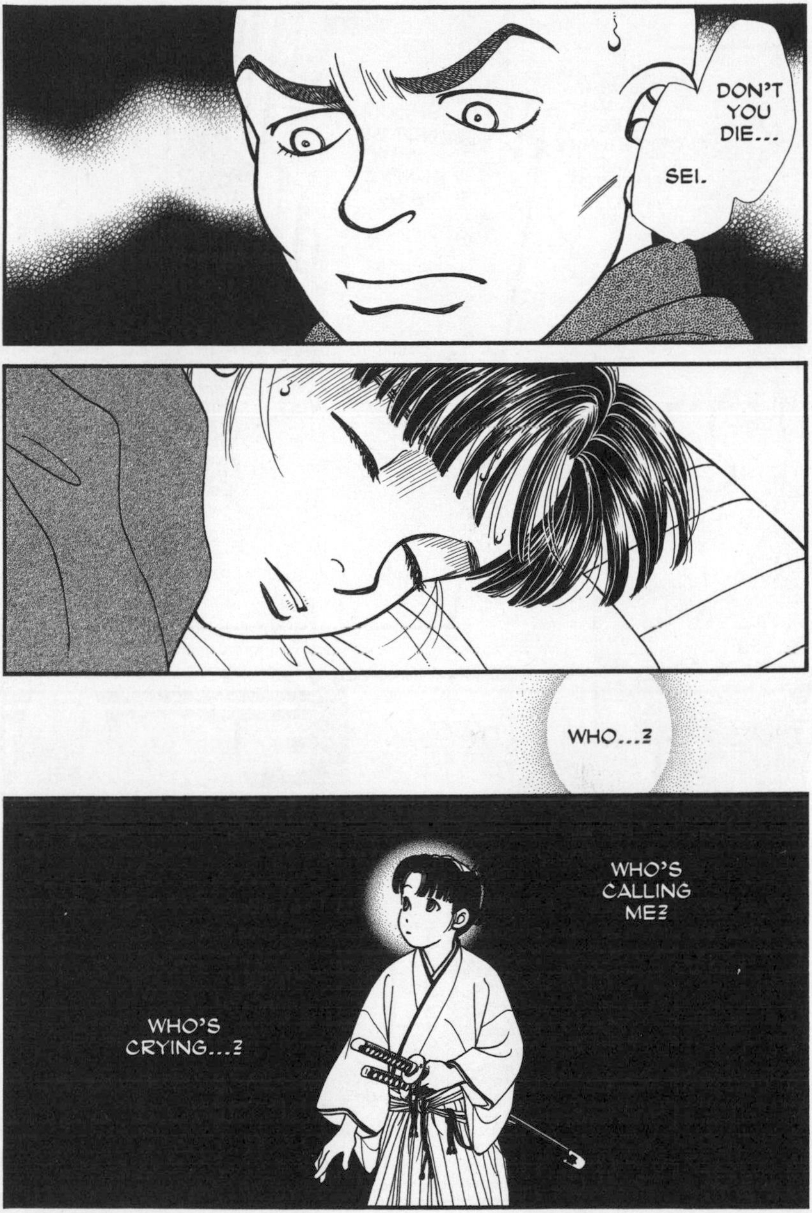
DON'T YOU DIE...
SEI.
WHO...?
WHO'S CALLING ME?
WHO'S CRYING...?

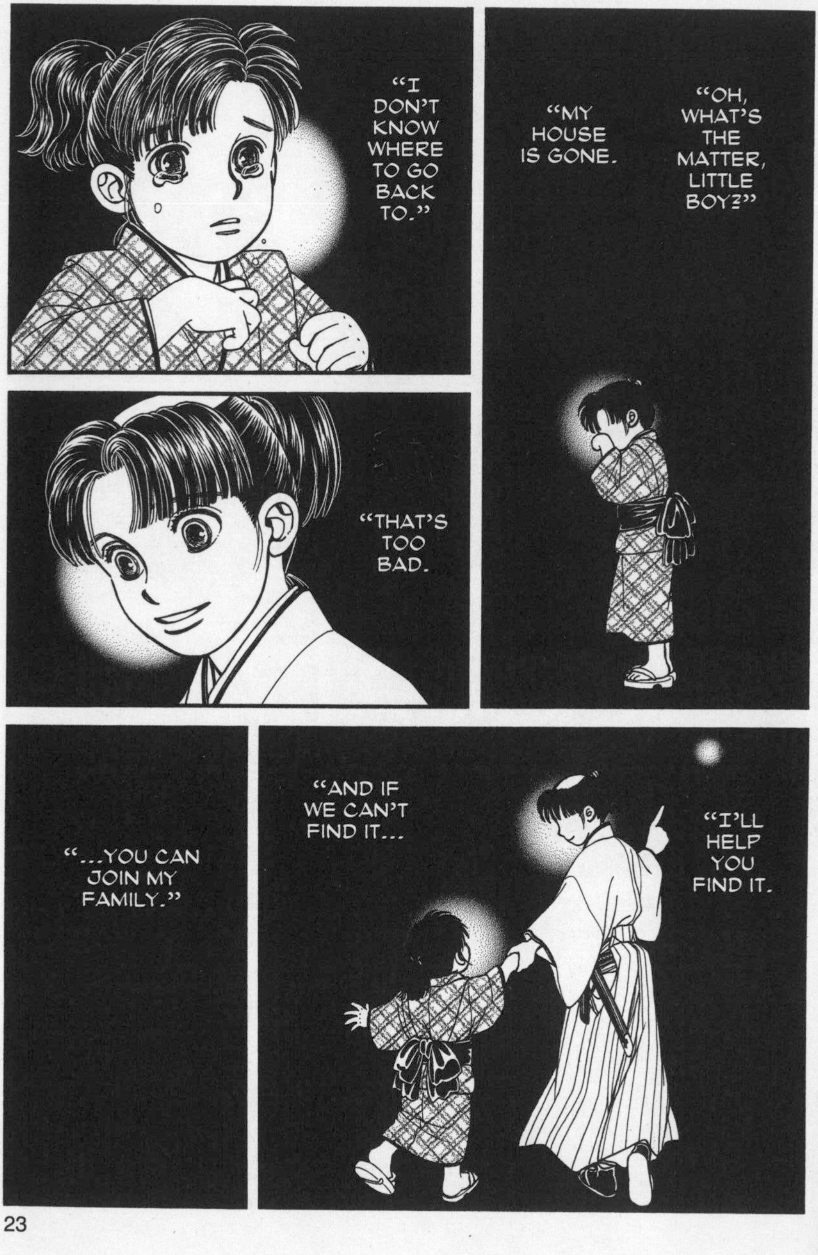
"OH, WHAT'S THE MATTER, LITTLE BOY?"
"MY HOUSE IS GONE.
"I DON'T KNOW WHERE TO GO BACK TO."
"THAT'S TOO BAD.
"I'LL HELP YOU FIND IT.
"AND IF WE CAN'T FIND IT...
"...YOU CAN JOIN MY FAMILY."

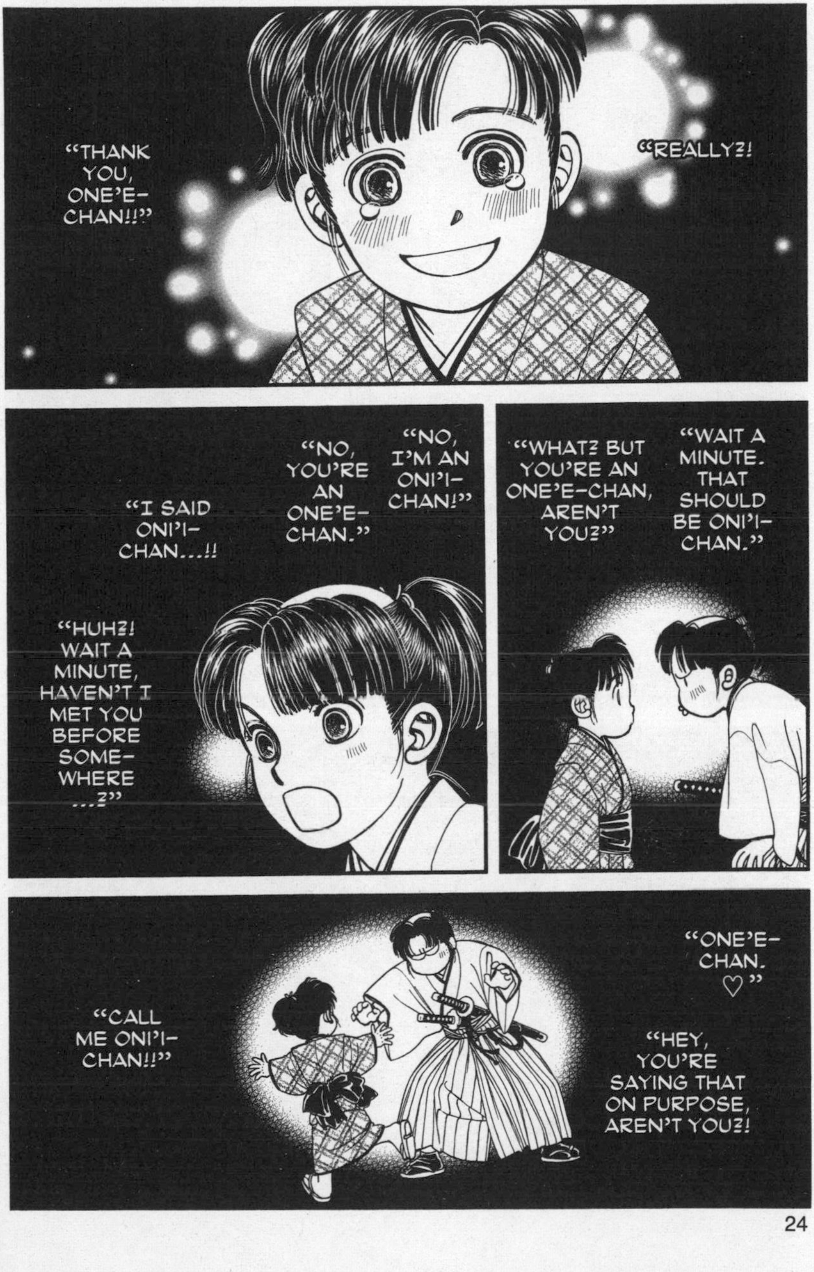
“REALLY?!
“THANK YOU, ONE’E-CHAN!!”
“WAIT A MINUTE. THAT SHOULD BE ONI’I-CHAN.”
“WHAT? BUT YOU’RE AN ONE’E-CHAN, AREN’T YOU?”
“NO, I’M AN ONI’I-CHAN!”
“NO, YOU’RE AN ONE’E-CHAN.”
“I SAID ONI’I-CHAN...!!
“HUH?! WAIT A MINUTE, HAVEN’T I MET YOU BEFORE SOMEWHERE...?”
“ONE’E-CHAN. ♡”
“HEY, YOU’RE SAYING THAT ON PURPOSE, AREN’T YOU?!
“CALL ME ONI’I-CHAN!!”

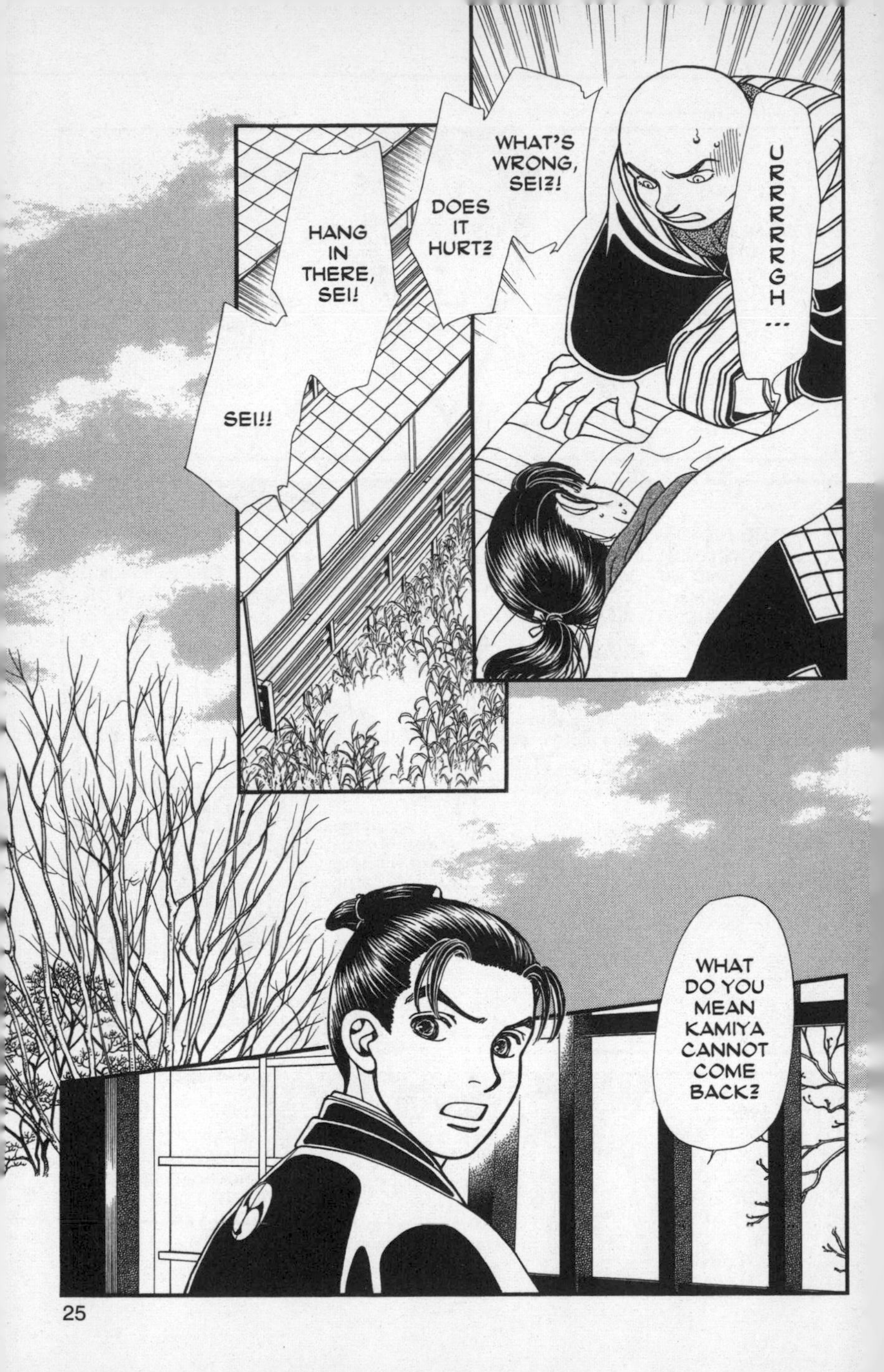
URRRRGH...
WHAT'S WRONG, SEI?!
DOES IT HURT?
HANG IN THERE, SEI!
SEI!!
WHAT DO YOU MEAN KAMIYA CANNOT COME BACK?

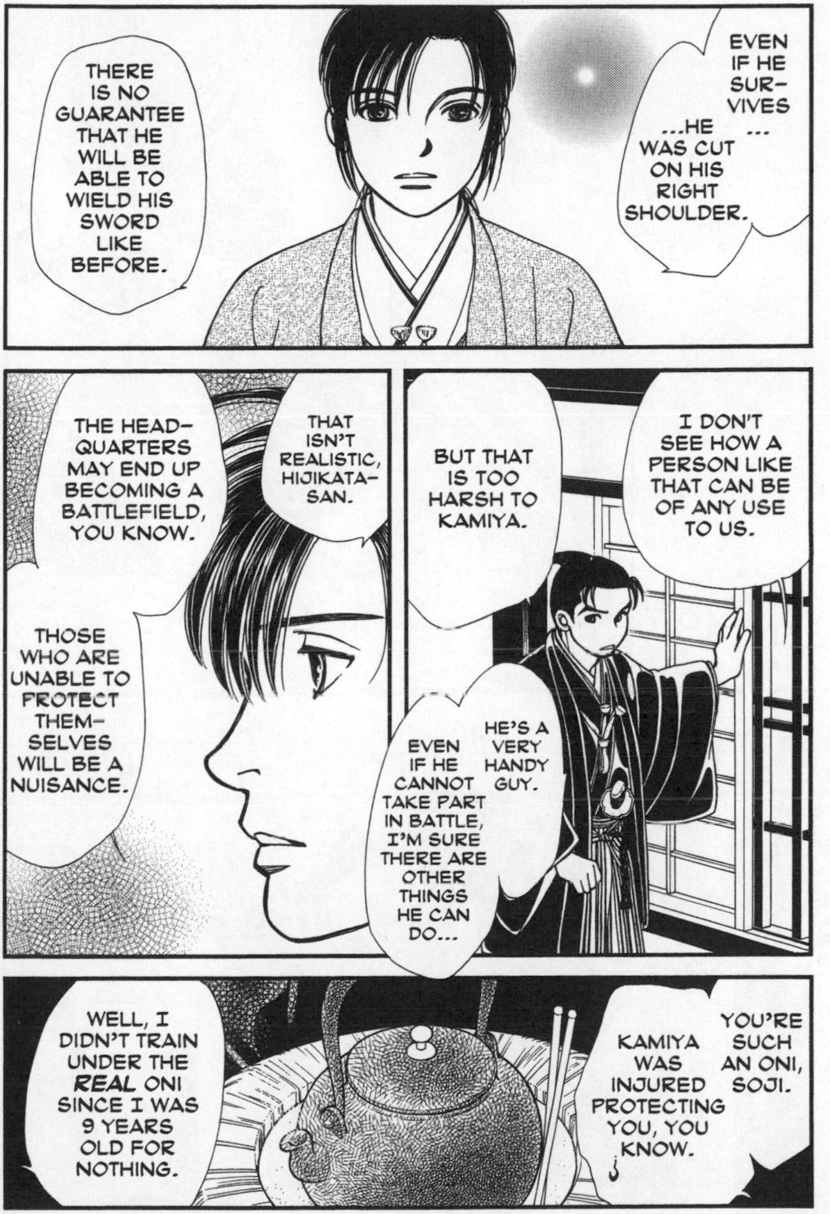
EVEN IF HE SURVIVES ...
...HE WAS CUT ON HIS RIGHT SHOULDER.
THERE IS NO GUARANTEE THAT HE WILL BE ABLE TO WIELD HIS SWORD LIKE BEFORE.
I DON'T SEE HOW A PERSON LIKE THAT CAN BE OF ANY USE TO US.
BUT THAT IS TOO HARSH TO KAMIYA.
HE'S A VERY HANDY GUY.
EVEN IF HE CANNOT TAKE PART IN BATTLE, I'M SURE THERE ARE OTHER THINGS HE CAN DO...
THAT ISN'T REALISTIC, HIJIKATA-SAN.
THE HEAD-QUARTERS MAY END UP BECOMING A BATTLEFIELD, YOU KNOW.
THOSE WHO ARE UNABLE TO PROTECT THEM-SELVES WILL BE A NUISANCE.
YOU'RE SUCH AN ONI, SOJI.
KAMIYA WAS INJURED PROTECTING YOU, YOU KNOW.
WELL, I DIDN'T TRAIN UNDER THE *REAL* ONI SINCE I WAS 9 YEARS OLD FOR NOTHING.

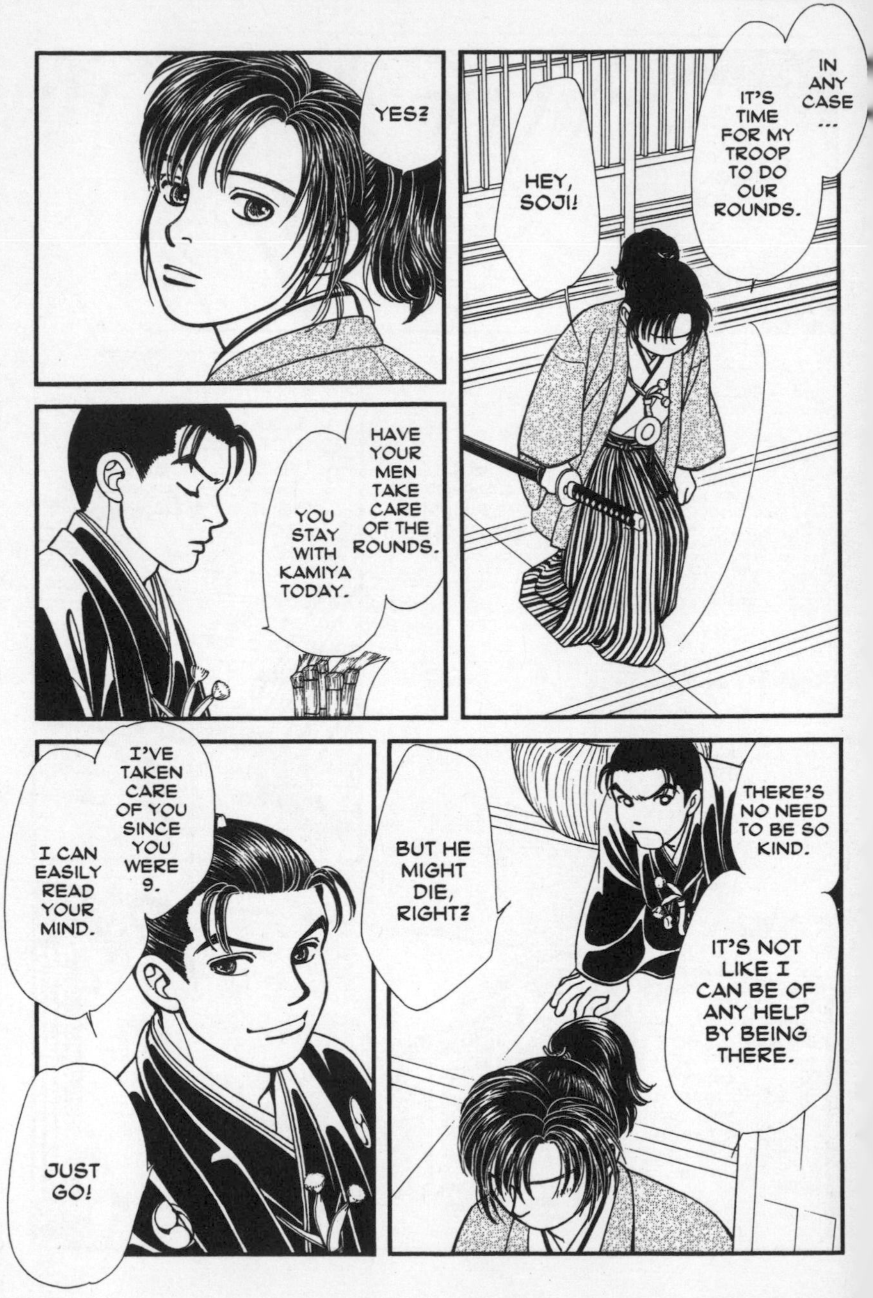
IN ANY CASE ...
IT'S TIME FOR MY TROOP TO DO OUR ROUNDS.
HEY, SOJI!
YES?
HAVE YOUR MEN TAKE CARE OF THE ROUNDS.
YOU STAY WITH KAMIYA TODAY.
THERE'S NO NEED TO BE SO KIND.
IT'S NOT LIKE I CAN BE OF ANY HELP BY BEING THERE.
BUT HE MIGHT DIE, RIGHT?
I'VE TAKEN CARE OF YOU SINCE YOU WERE 9.
I CAN EASILY READ YOUR MIND.
JUST GO!

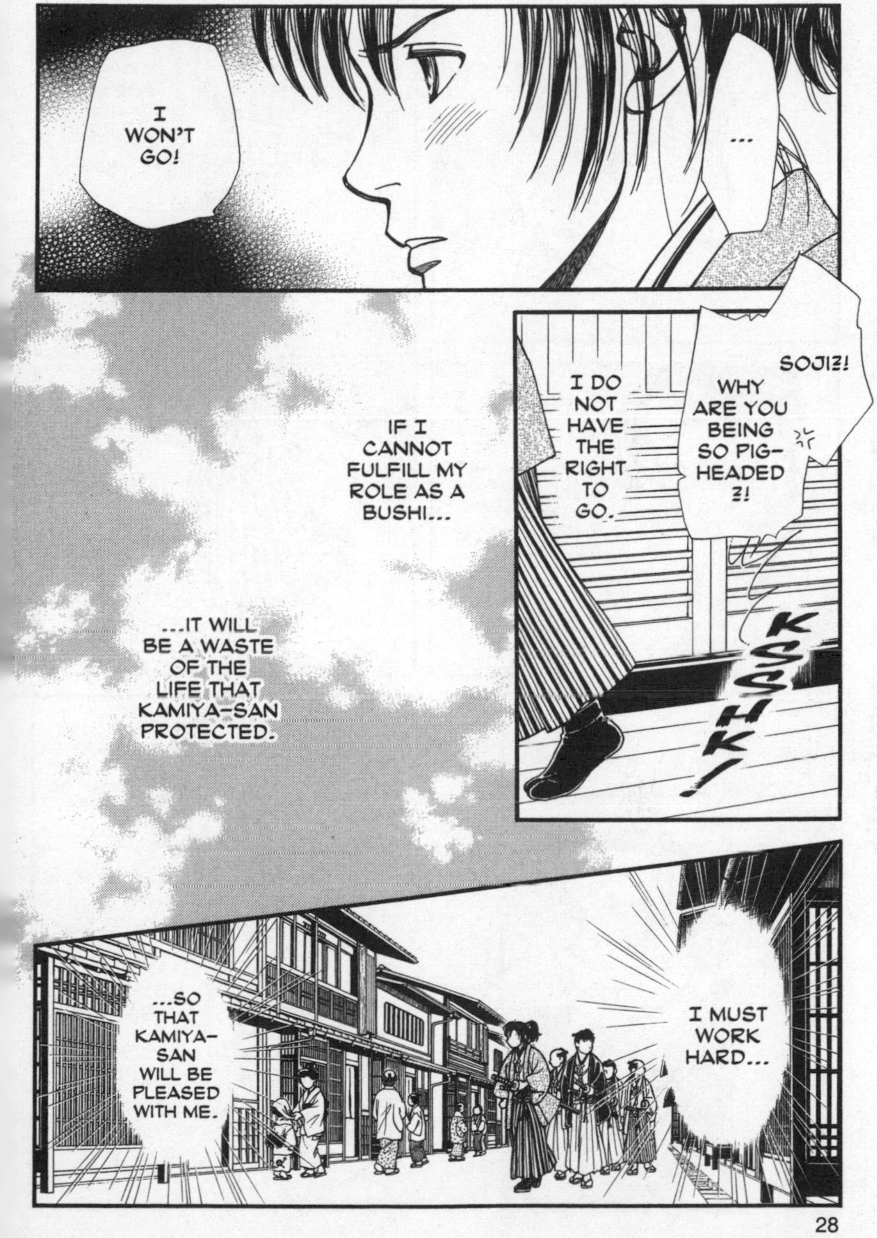
...
I WON'T GO!
SOJI?!
WHY ARE YOU BEING SO PIG-HEADED?!
I DO NOT HAVE THE RIGHT TO GO.
KSSHK!
IF I CANNOT FULFILL MY ROLE AS A BUSHI...
...IT WILL BE A WASTE OF THE LIFE THAT KAMIYA-SAN PROTECTED.
I MUST WORK HARD...
...SO THAT KAMIYA-SAN WILL BE PLEASED WITH ME.

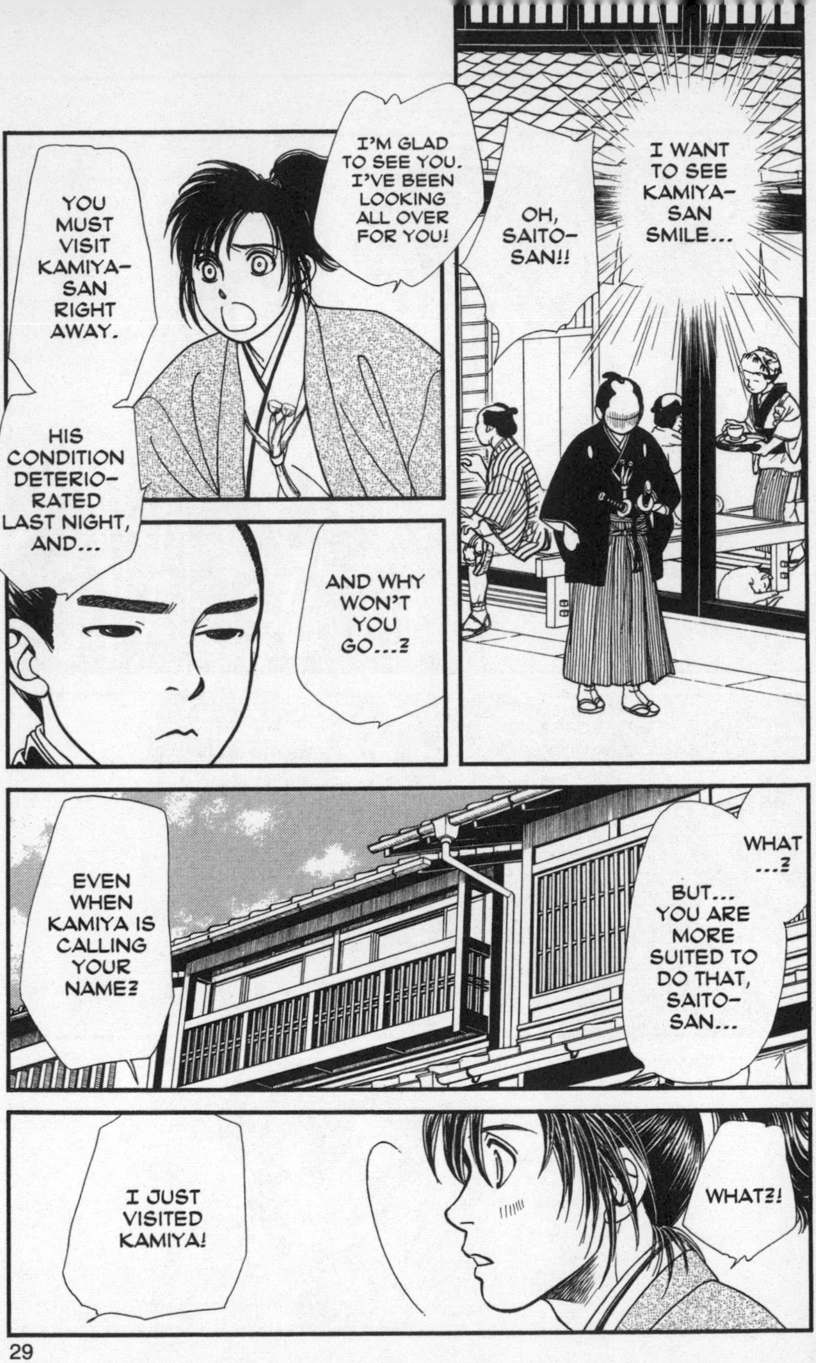
I WANT TO SEE KAMIYA-SAN SMILE...
OH, SAITO-SAN!!
I'M GLAD TO SEE YOU. I'VE BEEN LOOKING ALL OVER FOR YOU!
YOU MUST VISIT KAMIYA-SAN RIGHT AWAY.
HIS CONDITION DETERIORATED LAST NIGHT, AND...
AND WHY WON'T YOU GO...?
WHAT...?
BUT... YOU ARE MORE SUITED TO DO THAT, SAITO-SAN...
EVEN WHEN KAMIYA IS CALLING YOUR NAME?
WHAT?!
I JUST VISITED KAMIYA!

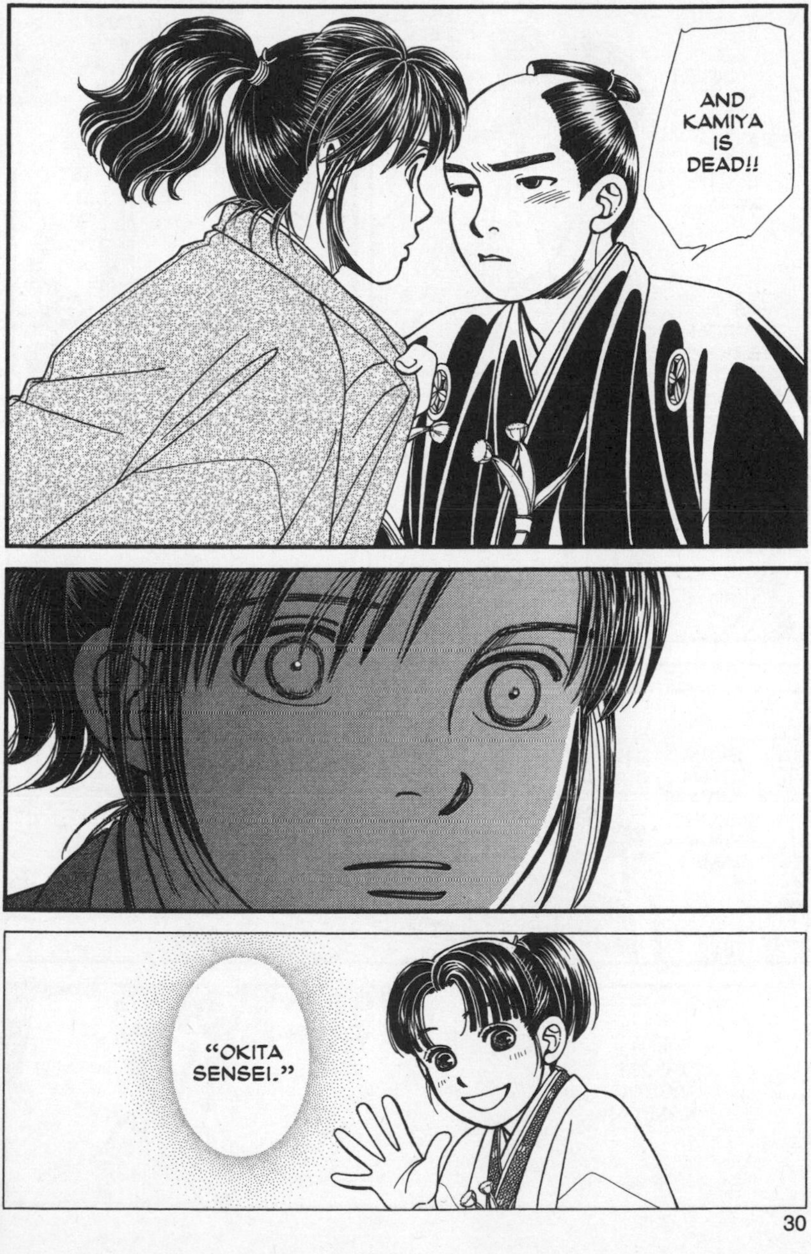
AND KAMIYA IS DEAD!!
"OKITA SENSEI."

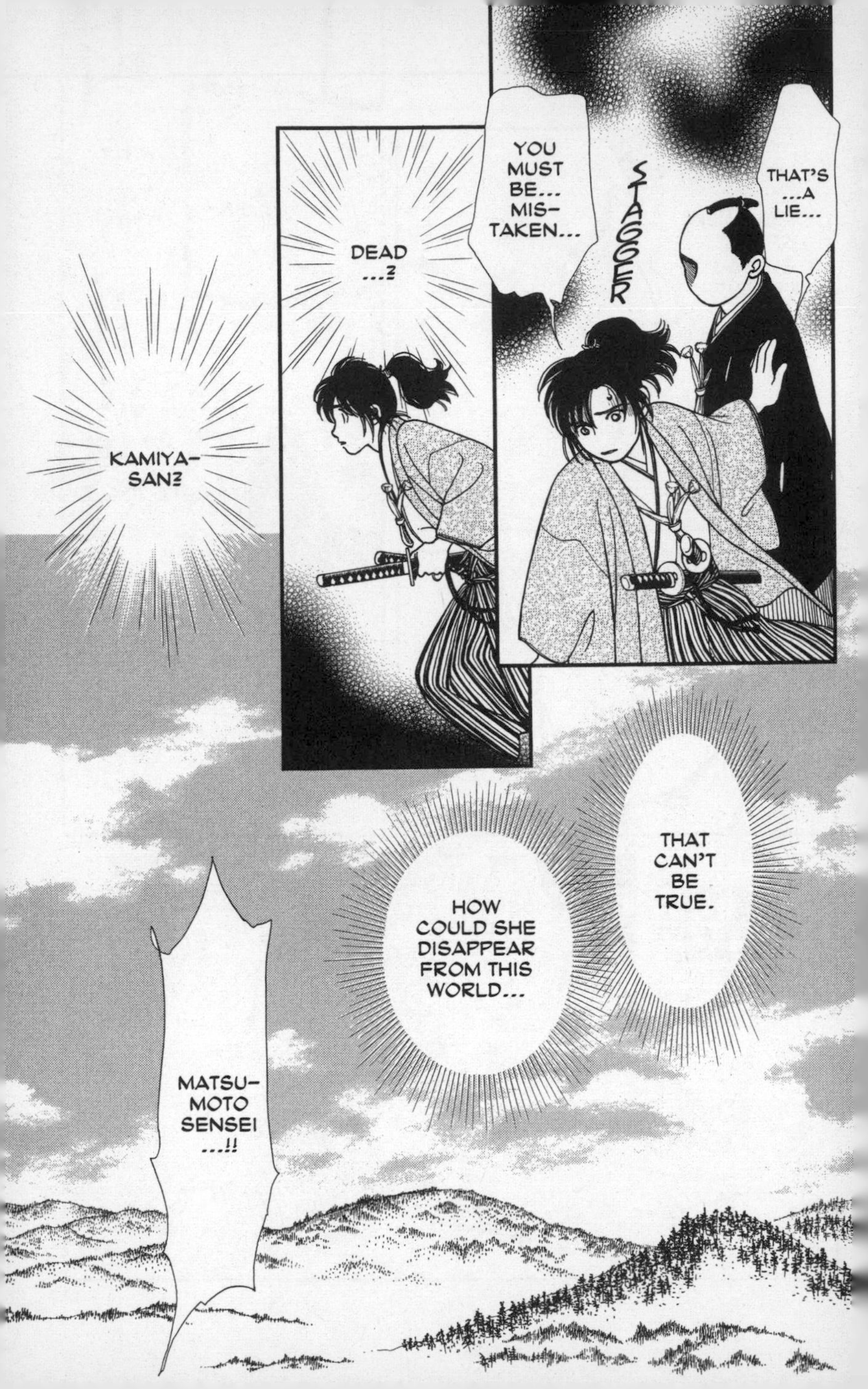
THAT'S ...A LIE...
STAGGER
YOU MUST BE... MIS-TAKEN...
DEAD ...?
KAMIYA-SAN?
THAT CAN'T BE TRUE.
HOW COULD SHE DISAPPEAR FROM THIS WORLD...
MATSU-MOTO SENSEI ...!!

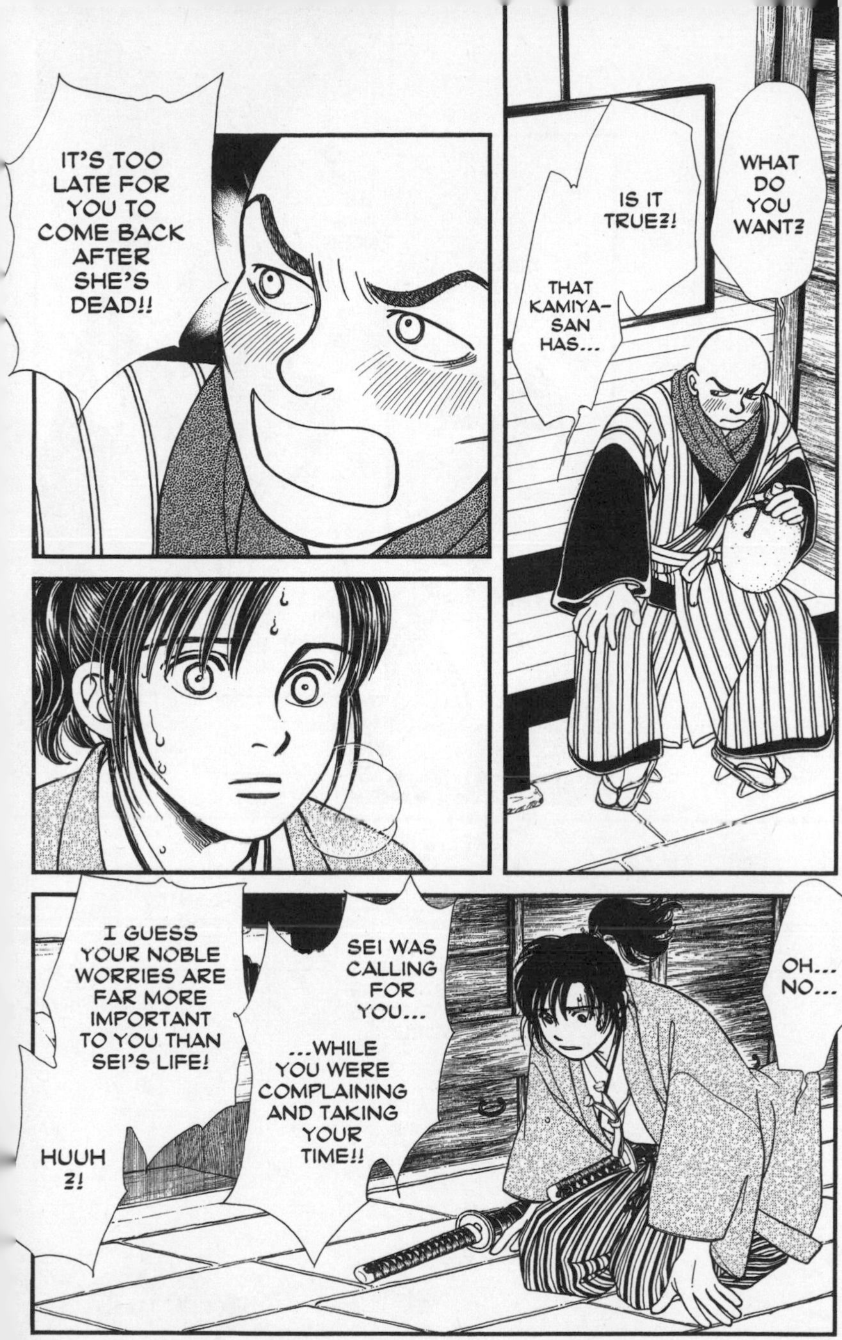
WHAT DO YOU WANT?
IS IT TRUE?!
THAT KAMIYA-SAN HAS...
IT'S TOO LATE FOR YOU TO COME BACK AFTER SHE'S DEAD!!
OH... NO...
SEI WAS CALLING FOR YOU...
...WHILE YOU WERE COMPLAINING AND TAKING YOUR TIME!!
I GUESS YOUR NOBLE WORRIES ARE FAR MORE IMPORTANT TO YOU THAN SEI'S LIFE!
HUUH ?!

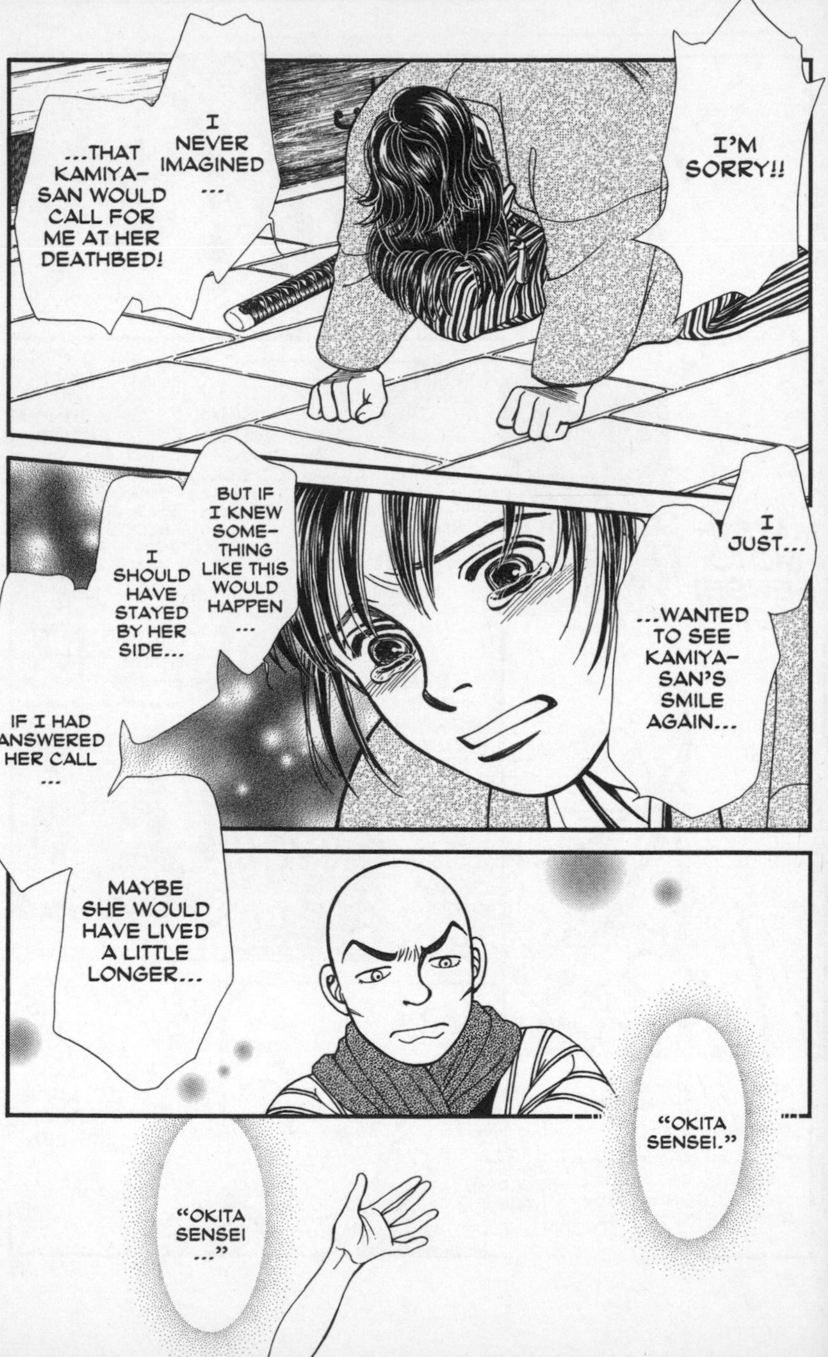
I'M SORRY!!
I NEVER IMAGINED ...
...THAT KAMIYA-SAN WOULD CALL FOR ME AT HER DEATHBED!
I JUST...
...WANTED TO SEE KAMIYA-SAN'S SMILE AGAIN...
BUT IF I KNEW SOMETHING LIKE THIS WOULD HAPPEN ...
I SHOULD HAVE STAYED BY HER SIDE...
IF I HAD ANSWERED HER CALL ...
MAYBE SHE WOULD HAVE LIVED A LITTLE LONGER...
"OKITA SENSEI."
"OKITA SENSEI ..."

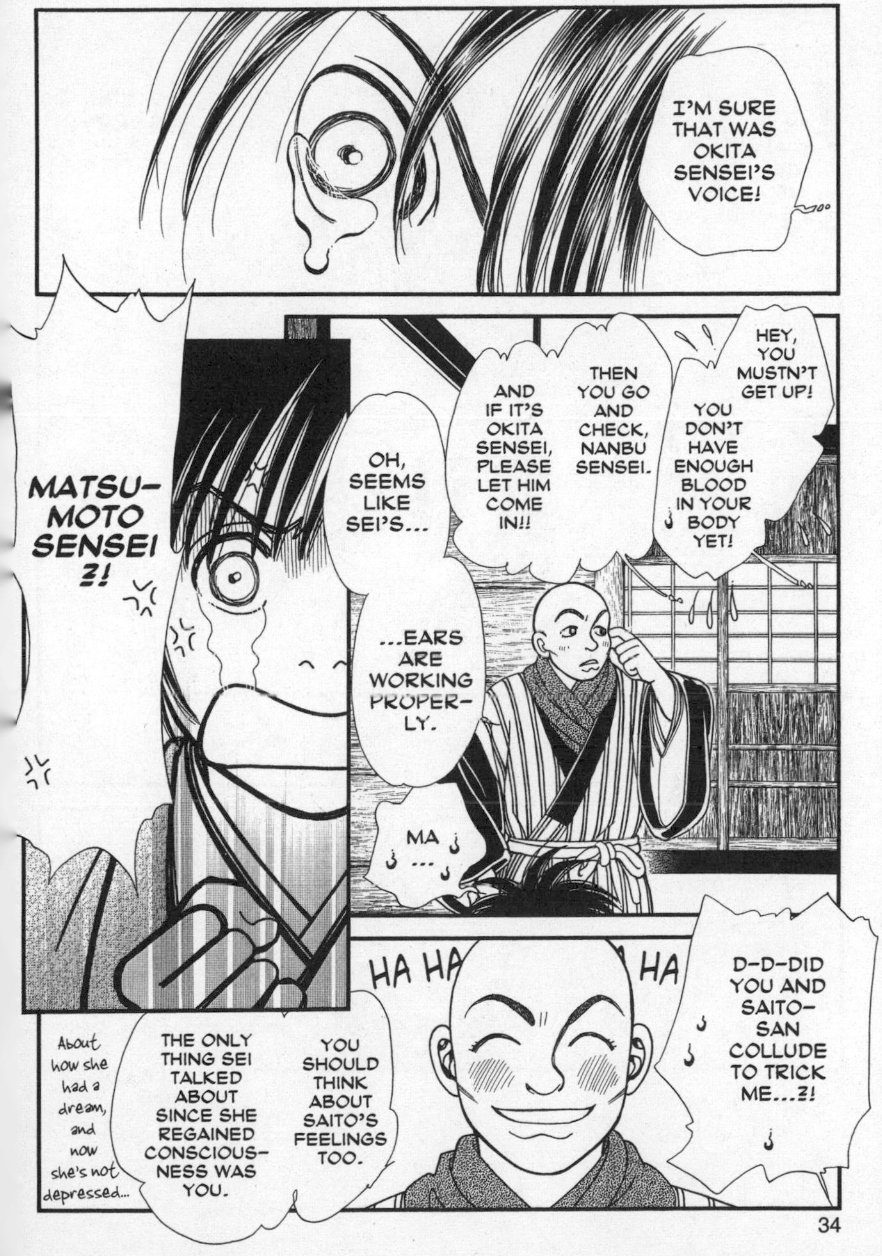
I'M SURE THAT WAS OKITA SENSEI'S VOICE!
HEY, YOU MUSTN'T GET UP!
YOU DON'T HAVE ENOUGH BLOOD IN YOUR BODY YET!
THEN YOU GO AND CHECK, NANBU SENSEI.
AND IF IT'S OKITA SENSEI, PLEASE LET HIM COME IN!!
OH, SEEMS LIKE SEI'S...
...EARS ARE WORKING PROPER-LY.
MA...
MATSU-MOTO SENSEI?!
HA HA HA HA
D-D-DID YOU AND SAITO-SAN COLLUDE TO TRICK ME...?!
YOU SHOULD THINK ABOUT SAITO'S FEELINGS TOO.
THE ONLY THING SEI TALKED ABOUT SINCE SHE REGAINED CONSCIOUS-NESS WAS YOU.
About how she had a dream, and now she's not depressed...

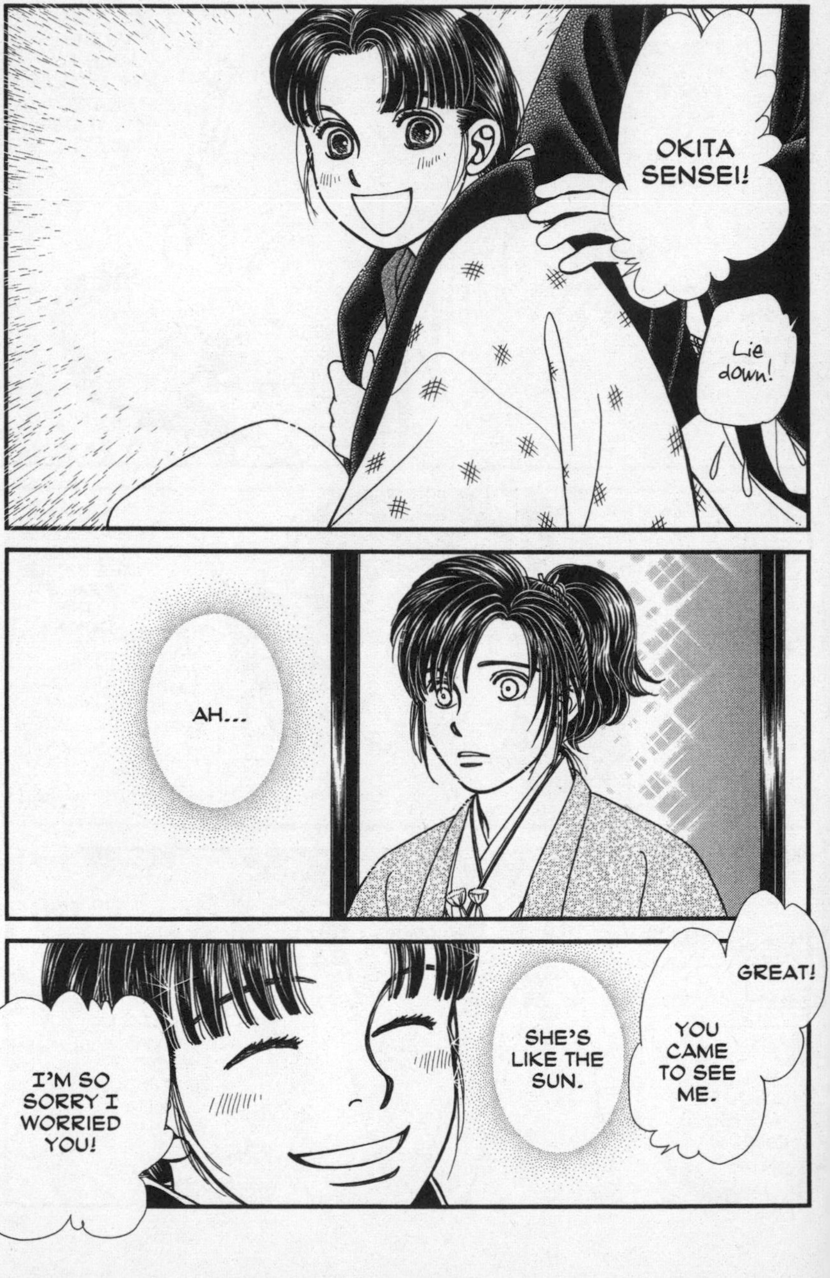
OKITA SENSEI!
Lie down!
AH...
GREAT!
YOU CAME TO SEE ME.
SHE'S LIKE THE SUN.
I'M SO SORRY I WORRIED YOU!

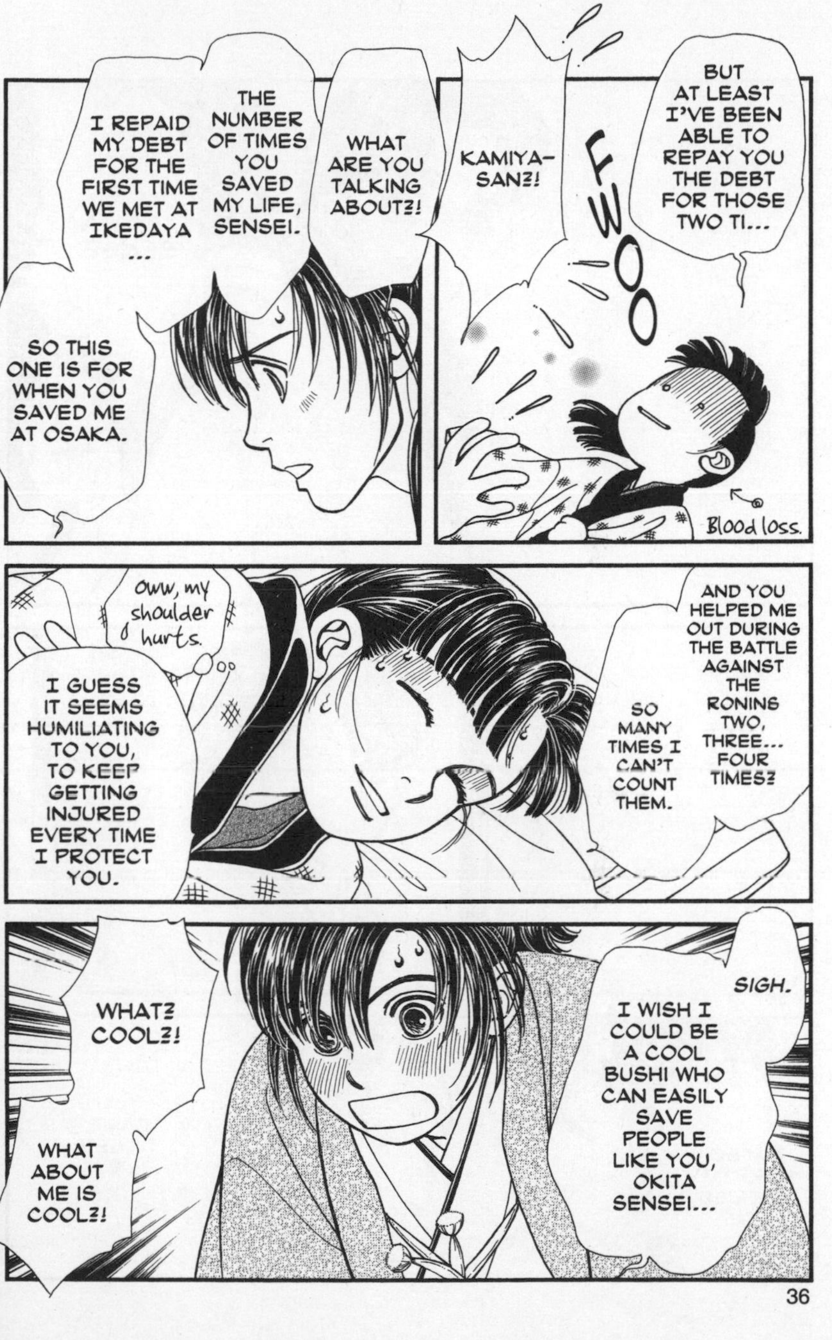
BUT AT LEAST I'VE BEEN ABLE TO REPAY YOU THE DEBT FOR THOSE TWO TI...
FWOOO
KAMIYA-SAN?!
Blood loss.
WHAT ARE YOU TALKING ABOUT?!
THE NUMBER OF TIMES YOU SAVED MY LIFE, SENSEI.
I REPAID MY DEBT FOR THE FIRST TIME WE MET AT IKEDAYA ...
SO THIS ONE IS FOR WHEN YOU SAVED ME AT OSAKA.
AND YOU HELPED ME OUT DURING THE BATTLE AGAINST THE RONINS TWO, THREE... FOUR TIMES?
SO MANY TIMES I CAN'T COUNT THEM.
Oww, my shoulder hurts.
I GUESS IT SEEMS HUMILIATING TO YOU, TO KEEP GETTING INJURED EVERY TIME I PROTECT YOU.
SIGH.
I WISH I COULD BE A COOL BUSHI WHO CAN EASILY SAVE PEOPLE LIKE YOU, OKITA SENSEI...
WHAT? COOL?!
WHAT ABOUT ME IS COOL?!

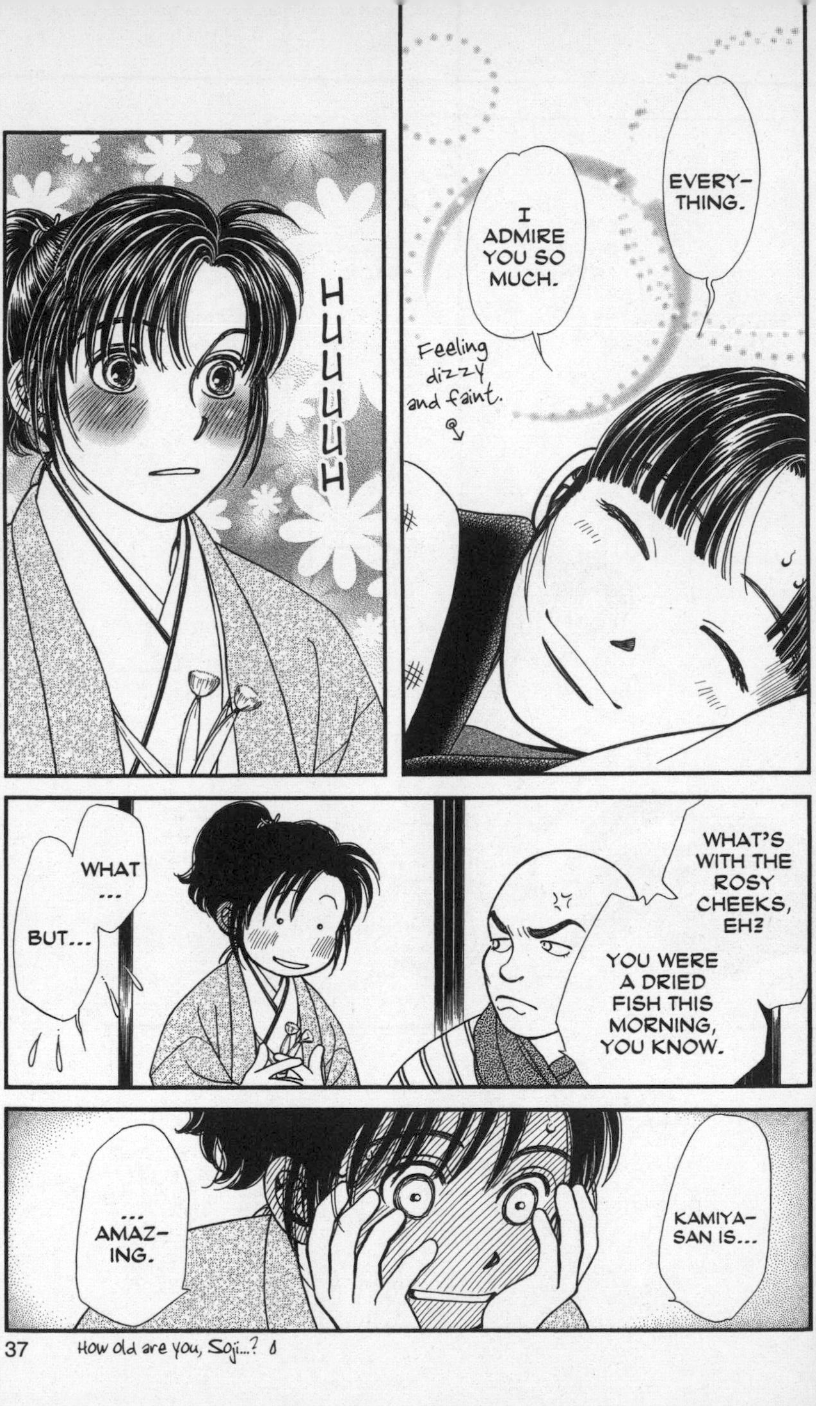
EVERY-THING.
I ADMIRE YOU SO MUCH.
Feeling dizzy and faint.
HUUUUUH
WHAT'S WITH THE ROSY CHEEKS, EH?
YOU WERE A DRIED FISH THIS MORNING, YOU KNOW.
WHAT ... BUT...
KAMIYA-SAN IS...
...AMAZ-ING.

 How old are you, Soji...?

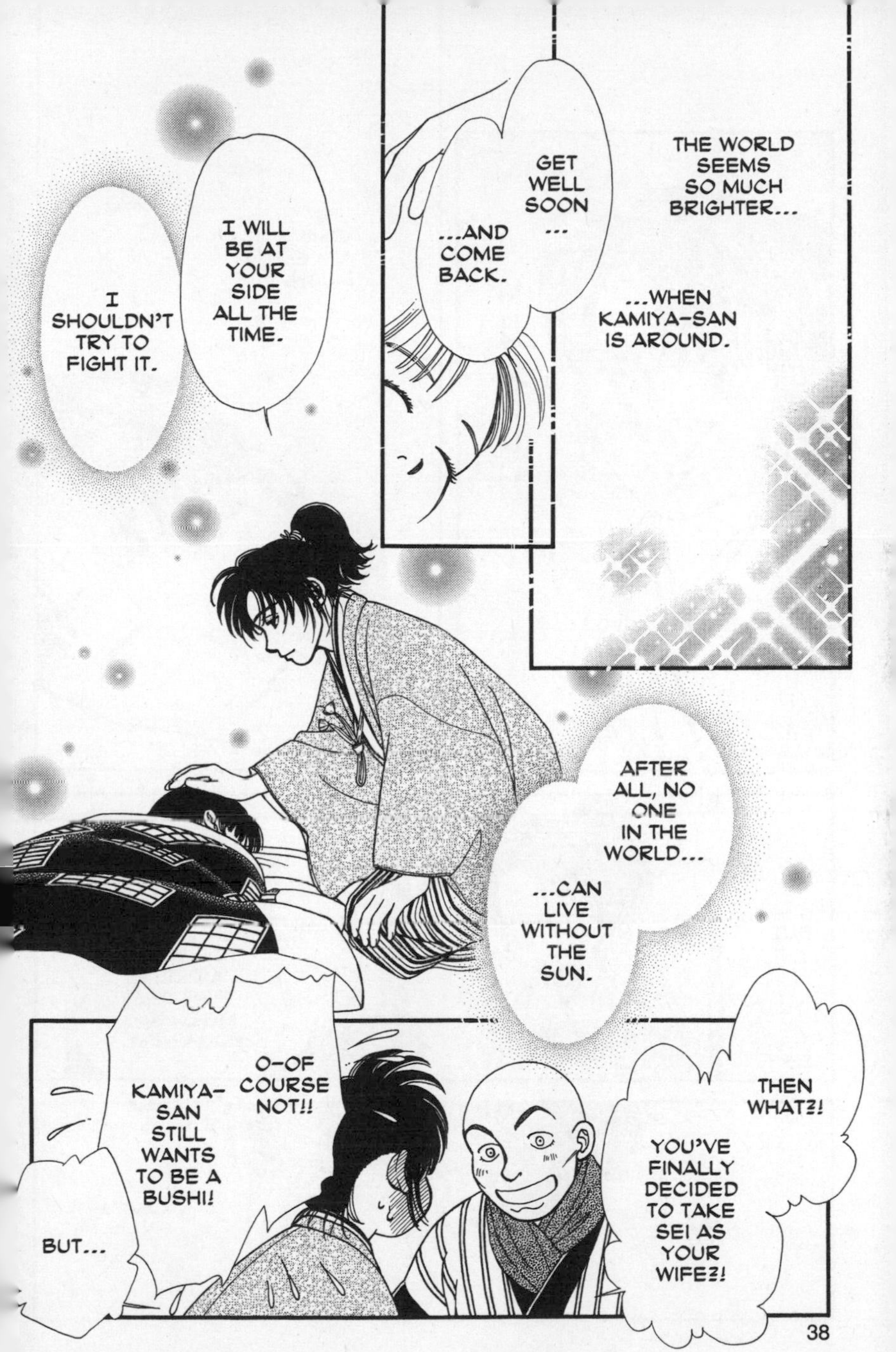
THE WORLD SEEMS SO MUCH BRIGHTER...
...WHEN KAMIYA-SAN IS AROUND.
GET WELL SOON...
...AND COME BACK.
I WILL BE AT YOUR SIDE ALL THE TIME.
I SHOULDN'T TRY TO FIGHT IT.
AFTER ALL, NO ONE IN THE WORLD...
...CAN LIVE WITHOUT THE SUN.
THEN WHAT?!
YOU'VE FINALLY DECIDED TO TAKE SEI AS YOUR WIFE?!
O-OF COURSE NOT!!
KAMIYA-SAN STILL WANTS TO BE A BUSHI!
BUT...

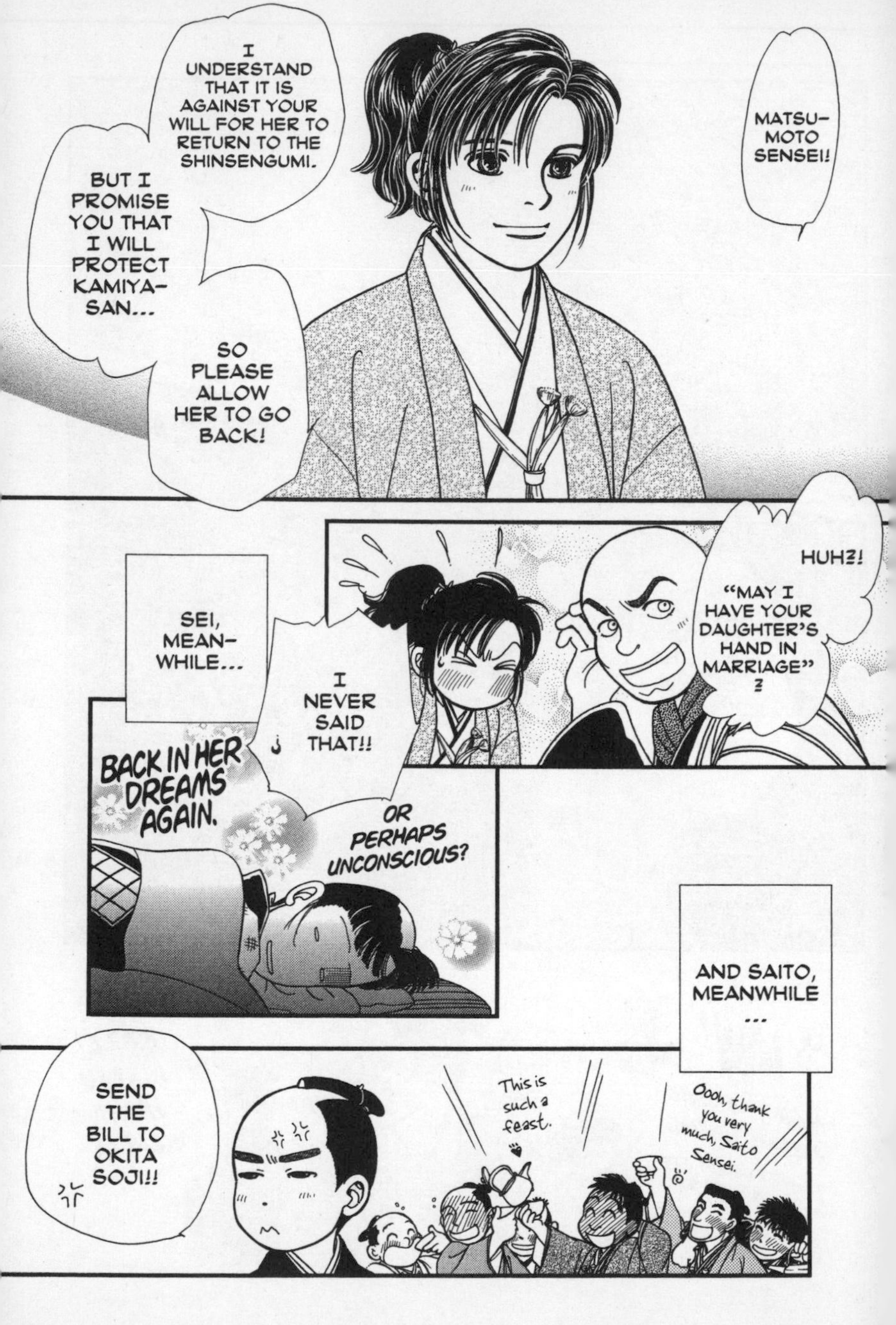
MATSU-MOTO SENSEI!
I UNDERSTAND THAT IT IS AGAINST YOUR WILL FOR HER TO RETURN TO THE SHINSENGUMI.
BUT I PROMISE YOU THAT I WILL PROTECT KAMIYA-SAN...
SO PLEASE ALLOW HER TO GO BACK!
HUH?!
"MAY I HAVE YOUR DAUGHTER'S HAND IN MARRIAGE"?
I NEVER SAID THAT!!
SEI, MEAN-WHILE...
BACK IN HER DREAMS AGAIN.
OR PERHAPS UNCONSCIOUS?
AND SAITO, MEANWHILE ...
Oooh, thank you very much, Saito Sensei.
This is such a feast.
SEND THE BILL TO OKITA SOJI!!

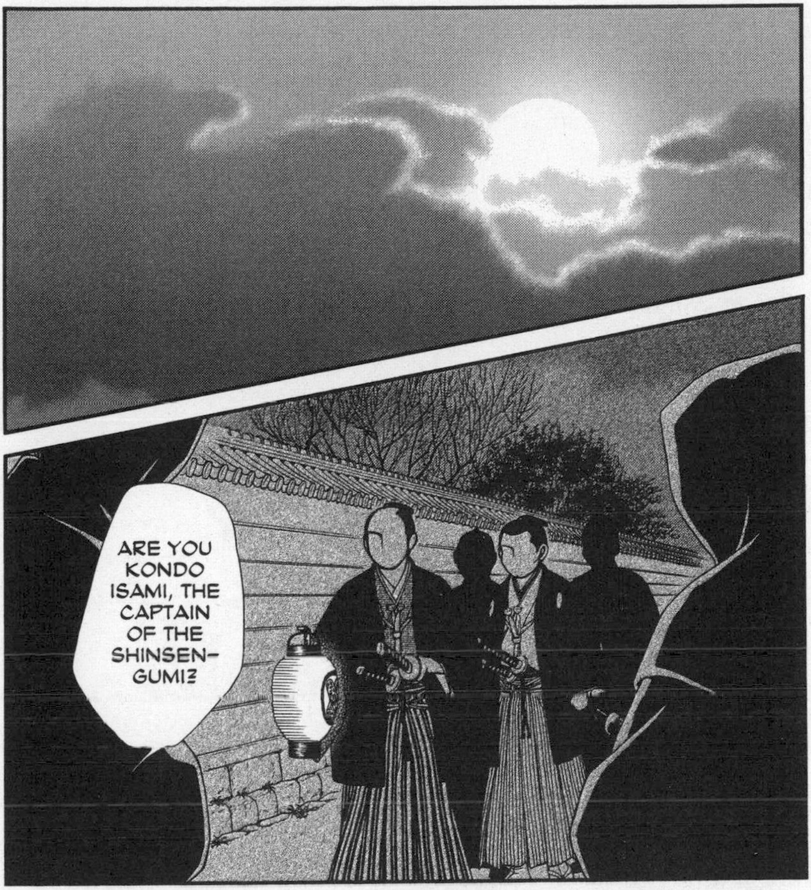
ARE YOU KONDO ISAMI, THE CAPTAIN OF THE SHINSEN-GUMI?

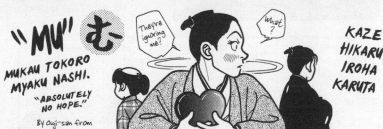

"MU" む

MUKAU TOKORO MYAKU NASHI.

"ABSOLUTELY NO HOPE."

By Ouji-san from Kanagawa

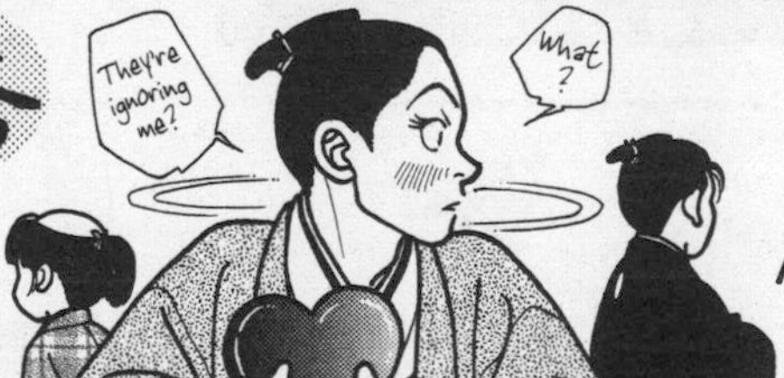
What?
They're ignoring me?

KAZE HIKARU IROHA KARUTA

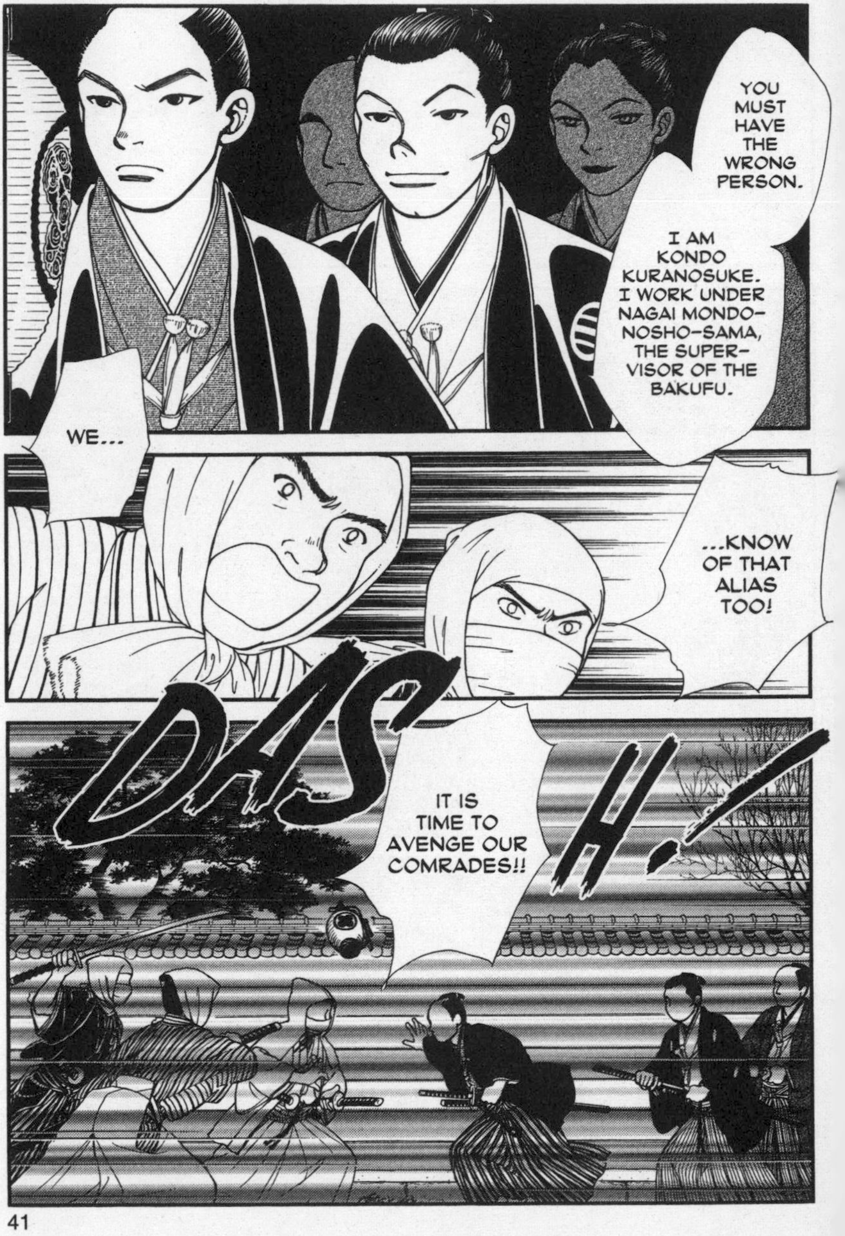
YOU MUST HAVE THE WRONG PERSON.
I AM KONDO KURANOSUKE. I WORK UNDER NAGAI MONDO-NOSHO-SAMA, THE SUPER-VISOR OF THE BAKUFU.
WE...
...KNOW OF THAT ALIAS TOO!
DASH!
IT IS TIME TO AVENGE OUR COMRADES!!

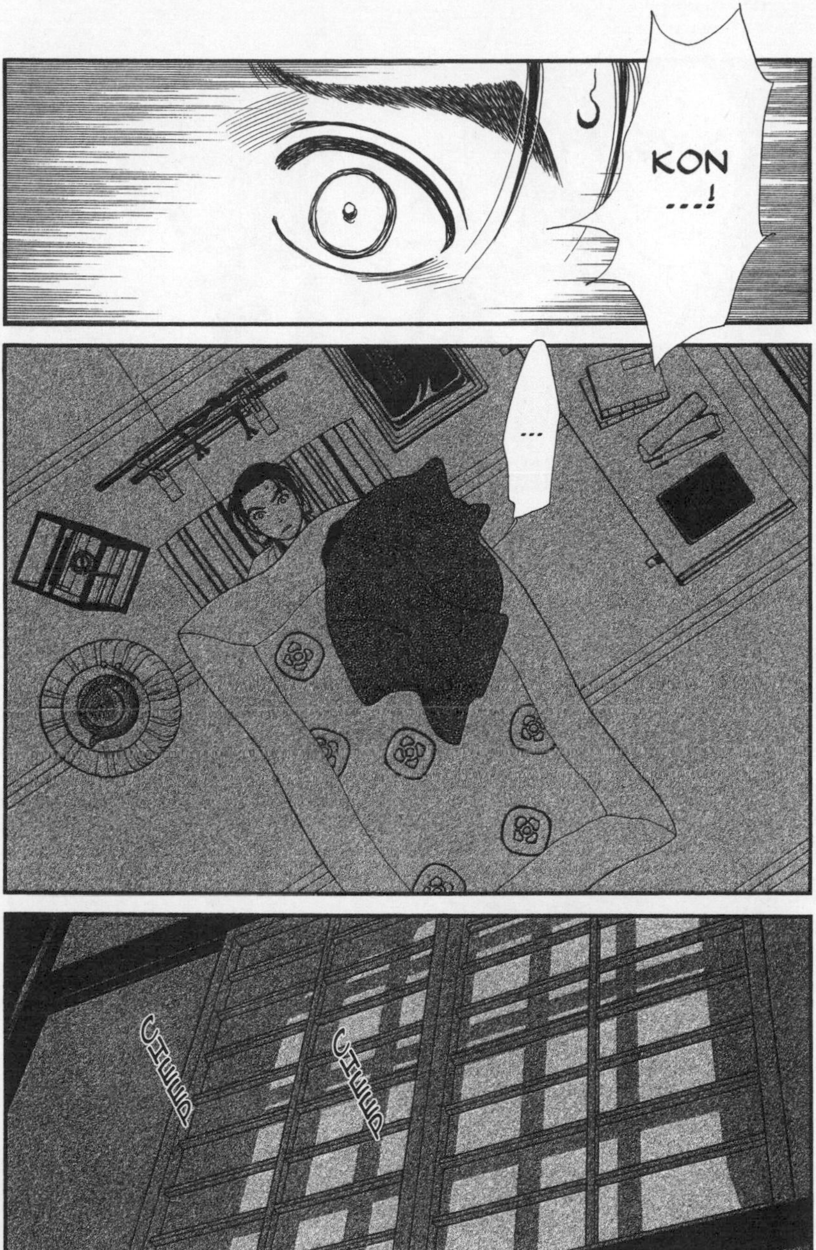
KON
...!
...

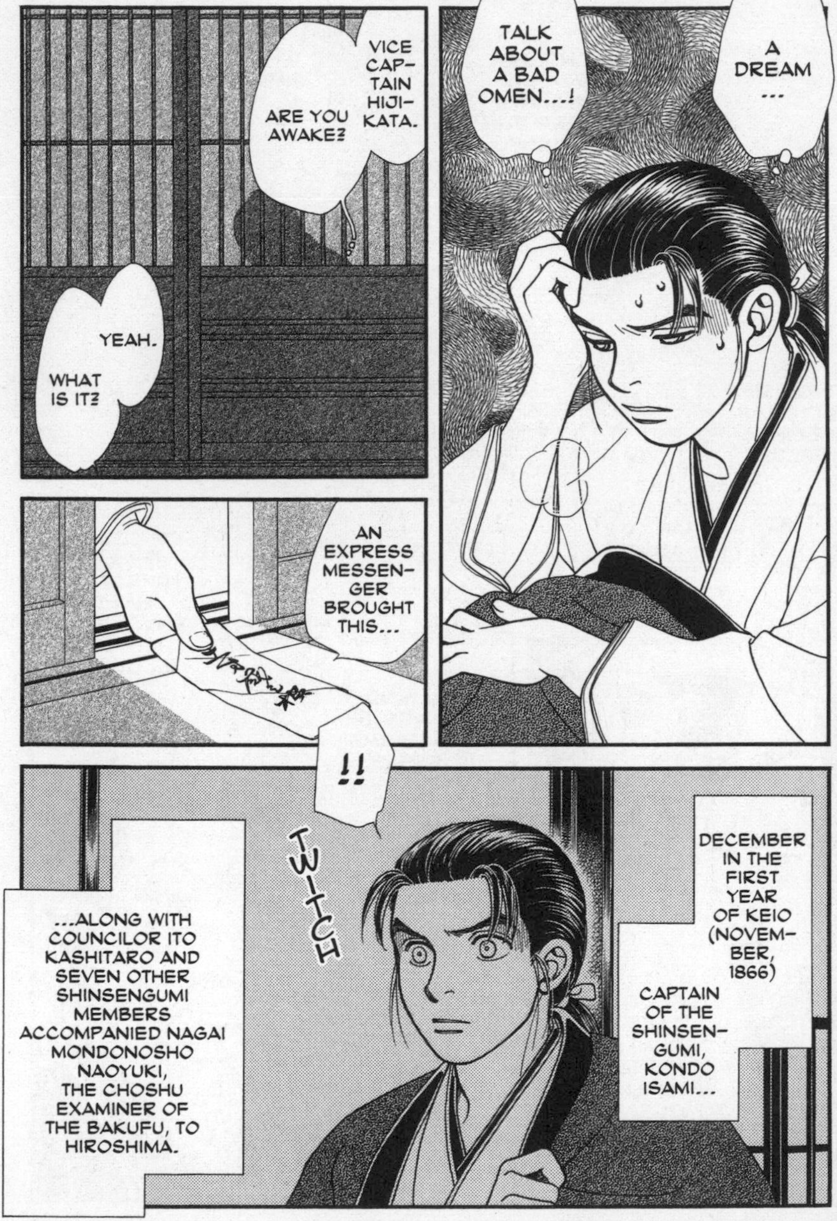
A DREAM ...
TALK ABOUT A BAD OMEN...!
VICE CAPTAIN HIJIKATA.
ARE YOU AWAKE?
YEAH.
WHAT IS IT?
AN EXPRESS MESSENGER BROUGHT THIS...
!!
TWITCH
DECEMBER IN THE FIRST YEAR OF KEIO (NOVEMBER, 1866)
CAPTAIN OF THE SHINSENGUMI, KONDO ISAMI...
...ALONG WITH COUNCILOR ITO KASHITARO AND SEVEN OTHER SHINSENGUMI MEMBERS ACCOMPANIED NAGAI MONDONOSHO NAOYUKI, THE CHOSHU EXAMINER OF THE BAKUFU, TO HIROSHIMA.

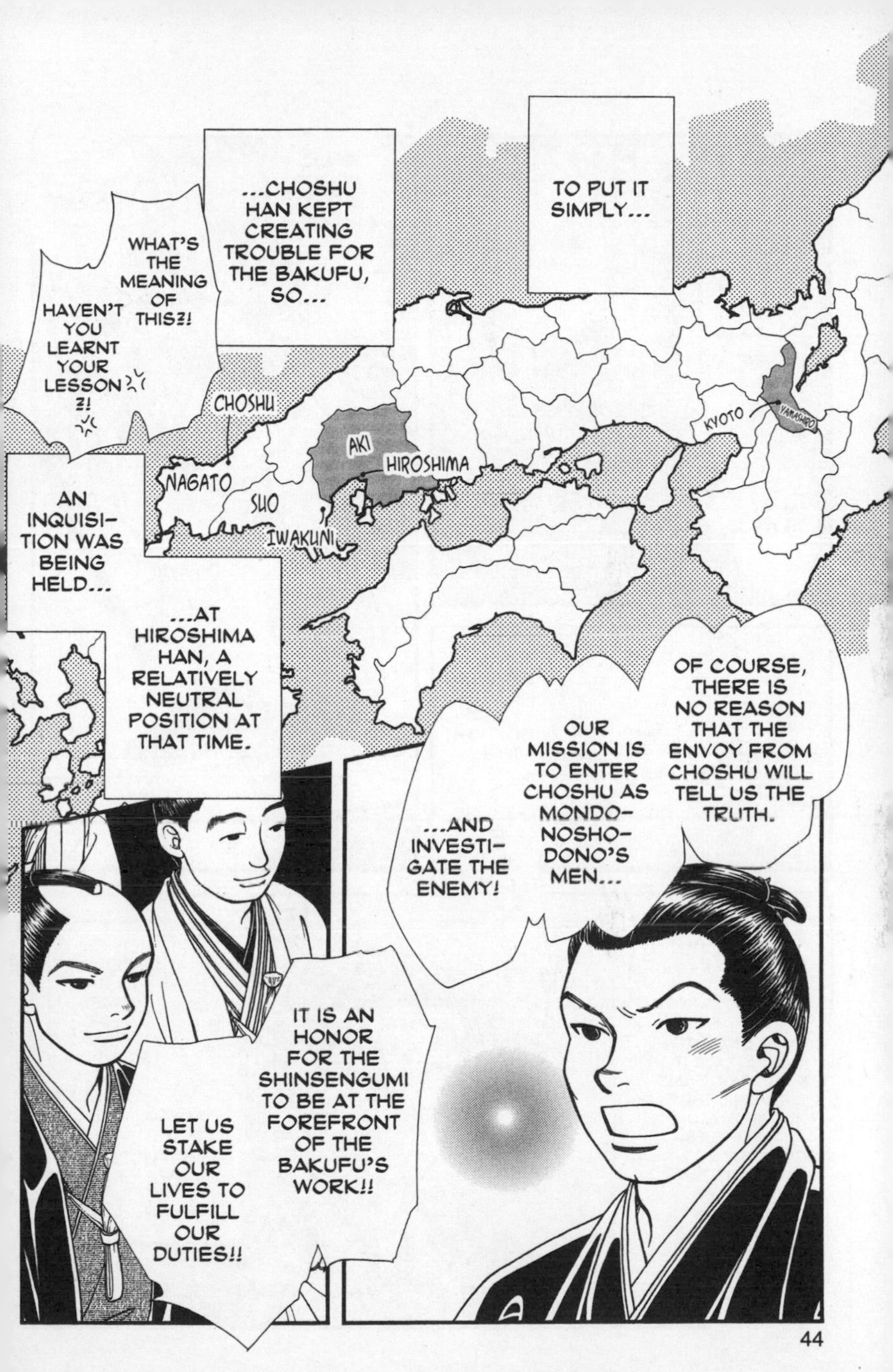
TO PUT IT SIMPLY...
...CHOSHU HAN KEPT CREATING TROUBLE FOR THE BAKUFU, SO...
WHAT'S THE MEANING OF THIS?!
HAVEN'T YOU LEARNT YOUR LESSON?!
CHOSHU
NAGATO
SUO
IWAKUNI
AKI
HIROSHIMA
KYOTO
YAMASHIRO
AN INQUISITION WAS BEING HELD...
...AT HIROSHIMA HAN, A RELATIVELY NEUTRAL POSITION AT THAT TIME.
OF COURSE, THERE IS NO REASON THAT THE ENVOY FROM CHOSHU WILL TELL US THE TRUTH.
OUR MISSION IS TO ENTER CHOSHU AS MONDO-NOSHO-DONO'S MEN...
...AND INVESTIGATE THE ENEMY!
IT IS AN HONOR FOR THE SHINSENGUMI TO BE AT THE FOREFRONT OF THE BAKUFU'S WORK!!
LET US STAKE OUR LIVES TO FULFILL OUR DUTIES!!

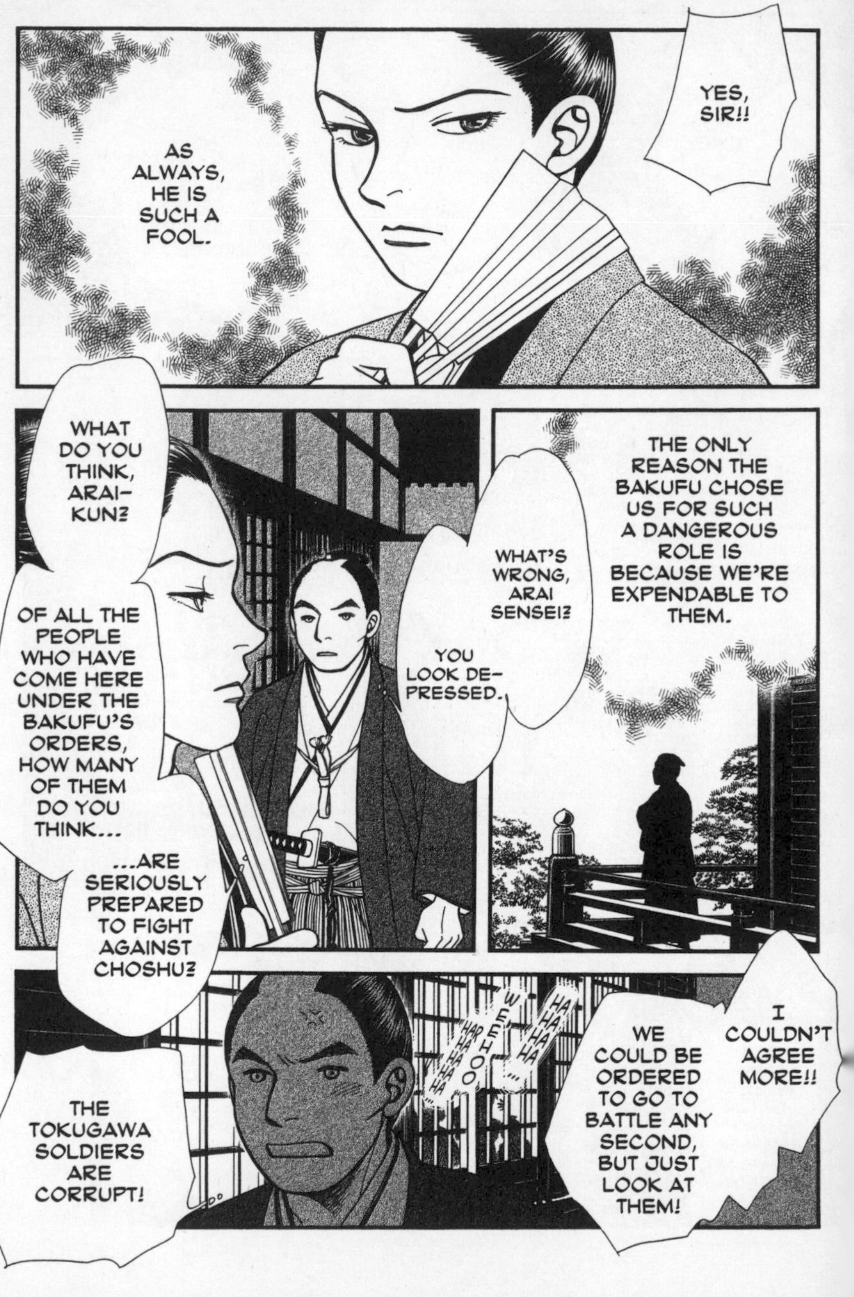

YES, SIR!!
AS ALWAYS, HE IS SUCH A FOOL.
THE ONLY REASON THE BAKUFU CHOSE US FOR SUCH A DANGEROUS ROLE IS BECAUSE WE'RE EXPENDABLE TO THEM.
WHAT'S WRONG, ARAI SENSEI!?
YOU LOOK DE-PRESSED.
WHAT DO YOU THINK, ARAI-KUN!?
OF ALL THE PEOPLE WHO HAVE COME HERE UNDER THE BAKUFU'S ORDERS, HOW MANY OF THEM DO YOU THINK...
...ARE SERIOUSLY PREPARED TO FIGHT AGAINST CHOSHU!?
I COULDN'T AGREE MORE!!
WE COULD BE ORDERED TO GO TO BATTLE ANY SECOND, BUT JUST LOOK AT THEM!
HA HA HA HA HA...
WEEHOO
HAR HA HA HA HA
THE TOKUGAWA SOLDIERS ARE CORRUPT!

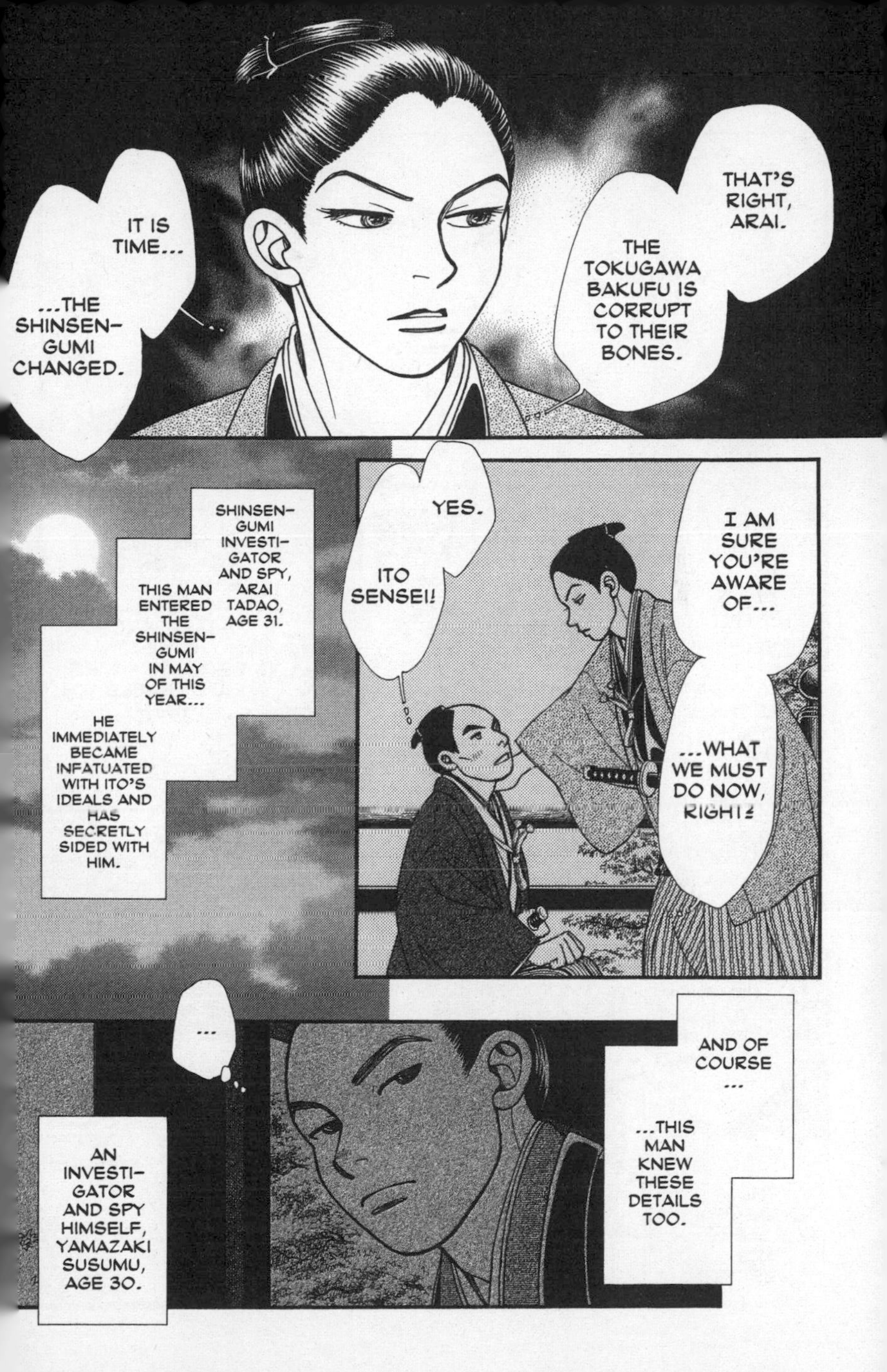
THAT'S RIGHT, ARAI.
THE TOKUGAWA BAKUFU IS CORRUPT TO THEIR BONES.
IT IS TIME...
...THE SHINSEN-GUMI CHANGED.
I AM SURE YOU'RE AWARE OF...
...WHAT WE MUST DO NOW, RIGHT?
YES.
ITO SENSEI!
SHINSEN-GUMI INVESTIGATOR AND SPY, ARAI TADAO, AGE 31.
THIS MAN ENTERED THE SHINSEN-GUMI IN MAY OF THIS YEAR...
HE IMMEDIATELY BECAME INFATUATED WITH ITO'S IDEALS AND HAS SECRETLY SIDED WITH HIM.
AND OF COURSE...
...THIS MAN KNEW THESE DETAILS TOO.
...
AN INVESTIGATOR AND SPY HIMSELF, YAMAZAKI SUSUMU, AGE 30.

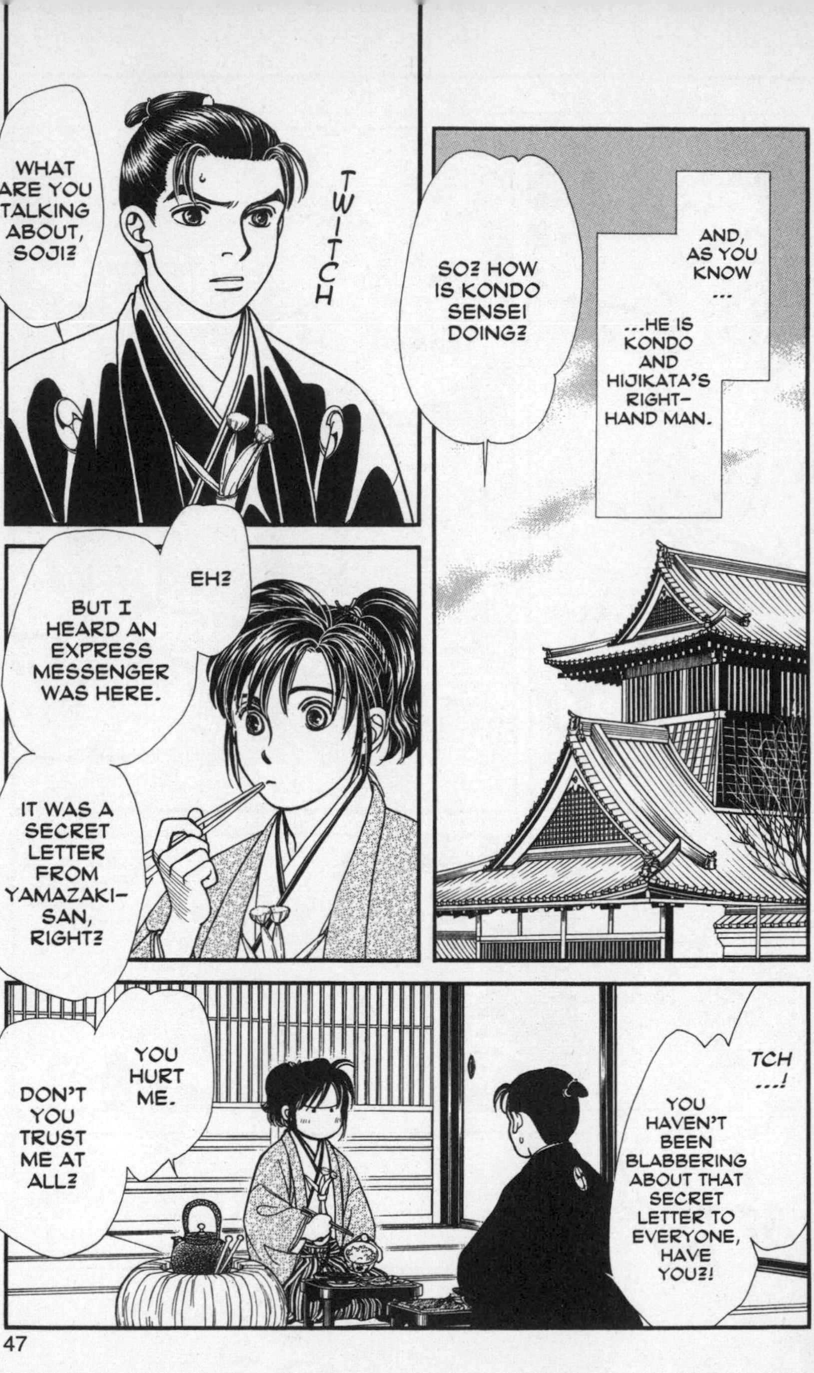
AND, AS YOU KNOW ... ...HE IS KONDO AND HIJIKATA'S RIGHT-HAND MAN.
SO? HOW IS KONDO SENSEI DOING?
TWITCH
WHAT ARE YOU TALKING ABOUT, SOJI?
EH?
BUT I HEARD AN EXPRESS MESSENGER WAS HERE.
IT WAS A SECRET LETTER FROM YAMAZAKI-SAN, RIGHT?
TCH ...!
YOU HAVEN'T BEEN BLABBERING ABOUT THAT SECRET LETTER TO EVERYONE, HAVE YOU?!
YOU HURT ME.
DON'T YOU TRUST ME AT ALL?

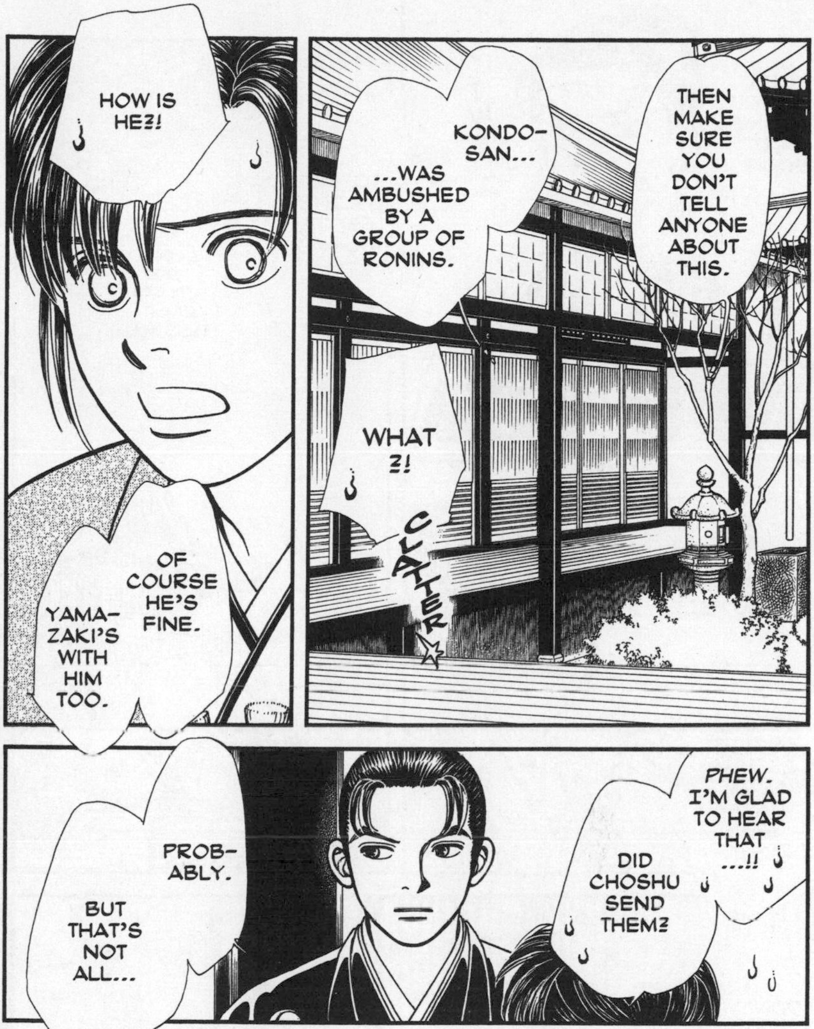
THEN MAKE SURE YOU DON'T TELL ANYONE ABOUT THIS.
KONDO-SAN...
...WAS AMBUSHED BY A GROUP OF RONINS.
WHAT?!
CLATTER
HOW IS HE?!
OF COURSE HE'S FINE.
YAMAZAKI'S WITH HIM TOO.
PHEW. I'M GLAD TO HEAR THAT...!!
DID CHOSHU SEND THEM?
PROBABLY.
BUT THAT'S NOT ALL...
WHAT?
what are those footsteps...?
TMP TMP TMP TMP TMP DMP

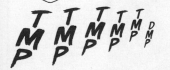

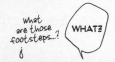

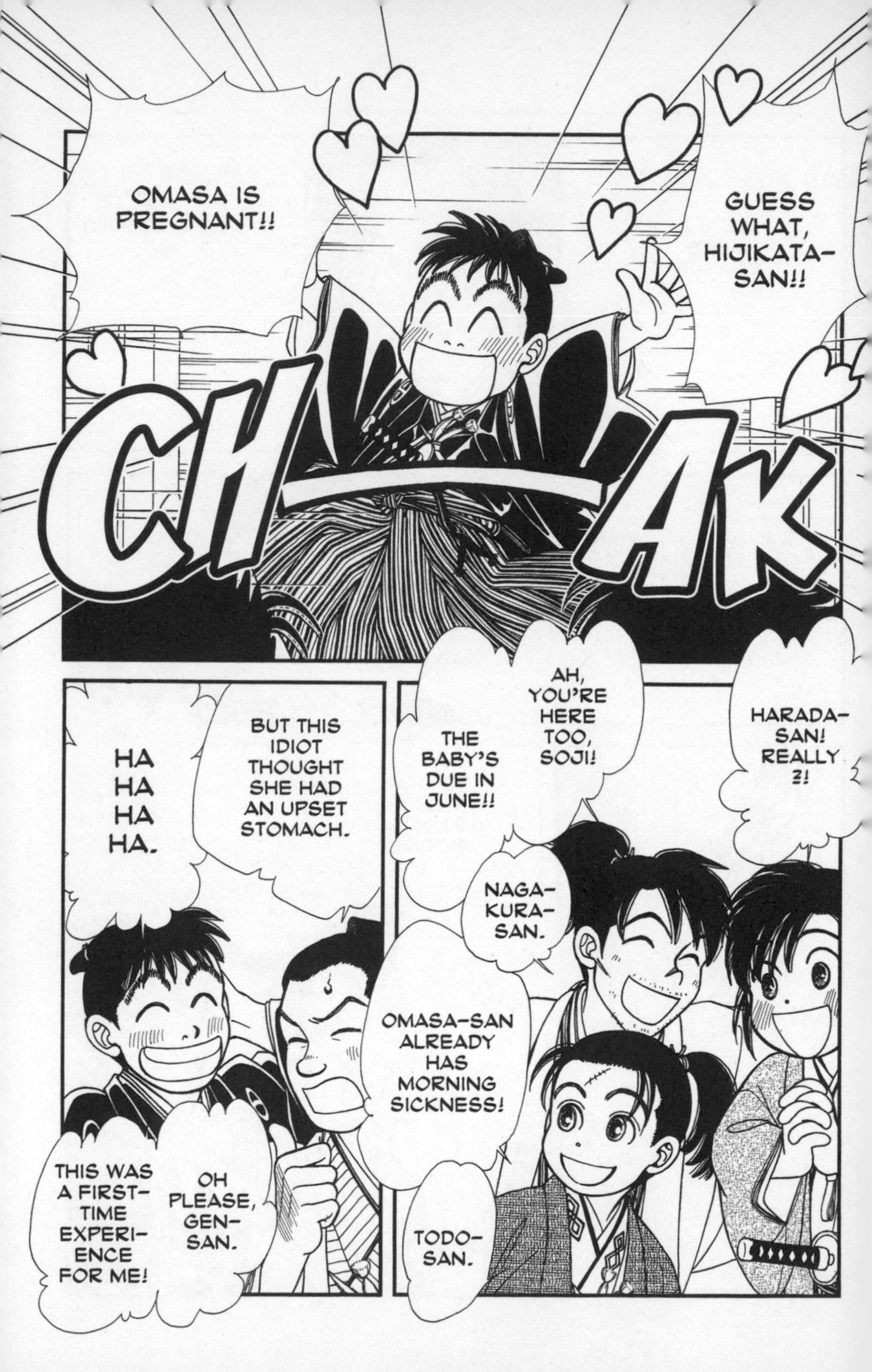
GUESS WHAT, HIJIKATA-SAN!!
OMASA IS PREGNANT!!
CHAK
HARADA-SAN! REALLY ?!
AH, YOU'RE HERE TOO, SOJI!
THE BABY'S DUE IN JUNE!!
NAGA-KURA-SAN.
OMASA-SAN ALREADY HAS MORNING SICKNESS!
TODO-SAN.
BUT THIS IDIOT THOUGHT SHE HAD AN UPSET STOMACH.
HA HA HA HA.
OH PLEASE, GEN-SAN.
THIS WAS A FIRST-TIME EXPERIENCE FOR ME!

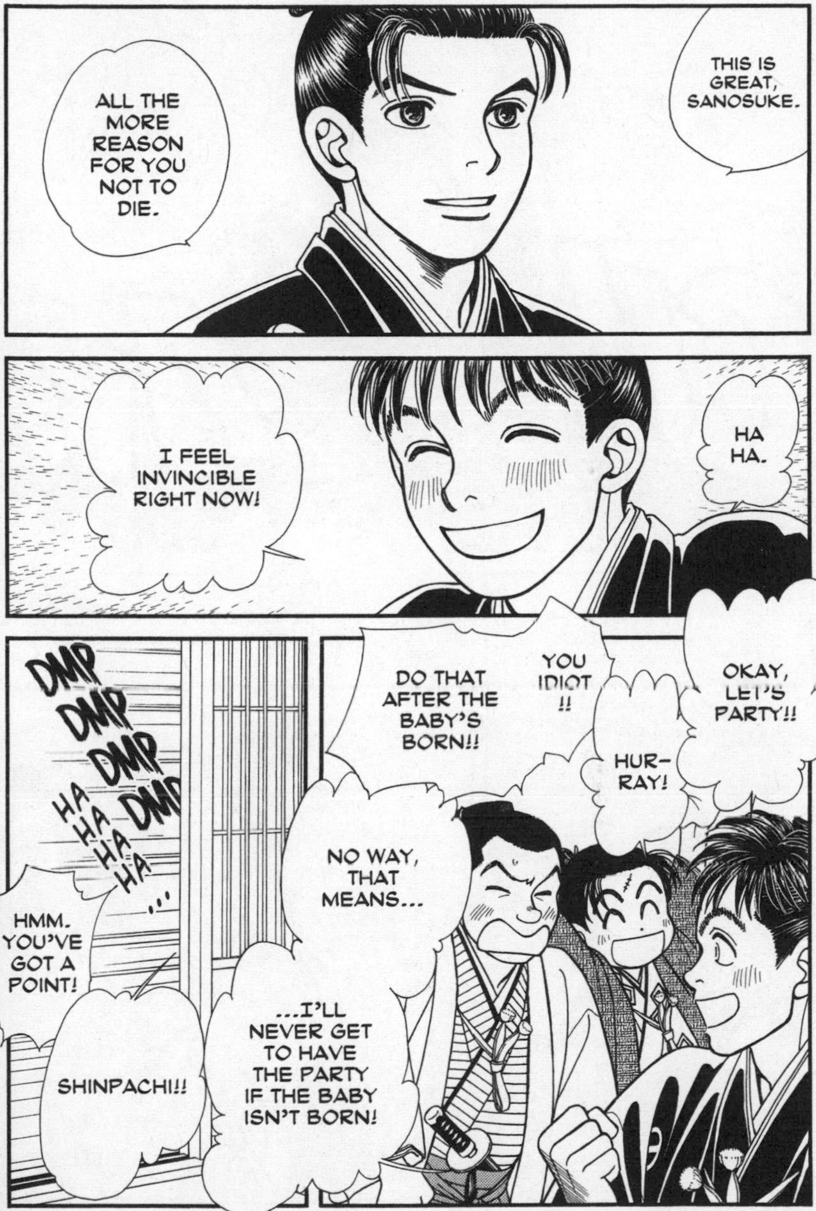
THIS IS GREAT, SANOSUKE.
ALL THE MORE REASON FOR YOU NOT TO DIE.
HA HA.
I FEEL INVINCIBLE RIGHT NOW!
OKAY, LET'S PARTY!!
HUR-RAY!
YOU IDIOT!!
DO THAT AFTER THE BABY'S BORN!!
NO WAY, THAT MEANS...
...I'LL NEVER GET TO HAVE THE PARTY IF THE BABY ISN'T BORN!
DMP DMP DMP DMP
HA HA HA HA
...
HMM. YOU'VE GOT A POINT!
SHINPACHI!!

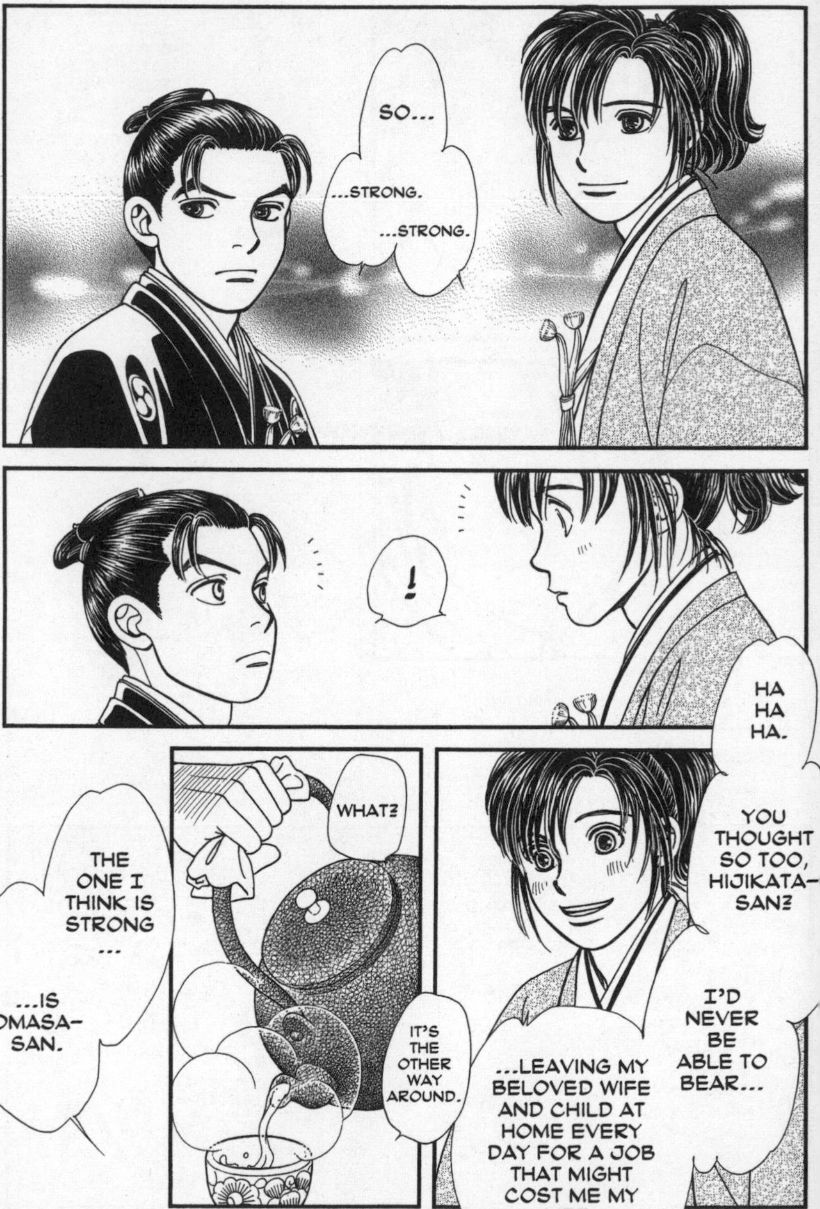
SO...
...STRONG.
...STRONG.
!
HA HA HA.
YOU THOUGHT SO TOO, HIJIKATA-SAN?
I'D NEVER BE ABLE TO BEAR...
...LEAVING MY BELOVED WIFE AND CHILD AT HOME EVERY DAY FOR A JOB THAT MIGHT COST ME MY LIFE.
WHAT?
IT'S THE OTHER WAY AROUND.
THE ONE I THINK IS STRONG...
...IS OMASA-SAN.

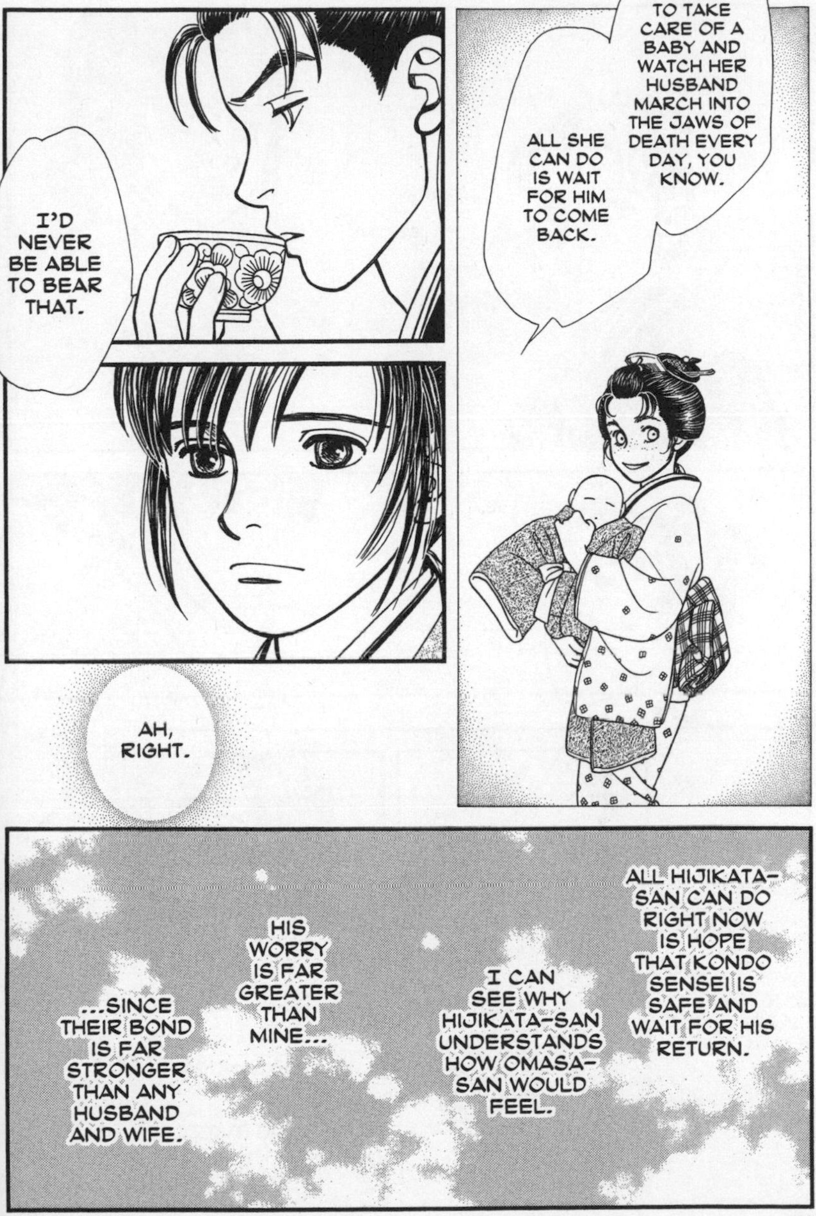
SHE HAS TO TAKE CARE OF A BABY AND WATCH HER HUSBAND MARCH INTO THE JAWS OF DEATH EVERY DAY, YOU KNOW.
ALL SHE CAN DO IS WAIT FOR HIM TO COME BACK.
I'D NEVER BE ABLE TO BEAR THAT.
AH, RIGHT.
ALL HIJIKATA-SAN CAN DO RIGHT NOW IS HOPE THAT KONDO SENSEI IS SAFE AND WAIT FOR HIS RETURN.
I CAN SEE WHY HIJIKATA-SAN UNDERSTANDS HOW OMASA-SAN WOULD FEEL.
HIS WORRY IS FAR GREATER THAN MINE...
...SINCE THEIR BOND IS FAR STRONGER THAN ANY HUSBAND AND WIFE.

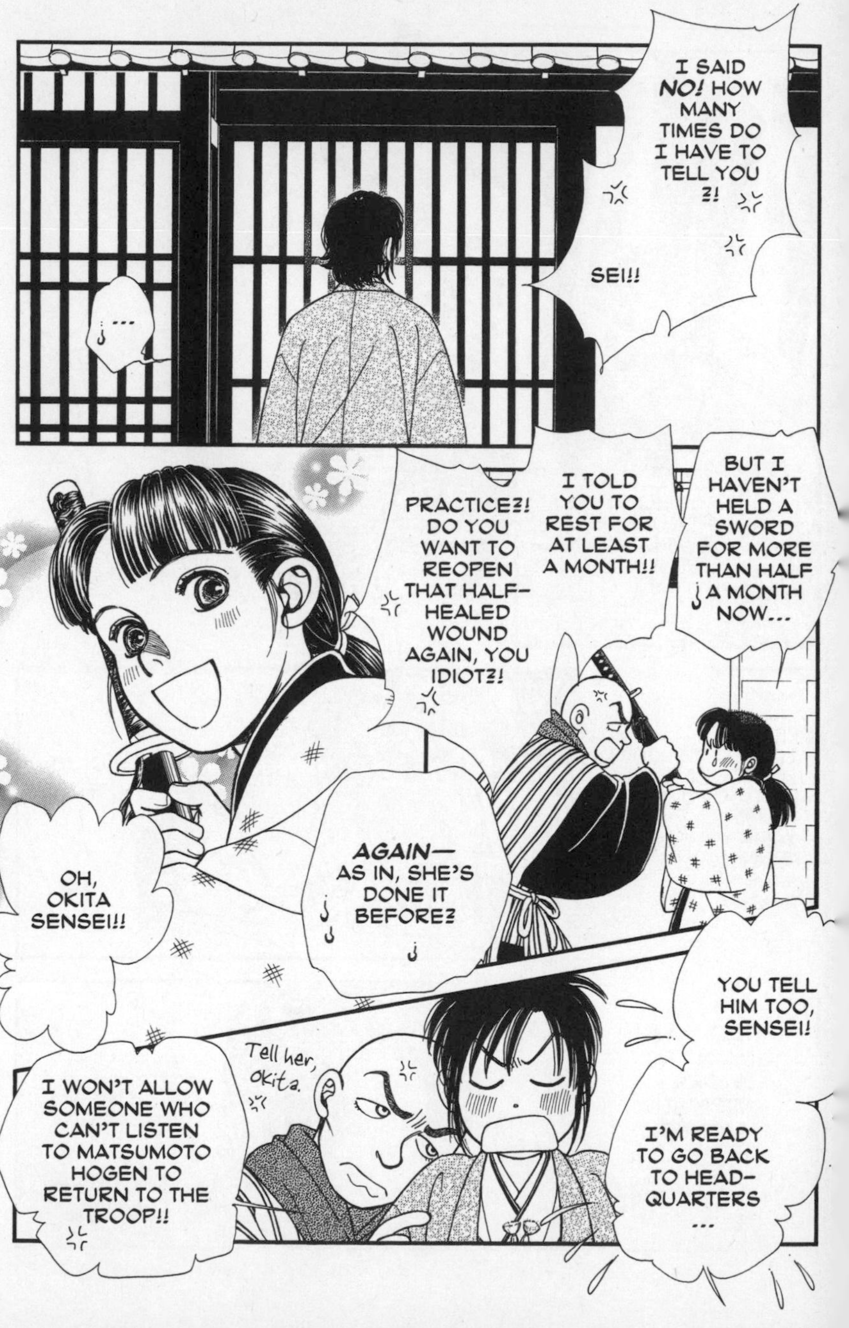
I SAID NO! HOW MANY TIMES DO I HAVE TO TELL YOU?!
SEI!!
...
BUT I HAVEN'T HELD A SWORD FOR MORE THAN HALF A MONTH NOW...
I TOLD YOU TO REST FOR AT LEAST A MONTH!!
PRACTICE?! DO YOU WANT TO REOPEN THAT HALF-HEALED WOUND AGAIN, YOU IDIOT?!
AGAIN— AS IN, SHE'S DONE IT BEFORE?
OH, OKITA SENSEI!!!
YOU TELL HIM TOO, SENSEI!
I'M READY TO GO BACK TO HEAD-QUARTERS ...
Tell her, Okita.
I WON'T ALLOW SOMEONE WHO CAN'T LISTEN TO MATSUMOTO HOGEN TO RETURN TO THE TROOP!!

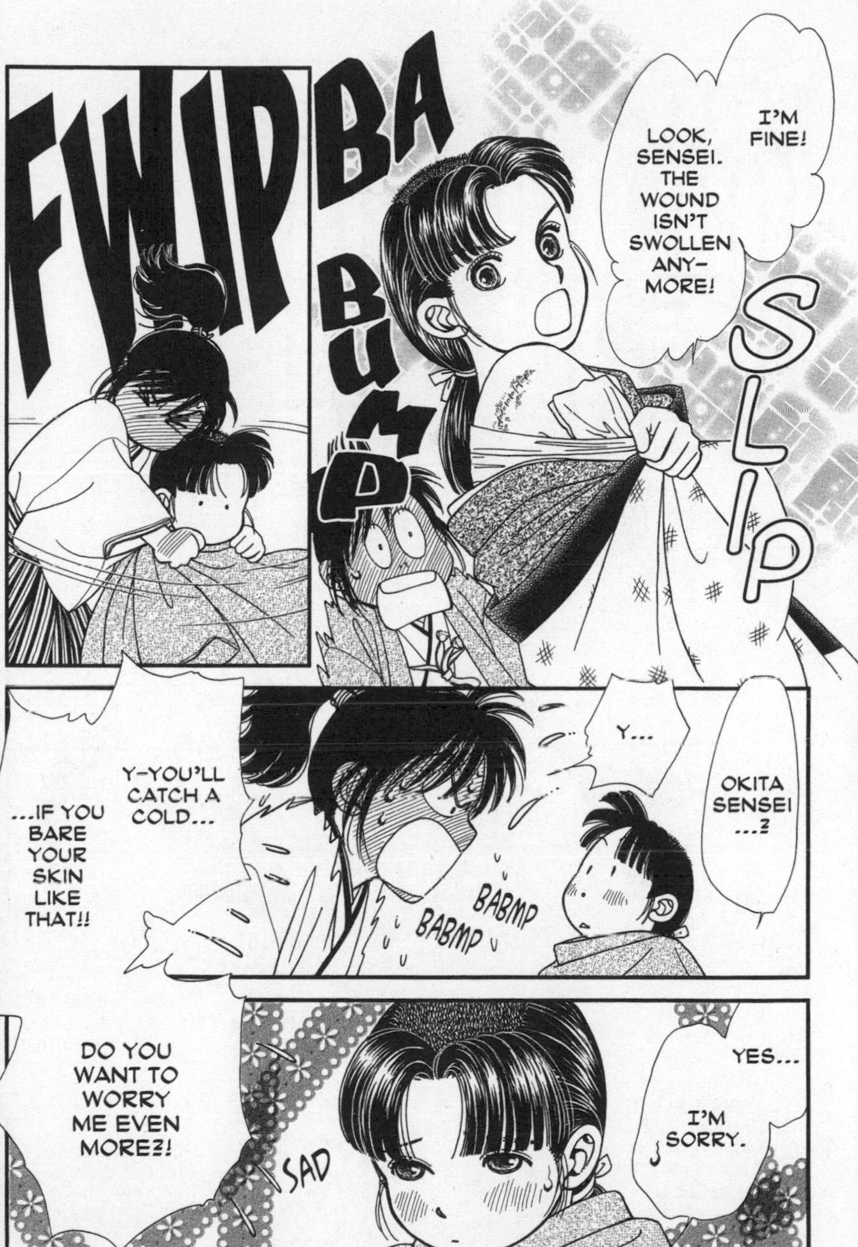
I'M FINE!
LOOK, SENSEI. THE WOUND ISN'T SWOLLEN ANY-MORE!
SLIP
BA BUMP
FWIP
OKITA SENSEI ...?
Y...
BABMP BABMP
Y-YOU'LL CATCH A COLD...
...IF YOU BARE YOUR SKIN LIKE THAT!!
YES...
I'M SORRY.
SAD
DO YOU WANT TO WORRY ME EVEN MORE?!

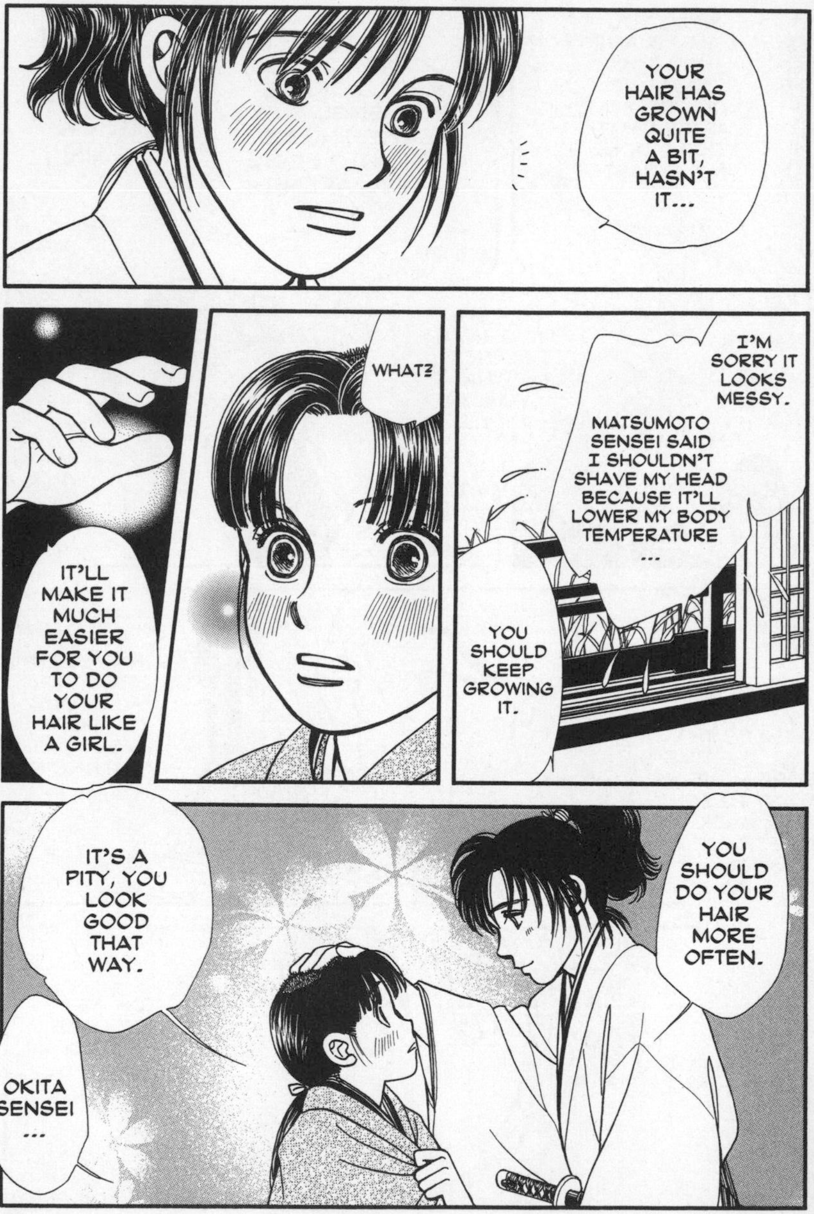
YOUR HAIR HAS GROWN QUITE A BIT, HASN'T IT...
I'M SORRY IT LOOKS MESSY.
MATSUMOTO SENSEI SAID I SHOULDN'T SHAVE MY HEAD BECAUSE IT'LL LOWER MY BODY TEMPERATURE ...
YOU SHOULD KEEP GROWING IT.
WHAT?
IT'LL MAKE IT MUCH EASIER FOR YOU TO DO YOUR HAIR LIKE A GIRL.
YOU SHOULD DO YOUR HAIR MORE OFTEN.
IT'S A PITY, YOU LOOK GOOD THAT WAY.
OKITA SENSEI ...

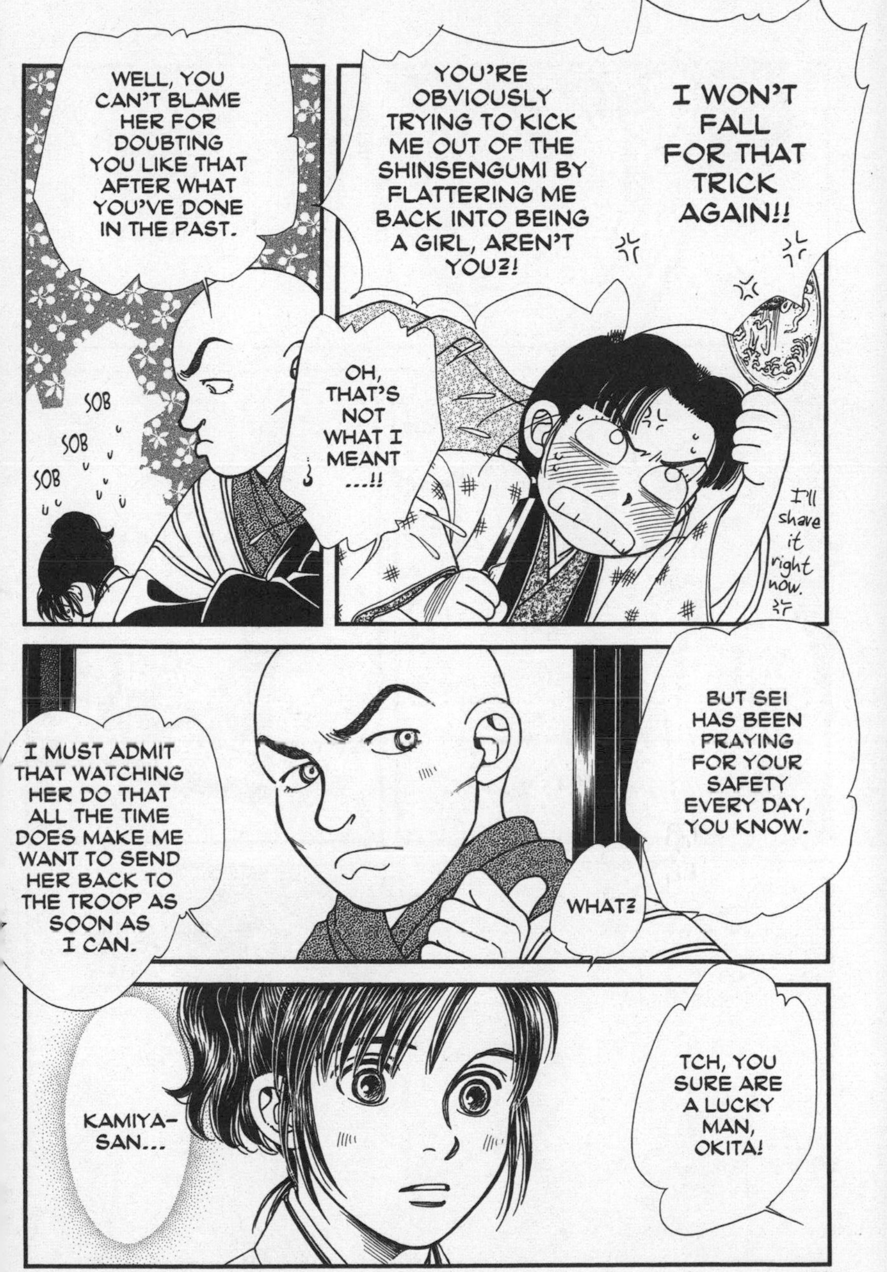
I WON'T FALL FOR THAT TRICK AGAIN!!
YOU'RE OBVIOUSLY TRYING TO KICK ME OUT OF THE SHINSENGUMI BY FLATTERING ME BACK INTO BEING A GIRL, AREN'T YOU?!
I'll shave it right now.
OH, THAT'S NOT WHAT I MEANT ...!!
WELL, YOU CAN'T BLAME HER FOR DOUBTING YOU LIKE THAT AFTER WHAT YOU'VE DONE IN THE PAST.
SOB
SOB
SOB
BUT SEI HAS BEEN PRAYING FOR YOUR SAFETY EVERY DAY, YOU KNOW.
WHAT?
I MUST ADMIT THAT WATCHING HER DO THAT ALL THE TIME DOES MAKE ME WANT TO SEND HER BACK TO THE TROOP AS SOON AS I CAN.
TCH, YOU SURE ARE A LUCKY MAN, OKITA!
KAMIYA-SAN...

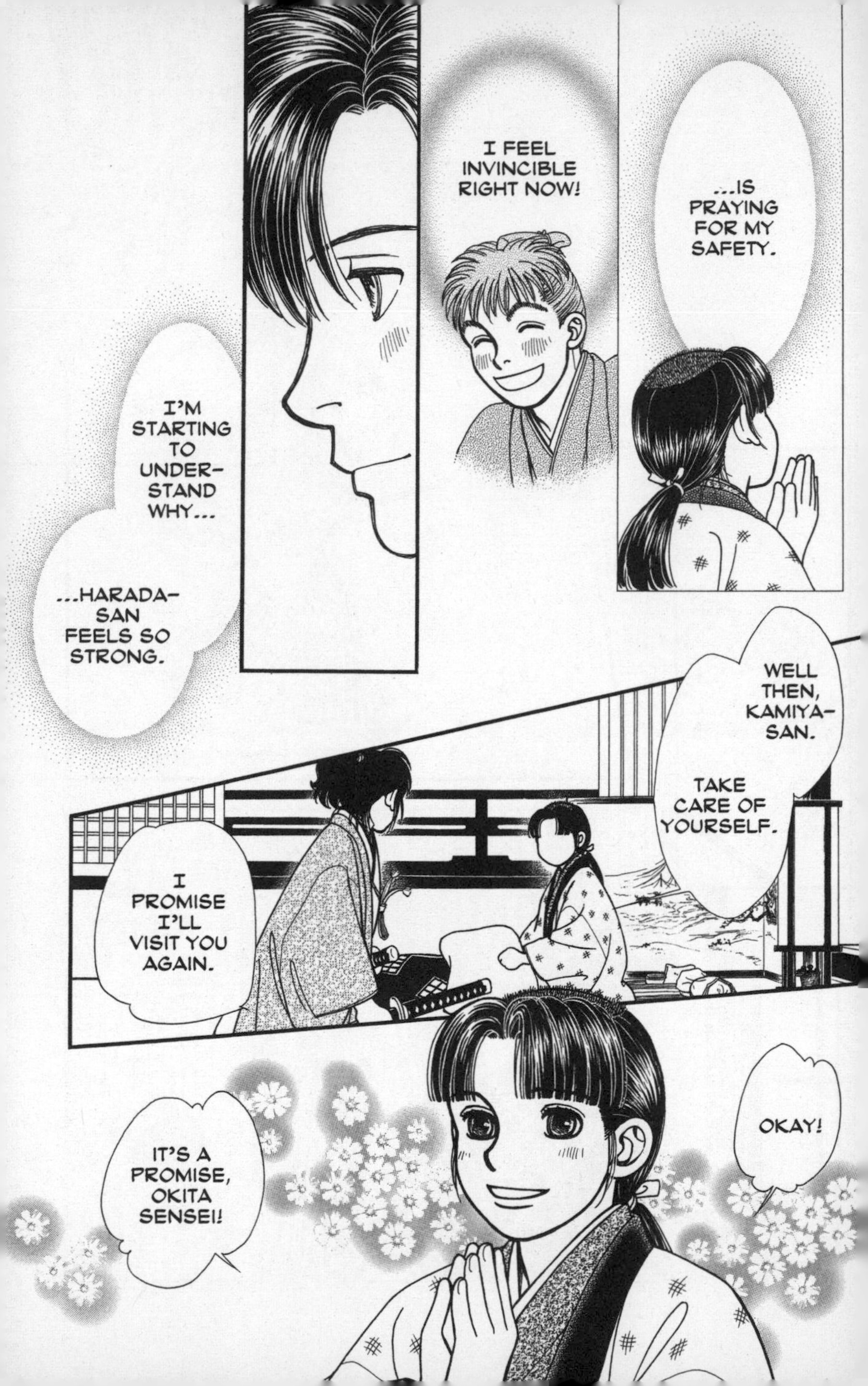
...IS PRAYING FOR MY SAFETY.
I FEEL INVINCIBLE RIGHT NOW!
I'M STARTING TO UNDER-STAND WHY...
...HARADA-SAN FEELS SO STRONG.
WELL THEN, KAMIYA-SAN.
TAKE CARE OF YOURSELF.
I PROMISE I'LL VISIT YOU AGAIN.
OKAY!
IT'S A PROMISE, OKITA SENSEI!

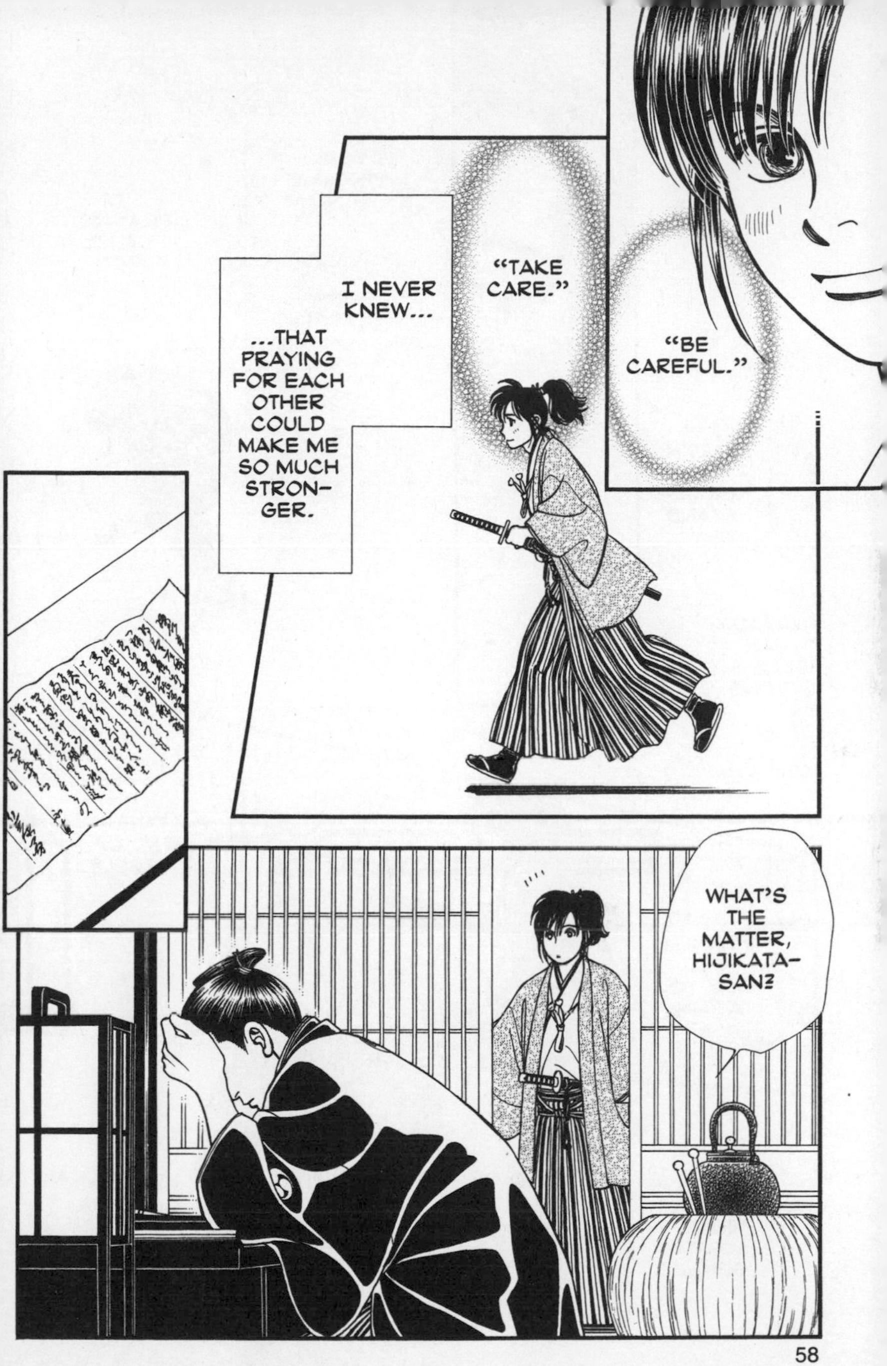
"BE CAREFUL."
"TAKE CARE."
I NEVER KNEW...
...THAT PRAYING FOR EACH OTHER COULD MAKE ME SO MUCH STRON-GER.
WHAT'S THE MATTER, HIJIKATA-SAN?

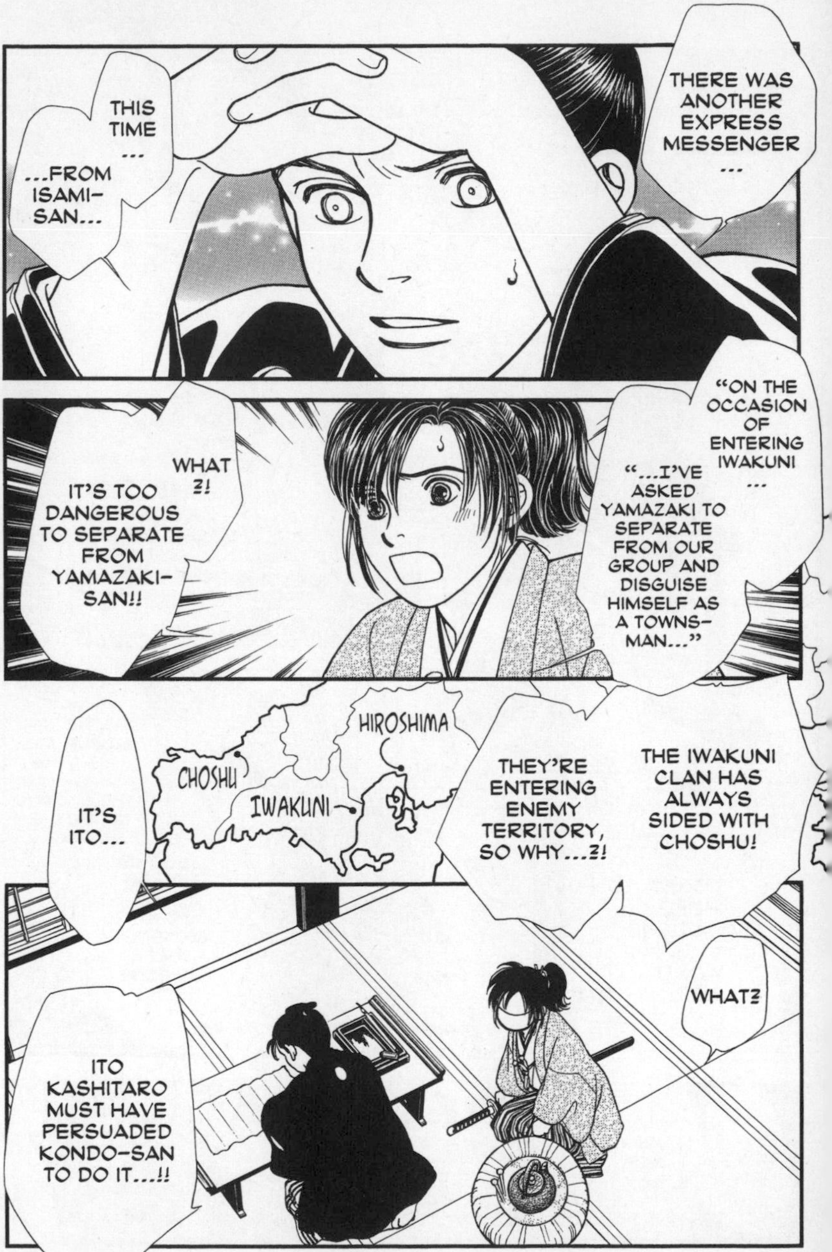
THERE WAS ANOTHER EXPRESS MESSENGER...
THIS TIME... ...FROM ISAMI-SAN...
"ON THE OCCASION OF ENTERING IWAKUNI...
"...I'VE ASKED YAMAZAKI TO SEPARATE FROM OUR GROUP AND DISGUISE HIMSELF AS A TOWNS-MAN..."
WHAT?!
IT'S TOO DANGEROUS TO SEPARATE FROM YAMAZAKI-SAN!!
THE IWAKUNI CLAN HAS ALWAYS SIDED WITH CHOSHU!
THEY'RE ENTERING ENEMY TERRITORY, SO WHY...?!
HIROSHIMA
CHOSHU
IWAKUNI
IT'S ITO...
WHAT?
ITO KASHITARO MUST HAVE PERSUADED KONDO-SAN TO DO IT...!!

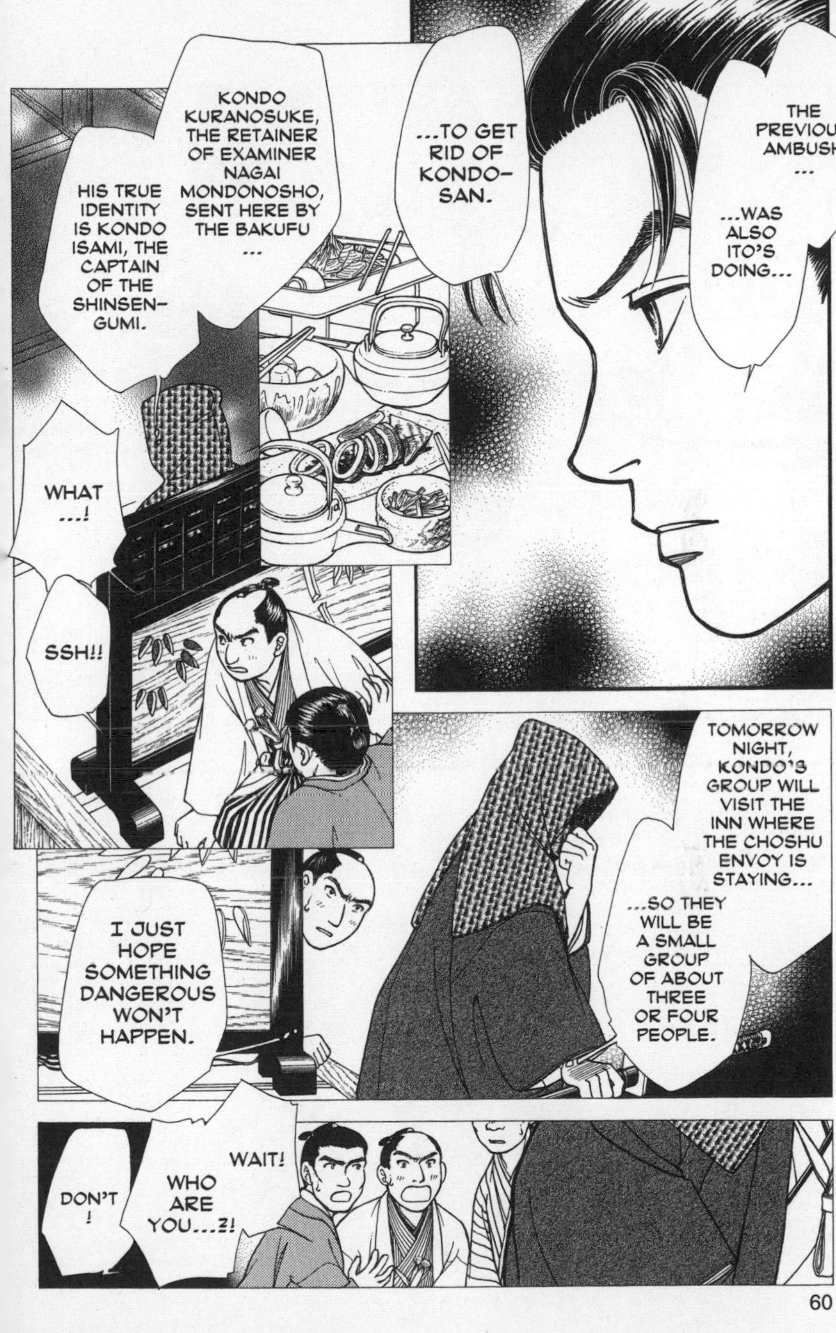
THE PREVIOUS AMBUSH ...
...WAS ALSO ITO'S DOING...
...TO GET RID OF KONDO-SAN.
KONDO KURANOSUKE, THE RETAINER OF EXAMINER NAGAI MONDONOSHO, SENT HERE BY THE BAKUFU ...
HIS TRUE IDENTITY IS KONDO ISAMI, THE CAPTAIN OF THE SHINSEN-GUMI.
WHAT ...!
SSH!!
TOMORROW NIGHT, KONDO'S GROUP WILL VISIT THE INN WHERE THE CHOSHU ENVOY IS STAYING...
...SO THEY WILL BE A SMALL GROUP OF ABOUT THREE OR FOUR PEOPLE.
I JUST HOPE SOMETHING DANGEROUS WON'T HAPPEN.
WAIT!
WHO ARE YOU...?!
DON'T !

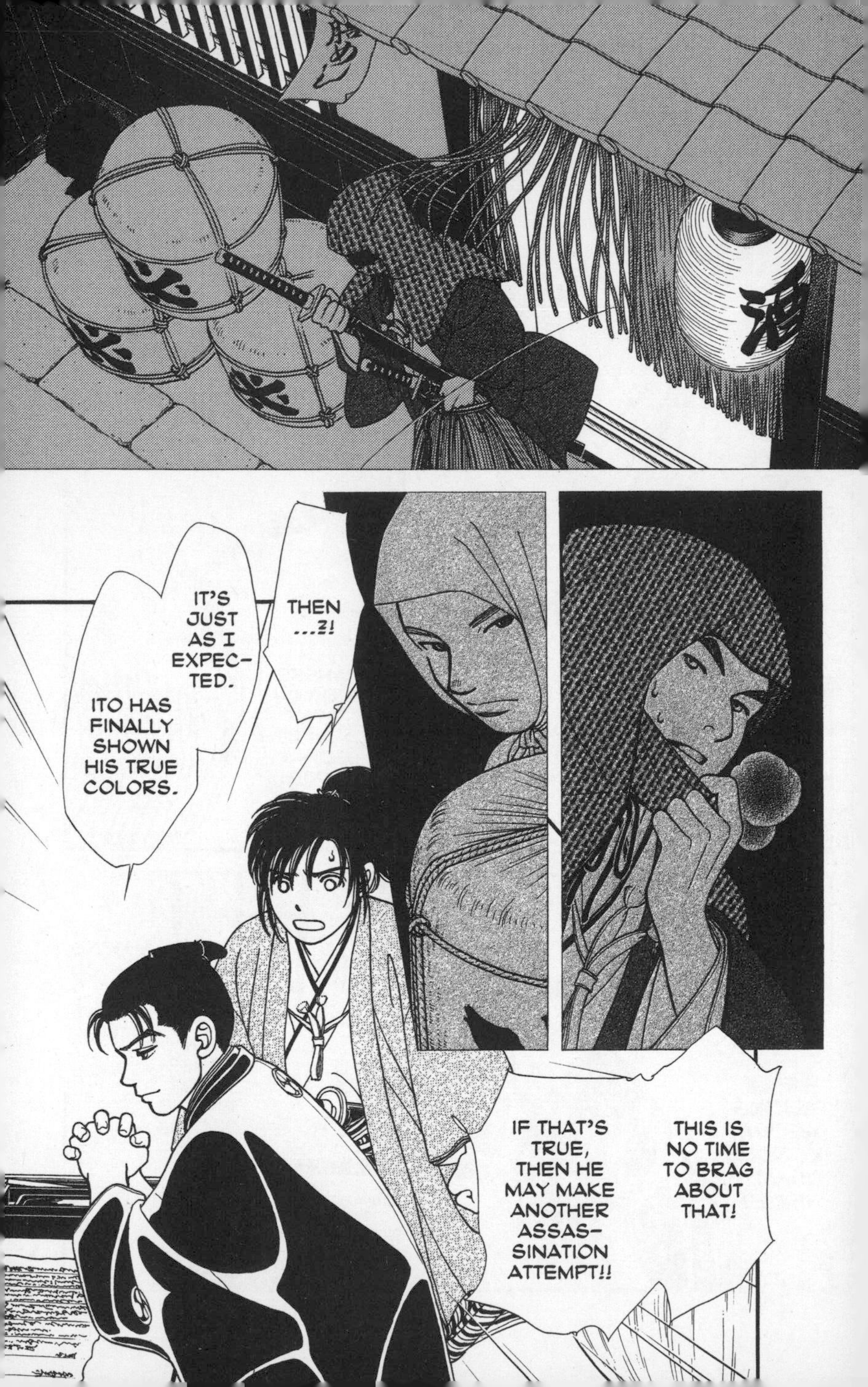
酒
THEN ...?!
IT'S JUST AS I EXPECTED.
ITO HAS FINALLY SHOWN HIS TRUE COLORS.
THIS IS NO TIME TO BRAG ABOUT THAT!
IF THAT'S TRUE, THEN HE MAY MAKE ANOTHER ASSASSINATION ATTEMPT!!

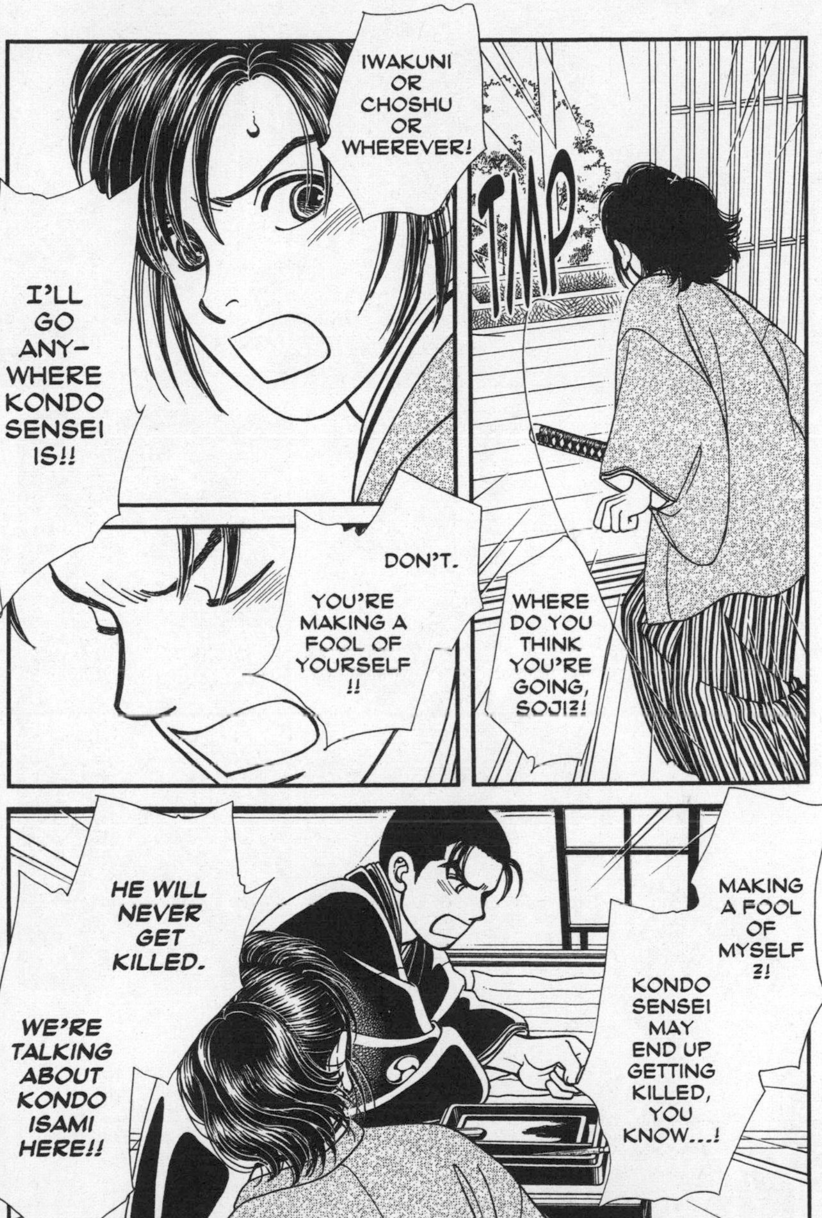
TMP
WHERE DO YOU THINK YOU'RE GOING, SOJI?!
I'LL GO ANY-WHERE KONDO SENSEI IS!!
IWAKUNI OR CHOSHU OR WHEREVER!
DON'T.
YOU'RE MAKING A FOOL OF YOURSELF!!
MAKING A FOOL OF MYSELF?!
KONDO SENSEI MAY END UP GETTING KILLED, YOU KNOW...!
HE WILL NEVER GET KILLED.
WE'RE TALKING ABOUT KONDO ISAMI HERE!!

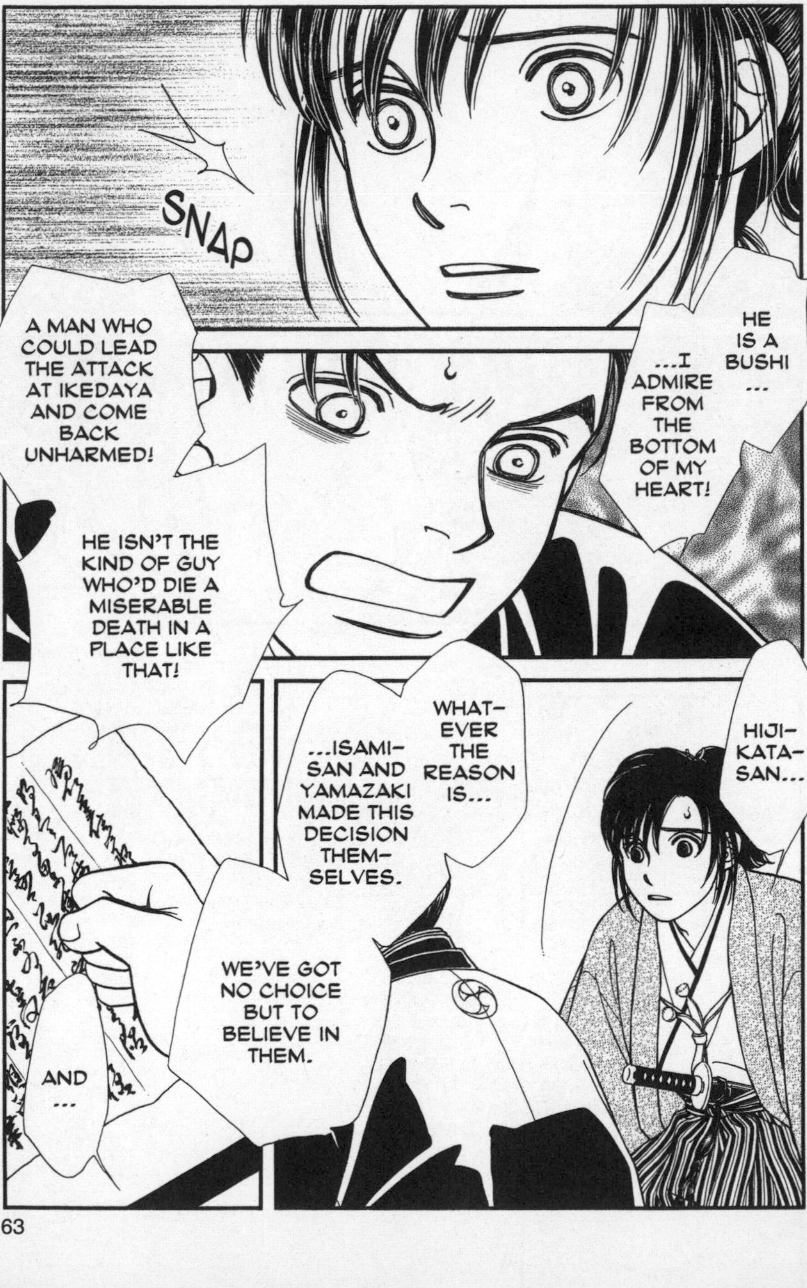
SNAP
HE IS A BUSHI ...
...I ADMIRE FROM THE BOTTOM OF MY HEART!
A MAN WHO COULD LEAD THE ATTACK AT IKEDAYA AND COME BACK UNHARMED!
HE ISN'T THE KIND OF GUY WHO'D DIE A MISERABLE DEATH IN A PLACE LIKE THAT!
HIJI-KATA-SAN...
WHAT-EVER THE REASON IS...
...ISAMI-SAN AND YAMAZAKI MADE THIS DECISION THEM-SELVES.
WE'VE GOT NO CHOICE BUT TO BELIEVE IN THEM.
AND ...

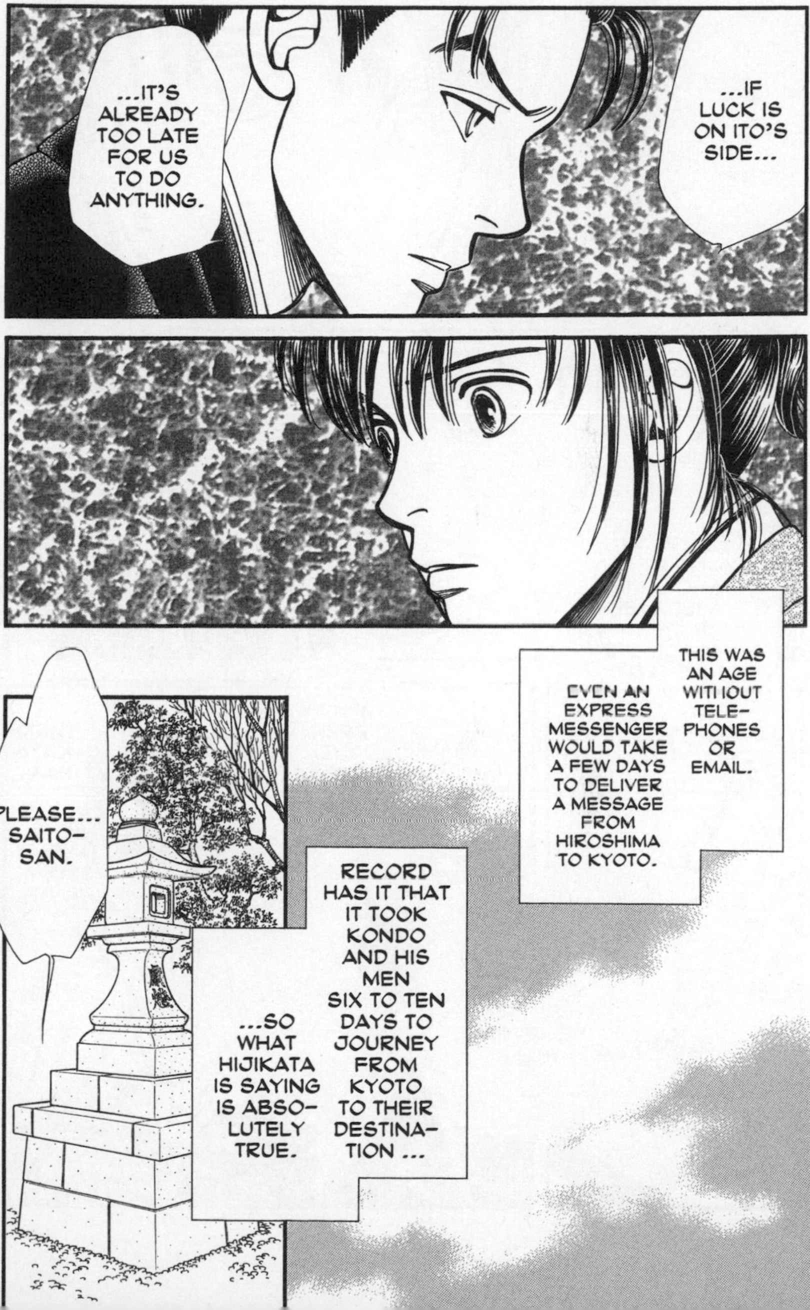
...IF LUCK IS ON ITO'S SIDE...
...IT'S ALREADY TOO LATE FOR US TO DO ANYTHING.
THIS WAS AN AGE WITHOUT TELE-PHONES OR EMAIL.
EVEN AN EXPRESS MESSENGER WOULD TAKE A FEW DAYS TO DELIVER A MESSAGE FROM HIROSHIMA TO KYOTO.
RECORD HAS IT THAT IT TOOK KONDO AND HIS MEN SIX TO TEN DAYS TO JOURNEY FROM KYOTO TO THEIR DESTINA-TION ...
...SO WHAT HIJIKATA IS SAYING IS ABSO-LUTELY TRUE.
PLEASE... SAITO-SAN.

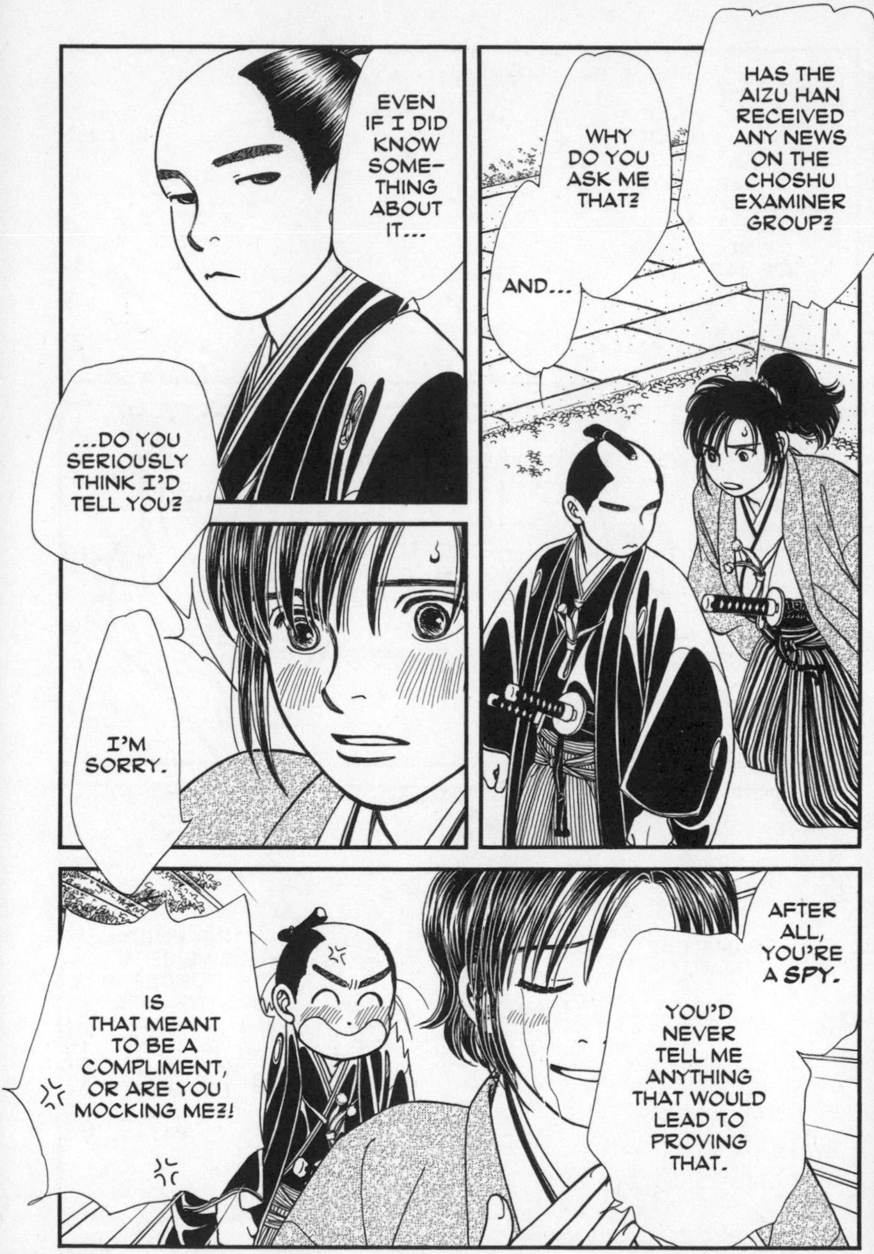
HAS THE AIZU HAN RECEIVED ANY NEWS ON THE CHOSHU EXAMINER GROUP?
WHY DO YOU ASK ME THAT?
AND...
EVEN IF I DID KNOW SOME-THING ABOUT IT...
...DO YOU SERIOUSLY THINK I'D TELL YOU?
I'M SORRY.
AFTER ALL, YOU'RE A *SPY*.
YOU'D NEVER TELL ME ANYTHING THAT WOULD LEAD TO PROVING THAT.
IS THAT MEANT TO BE A COMPLIMENT, OR ARE YOU MOCKING ME?!

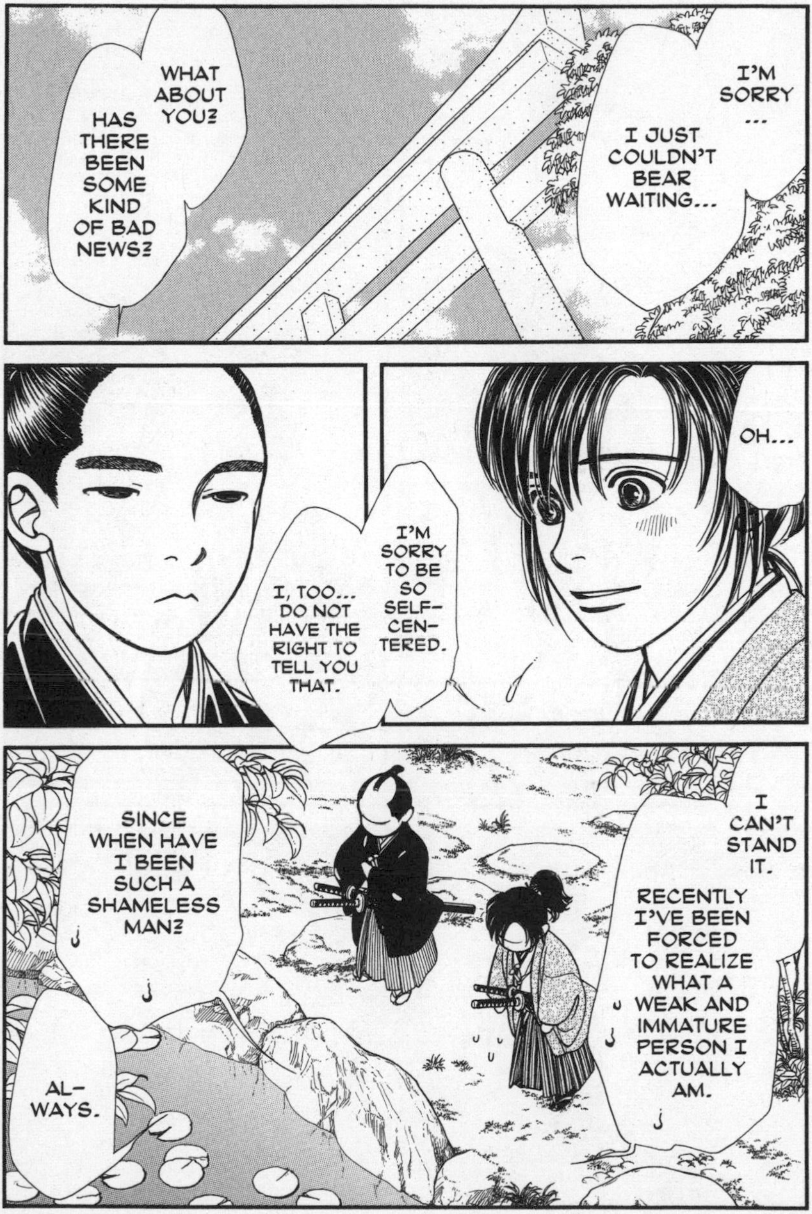

I'M SORRY...
I JUST COULDN'T BEAR WAITING...
WHAT ABOUT YOU?
HAS THERE BEEN SOME KIND OF BAD NEWS?
OH...
I'M SORRY TO BE SO SELF-CENTERED.
I, TOO... DO NOT HAVE THE RIGHT TO TELL YOU THAT.
I CAN'T STAND IT.
RECENTLY I'VE BEEN FORCED TO REALIZE WHAT A WEAK AND IMMATURE PERSON I ACTUALLY AM.
SINCE WHEN HAVE I BEEN SUCH A SHAMELESS MAN?
ALWAYS.

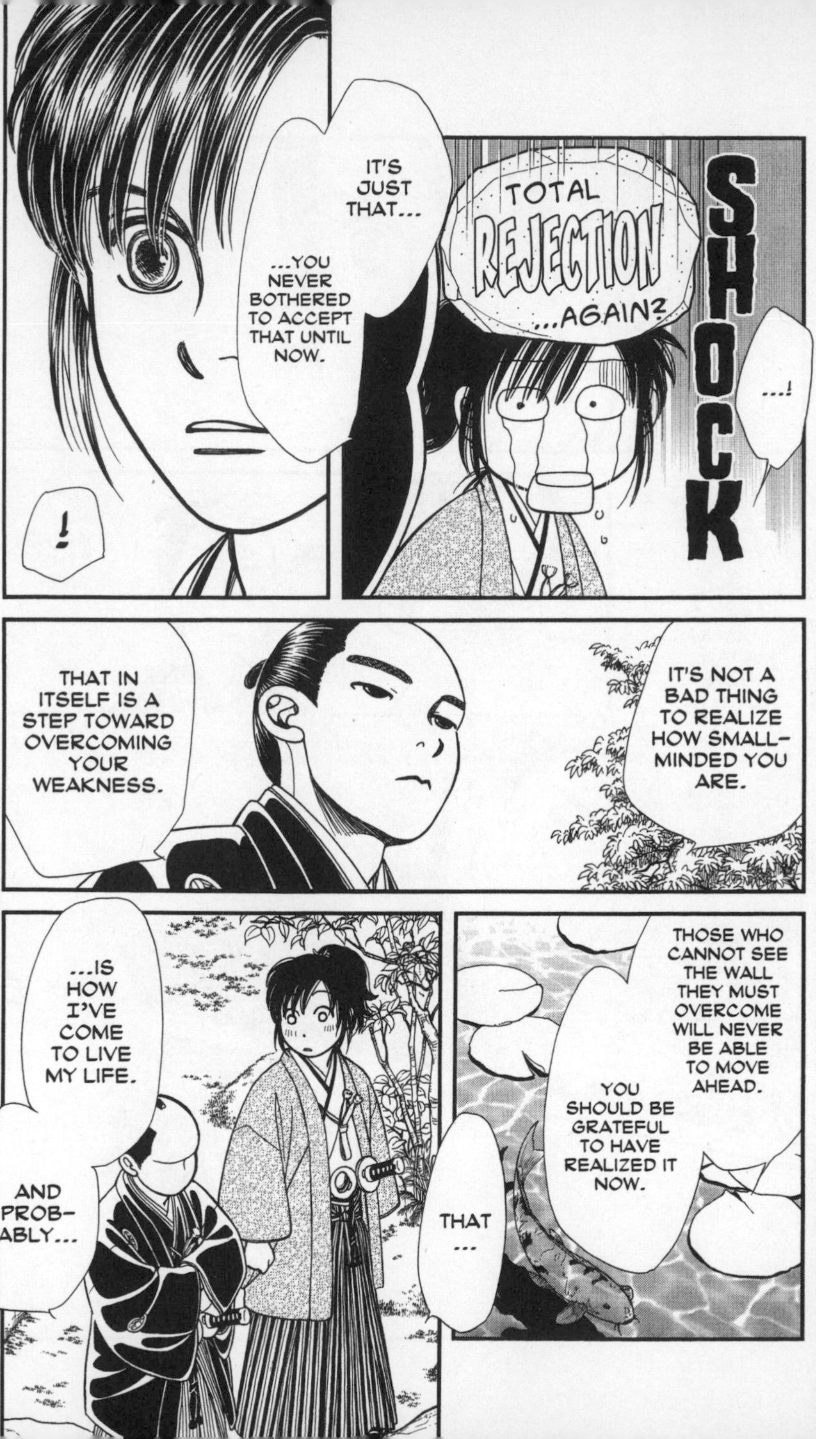
SHOCK
TOTAL REJECTION ...AGAIN?
...!
IT'S JUST THAT...
...YOU NEVER BOTHERED TO ACCEPT THAT UNTIL NOW.
!
IT'S NOT A BAD THING TO REALIZE HOW SMALL-MINDED YOU ARE.
THAT IN ITSELF IS A STEP TOWARD OVERCOMING YOUR WEAKNESS.
THOSE WHO CANNOT SEE THE WALL THEY MUST OVERCOME WILL NEVER BE ABLE TO MOVE AHEAD.
YOU SHOULD BE GRATEFUL TO HAVE REALIZED IT NOW.
THAT ...
...IS HOW I'VE COME TO LIVE MY LIFE.
AND PROB-ABLY...

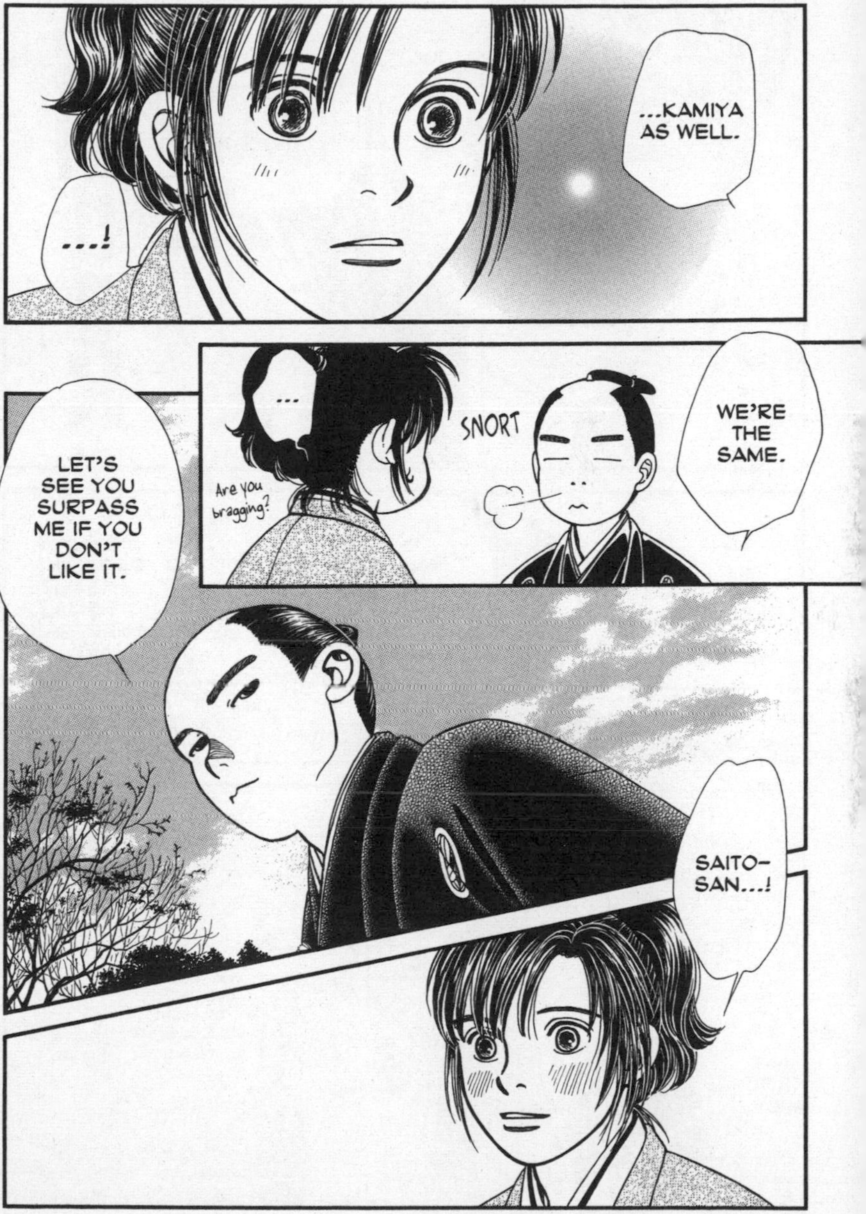
...KAMIYA AS WELL.
...!
WE'RE THE SAME.
SNORT
...
Are you bragging?
LET'S SEE YOU SURPASS ME IF YOU DON'T LIKE IT.
SAITO-SAN...!

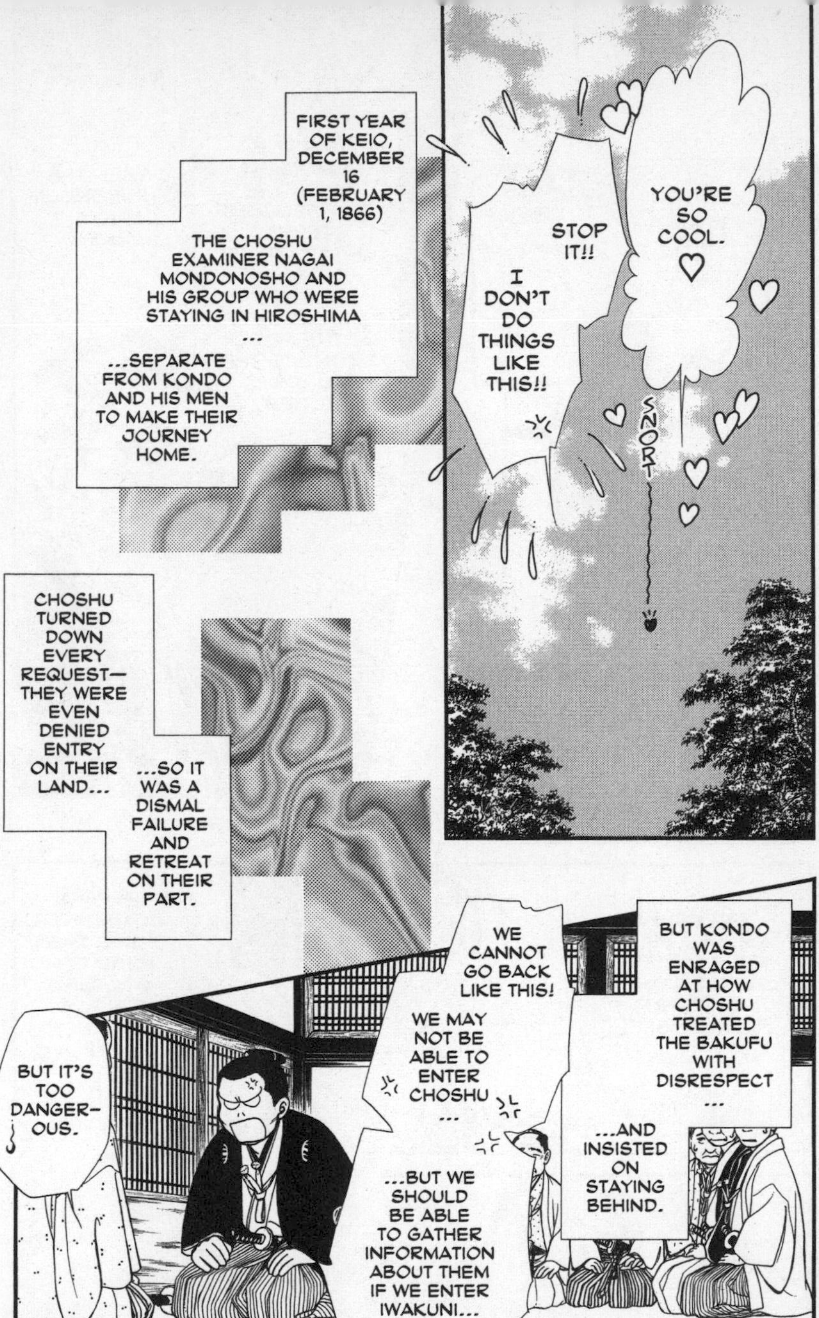
YOU'RE SO COOL. ♡
SNORT
STOP IT!!
I DON'T DO THINGS LIKE THIS!!
FIRST YEAR OF KEIO, DECEMBER 16 (FEBRUARY 1, 1866)
THE CHOSHU EXAMINER NAGAI MONDONOSHO AND HIS GROUP WHO WERE STAYING IN HIROSHIMA ...
...SEPARATE FROM KONDO AND HIS MEN TO MAKE THEIR JOURNEY HOME.
CHOSHU TURNED DOWN EVERY REQUEST—THEY WERE EVEN DENIED ENTRY ON THEIR LAND...
...SO IT WAS A DISMAL FAILURE AND RETREAT ON THEIR PART.
BUT KONDO WAS ENRAGED AT HOW CHOSHU TREATED THE BAKUFU WITH DISRESPECT ...
...AND INSISTED ON STAYING BEHIND.
WE CANNOT GO BACK LIKE THIS!
WE MAY NOT BE ABLE TO ENTER CHOSHU ...
...BUT WE SHOULD BE ABLE TO GATHER INFORMATION ABOUT THEM IF WE ENTER IWAKUNI...
BUT IT'S TOO DANGER-OUS.

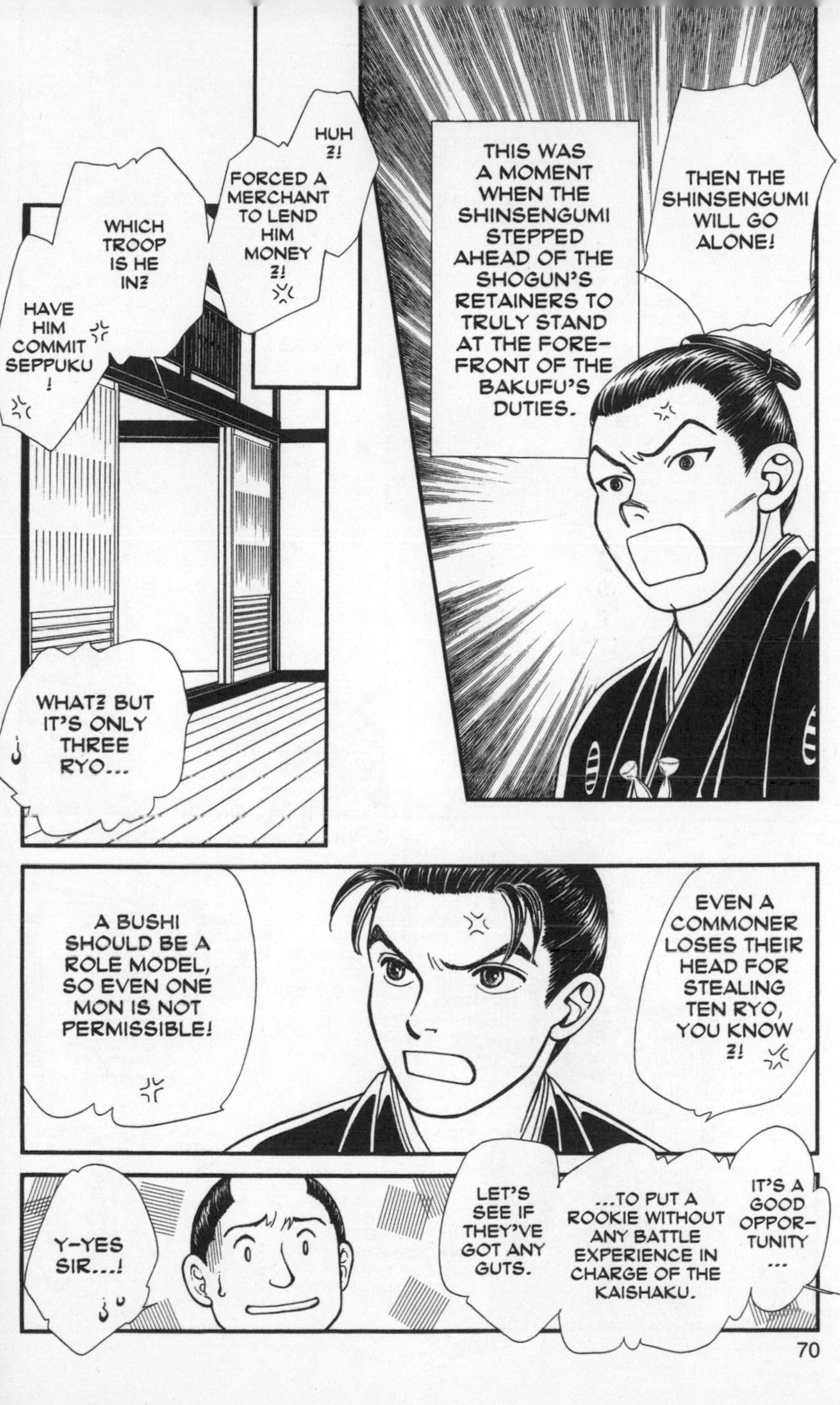
THEN THE SHINSENGUMI WILL GO ALONE!
THIS WAS A MOMENT WHEN THE SHINSENGUMI STEPPED AHEAD OF THE SHOGUN'S RETAINERS TO TRULY STAND AT THE FORE-FRONT OF THE BAKUFU'S DUTIES.
HUH?!
FORCED A MERCHANT TO LEND HIM MONEY?!
WHICH TROOP IS HE IN?
HAVE HIM COMMIT SEPPUKU!
WHAT? BUT IT'S ONLY THREE RYO...
EVEN A COMMONER LOSES THEIR HEAD FOR STEALING TEN RYO, YOU KNOW?!
A BUSHI SHOULD BE A ROLE MODEL, SO EVEN ONE MON IS NOT PERMISSIBLE!
IT'S A GOOD OPPORTUNITY...
...TO PUT A ROOKIE WITHOUT ANY BATTLE EXPERIENCE IN CHARGE OF THE KAISHAKU.
LET'S SEE IF THEY'VE GOT ANY GUTS.
Y-YES SIR...!

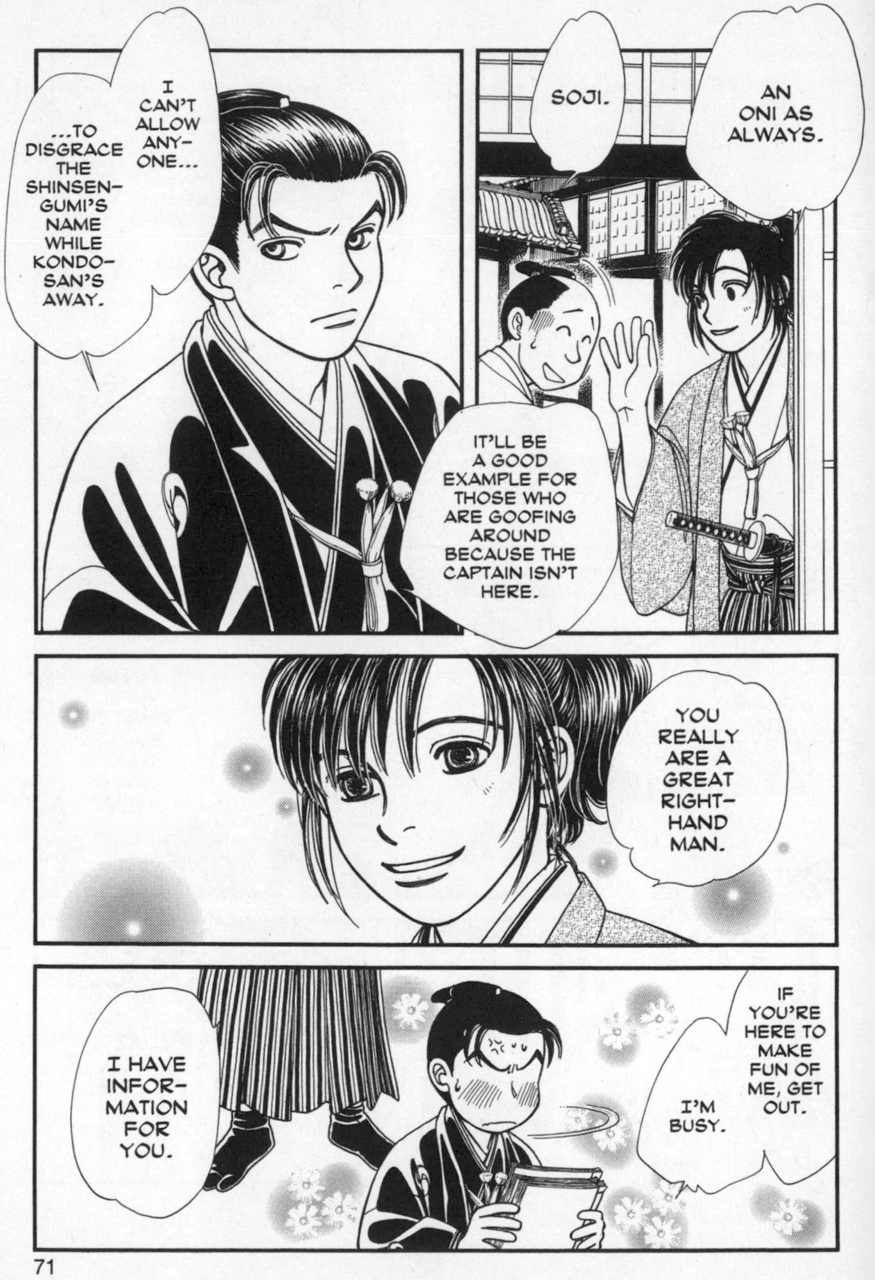
AN ONI AS ALWAYS.
SOJI.
IT'LL BE A GOOD EXAMPLE FOR THOSE WHO ARE GOOFING AROUND BECAUSE THE CAPTAIN ISN'T HERE.
I CAN'T ALLOW ANYONE...
...TO DISGRACE THE SHINSENGUMI'S NAME WHILE KONDO-SAN'S AWAY.
YOU REALLY ARE A GREAT RIGHT-HAND MAN.
IF YOU'RE HERE TO MAKE FUN OF ME, GET OUT.
I'M BUSY.
I HAVE INFORMATION FOR YOU.

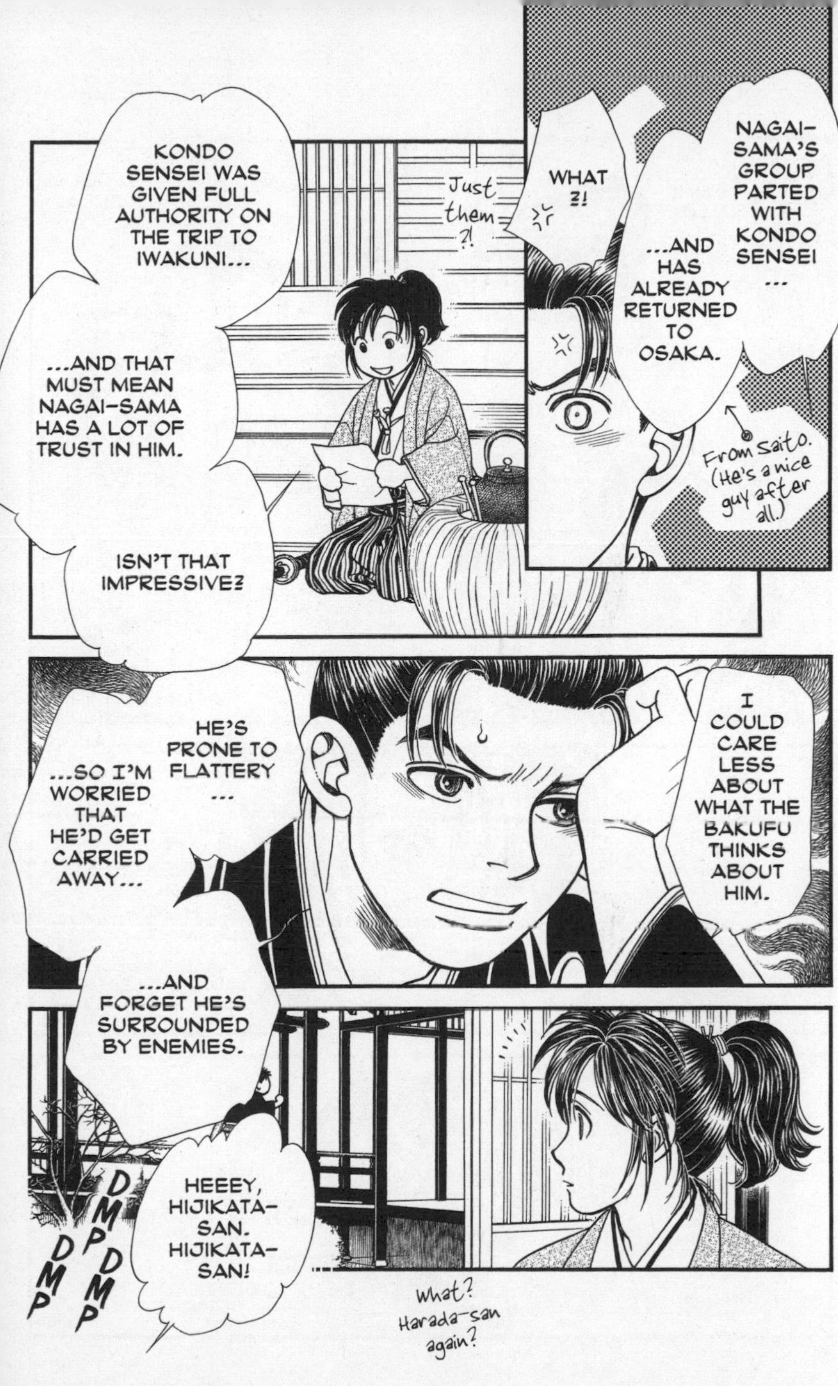
NAGAI-SAMA'S GROUP PARTED WITH KONDO SENSEI...
...AND HAS ALREADY RETURNED TO OSAKA.
WHAT?!
From Saito. (He's a nice guy after all.)
Just them?!
KONDO SENSEI WAS GIVEN FULL AUTHORITY ON THE TRIP TO IWAKUNI...
...AND THAT MUST MEAN NAGAI-SAMA HAS A LOT OF TRUST IN HIM.
ISN'T THAT IMPRESSIVE?
I COULD CARE LESS ABOUT WHAT THE BAKUFU THINKS ABOUT HIM.
HE'S PRONE TO FLATTERY...
...SO I'M WORRIED THAT HE'D GET CARRIED AWAY...
...AND FORGET HE'S SURROUNDED BY ENEMIES.
HEEEY, HIJIKATA-SAN. HIJIKATA-SAN!
DMP DMP
DMP DMP
What? Harada-san again?

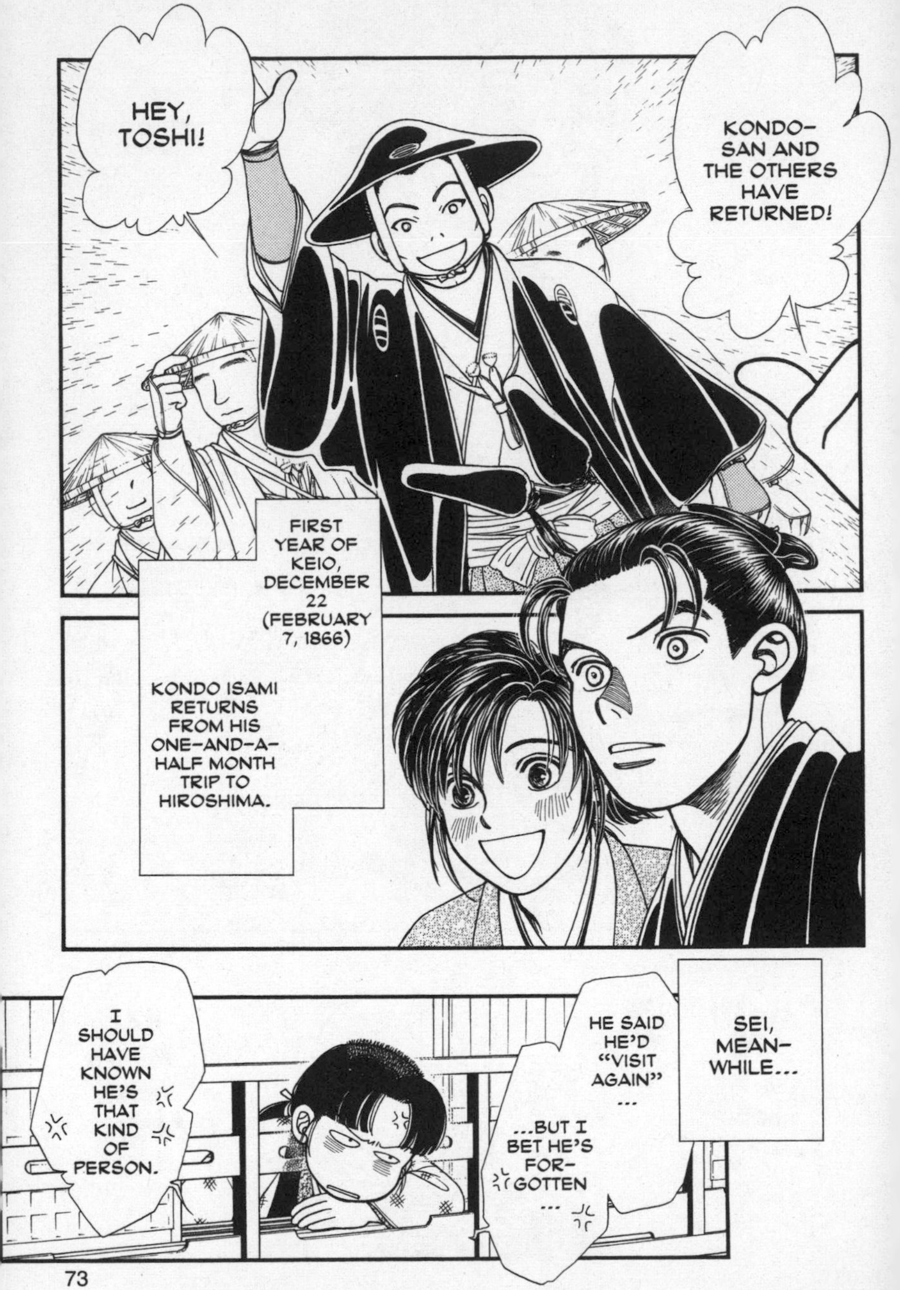
KONDO-SAN AND THE OTHERS HAVE RETURNED!
HEY, TOSHI!
FIRST YEAR OF KEIO, DECEMBER 22 (FEBRUARY 7, 1866)
KONDO ISAMI RETURNS FROM HIS ONE-AND-A-HALF MONTH TRIP TO HIROSHIMA.
SEI, MEANWHILE...
HE SAID HE'D "VISIT AGAIN"...
...BUT I BET HE'S FOR-GOTTEN...
I SHOULD HAVE KNOWN HE'S THAT KIND OF PERSON.

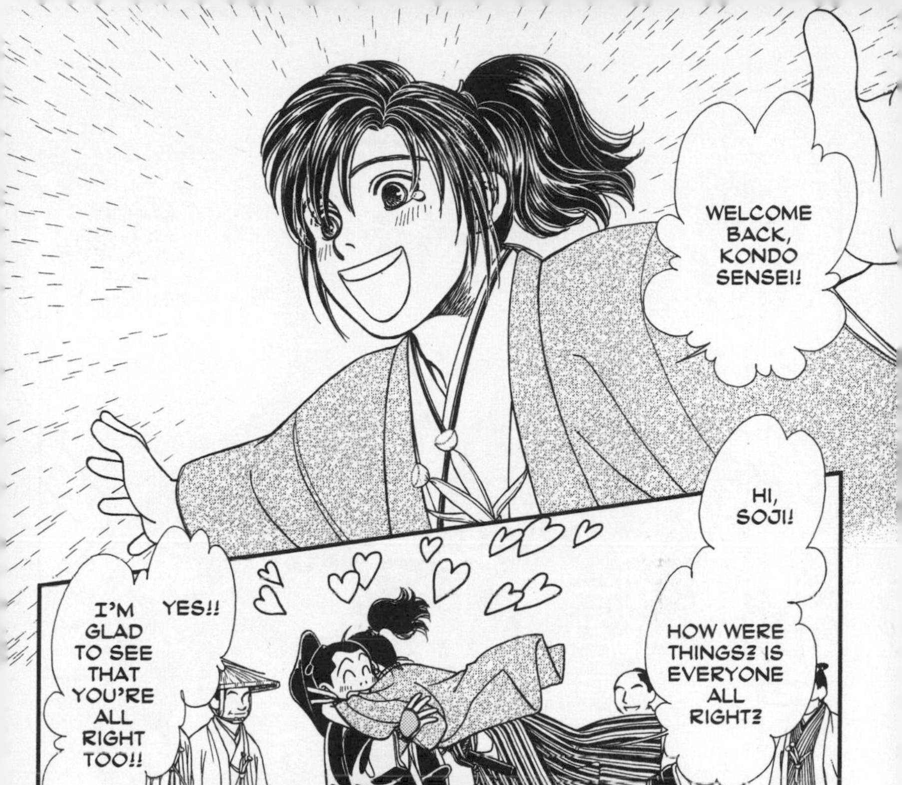
WELCOME BACK, KONDO SENSEI!
HI, SOJI!
HOW WERE THINGS? IS EVERYONE ALL RIGHT?
YES!!
I'M GLAD TO SEE THAT YOU'RE ALL RIGHT TOO!!
UH-HUH, EVERYONE IS FINE!

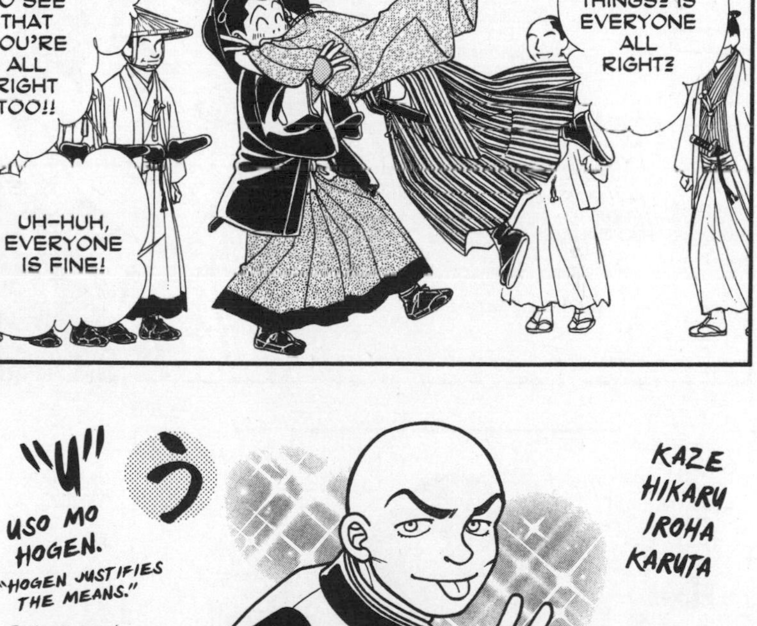
KAZE HIKARU IROHA KARUTA
"U"
う
USO MO HOGEN.
"HOGEN JUSTIFIES THE MEANS."
By Kocchi Takato-san from Chiba

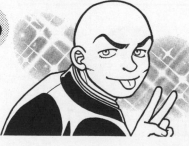

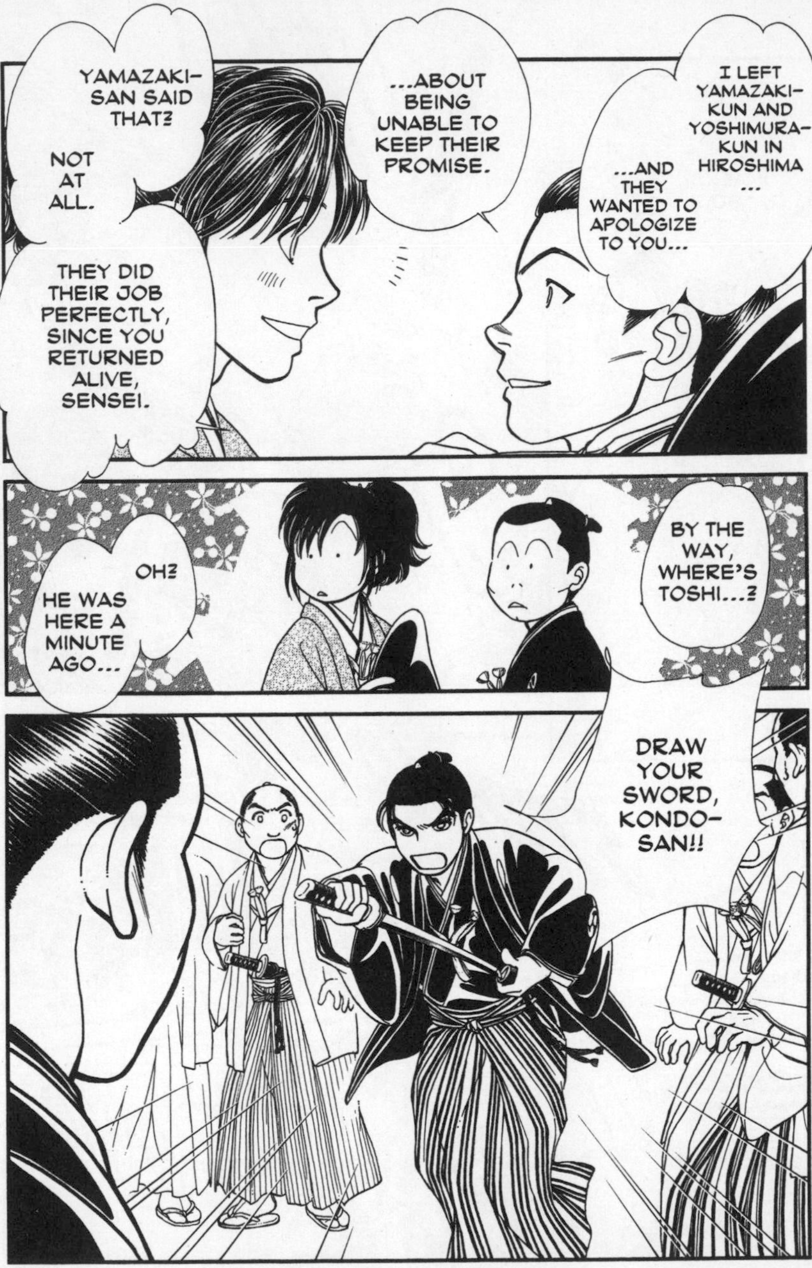
I LEFT YAMAZAKI-KUN AND YOSHIMURA-KUN IN HIROSHIMA...
...AND THEY WANTED TO APOLOGIZE TO YOU...
...ABOUT BEING UNABLE TO KEEP THEIR PROMISE.
YAMAZAKI-SAN SAID THAT?
NOT AT ALL.
THEY DID THEIR JOB PERFECTLY, SINCE YOU RETURNED ALIVE, SENSEI.
BY THE WAY, WHERE'S TOSHI...?
OH?
HE WAS HERE A MINUTE AGO...
DRAW YOUR SWORD, KONDO-SAN!!

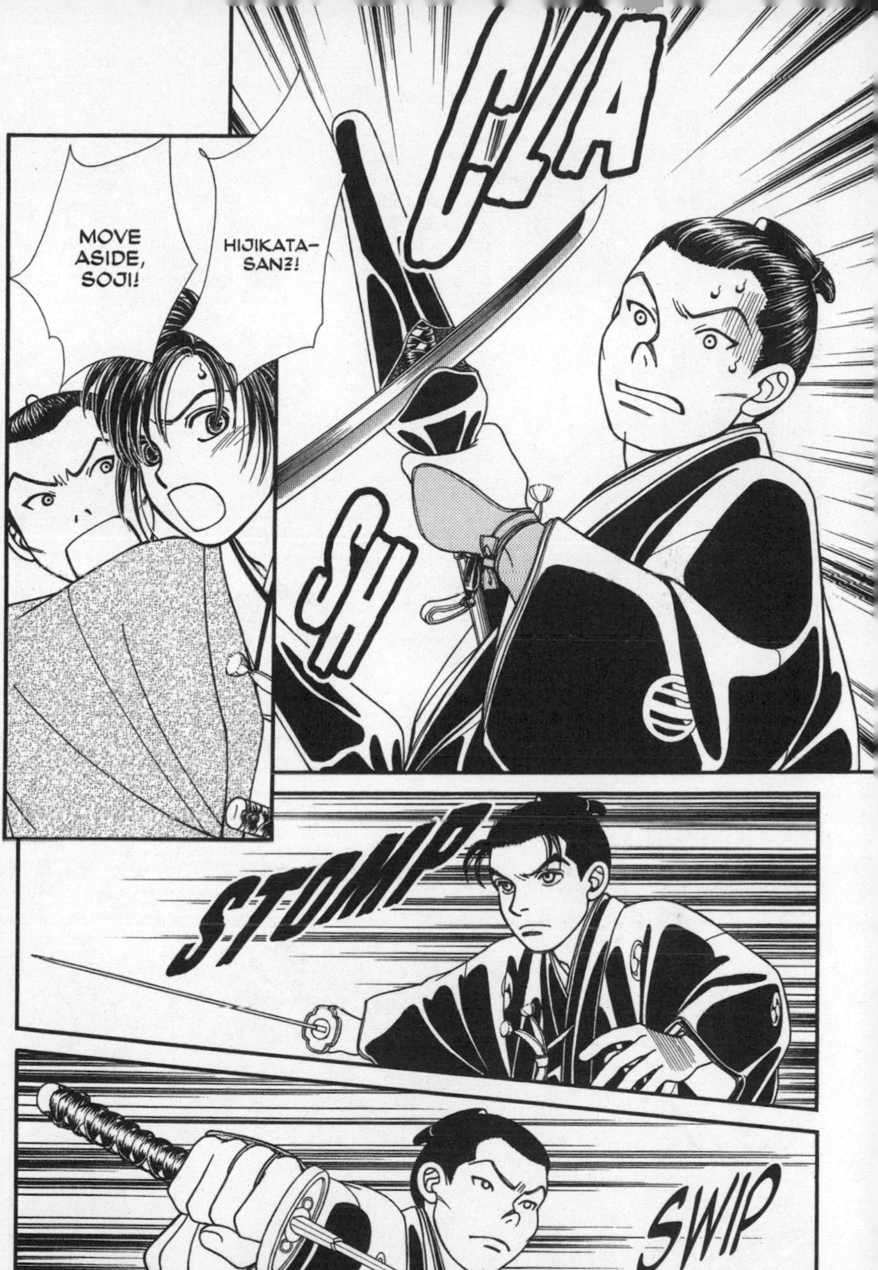
CLA
SH
HIJIKATA-SAN?!
MOVE ASIDE, SOJI!
STOMP
SWIP

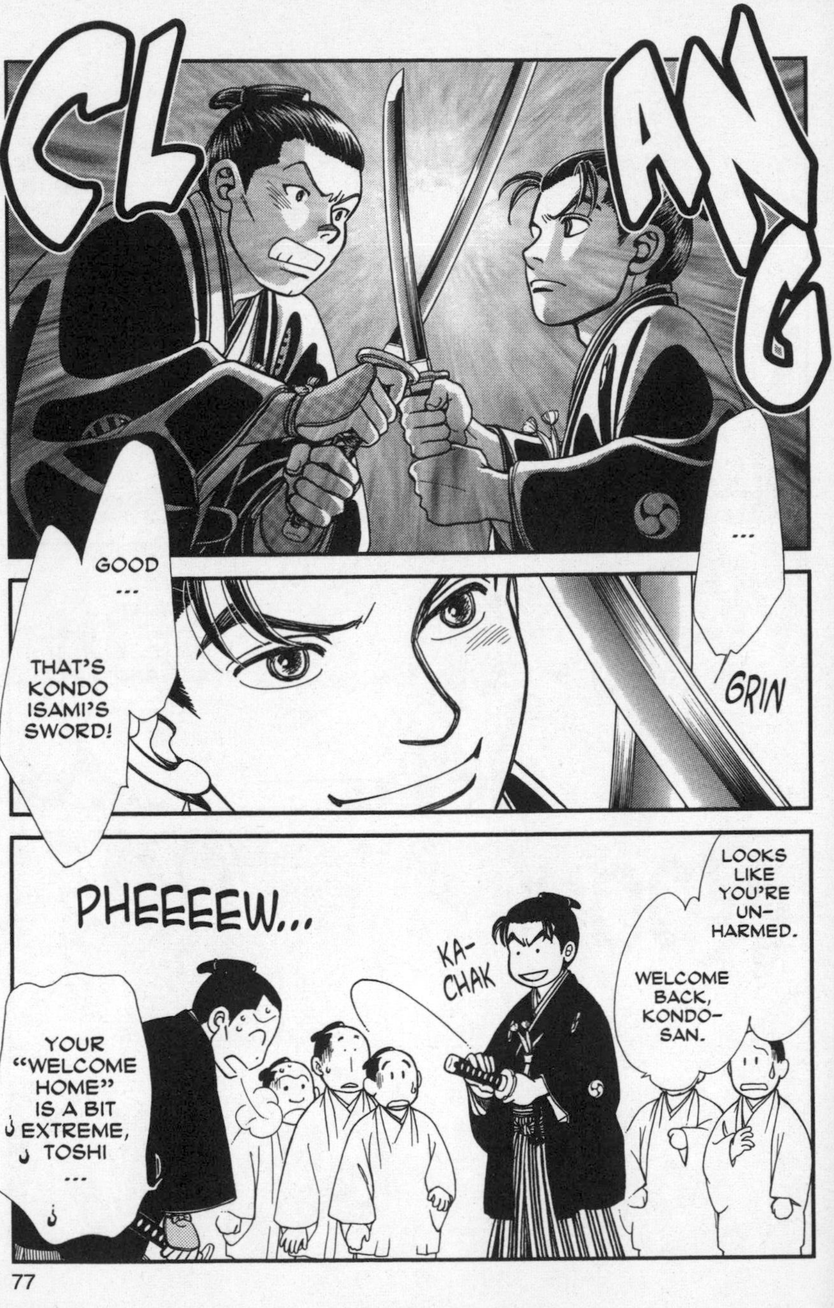
CLANG
...
GRIN
GOOD ...
THAT'S KONDO ISAMI'S SWORD!
LOOKS LIKE YOU'RE UN-HARMED.
WELCOME BACK, KONDO-SAN.
KA-CHAK
PHEEEEW...
YOUR "WELCOME HOME" IS A BIT EXTREME, TOSHI ...

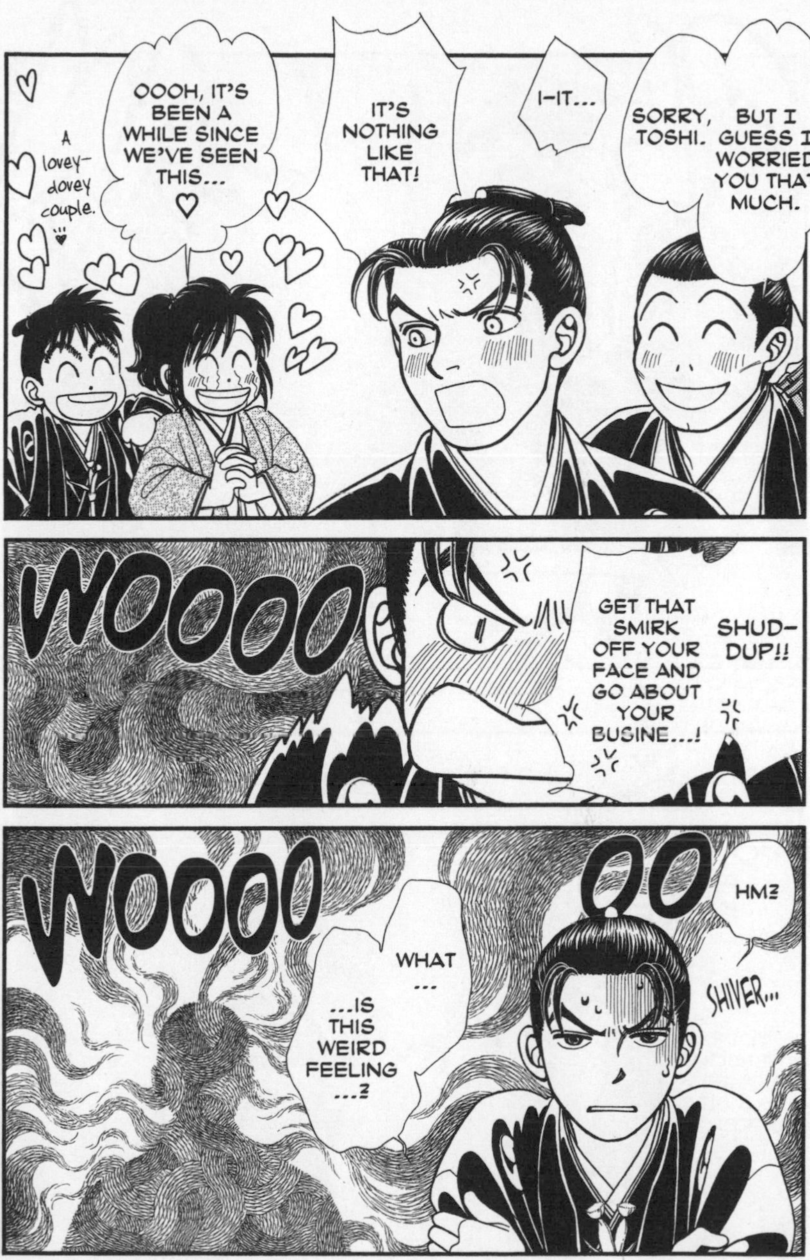

SORRY, TOSHI. BUT I GUESS I WORRIED YOU THAT MUCH.
I-IT...
IT'S NOTHING LIKE THAT!
OOOH, IT'S BEEN A WHILE SINCE WE'VE SEEN THIS...
A lovey-dovey couple.
WOOOO
SHUD-DUP!!
GET THAT SMIRK OFF YOUR FACE AND GO ABOUT YOUR BUSINE...!
WOOOOOO
HM?
SHIVER...
WHAT...
...IS THIS WEIRD FEELING...?

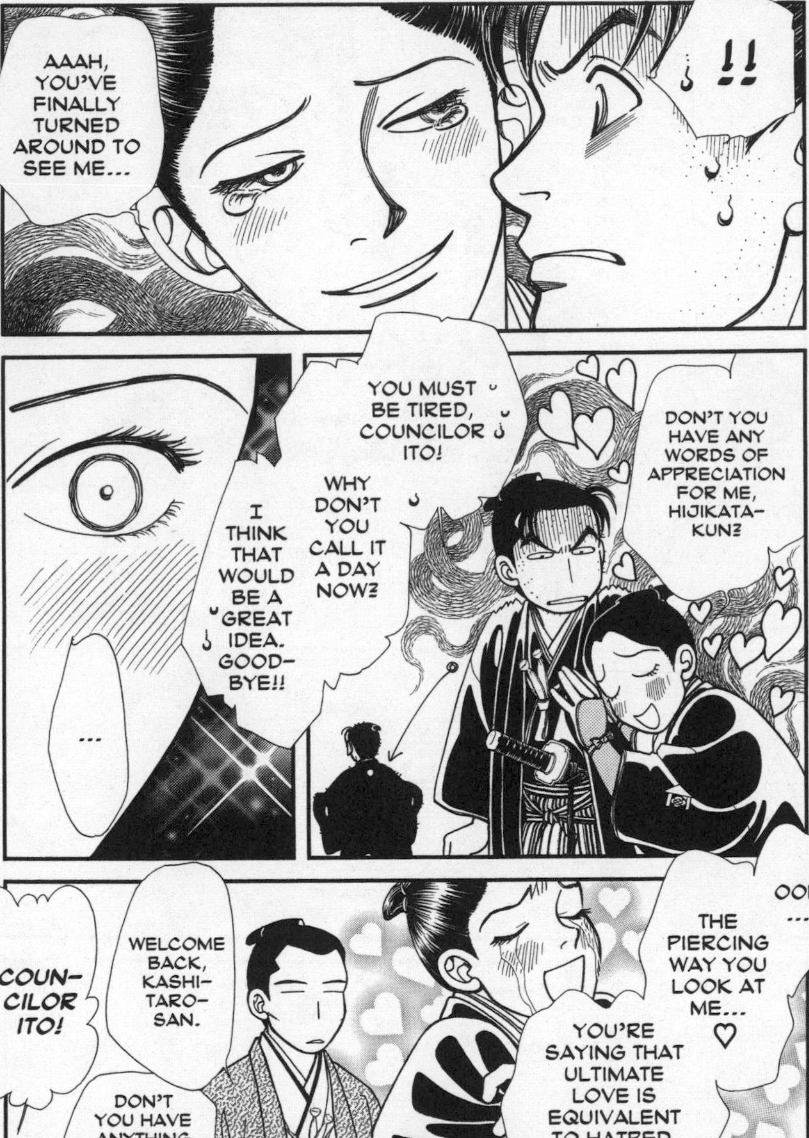
!!
AAAH, YOU'VE FINALLY TURNED AROUND TO SEE ME...
DON'T YOU HAVE ANY WORDS OF APPRECIATION FOR ME, HIJIKATA-KUN?
YOU MUST BE TIRED, COUNCILOR ITO!
WHY DON'T YOU CALL IT A DAY NOW?
I THINK THAT WOULD BE A GREAT IDEA. GOOD-BYE!!
...
OOH... THE PIERCING WAY YOU LOOK AT ME... ♡
YOU'RE SAYING THAT ULTIMATE LOVE IS EQUIVALENT TO HATRED, AREN'T YOU HIJIKATA-KUN...
WELCOME BACK, KASHITARO-SAN.
COUNCILOR ITO!
DON'T YOU HAVE ANYTHING ELSE TO SAY, UTSUMI?

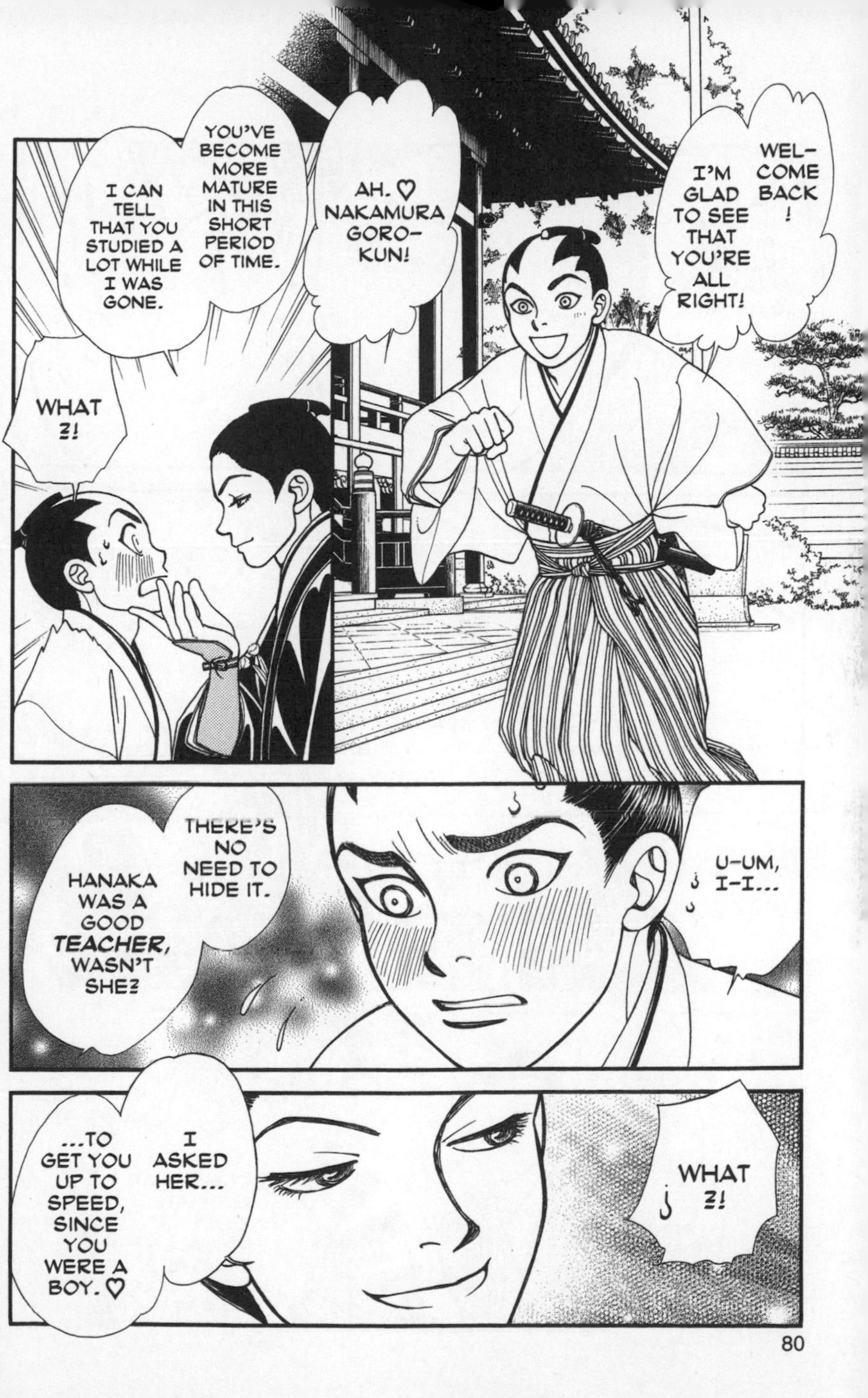
WEL-COME BACK!
I'M GLAD TO SEE THAT YOU'RE ALL RIGHT!
AH. ♡ NAKAMURA GORO-KUN!
YOU'VE BECOME MORE MATURE IN THIS SHORT PERIOD OF TIME.
I CAN TELL THAT YOU STUDIED A LOT WHILE I WAS GONE.
WHAT?!
U-UM, I-I...
THERE'S NO NEED TO HIDE IT.
HANAKA WAS A GOOD *TEACHER*, WASN'T SHE?
WHAT?!
I ASKED HER...
...TO GET YOU UP TO SPEED, SINCE YOU WERE A BOY. ♡

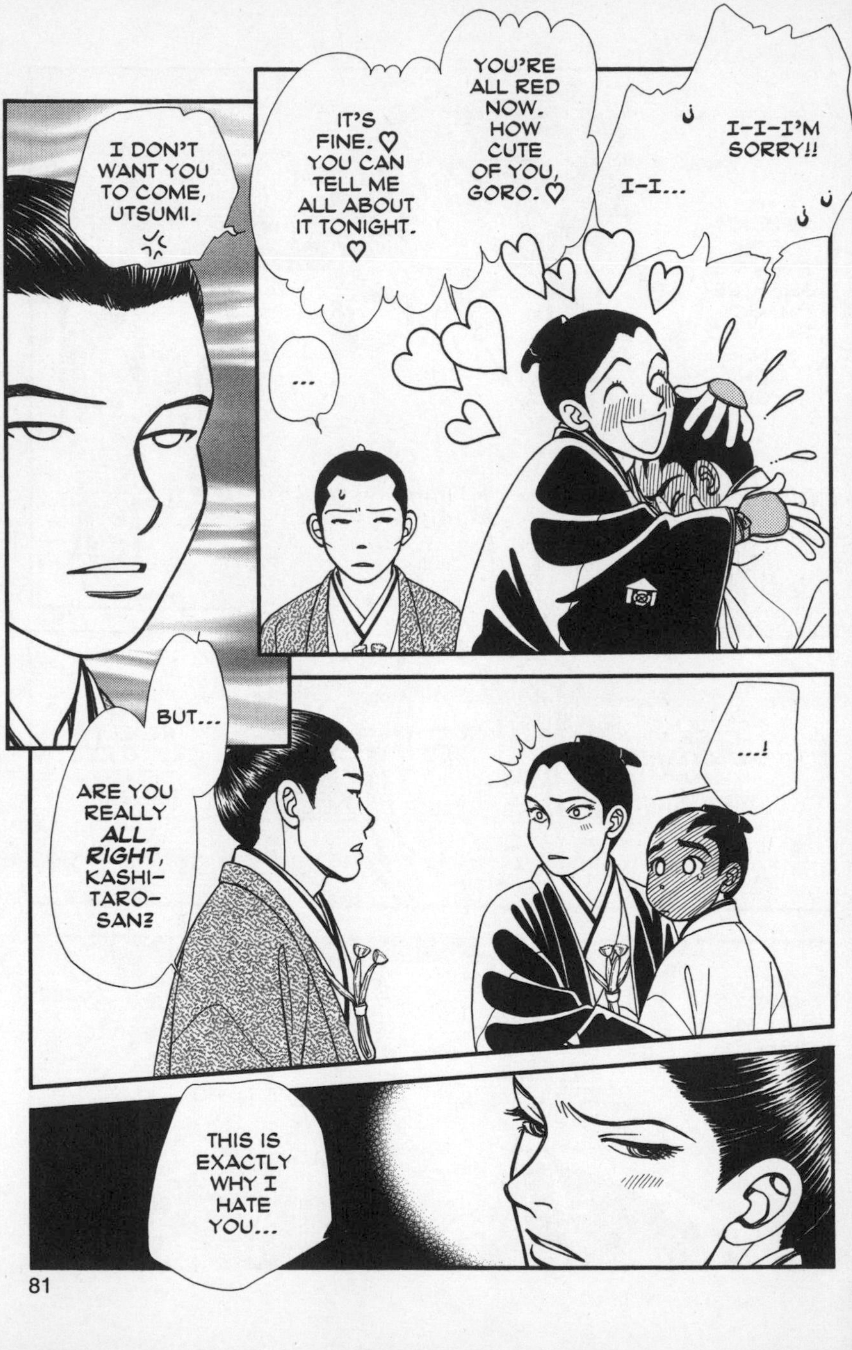
I-I...
I-I-I'M SORRY!!
YOU'RE ALL RED NOW. HOW CUTE OF YOU, GORO. ♡
IT'S FINE. ♡ YOU CAN TELL ME ALL ABOUT IT TONIGHT. ♡
...
I DON'T WANT YOU TO COME, UTSUMI.
...!
BUT...
ARE YOU REALLY ***ALL RIGHT***, KASHITARO-SAN?
THIS IS EXACTLY WHY I HATE YOU...

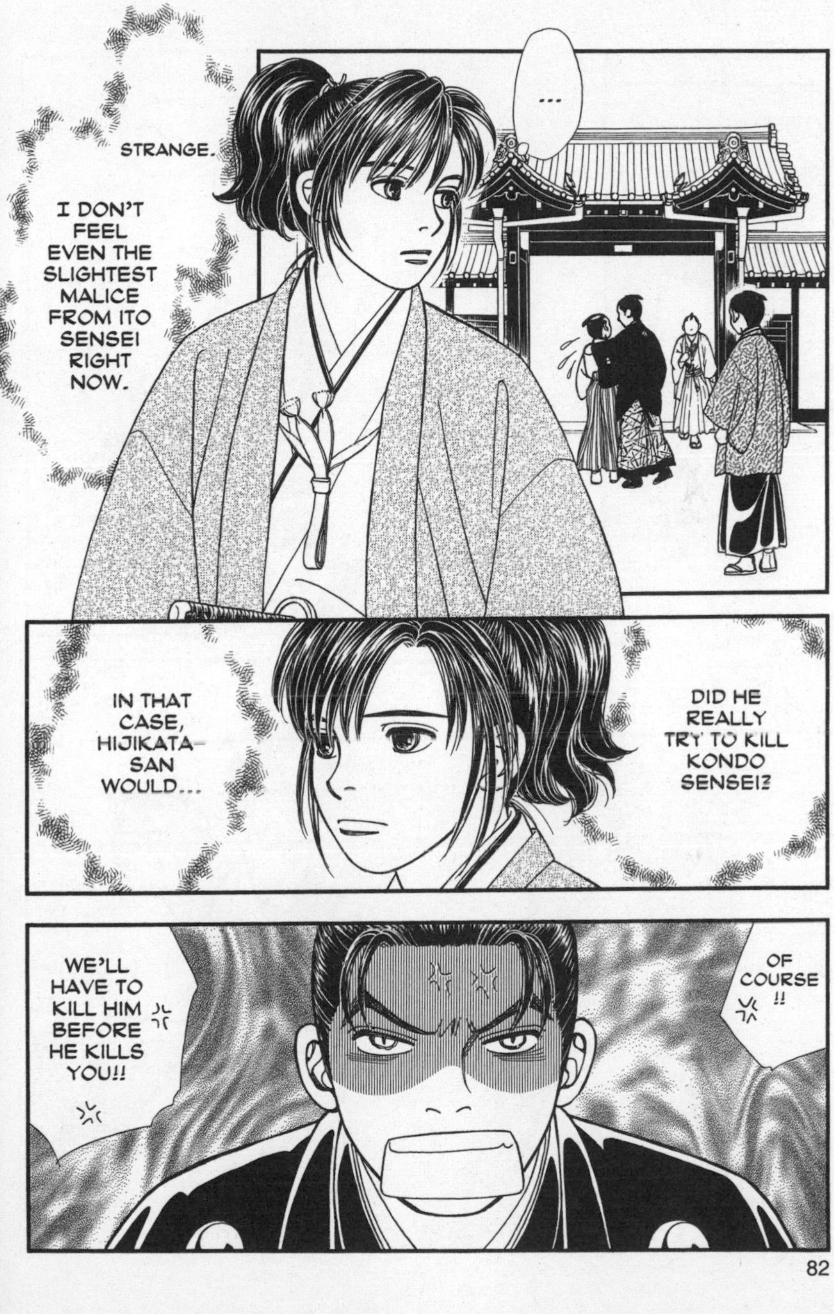
...
STRANGE.
I DON'T FEEL EVEN THE SLIGHTEST MALICE FROM ITO SENSEI RIGHT NOW.
DID HE REALLY TRY TO KILL KONDO SENSEI!?
IN THAT CASE, HIJIKATA-SAN WOULD...
OF COURSE!!
WE'LL HAVE TO KILL HIM BEFORE HE KILLS YOU!!

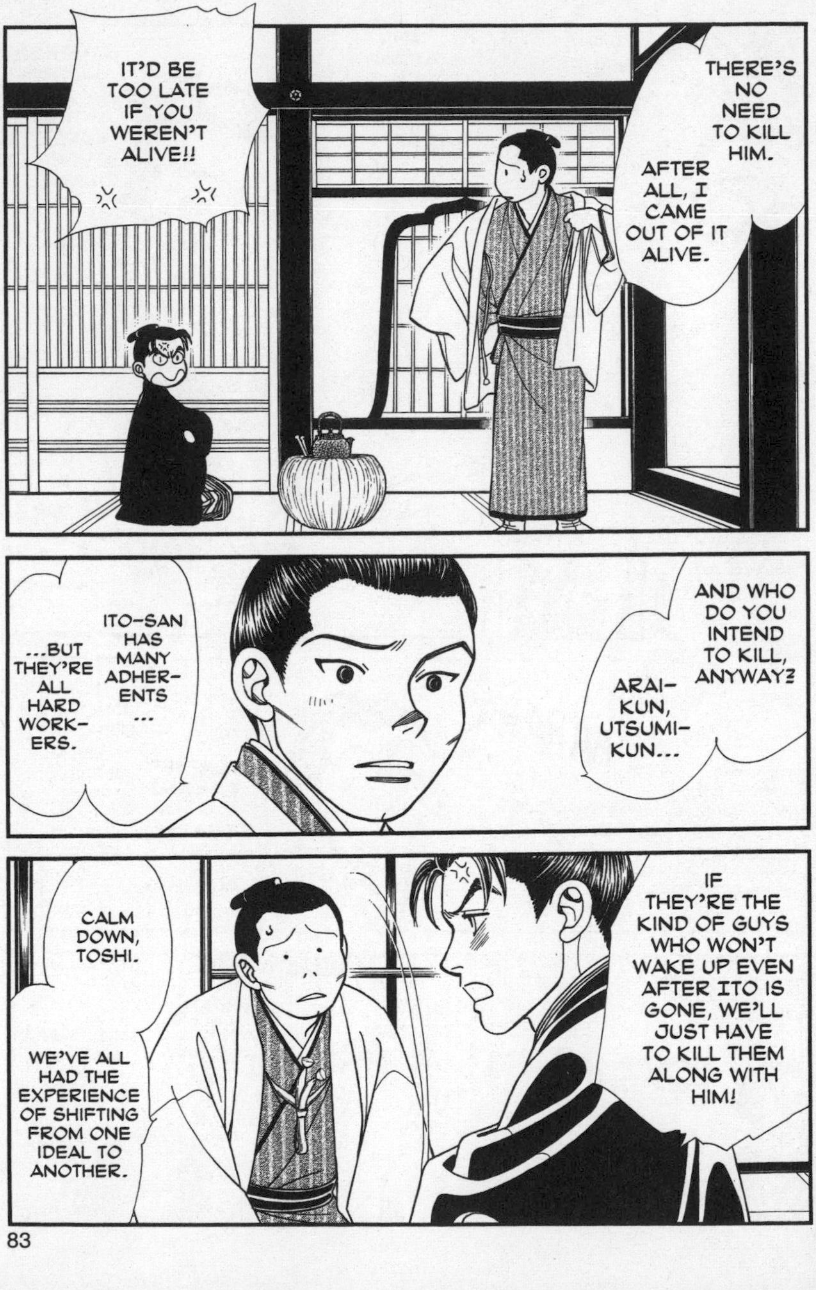

THERE'S NO NEED TO KILL HIM.
AFTER ALL, I CAME OUT OF IT ALIVE.
IT'D BE TOO LATE IF YOU WEREN'T ALIVE!!
AND WHO DO YOU INTEND TO KILL, ANYWAY?
ARAI-KUN, UTSUMI-KUN...
ITO-SAN HAS MANY ADHER-ENTS...
...BUT THEY'RE ALL HARD WORK-ERS.
IF THEY'RE THE KIND OF GUYS WHO WON'T WAKE UP EVEN AFTER ITO IS GONE, WE'LL JUST HAVE TO KILL THEM ALONG WITH HIM!
CALM DOWN, TOSHI.
WE'VE ALL HAD THE EXPERIENCE OF SHIFTING FROM ONE IDEAL TO ANOTHER.

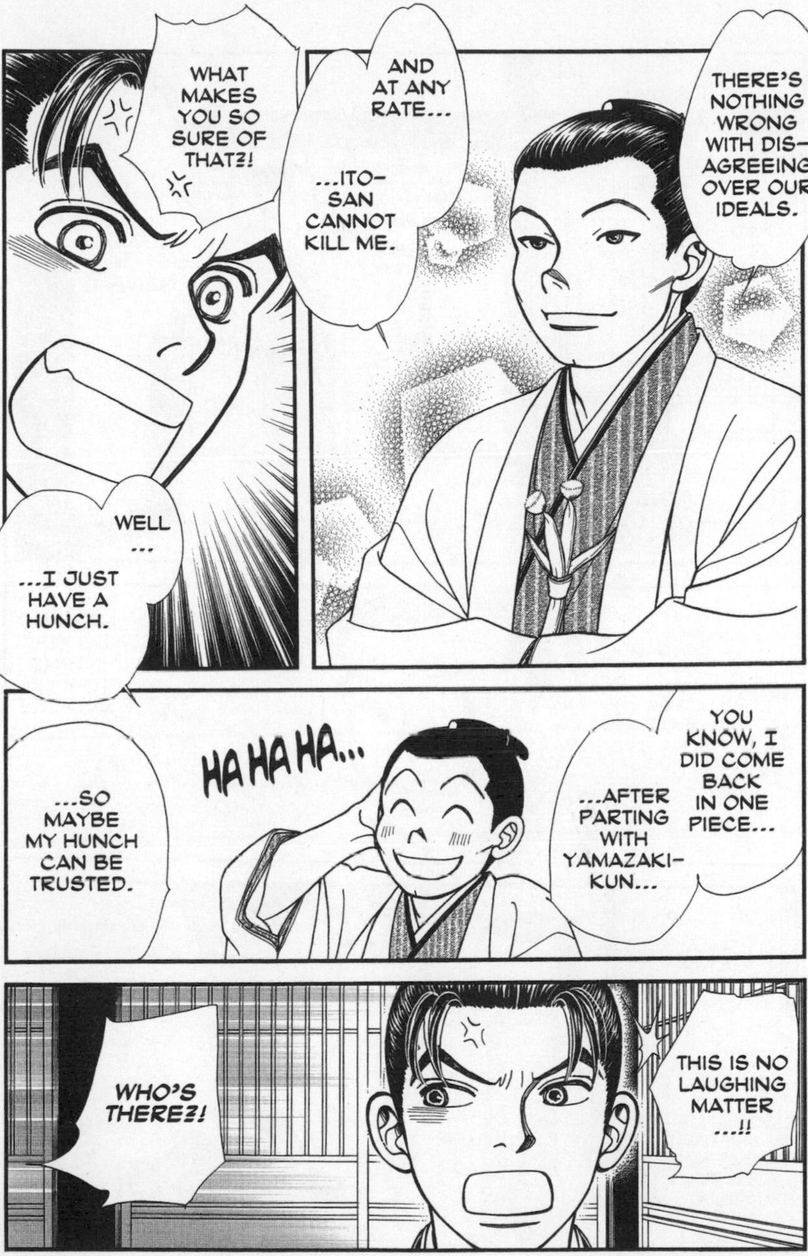
THERE'S NOTHING WRONG WITH DIS-AGREEING OVER OUR IDEALS.
AND AT ANY RATE...
...ITO-SAN CANNOT KILL ME.
WHAT MAKES YOU SO SURE OF THAT?!
WELL ...
...I JUST HAVE A HUNCH.
YOU KNOW, I DID COME BACK IN ONE PIECE...
...AFTER PARTING WITH YAMAZAKI-KUN...
HA HA HA...
...SO MAYBE MY HUNCH CAN BE TRUSTED.
THIS IS NO LAUGHING MATTER ...!!
WHO'S THERE?!

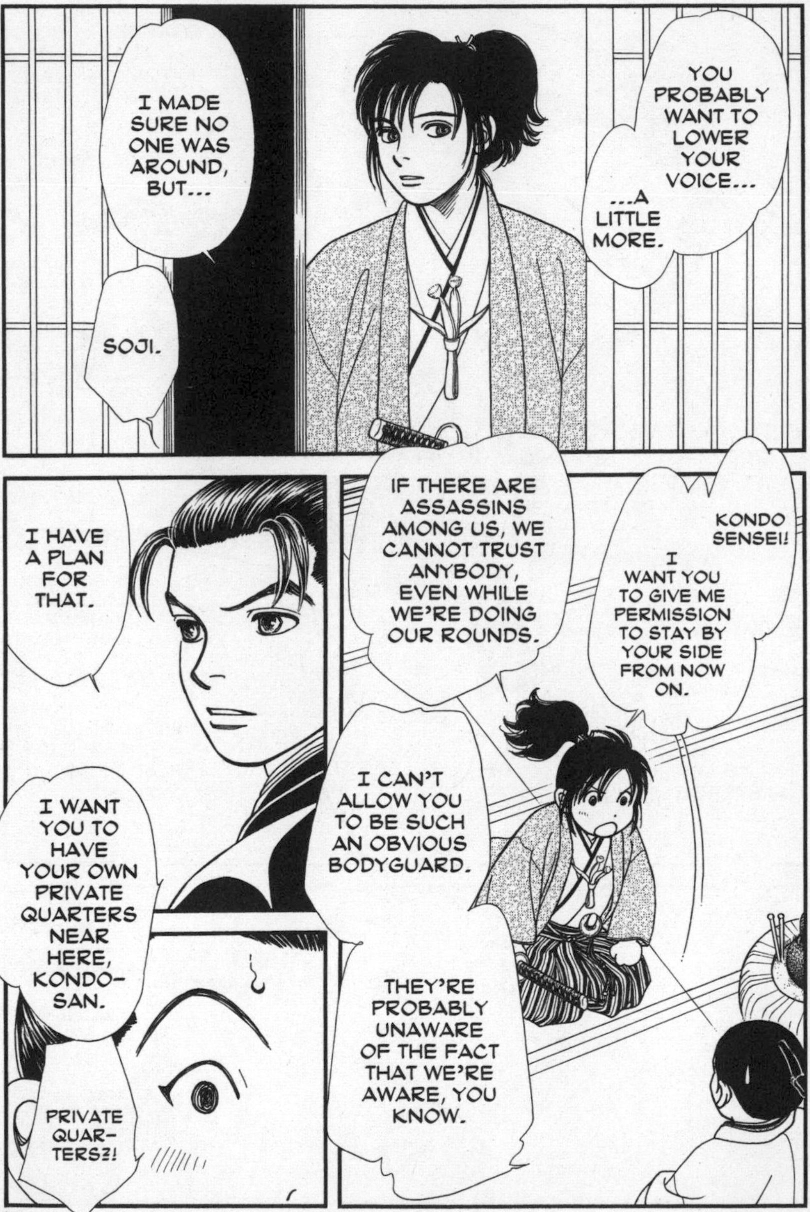
YOU PROBABLY WANT TO LOWER YOUR VOICE...
...A LITTLE MORE.
I MADE SURE NO ONE WAS AROUND, BUT...
SOJI.
KONDO SENSEI!
I WANT YOU TO GIVE ME PERMISSION TO STAY BY YOUR SIDE FROM NOW ON.
IF THERE ARE ASSASSINS AMONG US, WE CANNOT TRUST ANYBODY, EVEN WHILE WE'RE DOING OUR ROUNDS.
I CAN'T ALLOW YOU TO BE SUCH AN OBVIOUS BODYGUARD.
THEY'RE PROBABLY UNAWARE OF THE FACT THAT WE'RE AWARE, YOU KNOW.
I HAVE A PLAN FOR THAT.
I WANT YOU TO HAVE YOUR OWN PRIVATE QUARTERS NEAR HERE, KONDO-SAN.
PRIVATE QUARTERS?!

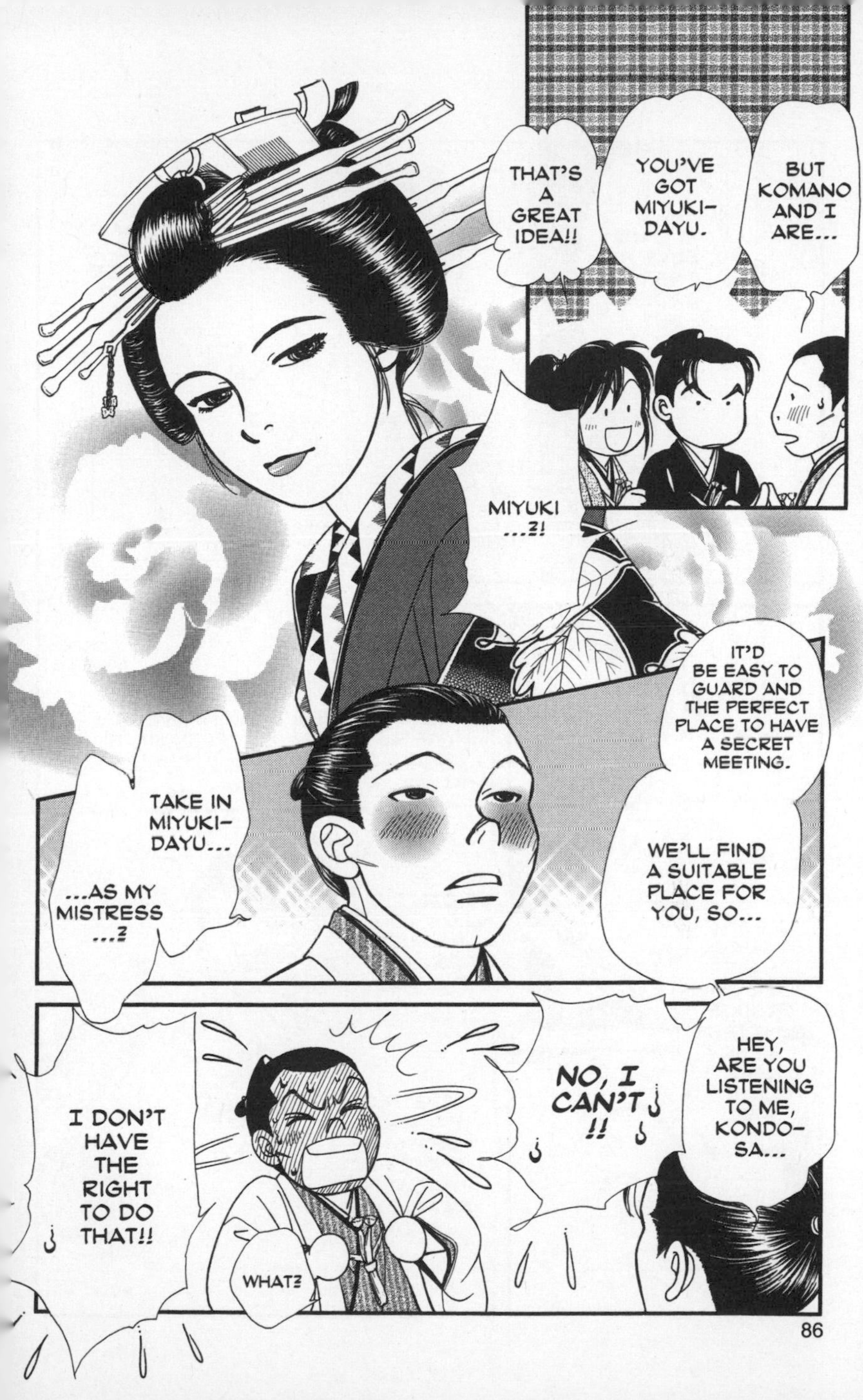
BUT KOMANO AND I ARE...
YOU'VE GOT MIYUKI-DAYU.
THAT'S A GREAT IDEA!!
MIYUKI ...?!
IT'D BE EASY TO GUARD AND THE PERFECT PLACE TO HAVE A SECRET MEETING.
WE'LL FIND A SUITABLE PLACE FOR YOU, SO...
TAKE IN MIYUKI-DAYU...
...AS MY MISTRESS ...?
HEY, ARE YOU LISTENING TO ME, KONDO-SA...
NO, I CAN'T!!
I DON'T HAVE THE RIGHT TO DO THAT!!
WHAT?

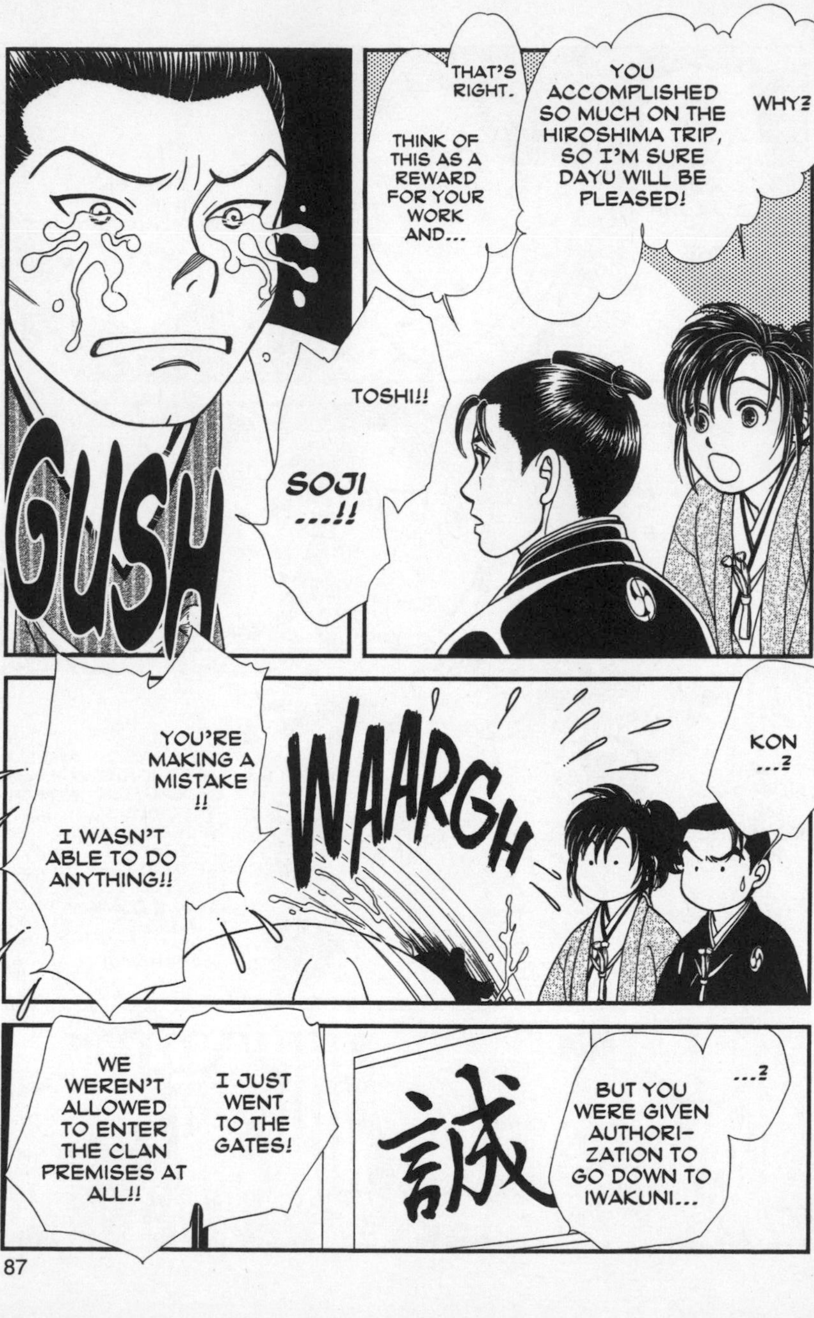
WHY?
YOU ACCOMPLISHED SO MUCH ON THE HIROSHIMA TRIP, SO I'M SURE DAYU WILL BE PLEASED!
THAT'S RIGHT.
THINK OF THIS AS A REWARD FOR YOUR WORK AND...
TOSHI!!
SOJI ...!!
GUSH
KON ...?
WAARGH
YOU'RE MAKING A MISTAKE !!
I WASN'T ABLE TO DO ANYTHING!!
...?
BUT YOU WERE GIVEN AUTHORI-ZATION TO GO DOWN TO IWAKUNI...
誠
I JUST WENT TO THE GATES!
WE WEREN'T ALLOWED TO ENTER THE CLAN PREMISES AT ALL!!

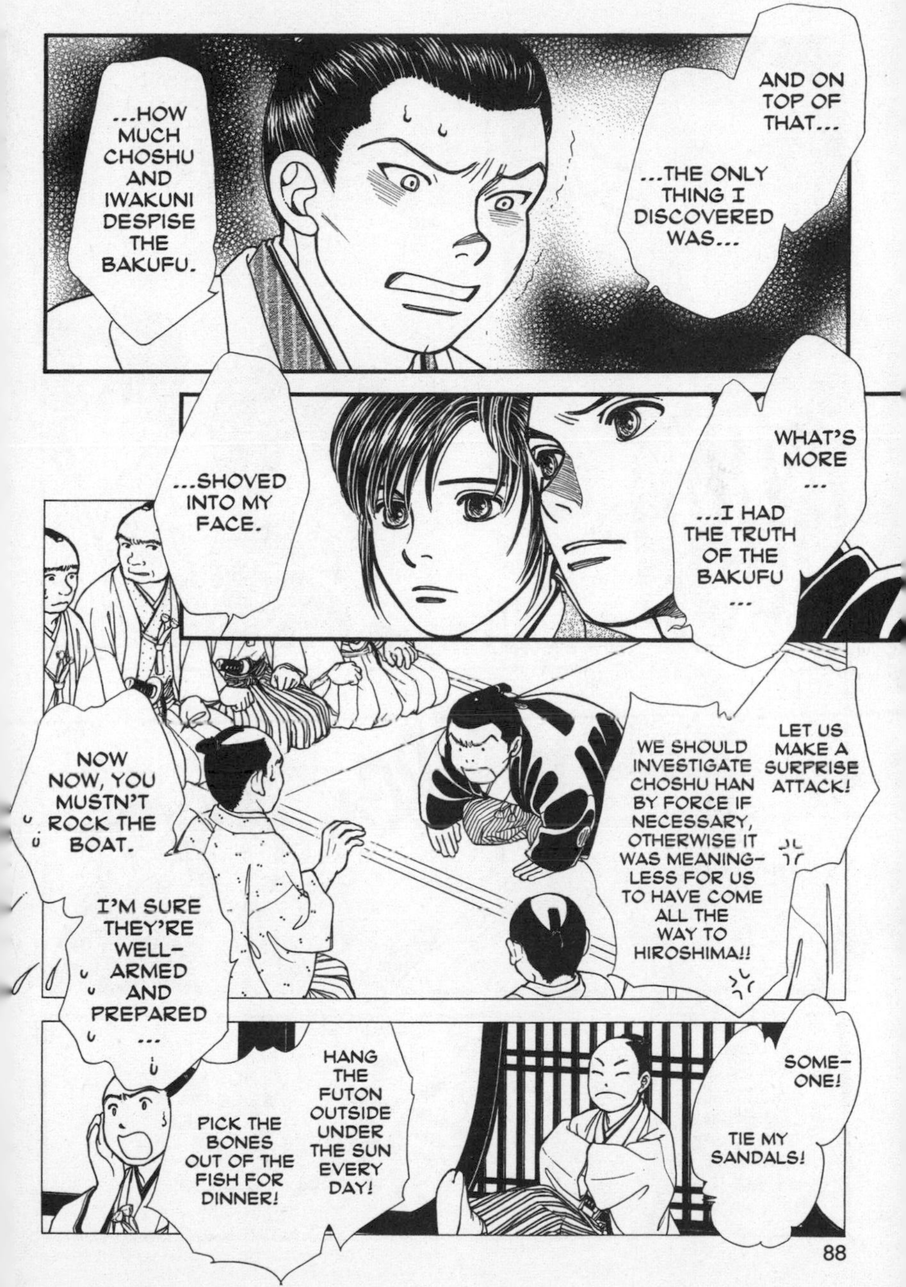
AND ON TOP OF THAT...
...THE ONLY THING I DISCOVERED WAS...
...HOW MUCH CHOSHU AND IWAKUNI DESPISE THE BAKUFU.
WHAT'S MORE...
...I HAD THE TRUTH OF THE BAKUFU...
...SHOVED INTO MY FACE.
LET US MAKE A SURPRISE ATTACK!
WE SHOULD INVESTIGATE CHOSHU HAN BY FORCE IF NECESSARY, OTHERWISE IT WAS MEANING-LESS FOR US TO HAVE COME ALL THE WAY TO HIROSHIMA!!
NOW NOW, YOU MUSTN'T ROCK THE BOAT.
I'M SURE THEY'RE WELL-ARMED AND PREPARED...
SOME-ONE!
TIE MY SANDALS!
HANG THE FUTON OUTSIDE UNDER THE SUN EVERY DAY!
PICK THE BONES OUT OF THE FISH FOR DINNER!

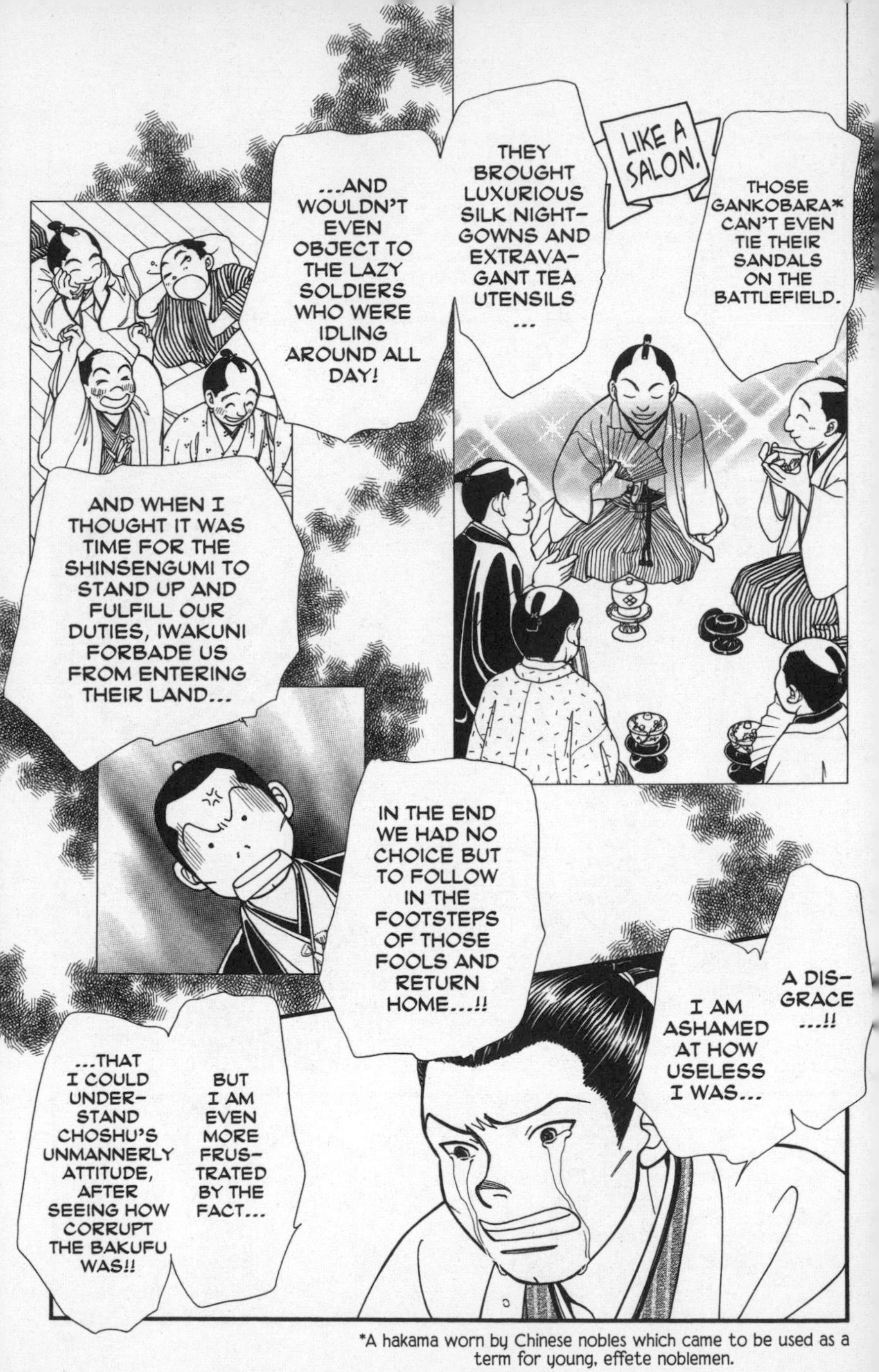
THOSE GANKOBARA* CAN'T EVEN TIE THEIR SANDALS ON THE BATTLEFIELD.
LIKE A SALON.
THEY BROUGHT LUXURIOUS SILK NIGHT-GOWNS AND EXTRAVA-GANT TEA UTENSILS ...
...AND WOULDN'T EVEN OBJECT TO THE LAZY SOLDIERS WHO WERE IDLING AROUND ALL DAY!
AND WHEN I THOUGHT IT WAS TIME FOR THE SHINSENGUMI TO STAND UP AND FULFILL OUR DUTIES, IWAKUNI FORBADE US FROM ENTERING THEIR LAND...
IN THE END WE HAD NO CHOICE BUT TO FOLLOW IN THE FOOTSTEPS OF THOSE FOOLS AND RETURN HOME...!!
A DIS-GRACE ...!!
I AM ASHAMED AT HOW USELESS I WAS...
BUT I AM EVEN MORE FRUS-TRATED BY THE FACT...
...THAT I COULD UNDER-STAND CHOSHU'S UNMANNERLY ATTITUDE, AFTER SEEING HOW CORRUPT THE BAKUFU WAS!!

*A hakama worn by Chinese nobles which came to be used as a term for young, effete noblemen.

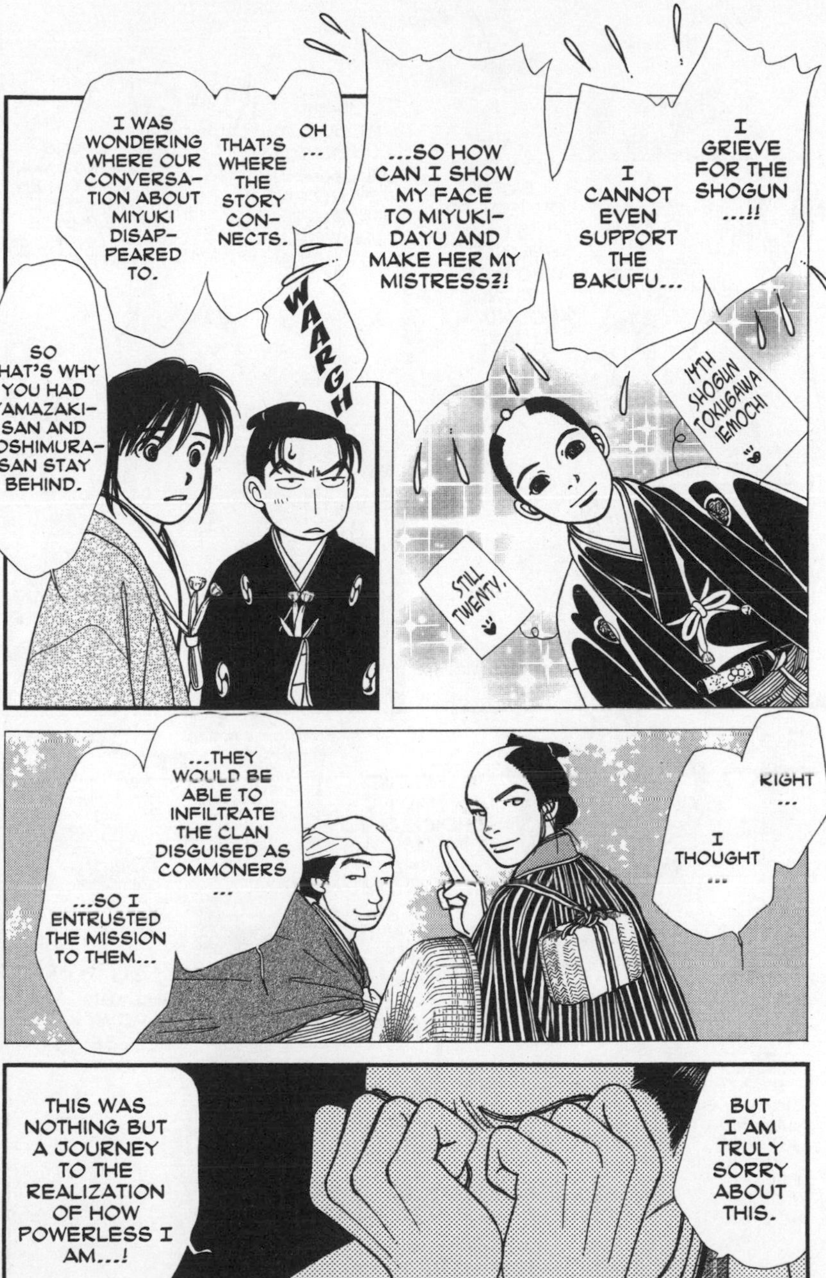
I GRIEVE FOR THE SHOGUN ...!!
I CANNOT EVEN SUPPORT THE BAKUFU...
...SO HOW CAN I SHOW MY FACE TO MIYUKI-DAYU AND MAKE HER MY MISTRESS?!
14TH SHOGUN TOKUGAWA IEMOCHI
STILL TWENTY.
OH ...
THAT'S WHERE THE STORY CONNECTS.
I WAS WONDERING WHERE OUR CONVERSATION ABOUT MIYUKI DISAPPEARED TO.
WAARGH
SO THAT'S WHY YOU HAD YAMAZAKI-SAN AND YOSHIMURA-SAN STAY BEHIND.
RIGHT ... I THOUGHT ...
...THEY WOULD BE ABLE TO INFILTRATE THE CLAN DISGUISED AS COMMONERS ...
...SO I ENTRUSTED THE MISSION TO THEM...
BUT I AM TRULY SORRY ABOUT THIS.
THIS WAS NOTHING BUT A JOURNEY TO THE REALIZATION OF HOW POWERLESS I AM...!

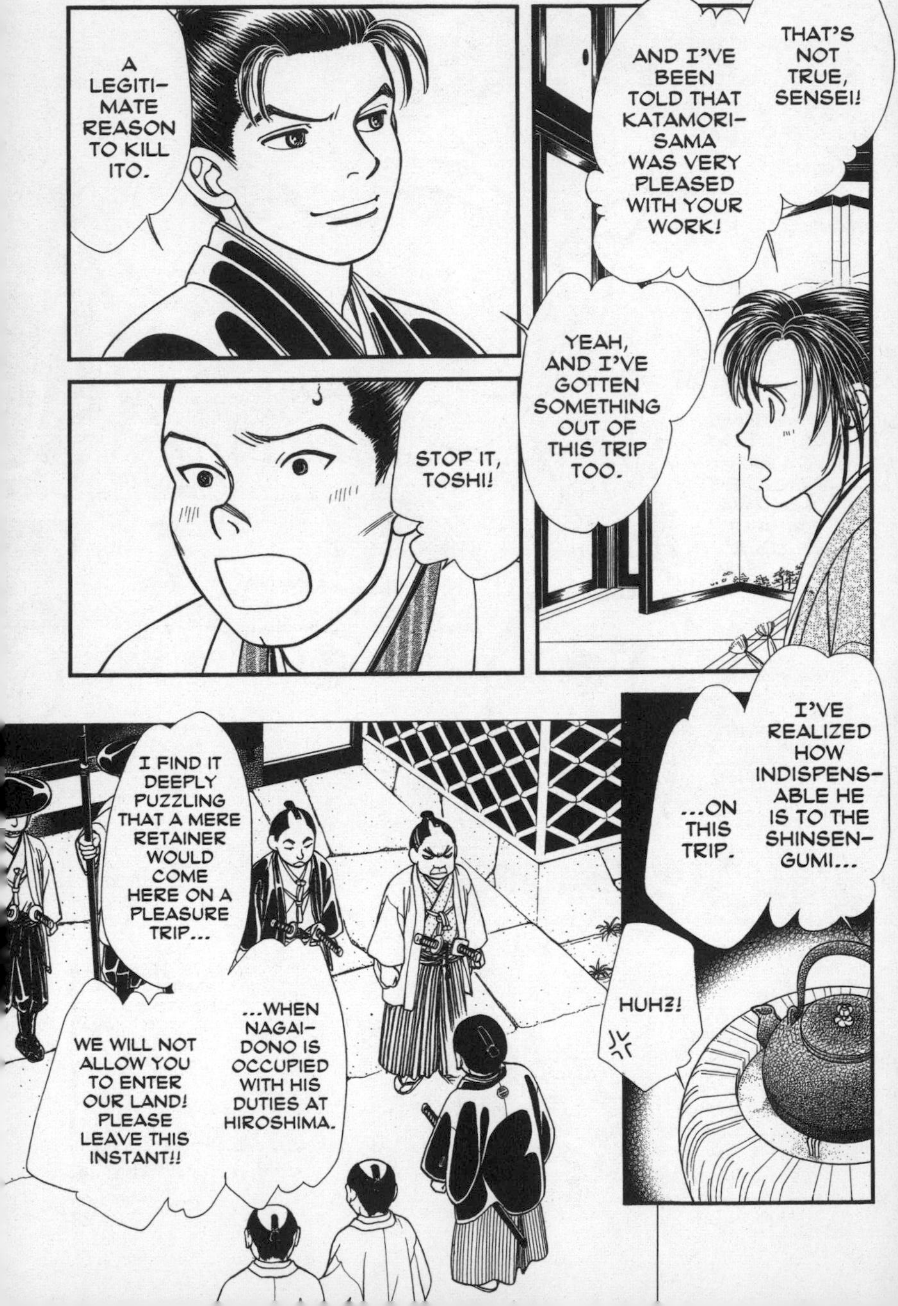
THAT'S NOT TRUE, SENSEI!
AND I'VE BEEN TOLD THAT KATAMORI-SAMA WAS VERY PLEASED WITH YOUR WORK!
YEAH, AND I'VE GOTTEN SOMETHING OUT OF THIS TRIP TOO.
A LEGITI-MATE REASON TO KILL ITO.
STOP IT, TOSHI!
I'VE REALIZED HOW INDISPENS-ABLE HE IS TO THE SHINSEN-GUMI...
...ON THIS TRIP.
HUH?!
I FIND IT DEEPLY PUZZLING THAT A MERE RETAINER WOULD COME HERE ON A PLEASURE TRIP...
...WHEN NAGAI-DONO IS OCCUPIED WITH HIS DUTIES AT HIROSHIMA.
WE WILL NOT ALLOW YOU TO ENTER OUR LAND! PLEASE LEAVE THIS INSTANT!!

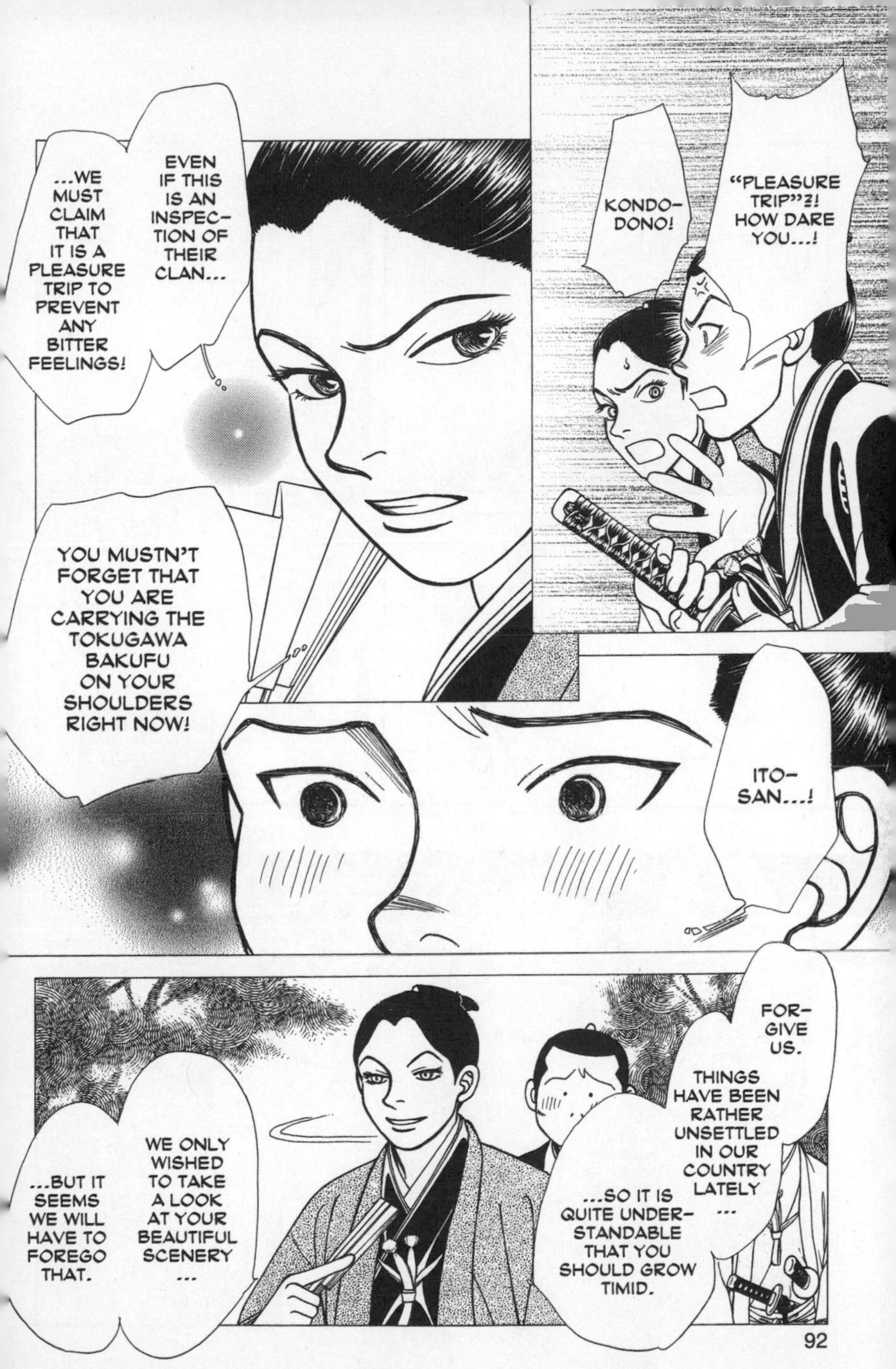
"PLEASURE TRIP"?! HOW DARE YOU...!
KONDO-DONO!
EVEN IF THIS IS AN INSPECTION OF THEIR CLAN...
...WE MUST CLAIM THAT IT IS A PLEASURE TRIP TO PREVENT ANY BITTER FEELINGS!
YOU MUSTN'T FORGET THAT YOU ARE CARRYING THE TOKUGAWA BAKUFU ON YOUR SHOULDERS RIGHT NOW!
ITO-SAN...!
FORGIVE US.
THINGS HAVE BEEN RATHER UNSETTLED IN OUR COUNTRY LATELY...
...SO IT IS QUITE UNDERSTANDABLE THAT YOU SHOULD GROW TIMID.
WE ONLY WISHED TO TAKE A LOOK AT YOUR BEAUTIFUL SCENERY...
...BUT IT SEEMS WE WILL HAVE TO FOREGO THAT.

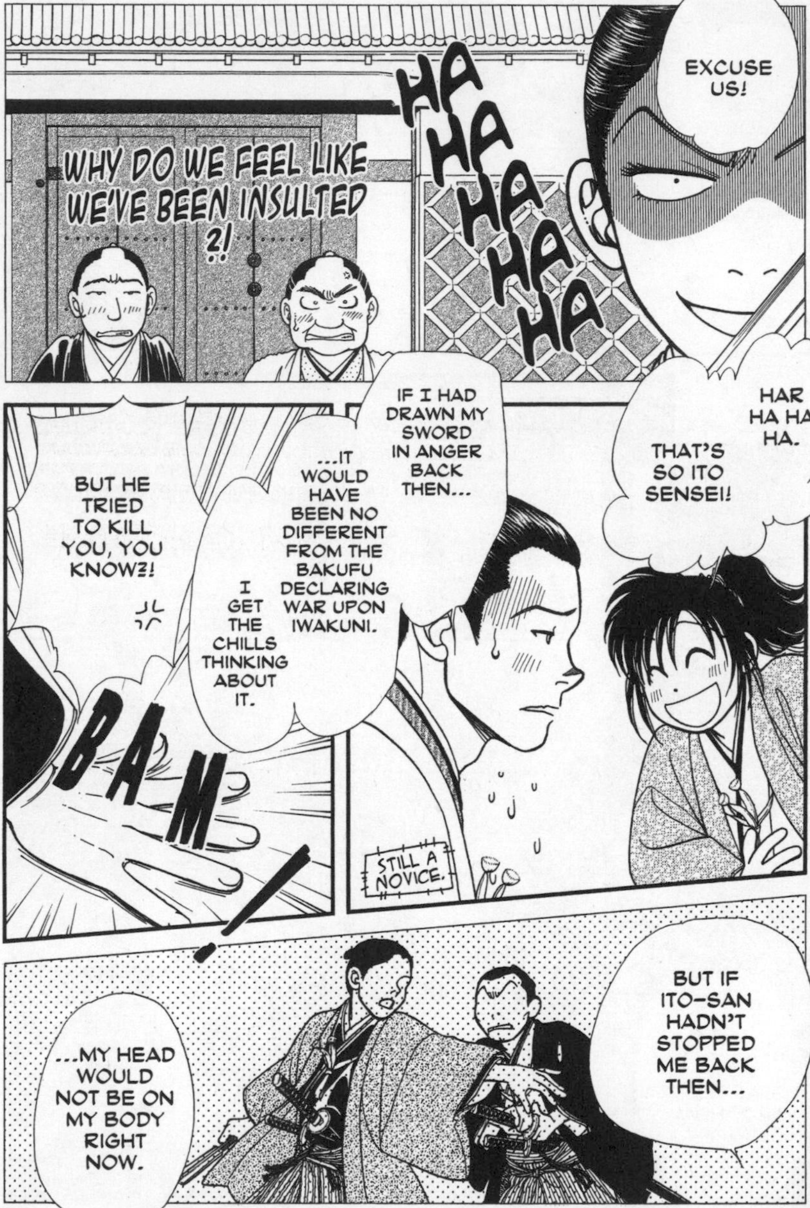
EXCUSE US!
HA HA HA HA HA HA
WHY DO WE FEEL LIKE WE'VE BEEN INSULTED ?!
HAR HA HA HA.
THAT'S SO ITO SENSEI!
IF I HAD DRAWN MY SWORD IN ANGER BACK THEN...
...IT WOULD HAVE BEEN NO DIFFERENT FROM THE BAKUFU DECLARING WAR UPON IWAKUNI.
I GET THE CHILLS THINKING ABOUT IT.
STILL A NOVICE.
BUT HE TRIED TO KILL YOU, YOU KNOW?!
BAM
BUT IF ITO-SAN HADN'T STOPPED ME BACK THEN...
...MY HEAD WOULD NOT BE ON MY BODY RIGHT NOW.

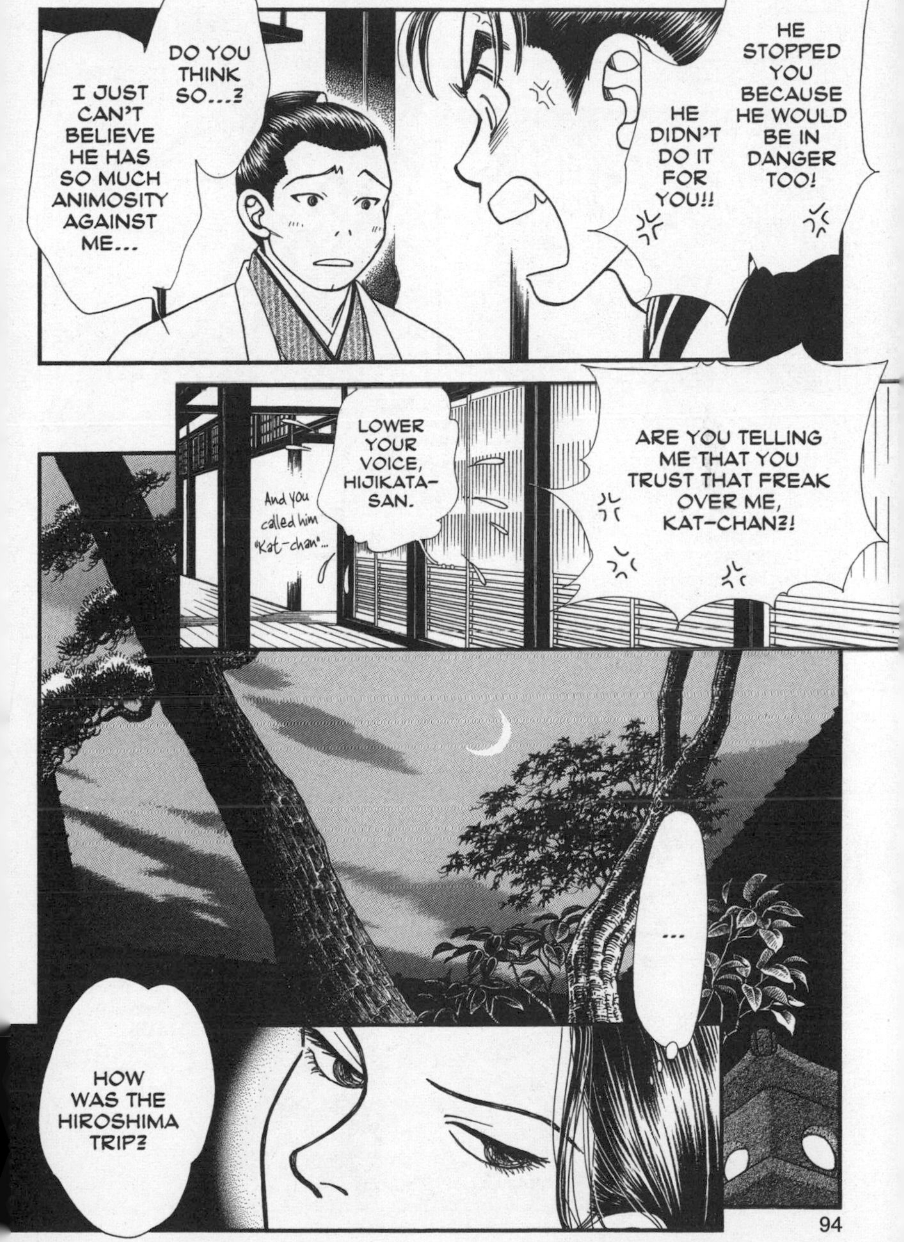
HE STOPPED YOU BECAUSE HE WOULD BE IN DANGER TOO!
HE DIDN'T DO IT FOR YOU!!
DO YOU THINK SO...?
I JUST CAN'T BELIEVE HE HAS SO MUCH ANIMOSITY AGAINST ME...
ARE YOU TELLING ME THAT YOU TRUST THAT FREAK OVER ME, KAT-CHAN?!
LOWER YOUR VOICE, HIJIKATA-SAN.
And you called him "Kat-chan"...
...
HOW WAS THE HIROSHIMA TRIP?

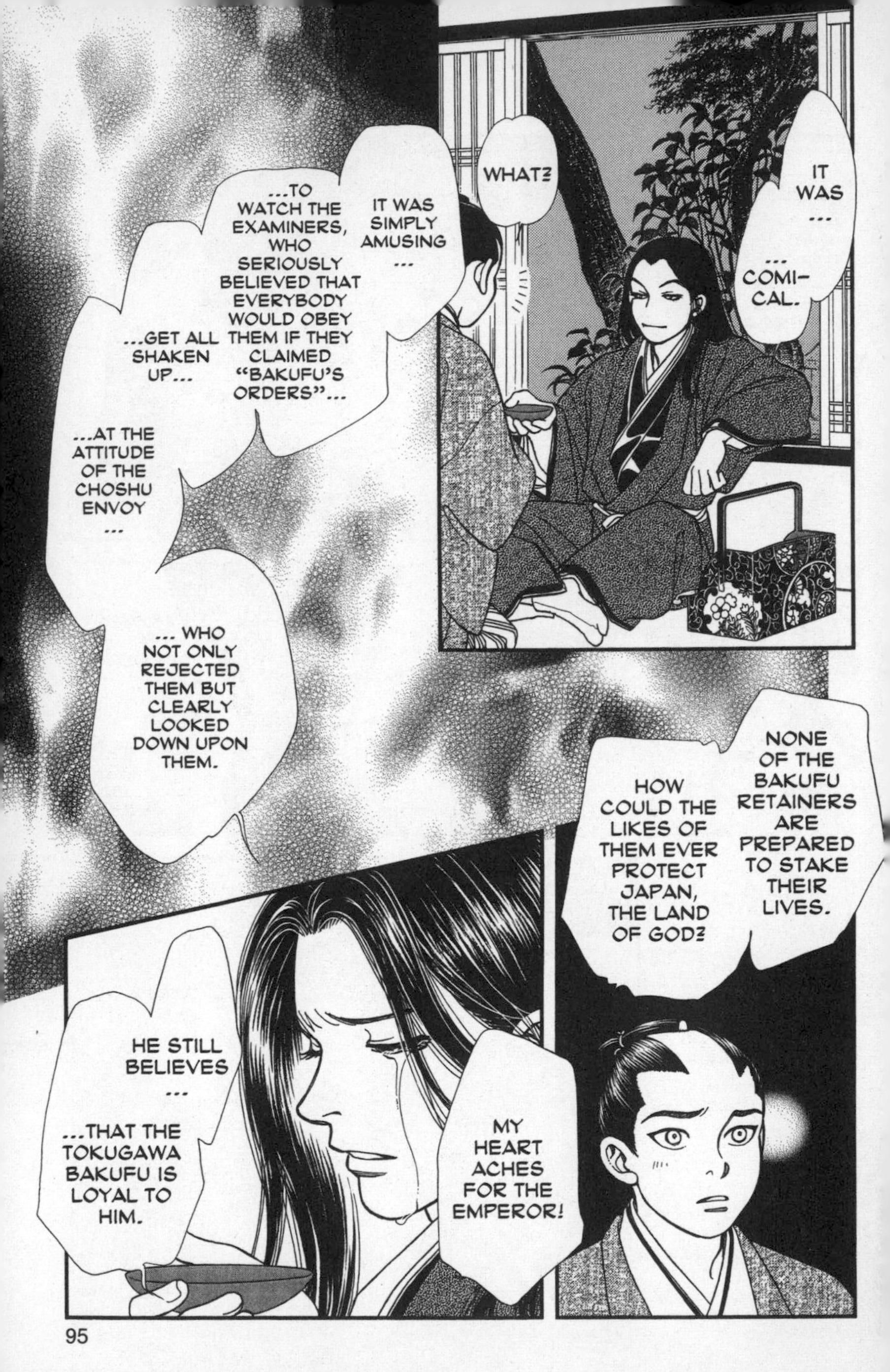
IT WAS ...
... COMI-CAL.
WHAT?
IT WAS SIMPLY AMUSING ...
...TO WATCH THE EXAMINERS, WHO SERIOUSLY BELIEVED THAT EVERYBODY WOULD OBEY THEM IF THEY CLAIMED "BAKUFU'S ORDERS"...
...GET ALL SHAKEN UP...
...AT THE ATTITUDE OF THE CHOSHU ENVOY ...
... WHO NOT ONLY REJECTED THEM BUT CLEARLY LOOKED DOWN UPON THEM.
NONE OF THE BAKUFU RETAINERS ARE PREPARED TO STAKE THEIR LIVES.
HOW COULD THE LIKES OF THEM EVER PROTECT JAPAN, THE LAND OF GOD?
MY HEART ACHES FOR THE EMPEROR!
HE STILL BELIEVES ...
...THAT THE TOKUGAWA BAKUFU IS LOYAL TO HIM.

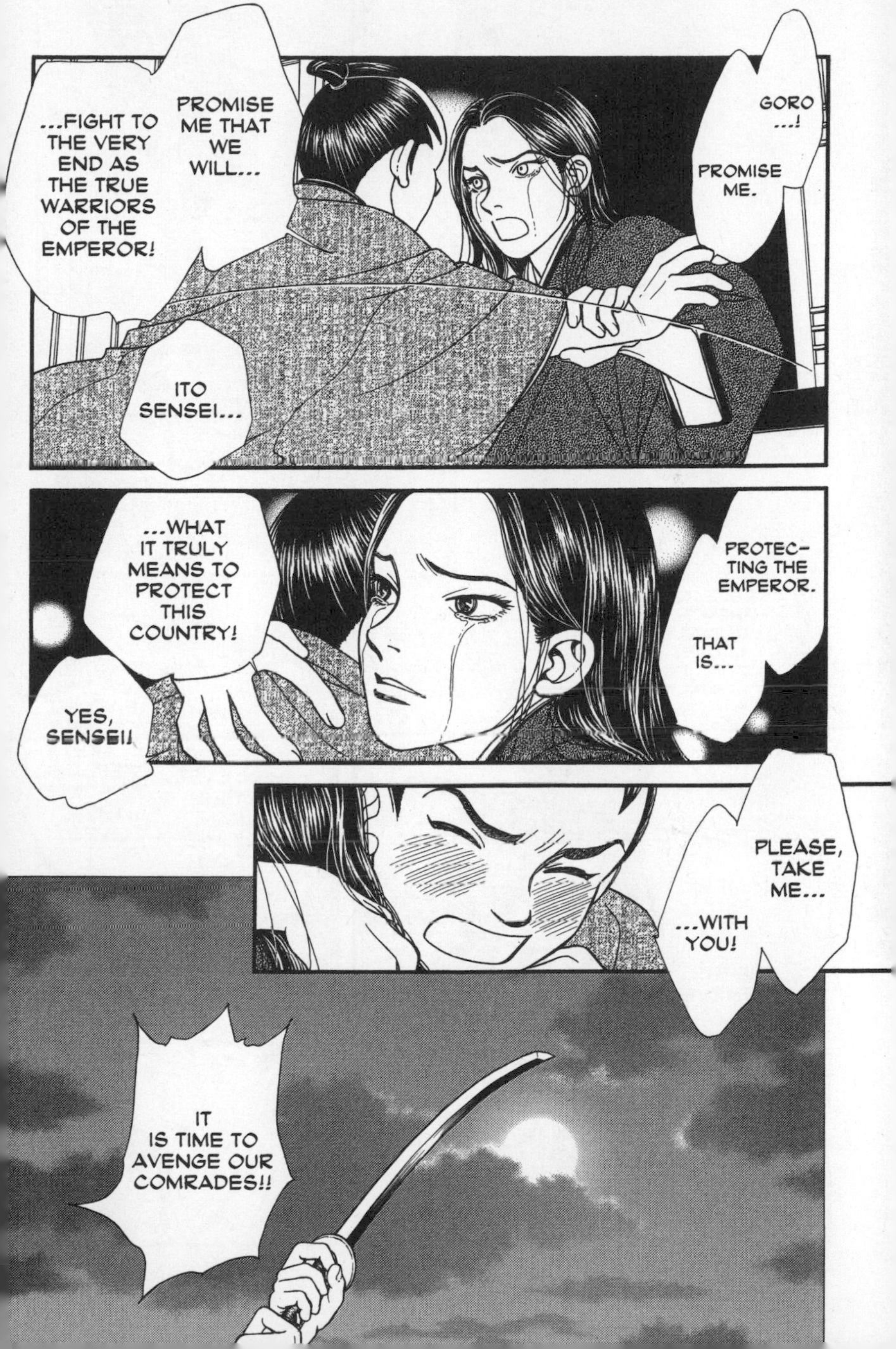
GORO ...!
PROMISE ME.
PROMISE ME THAT WE WILL...
...FIGHT TO THE VERY END AS THE TRUE WARRIORS OF THE EMPEROR!
ITO SENSEI...
PROTEC-TING THE EMPEROR.
THAT IS...
...WHAT IT TRULY MEANS TO PROTECT THIS COUNTRY!
YES, SENSEI!
PLEASE, TAKE ME...
...WITH YOU!
IT IS TIME TO AVENGE OUR COMRADES!!

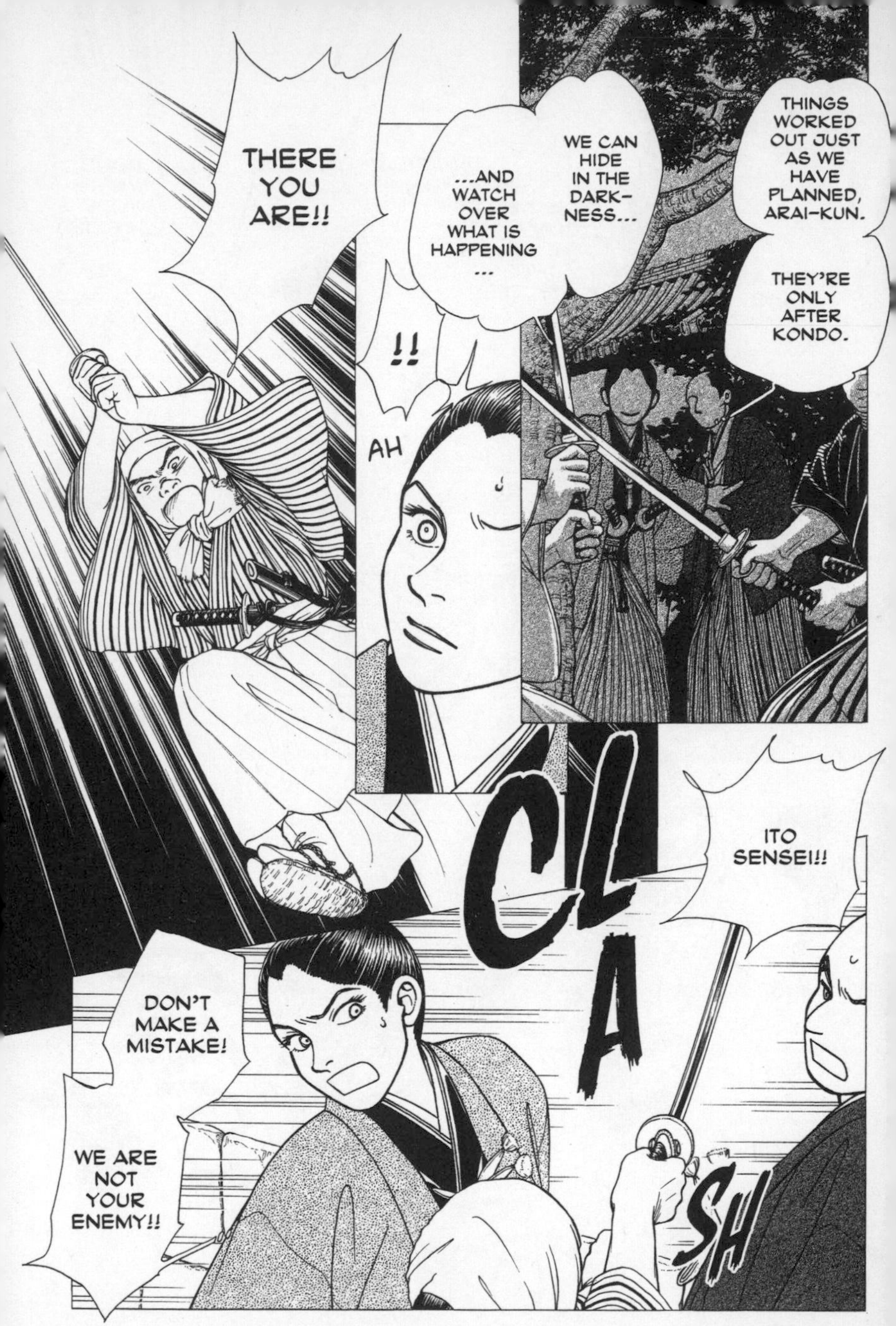
THINGS WORKED OUT JUST AS WE HAVE PLANNED, ARAI-KUN.
THEY'RE ONLY AFTER KONDO.
WE CAN HIDE IN THE DARK-NESS...
...AND WATCH OVER WHAT IS HAPPENING ...
!!
AH
THERE YOU ARE!!
ITO SENSEI!!
CLA
DON'T MAKE A MISTAKE!
WE ARE NOT YOUR ENEMY!!
SH

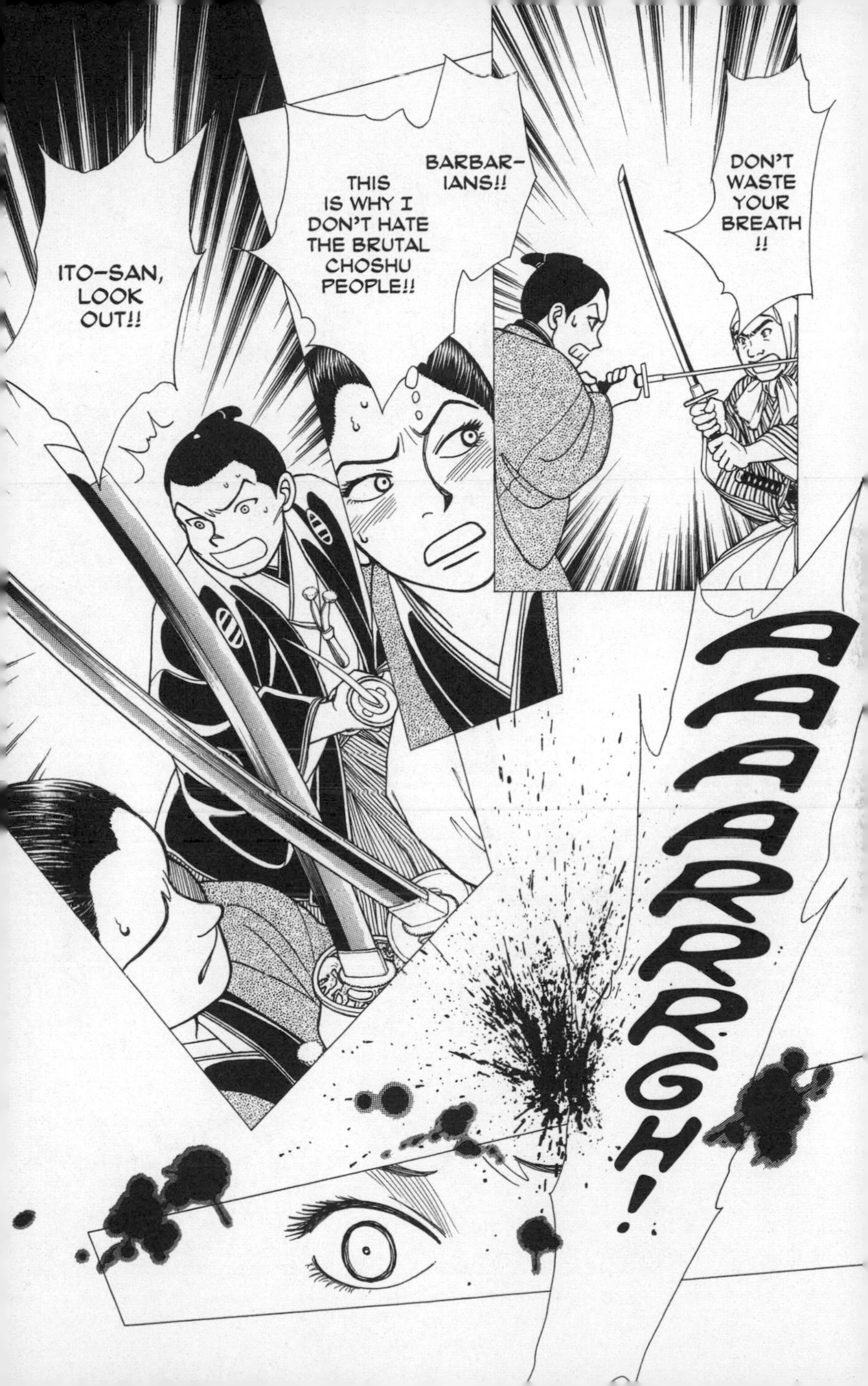
DON'T WASTE YOUR BREATH !!
BARBAR-IANS!!
THIS IS WHY I DON'T HATE THE BRUTAL CHOSHU PEOPLE!!
ITO-SAN, LOOK OUT!!
AAAARRRGH!

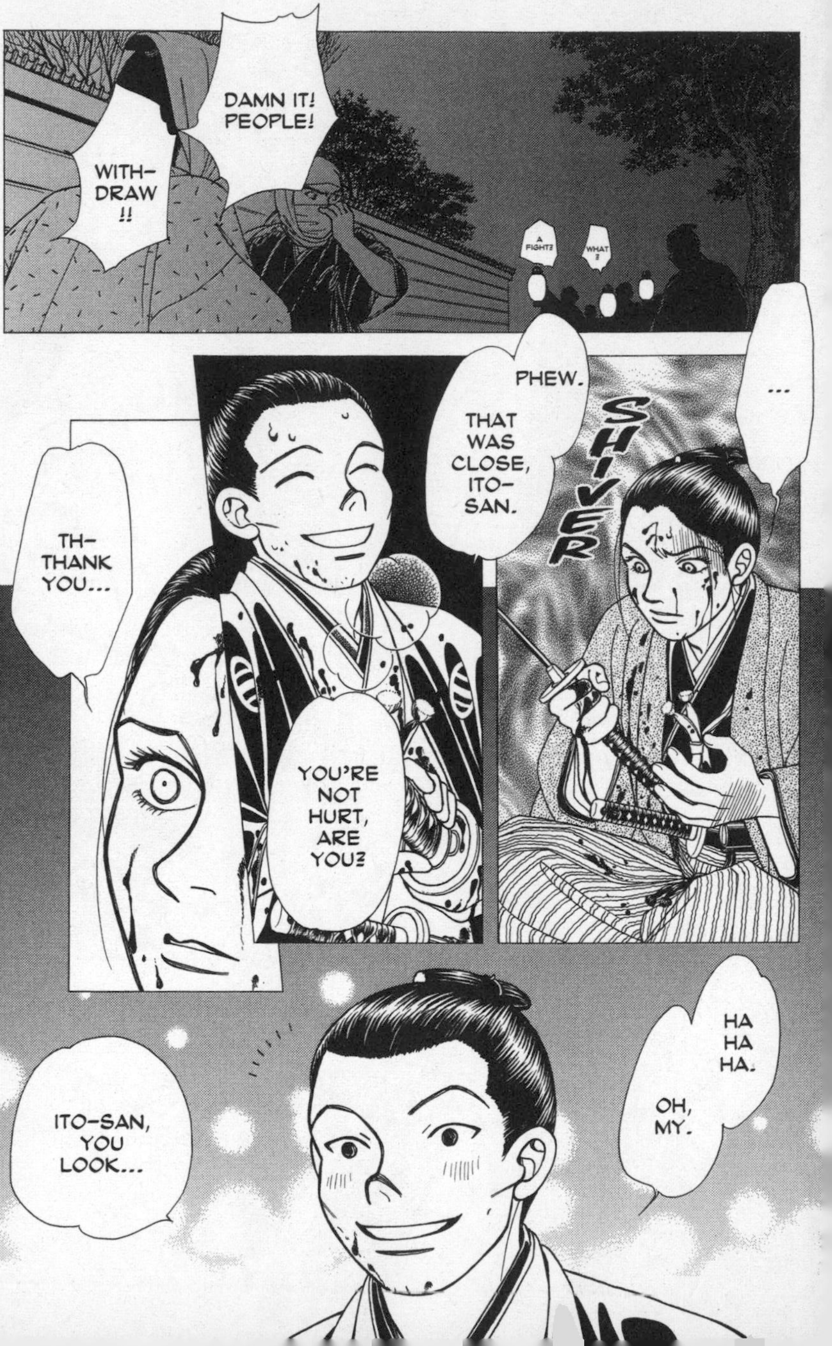
DAMN IT! PEOPLE!
WITH-DRAW!!
WHAT?
A FIGHT?
...
SHIVER
PHEW. THAT WAS CLOSE, ITO-SAN.
YOU'RE NOT HURT, ARE YOU?
TH-THANK YOU...
HA HA HA.
OH, MY.
ITO-SAN, YOU LOOK...

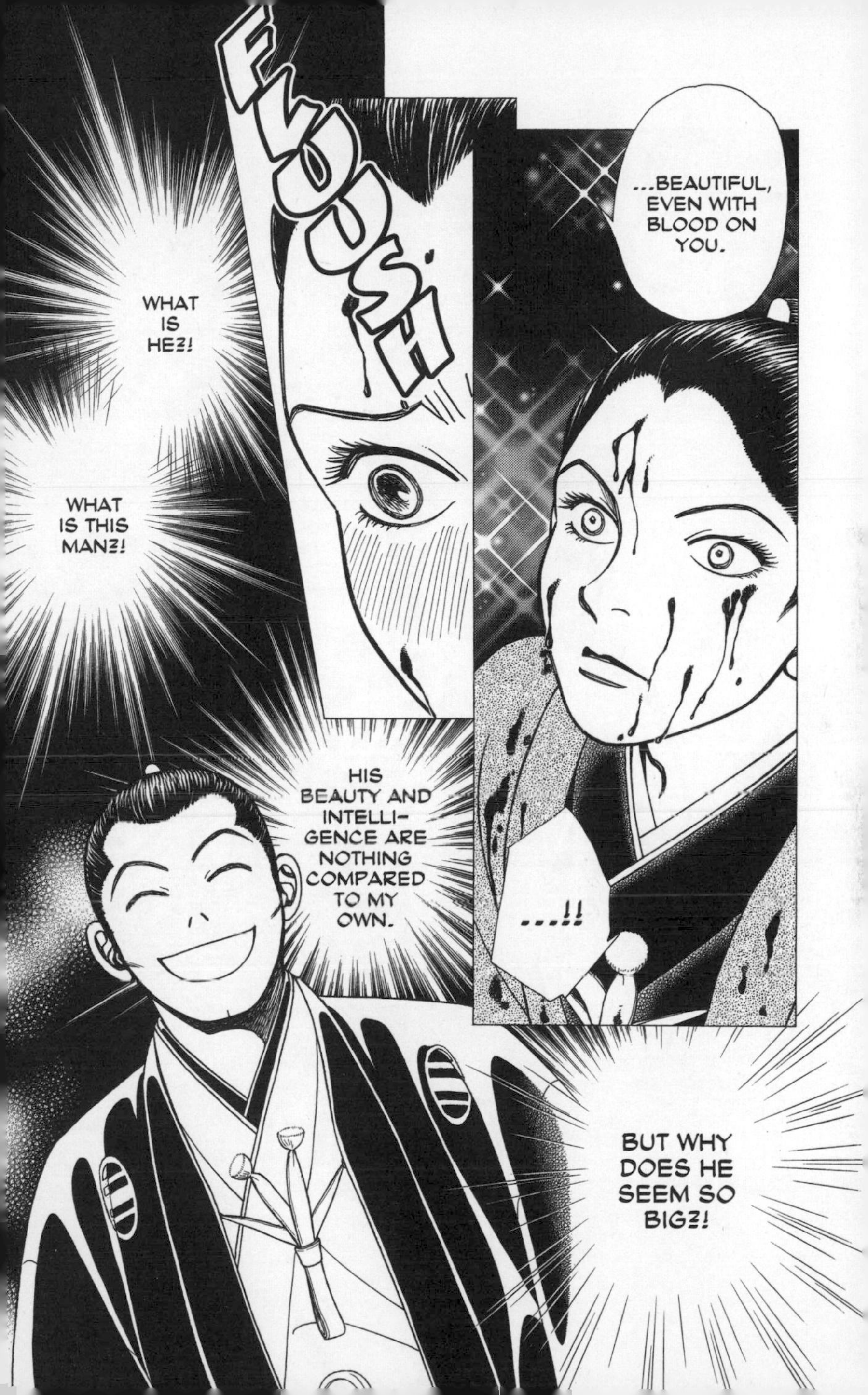
...BEAUTIFUL, EVEN WITH BLOOD ON YOU.
FWOOSH!
WHAT IS HE?!
WHAT IS THIS MAN?!
...!!
HIS BEAUTY AND INTELLI- GENCE ARE NOTHING COMPARED TO MY OWN.
BUT WHY DOES HE SEEM SO BIG?!

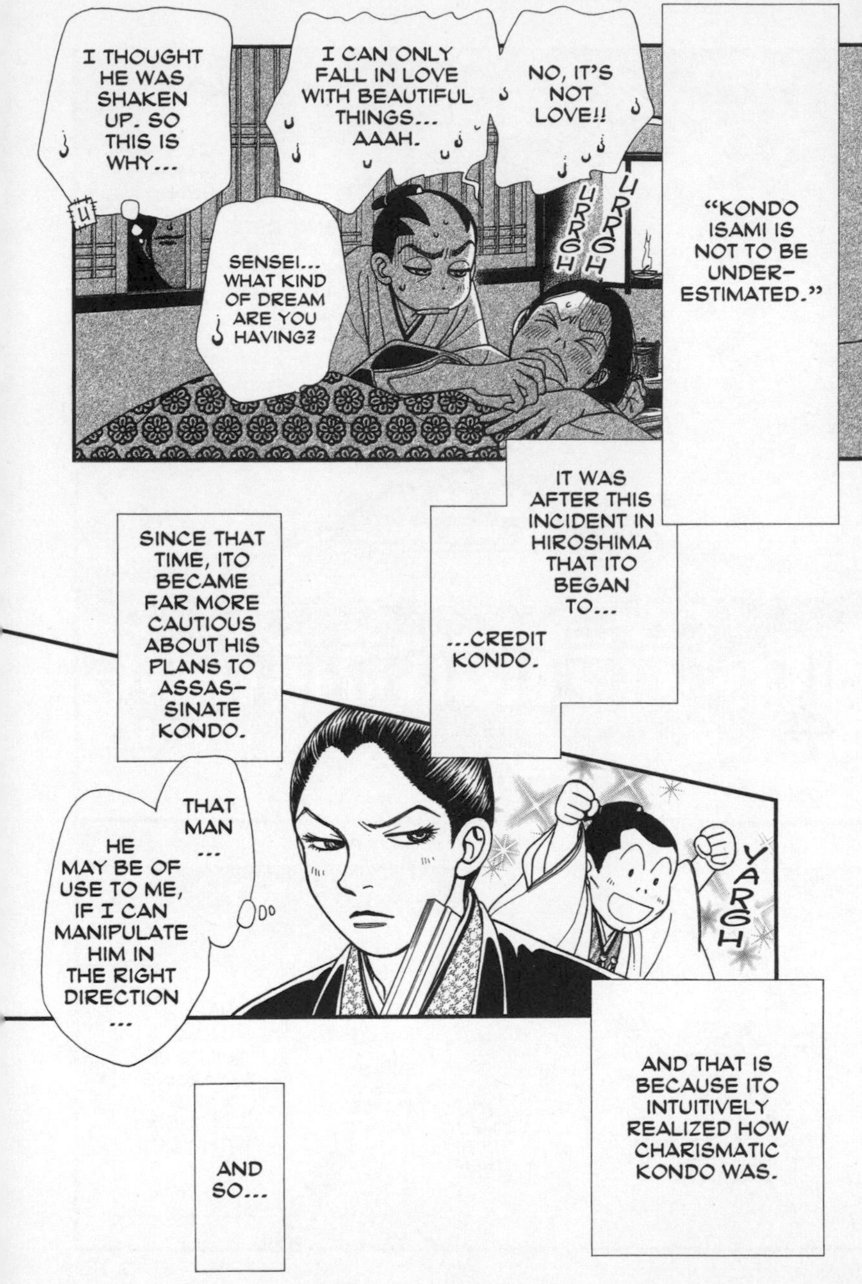
"KONDO ISAMI IS NOT TO BE UNDER-ESTIMATED."
NO, IT'S NOT LOVE!!
I CAN ONLY FALL IN LOVE WITH BEAUTIFUL THINGS... AAAH.
I THOUGHT HE WAS SHAKEN UP. SO THIS IS WHY...
URRGH
URRGH
SENSEI... WHAT KIND OF DREAM ARE YOU HAVING?
IT WAS AFTER THIS INCIDENT IN HIROSHIMA THAT ITO BEGAN TO...
...CREDIT KONDO.
SINCE THAT TIME, ITO BECAME FAR MORE CAUTIOUS ABOUT HIS PLANS TO ASSAS-SINATE KONDO.
YARGH
THAT MAN...
HE MAY BE OF USE TO ME, IF I CAN MANIPULATE HIM IN THE RIGHT DIRECTION...
AND THAT IS BECAUSE ITO INTUITIVELY REALIZED HOW CHARISMATIC KONDO WAS.
AND SO...

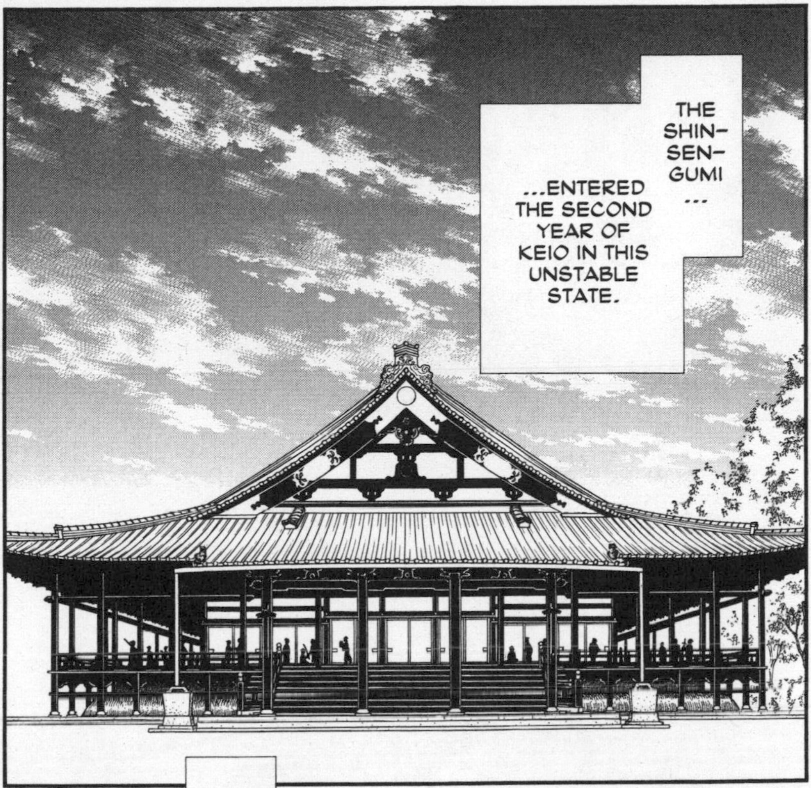
THE SHINSENGUMI...
...ENTERED THE SECOND YEAR OF KEIO IN THIS UNSTABLE STATE.

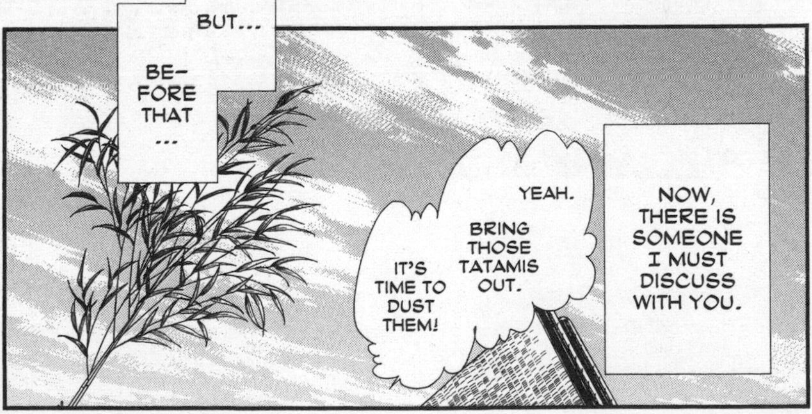
BUT...
BEFORE THAT...
NOW, THERE IS SOMEONE I MUST DISCUSS WITH YOU.
YEAH.
BRING THOSE TATAMIS OUT.
IT'S TIME TO DUST THEM!

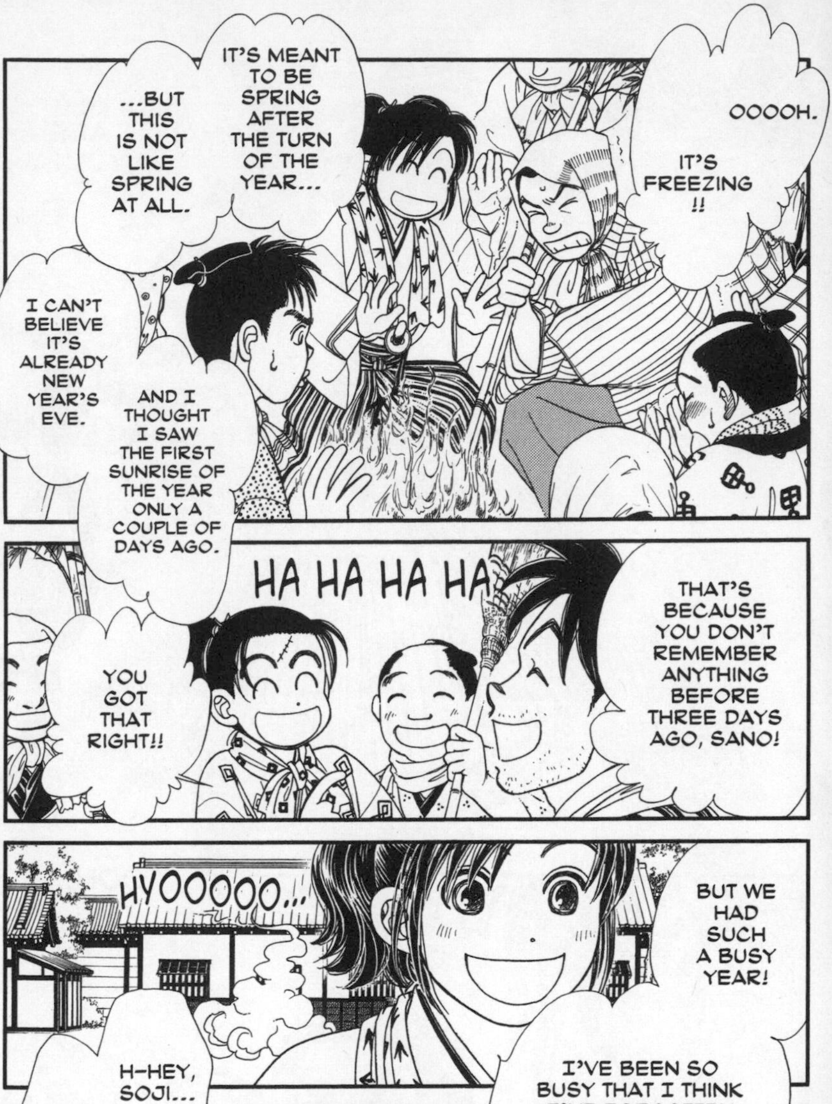
OOOOH.
IT'S FREEZING!!
IT'S MEANT TO BE SPRING AFTER THE TURN OF THE YEAR...
...BUT THIS IS NOT LIKE SPRING AT ALL.
I CAN'T BELIEVE IT'S ALREADY NEW YEAR'S EVE.
AND I THOUGHT I SAW THE FIRST SUNRISE OF THE YEAR ONLY A COUPLE OF DAYS AGO.
THAT'S BECAUSE YOU DON'T REMEMBER ANYTHING BEFORE THREE DAYS AGO, SANO!
HA HA HA HA
YOU GOT THAT RIGHT!!
BUT WE HAD SUCH A BUSY YEAR!
HYOOOOO...
I'VE BEEN SO BUSY THAT I THINK I'VE FORGOTTEN SOMETHING VERY IMPORTANT...
H-HEY, SOJI...
GOOOOOO...
WHAT'S THAT...?

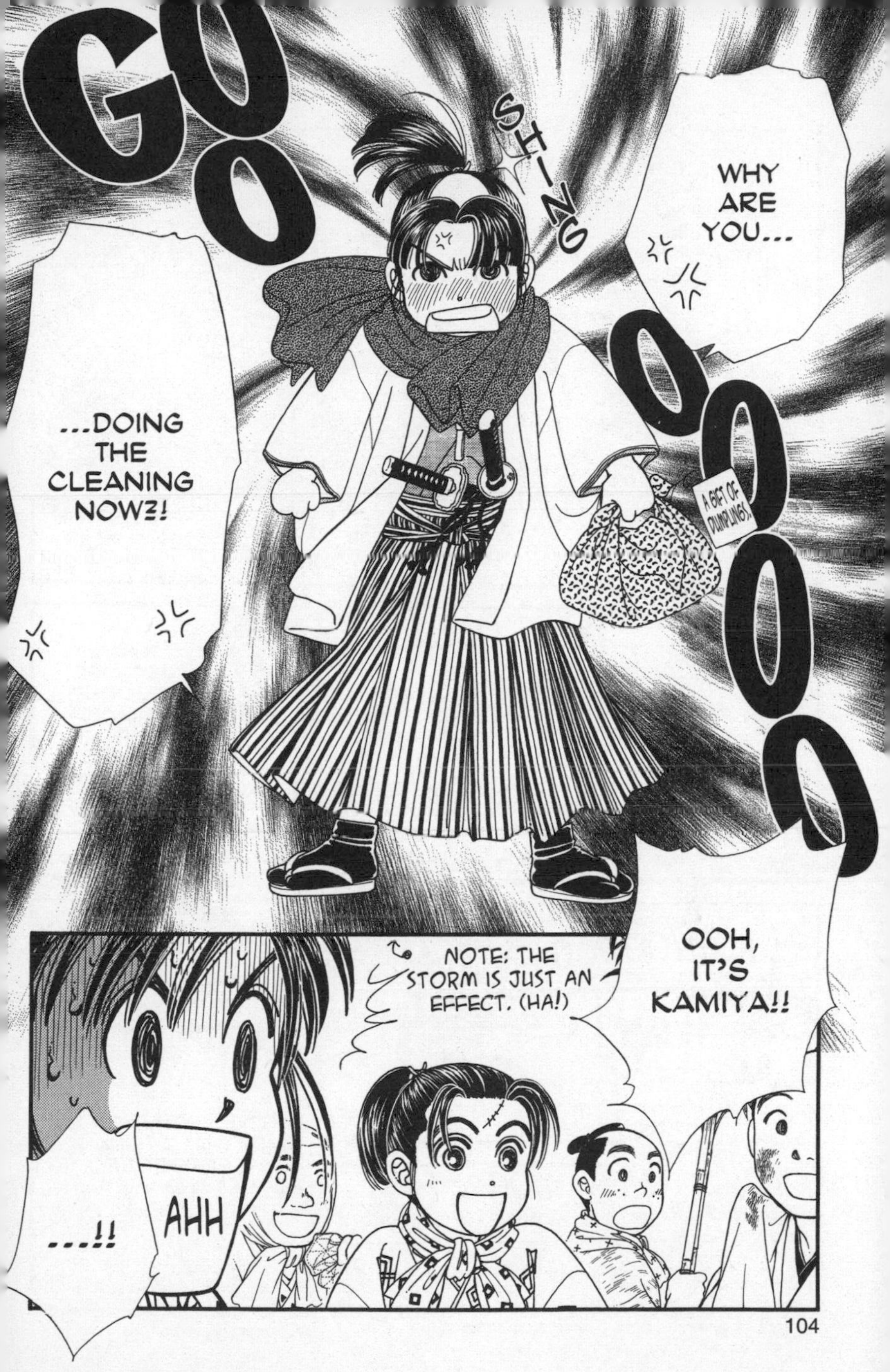
WHY ARE YOU...
SHING
GOOOOOOOO
A GIFT OF DUMPLINGS
...DOING THE CLEANING NOW?!
OOH, IT'S KAMIYA!!
NOTE: THE STORM IS JUST AN EFFECT. (HA!)
AHH
...!!

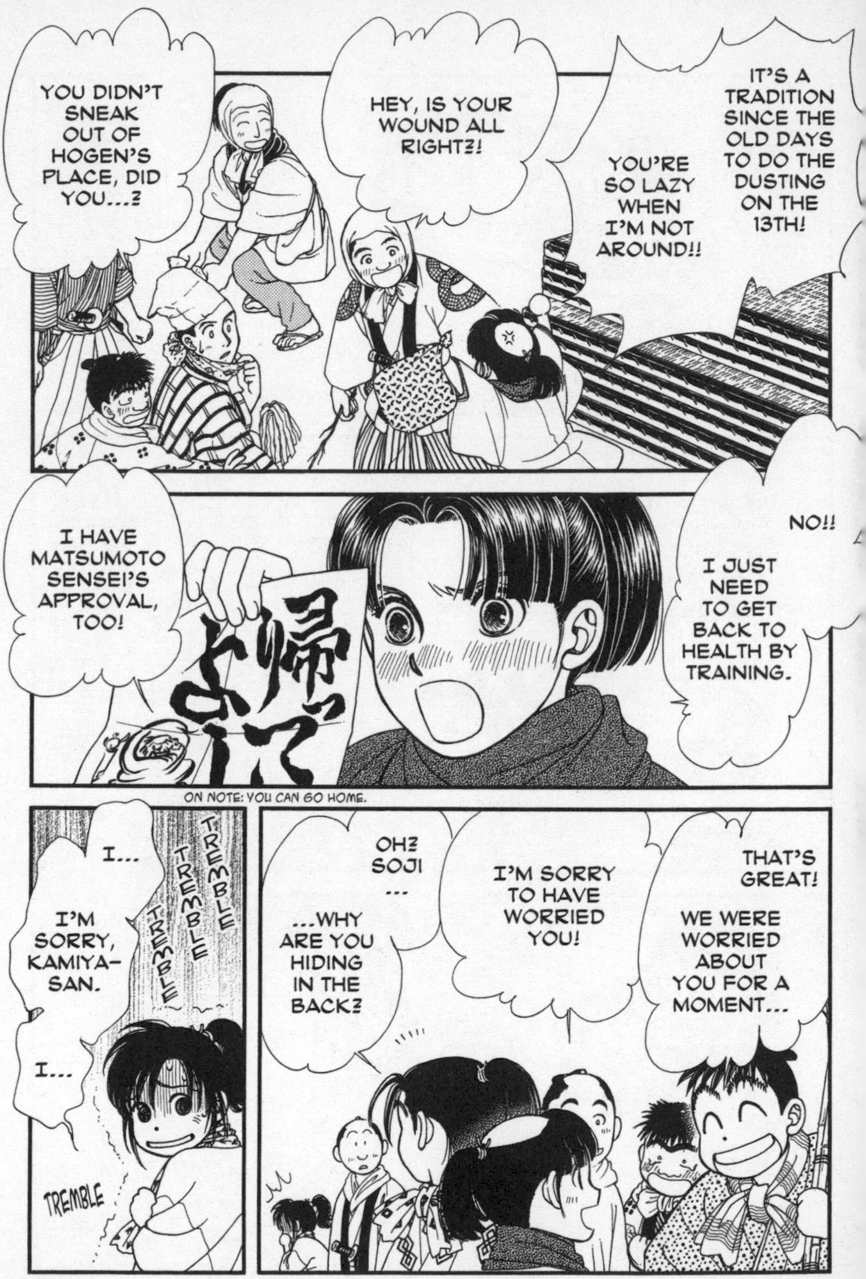
IT'S A TRADITION SINCE THE OLD DAYS TO DO THE DUSTING ON THE 13TH!
YOU'RE SO LAZY WHEN I'M NOT AROUND!!
HEY, IS YOUR WOUND ALL RIGHT?!
YOU DIDN'T SNEAK OUT OF HOGEN'S PLACE, DID YOU...?
NO!!
I JUST NEED TO GET BACK TO HEALTH BY TRAINING.
I HAVE MATSUMOTO SENSEI'S APPROVAL, TOO!
帰ってよし
ON NOTE: YOU CAN GO HOME.
THAT'S GREAT!
WE WERE WORRIED ABOUT YOU FOR A MOMENT...
I'M SORRY TO HAVE WORRIED YOU!
OH? SOJI ...
...WHY ARE YOU HIDING IN THE BACK?
TREMBLE TREMBLE TREMBLE
I...
I'M SORRY, KAMIYA-SAN.
I...
TREMBLE

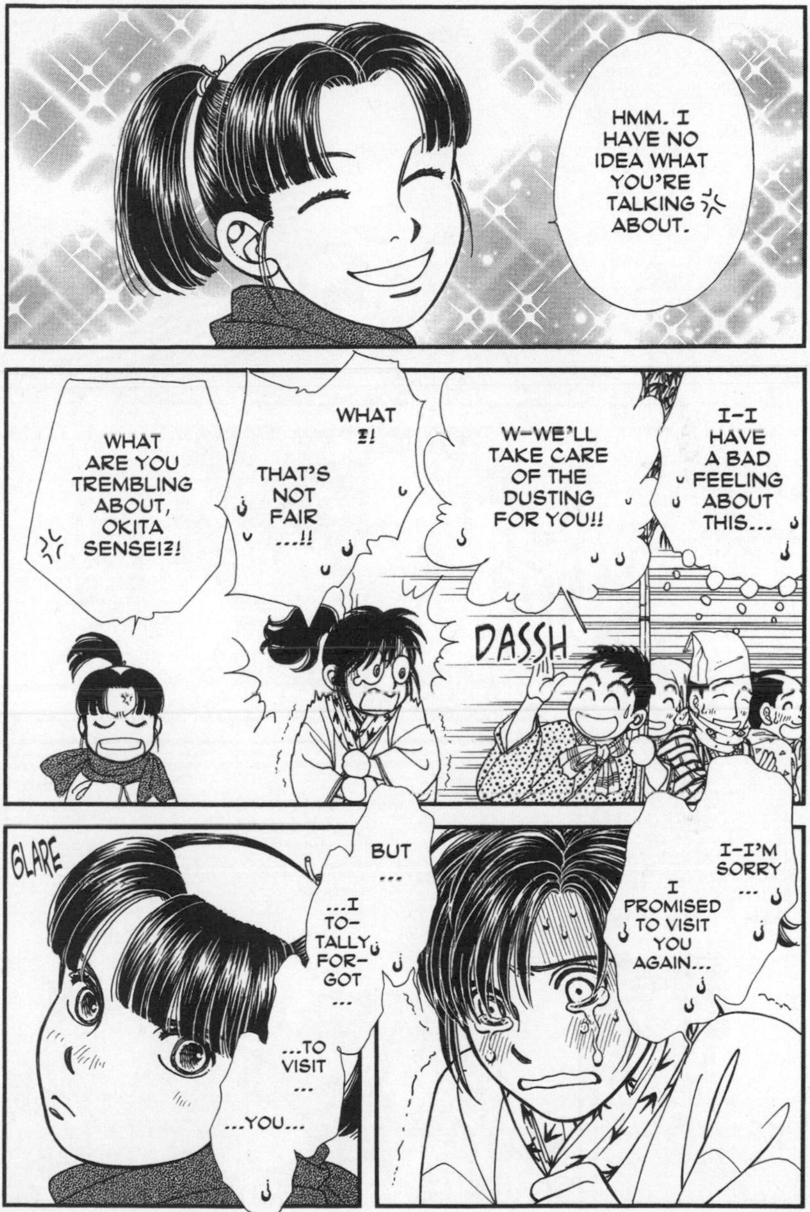
HMM. I HAVE NO IDEA WHAT YOU'RE TALKING ABOUT.
I-I HAVE A BAD FEELING ABOUT THIS...
W-WE'LL TAKE CARE OF THE DUSTING FOR YOU!!
DASSH
WHAT?!
THAT'S NOT FAIR...!!
WHAT ARE YOU TREMBLING ABOUT, OKITA SENSEI?!
I-I'M SORRY...
I PROMISED TO VISIT YOU AGAIN...
BUT...
...I TOTALLY FORGOT...
...TO VISIT...
...YOU...
GLARE

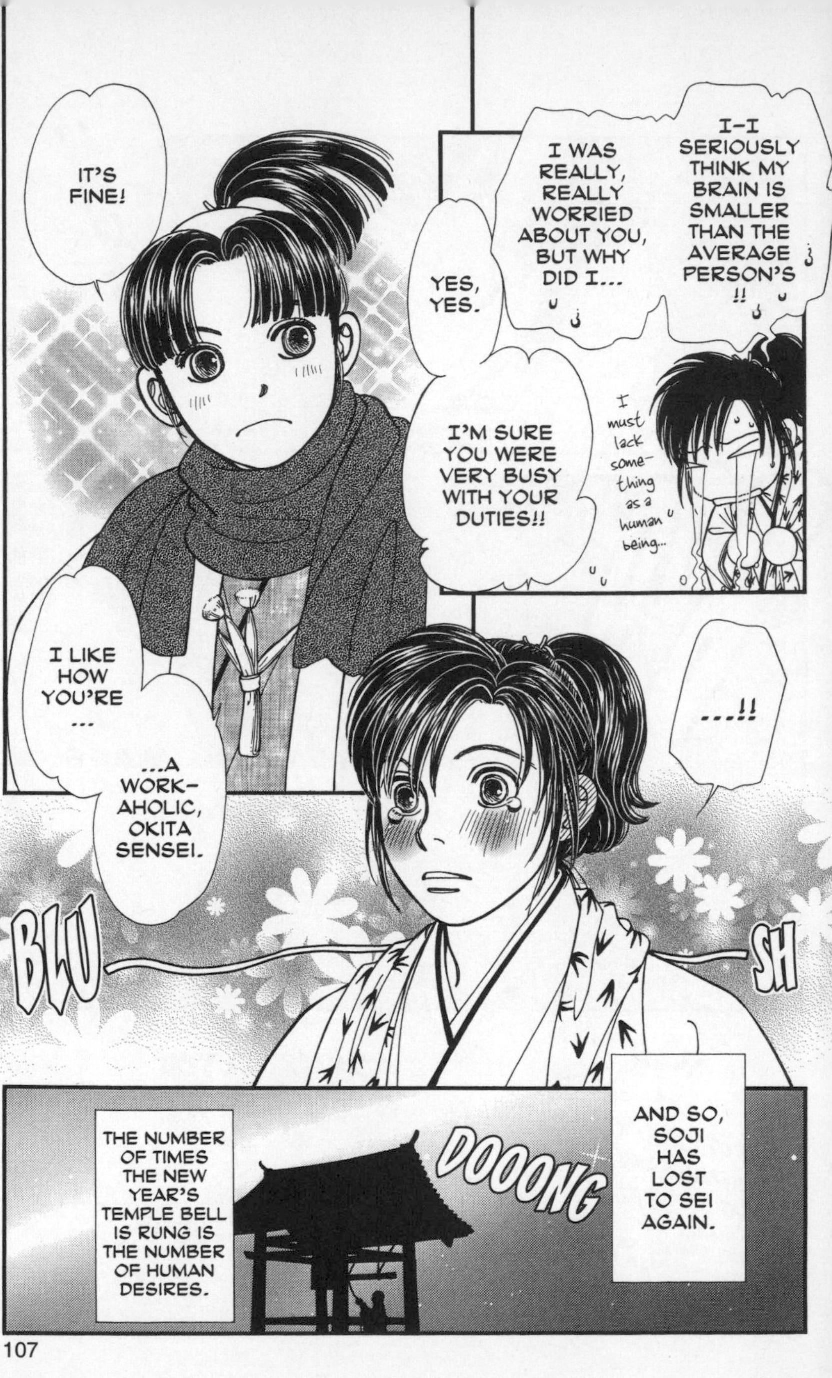
I–I SERIOUSLY THINK MY BRAIN IS SMALLER THAN THE AVERAGE PERSON'S !!
I WAS REALLY, REALLY WORRIED ABOUT YOU, BUT WHY DID I...
YES, YES.
I'M SURE YOU WERE VERY BUSY WITH YOUR DUTIES!!
I must lack some-thing as a human being...
IT'S FINE!
I LIKE HOW YOU'RE ...
...A WORK-AHOLIC, OKITA SENSEI.
...!!
BLU
SH
AND SO, SOJI HAS LOST TO SEI AGAIN.
DOOONG
THE NUMBER OF TIMES THE NEW YEAR'S TEMPLE BELL IS RUNG IS THE NUMBER OF HUMAN DESIRES.

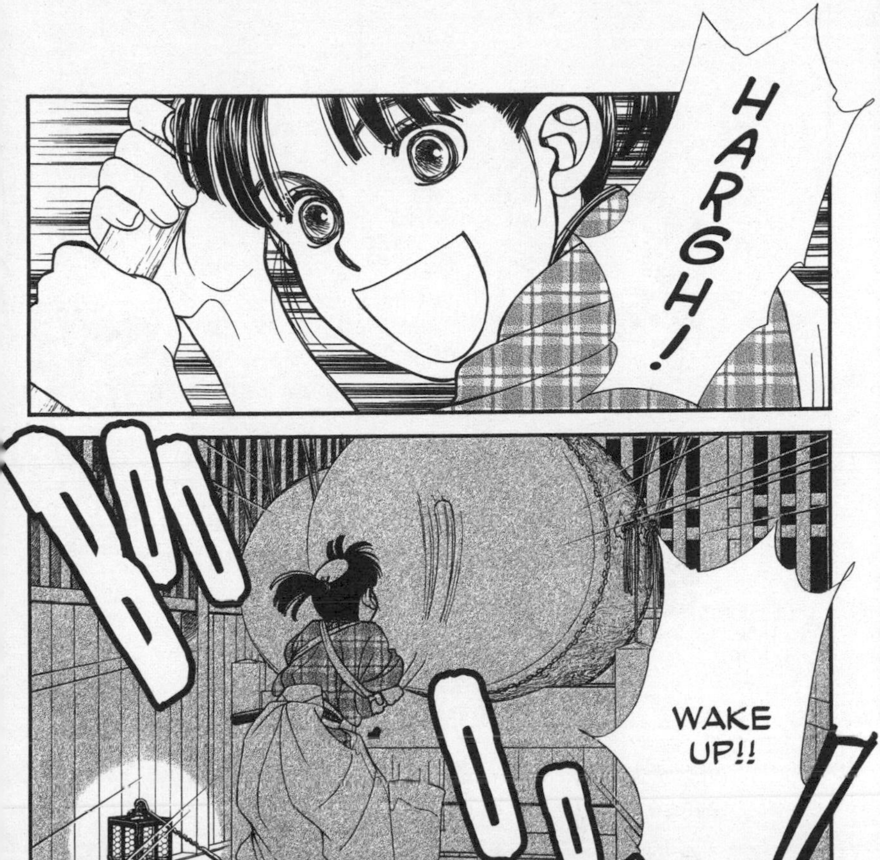
HARGH!
WAKE UP!!
BOOOOM!

KAZE HIKARU IROHA KARUTA

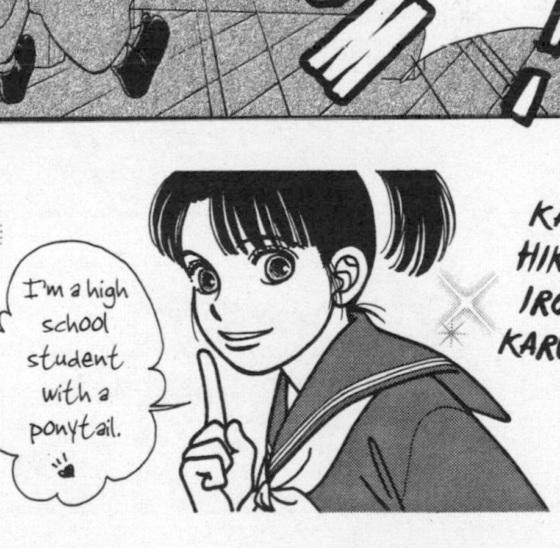
I'm a high school student with a ponytail.

"ゐ"

ゐ

ITOTEKINI SAKAYAKI KAKUSU KATTO WARI.

"A PANEL THAT HIDES THE SHAVED HEAD ON PURPOSE."

By Jun-san from Saitama

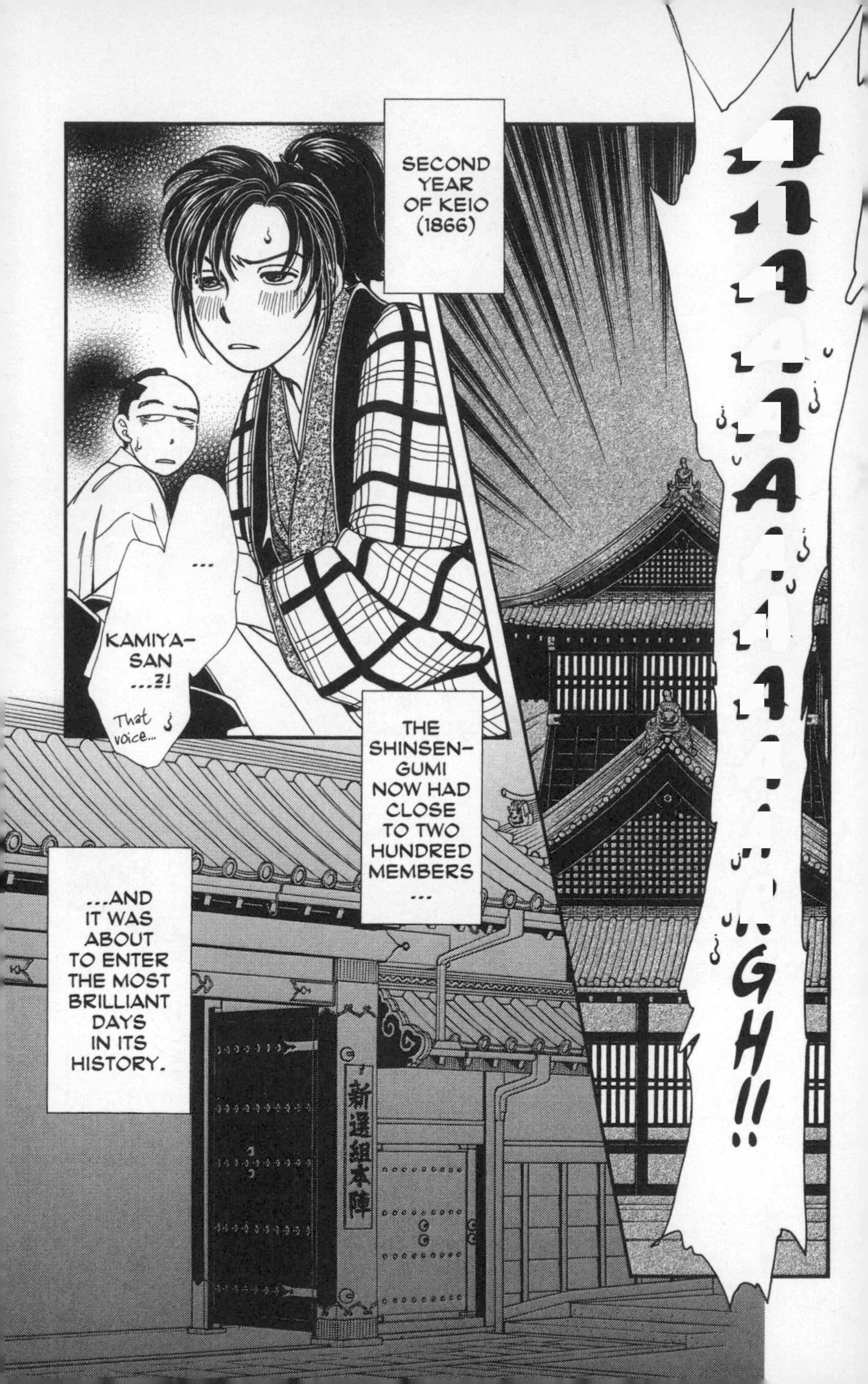
GH!!
SECOND YEAR OF KEIO (1866)
...
KAMIYA-SAN ...?!
That voice...
THE SHINSEN-GUMI NOW HAD CLOSE TO TWO HUNDRED MEMBERS ...
...AND IT WAS ABOUT TO ENTER THE MOST BRILLIANT DAYS IN ITS HISTORY.
新選組本陣

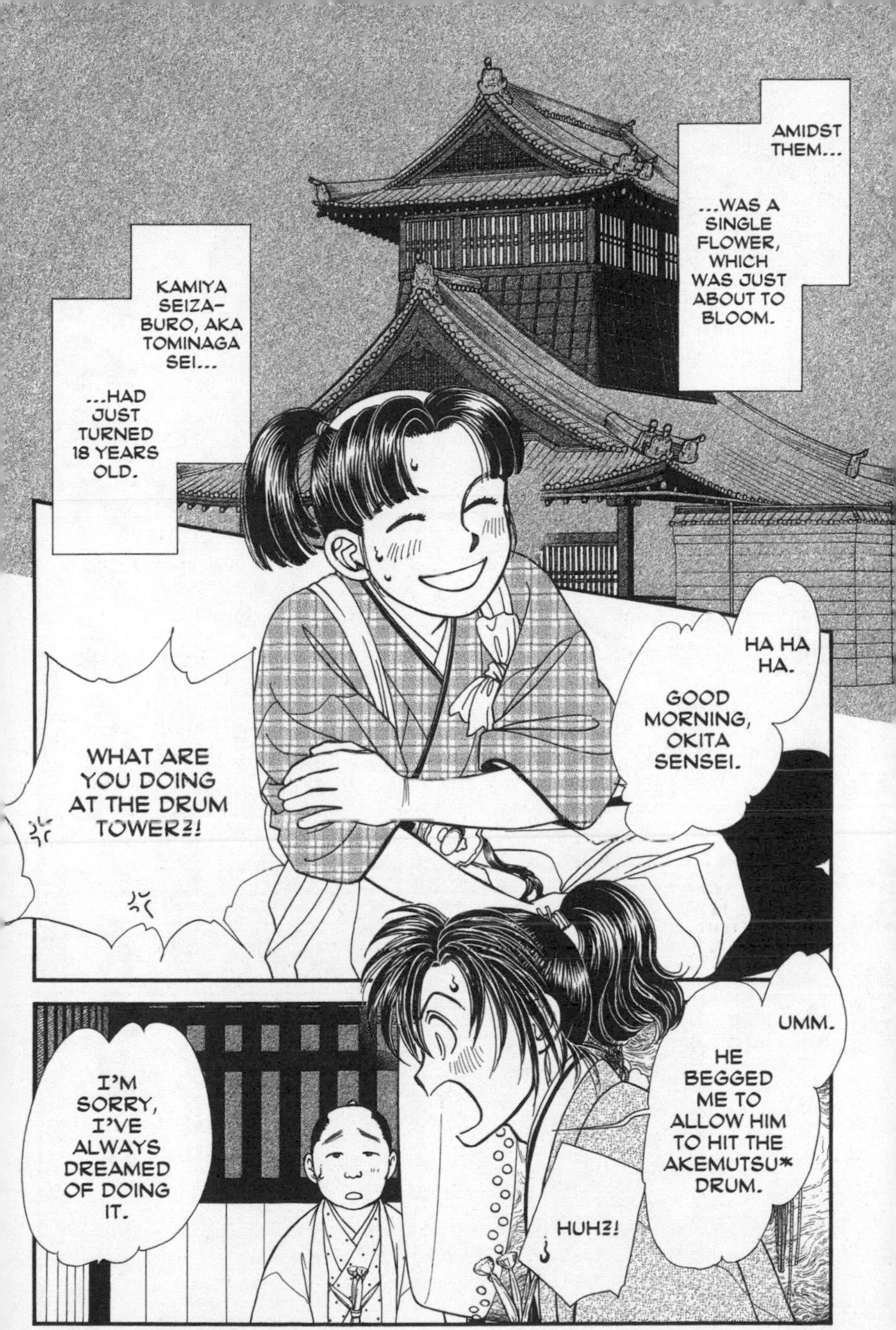
AMIDST THEM...
...WAS A SINGLE FLOWER, WHICH WAS JUST ABOUT TO BLOOM.
KAMIYA SEIZA-BURO, AKA TOMINAGA SEI...
...HAD JUST TURNED 18 YEARS OLD.
HA HA HA.
GOOD MORNING, OKITA SENSEI.
WHAT ARE YOU DOING AT THE DRUM TOWER?!
UMM.
HE BEGGED ME TO ALLOW HIM TO HIT THE AKEMUTSU* DRUM.
HUH?!
I'M SORRY, I'VE ALWAYS DREAMED OF DOING IT.

* Drum to wake members of the Shinsengumi at thirty minutes before sunrise.

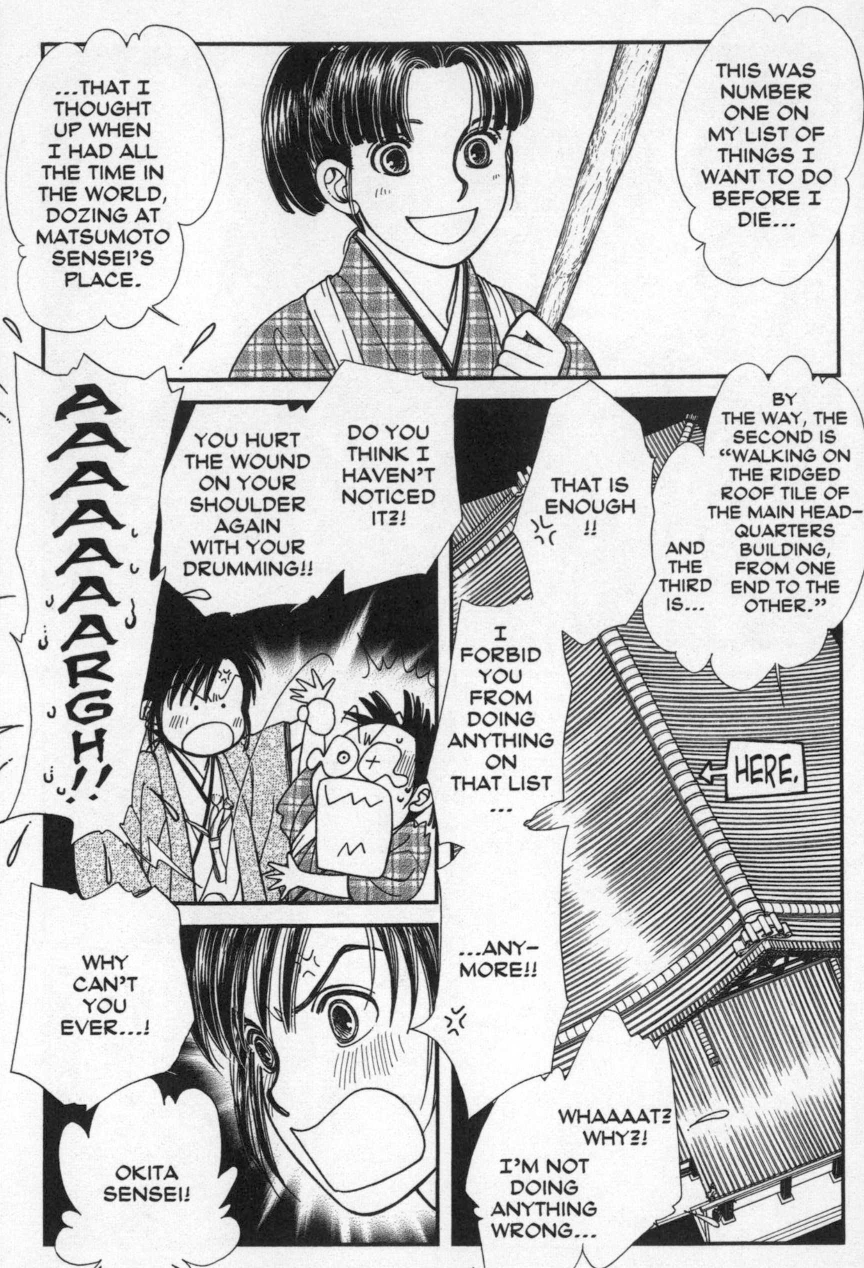
THIS WAS NUMBER ONE ON MY LIST OF THINGS I WANT TO DO BEFORE I DIE...
...THAT I THOUGHT UP WHEN I HAD ALL THE TIME IN THE WORLD, DOZING AT MATSUMOTO SENSEI'S PLACE.
BY THE WAY, THE SECOND IS "WALKING ON THE RIDGED ROOF TILE OF THE MAIN HEAD-QUARTERS BUILDING, FROM ONE END TO THE OTHER."
AND THE THIRD IS...
HERE.
THAT IS ENOUGH!!
I FORBID YOU FROM DOING ANYTHING ON THAT LIST...
...ANY-MORE!!
DO YOU THINK I HAVEN'T NOTICED IT?!
YOU HURT THE WOUND ON YOUR SHOULDER AGAIN WITH YOUR DRUMMING!!
AAAAAAARGH!!
WHAAAAT?! WHY?!
I'M NOT DOING ANYTHING WRONG...
WHY CAN'T YOU EVER...!
OKITA SENSEI!

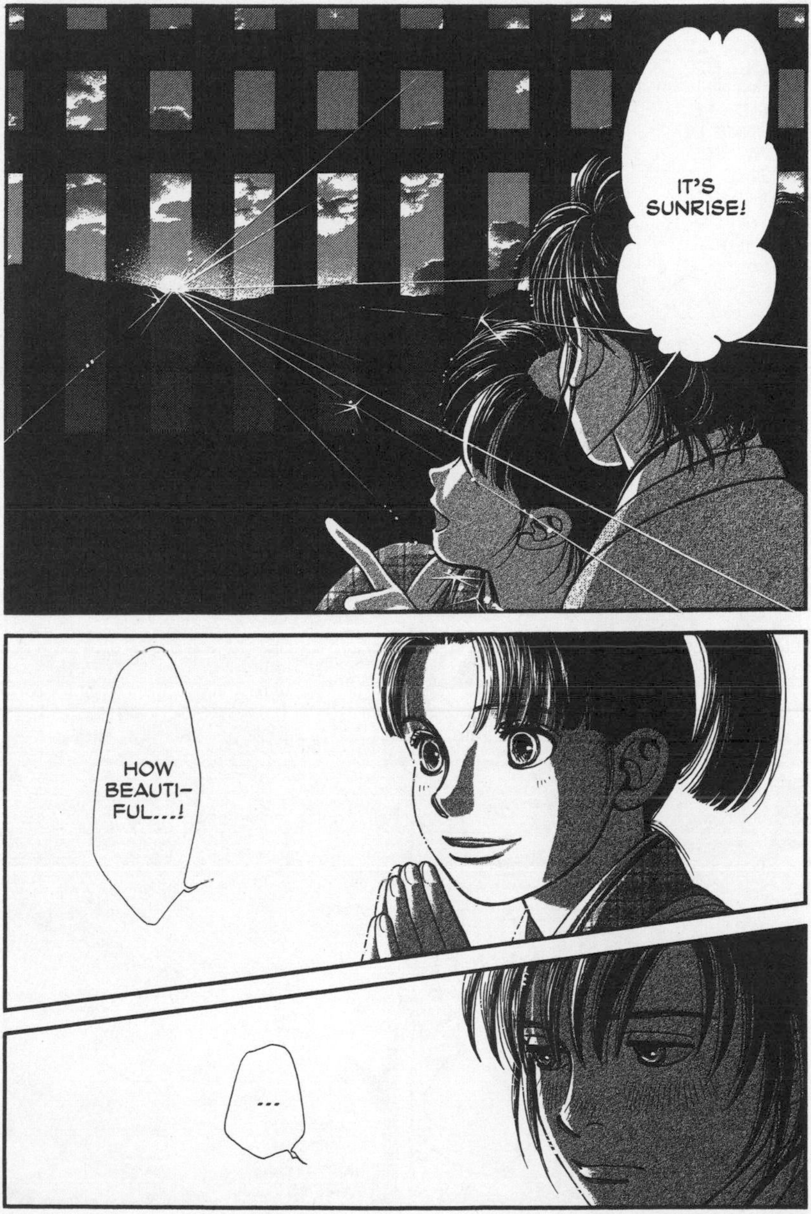
IT'S SUNRISE!
HOW BEAUTI-FUL...!
...

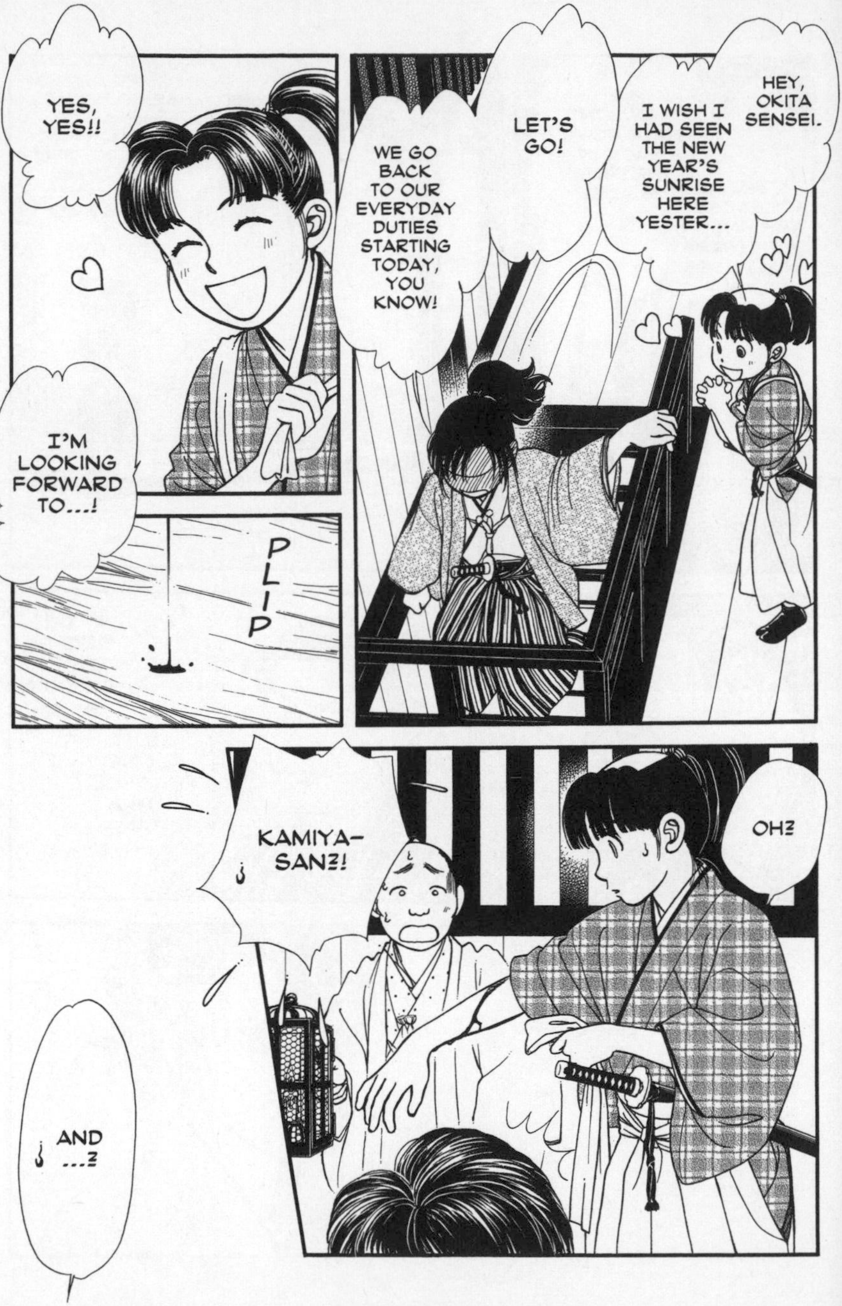
HEY, OKITA SENSEI.
I WISH I HAD SEEN THE NEW YEAR'S SUNRISE HERE YESTER...
LET'S GO!
WE GO BACK TO OUR EVERYDAY DUTIES STARTING TODAY, YOU KNOW!
YES, YES!!
I'M LOOKING FORWARD TO...!
PLIP
OH?
KAMIYA-SAN?!
AND ...?

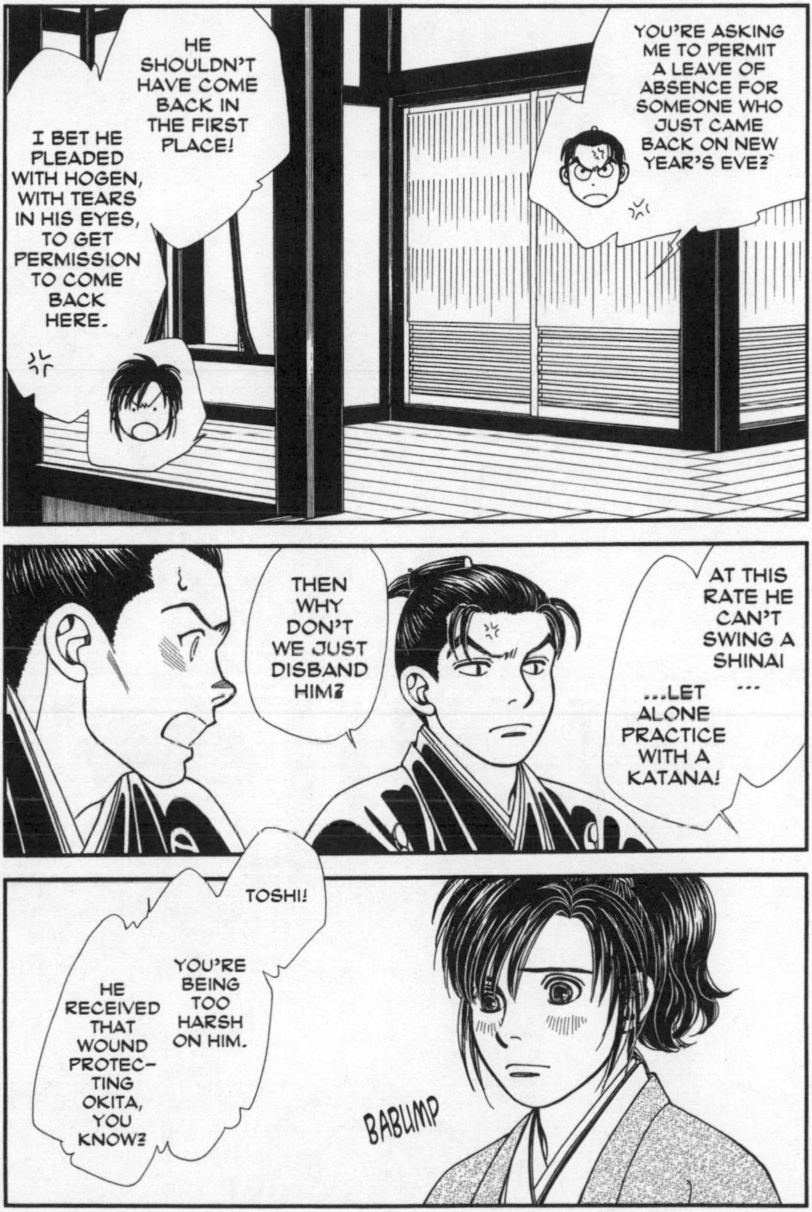
YOU'RE ASKING ME TO PERMIT A LEAVE OF ABSENCE FOR SOMEONE WHO JUST CAME BACK ON NEW YEAR'S EVE?
HE SHOULDN'T HAVE COME BACK IN THE FIRST PLACE!
I BET HE PLEADED WITH HOGEN, WITH TEARS IN HIS EYES, TO GET PERMISSION TO COME BACK HERE.
AT THIS RATE HE CAN'T SWING A SHINAI...
...LET ALONE PRACTICE WITH A KATANA!
THEN WHY DON'T WE JUST DISBAND HIM?
TOSHI!
YOU'RE BEING TOO HARSH ON HIM.
HE RECEIVED THAT WOUND PROTECTING OKITA, YOU KNOW?
BABUMP

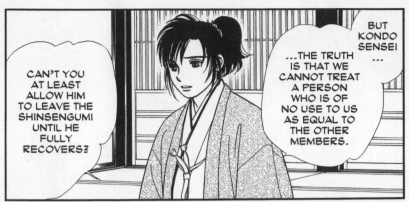

BUT KONDO SENSEI ...
...THE TRUTH IS THAT WE CANNOT TREAT A PERSON WHO IS OF NO USE TO US AS EQUAL TO THE OTHER MEMBERS.
CAN'T YOU AT LEAST ALLOW HIM TO LEAVE THE SHINSENGUMI UNTIL HE FULLY RECOVERS?
BUT HOW WOULD HE MAKE A LIVING DURING THAT TIME?
AND WHAT IF HE NEVER FULLY RECOVERS?
I'LL TAKE CARE OF HIM.
EVEN IF THAT MEANS I'LL HAVE TO LOOK AFTER HIM FOR THE REST OF MY LIFE.
誠
I FEEL THAT...
...I OWE HIM THAT MUCH...
SOJI...

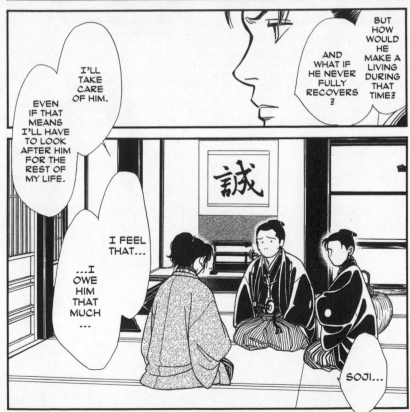

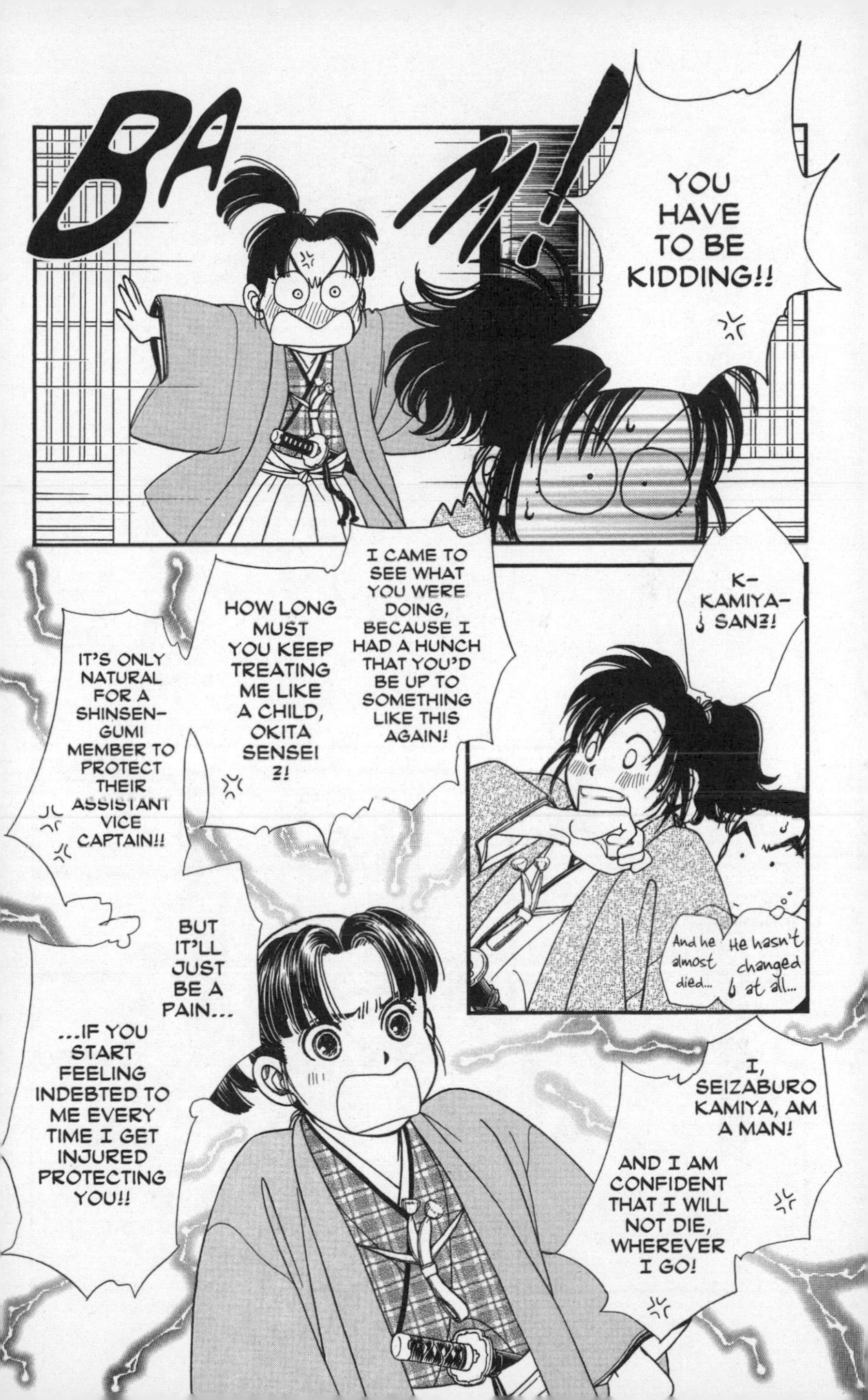
BAM!
YOU HAVE TO BE KIDDING!!
K-KAMIYA-SAN?!
He hasn't changed at all...
And he almost died...
I CAME TO SEE WHAT YOU WERE DOING, BECAUSE I HAD A HUNCH THAT YOU'D BE UP TO SOMETHING LIKE THIS AGAIN!
HOW LONG MUST YOU KEEP TREATING ME LIKE A CHILD, OKITA SENSEI?!
IT'S ONLY NATURAL FOR A SHINSEN-GUMI MEMBER TO PROTECT THEIR ASSISTANT VICE CAPTAIN!!
I, SEIZABURO KAMIYA, AM A MAN!
AND I AM CONFIDENT THAT I WILL NOT DIE, WHEREVER I GO!
BUT IT'LL JUST BE A PAIN...
...IF YOU START FEELING INDEBTED TO ME EVERY TIME I GET INJURED PROTECTING YOU!!

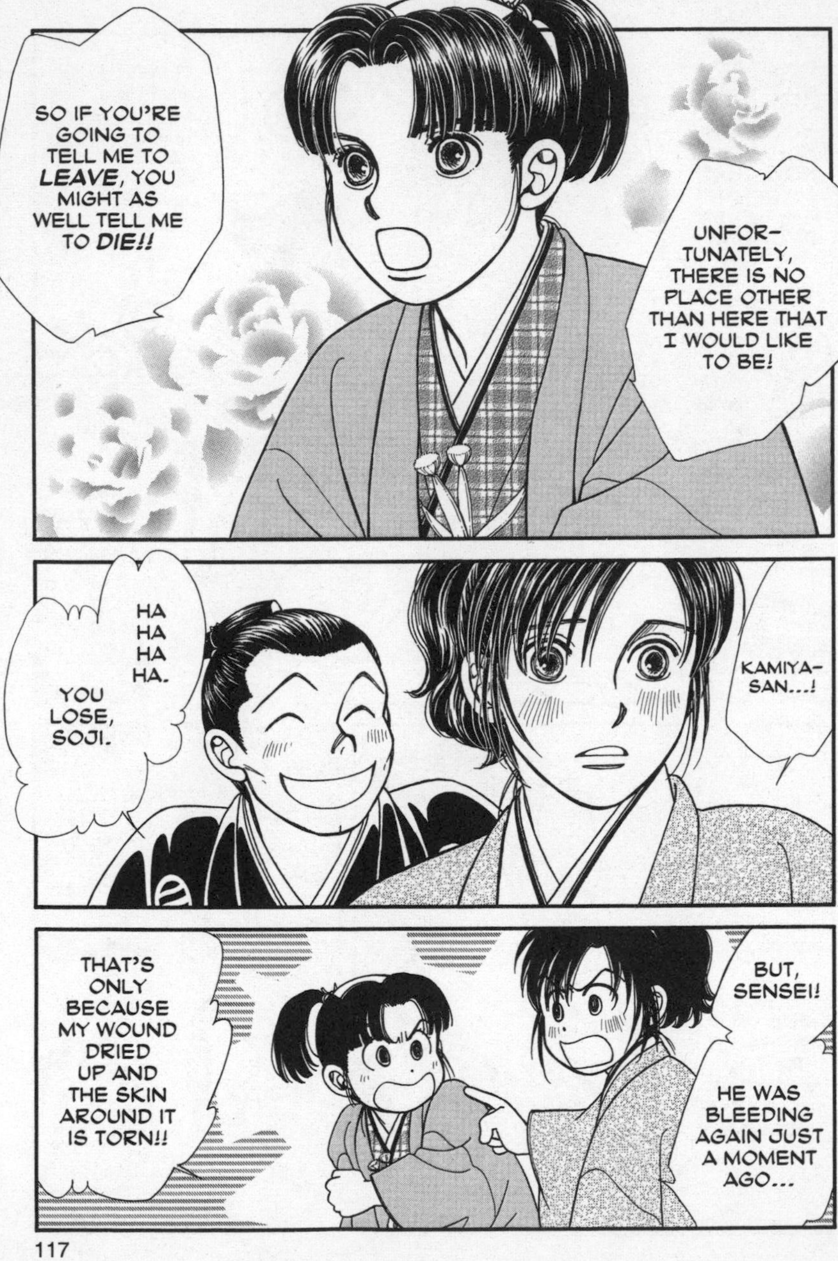
UNFOR-TUNATELY, THERE IS NO PLACE OTHER THAN HERE THAT I WOULD LIKE TO BE!
SO IF YOU'RE GOING TO TELL ME TO *LEAVE*, YOU MIGHT AS WELL TELL ME TO *DIE!!*
KAMIYA-SAN...!
HA HA HA HA.
YOU LOSE, SOJI.
BUT, SENSEI!
HE WAS BLEEDING AGAIN JUST A MOMENT AGO...
THAT'S ONLY BECAUSE MY WOUND DRIED UP AND THE SKIN AROUND IT IS TORN!!

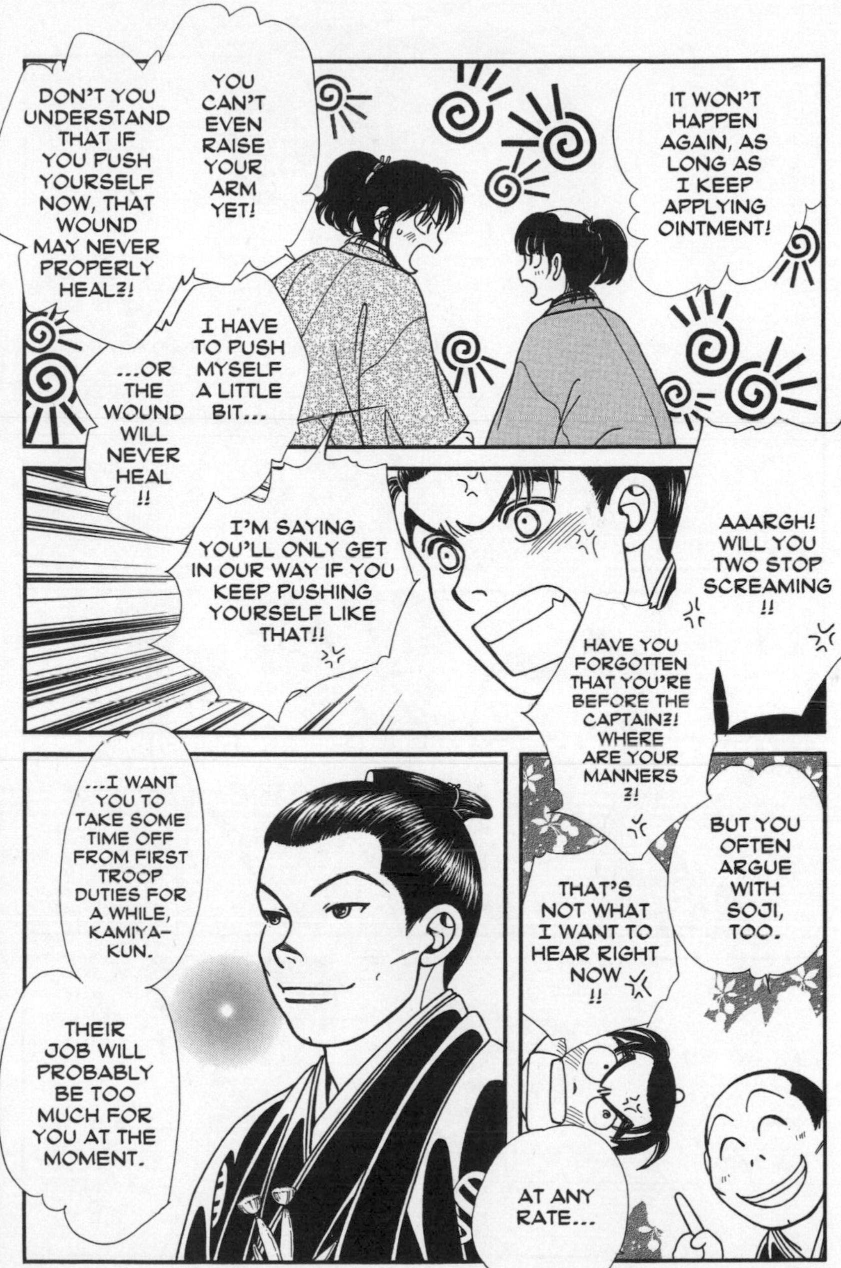
IT WON'T HAPPEN AGAIN, AS LONG AS I KEEP APPLYING OINTMENT!
YOU CAN'T EVEN RAISE YOUR ARM YET!
DON'T YOU UNDERSTAND THAT IF YOU PUSH YOURSELF NOW, THAT WOUND MAY NEVER PROPERLY HEAL?!
I HAVE TO PUSH MYSELF A LITTLE BIT...
...OR THE WOUND WILL NEVER HEAL!!
AAARGH! WILL YOU TWO STOP SCREAMING!!
I'M SAYING YOU'LL ONLY GET IN OUR WAY IF YOU KEEP PUSHING YOURSELF LIKE THAT!!
HAVE YOU FORGOTTEN THAT YOU'RE BEFORE THE CAPTAIN?! WHERE ARE YOUR MANNERS?!
BUT YOU OFTEN ARGUE WITH SOJI, TOO.
THAT'S NOT WHAT I WANT TO HEAR RIGHT NOW!!
AT ANY RATE...
...I WANT YOU TO TAKE SOME TIME OFF FROM FIRST TROOP DUTIES FOR A WHILE, KAMIYA-KUN.
THEIR JOB WILL PROBABLY BE TOO MUCH FOR YOU AT THE MOMENT.

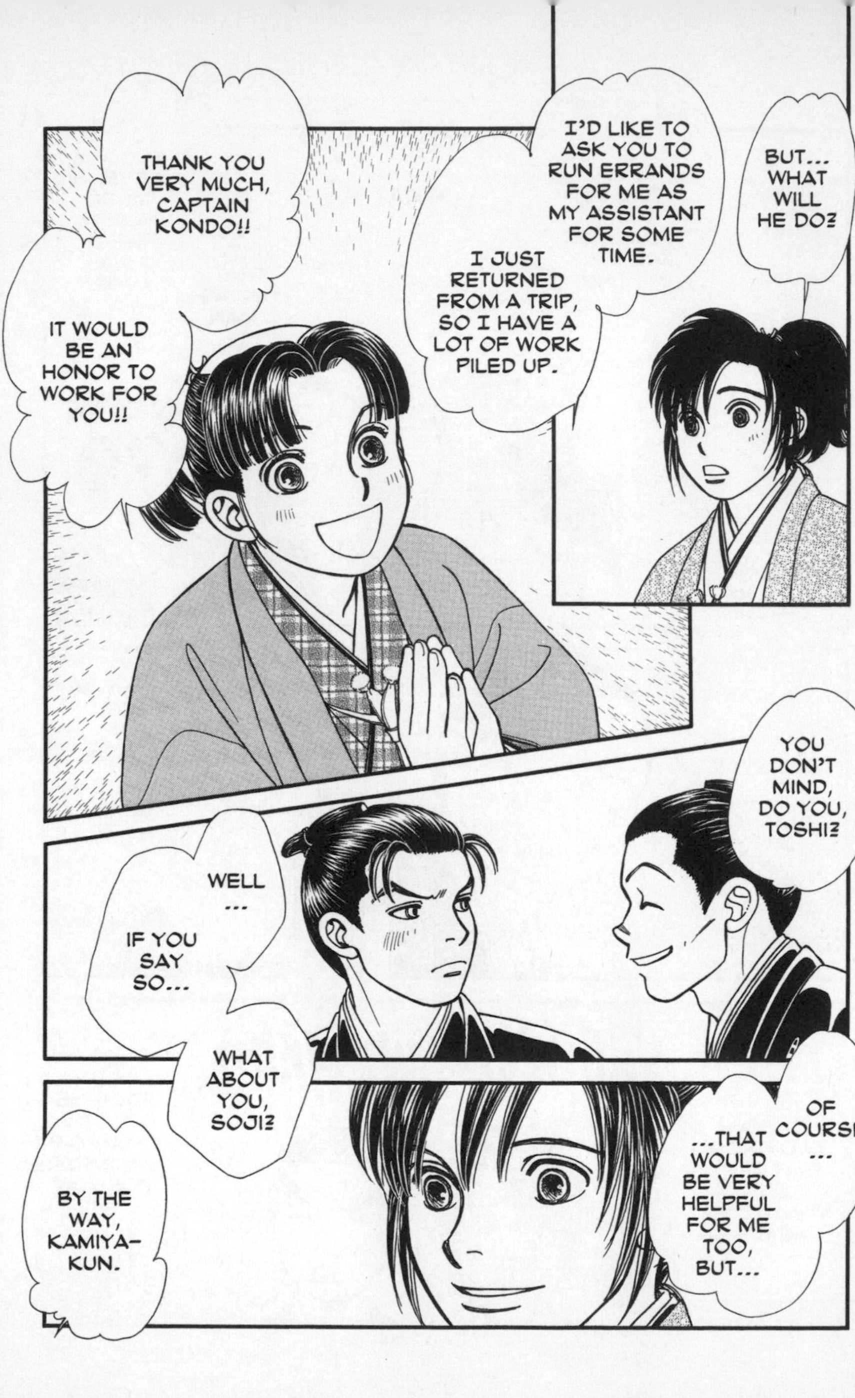
BUT... WHAT WILL HE DO?
I'D LIKE TO ASK YOU TO RUN ERRANDS FOR ME AS MY ASSISTANT FOR SOME TIME.
I JUST RETURNED FROM A TRIP, SO I HAVE A LOT OF WORK PILED UP.
THANK YOU VERY MUCH, CAPTAIN KONDO!!
IT WOULD BE AN HONOR TO WORK FOR YOU!!
YOU DON'T MIND, DO YOU, TOSHI?
WELL...
IF YOU SAY SO...
WHAT ABOUT YOU, SOJI?
OF COURSE...
...THAT WOULD BE VERY HELPFUL FOR ME TOO, BUT...
BY THE WAY, KAMIYA-KUN.

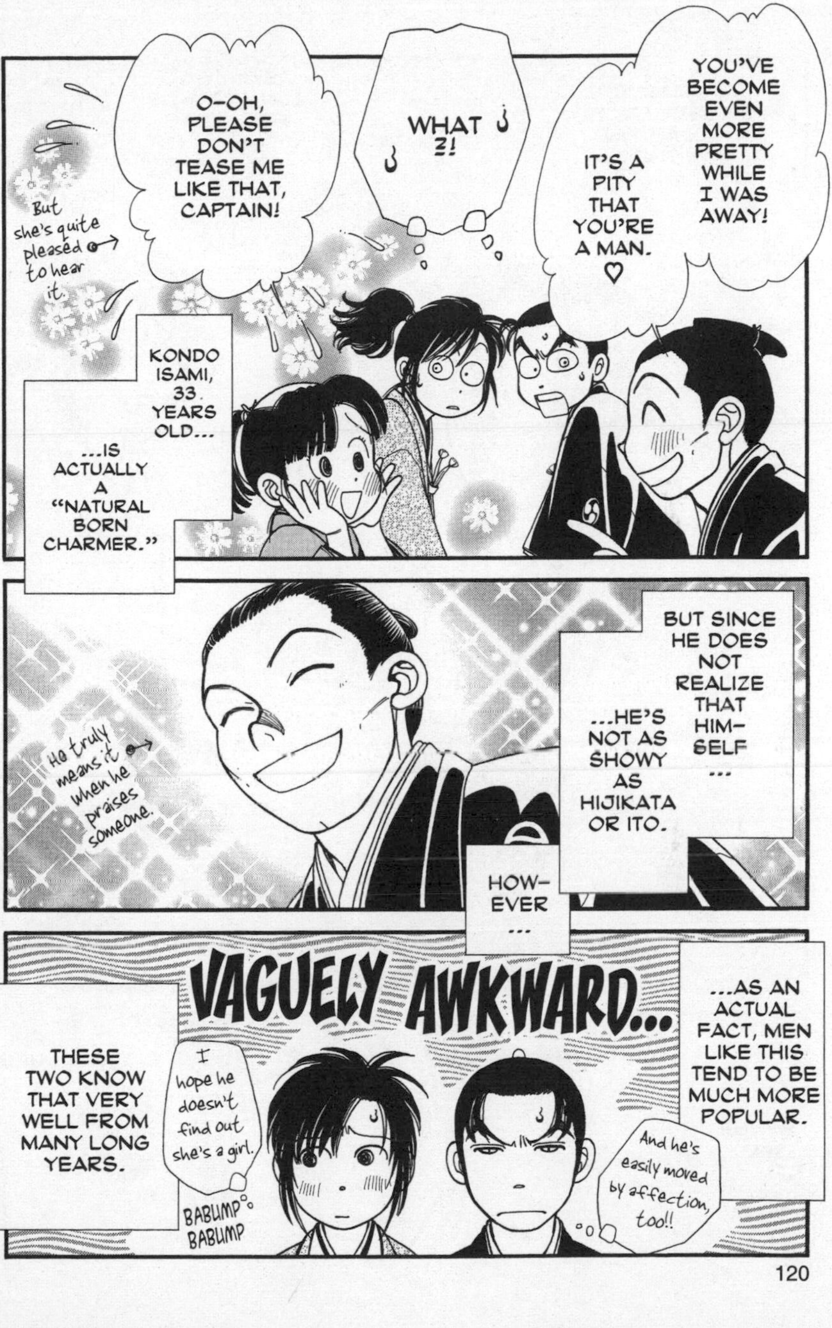
YOU'VE BECOME EVEN MORE PRETTY WHILE I WAS AWAY!
IT'S A PITY THAT YOU'RE A MAN. ♡
WHAT?!
O-OH, PLEASE DON'T TEASE ME LIKE THAT, CAPTAIN!
But she's quite pleased to hear it.
KONDO ISAMI, 33 YEARS OLD...
...IS ACTUALLY A "NATURAL BORN CHARMER."
BUT SINCE HE DOES NOT REALIZE THAT HIMSELF...
...HE'S NOT AS SHOWY AS HIJIKATA OR ITO.
He truly means it when he praises someone.
HOWEVER...
...AS AN ACTUAL FACT, MEN LIKE THIS TEND TO BE MUCH MORE POPULAR.
VAGUELY AWKWARD...
And he's easily moved by affection, too!!
I hope he doesn't find out she's a girl.
BABUMP BABUMP
THESE TWO KNOW THAT VERY WELL FROM MANY LONG YEARS.

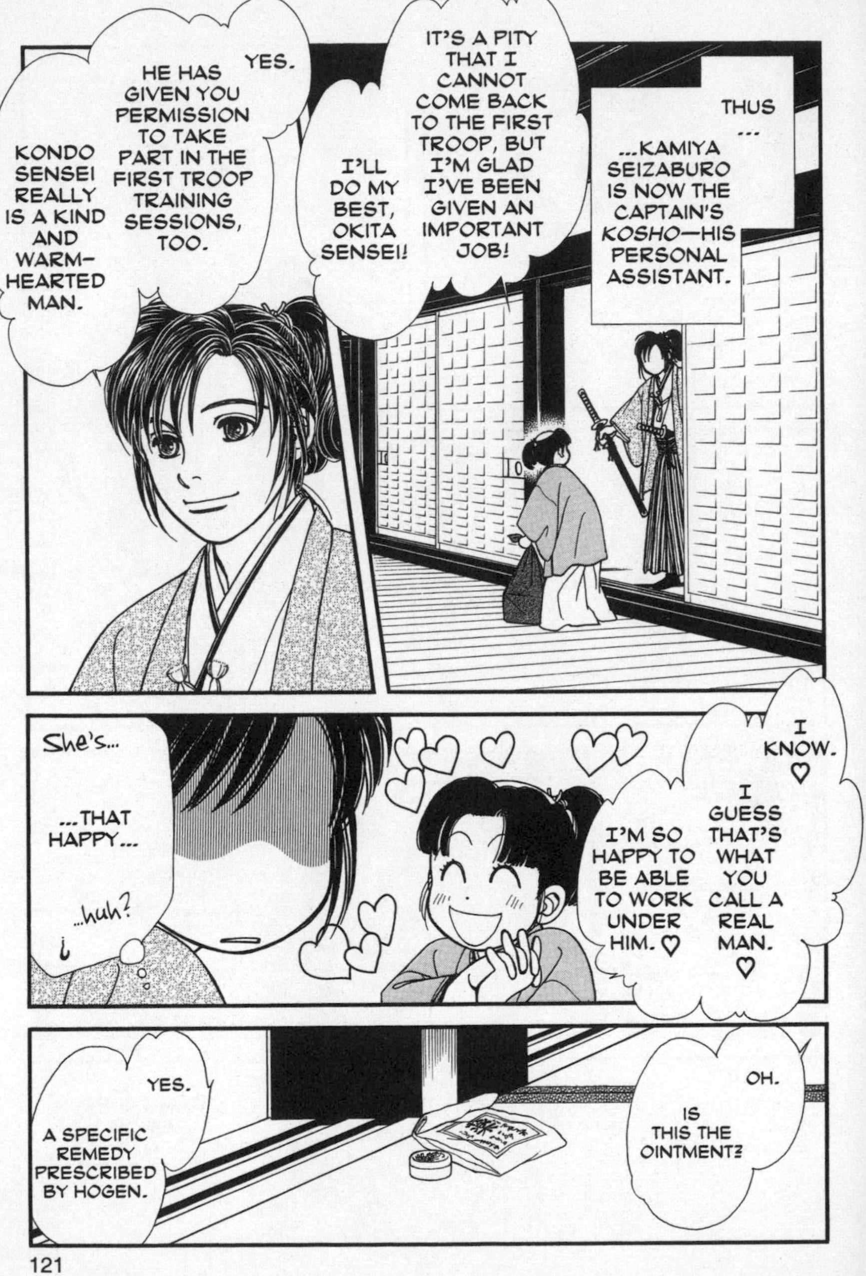
THUS ...
...KAMIYA SEIZABURO IS NOW THE CAPTAIN'S *KOSHO*—HIS PERSONAL ASSISTANT.
IT'S A PITY THAT I CANNOT COME BACK TO THE FIRST TROOP, BUT I'M GLAD I'VE BEEN GIVEN AN IMPORTANT JOB!
I'LL DO MY BEST, OKITA SENSEI!
YES.
HE HAS GIVEN YOU PERMISSION TO TAKE PART IN THE FIRST TROOP TRAINING SESSIONS, TOO.
KONDO SENSEI REALLY IS A KIND AND WARM-HEARTED MAN.
I KNOW. ♡
I GUESS THAT'S WHAT YOU CALL A REAL MAN. ♡
I'M SO HAPPY TO BE ABLE TO WORK UNDER HIM. ♡
She's...
...THAT HAPPY...
...huh?
OH.
IS THIS THE OINTMENT?
YES.
A SPECIFIC REMEDY PRESCRIBED BY HOGEN.

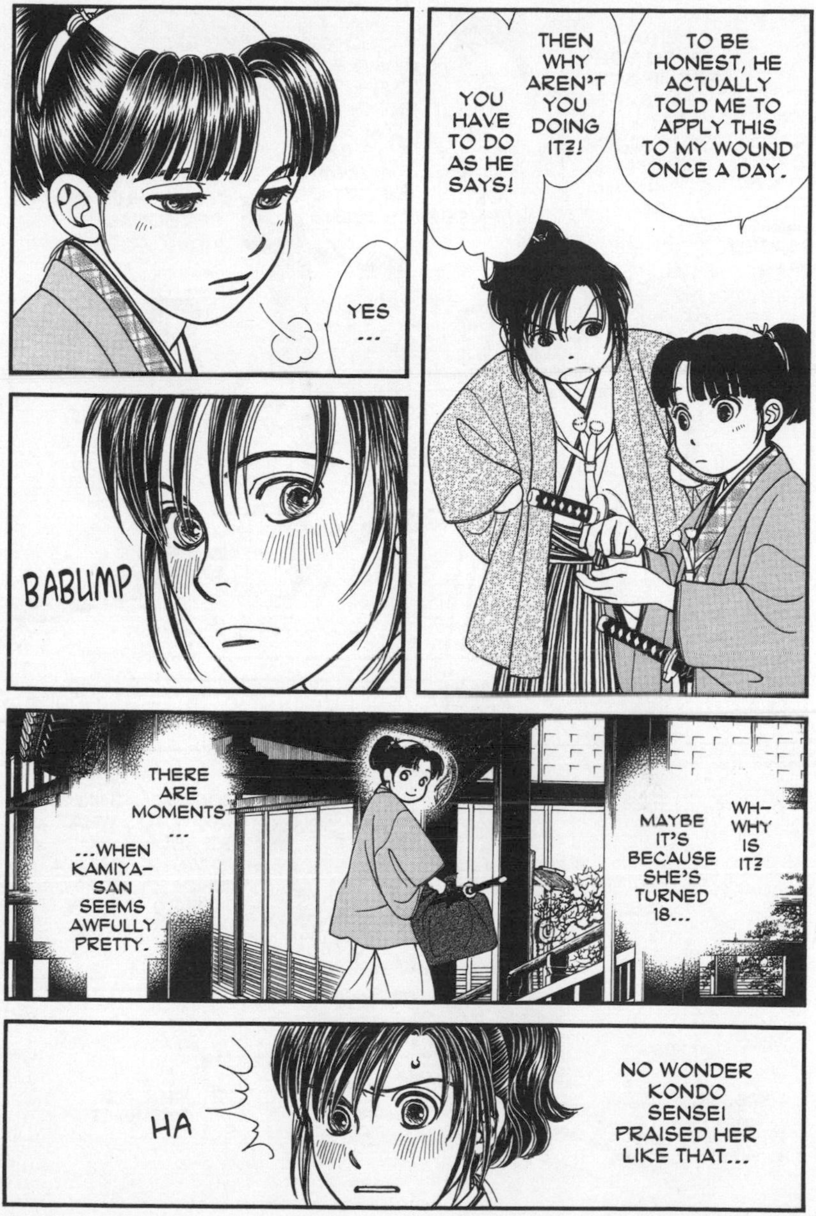
TO BE HONEST, HE ACTUALLY TOLD ME TO APPLY THIS TO MY WOUND ONCE A DAY.
THEN WHY AREN'T YOU DOING IT?!
YOU HAVE TO DO AS HE SAYS!
YES ...
BABUMP
WH- WHY IS IT?
MAYBE IT'S BECAUSE SHE'S TURNED 18...
THERE ARE MOMENTS ...
...WHEN KAMIYA-SAN SEEMS AWFULLY PRETTY.
NO WONDER KONDO SENSEI PRAISED HER LIKE THAT...
HA

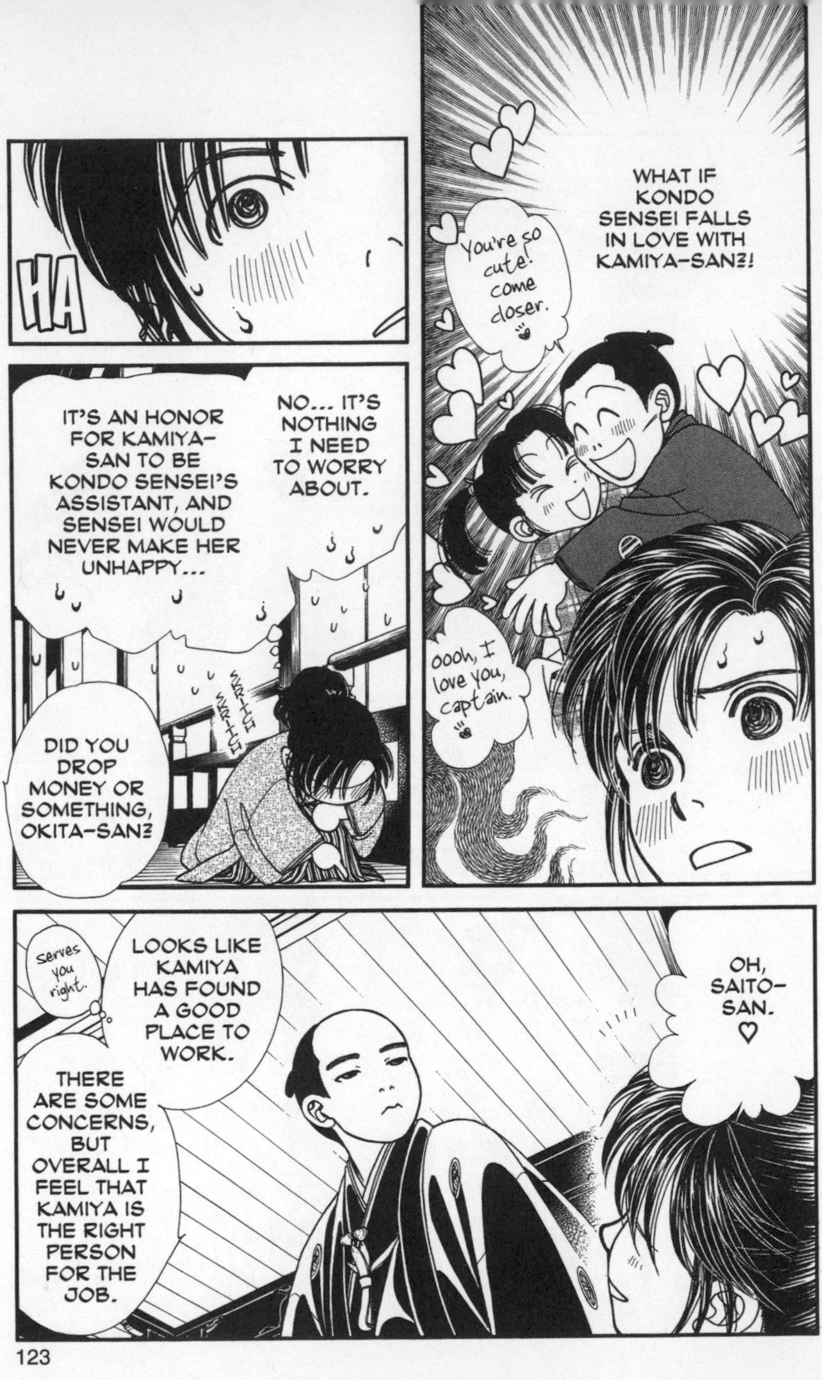
WHAT IF KONDO SENSEI FALLS IN LOVE WITH KAMIYA-SAN?!
You're so cute! come closer.
oooh, I love you, captain.
HA
NO... IT'S NOTHING I NEED TO WORRY ABOUT.
IT'S AN HONOR FOR KAMIYA-SAN TO BE KONDO SENSEI'S ASSISTANT, AND SENSEI WOULD NEVER MAKE HER UNHAPPY...
SKRITCH SKRITCH
DID YOU DROP MONEY OR SOMETHING, OKITA-SAN?
OH, SAITO-SAN. ♡
LOOKS LIKE KAMIYA HAS FOUND A GOOD PLACE TO WORK.
serves you right.
THERE ARE SOME CONCERNS, BUT OVERALL I FEEL THAT KAMIYA IS THE RIGHT PERSON FOR THE JOB.

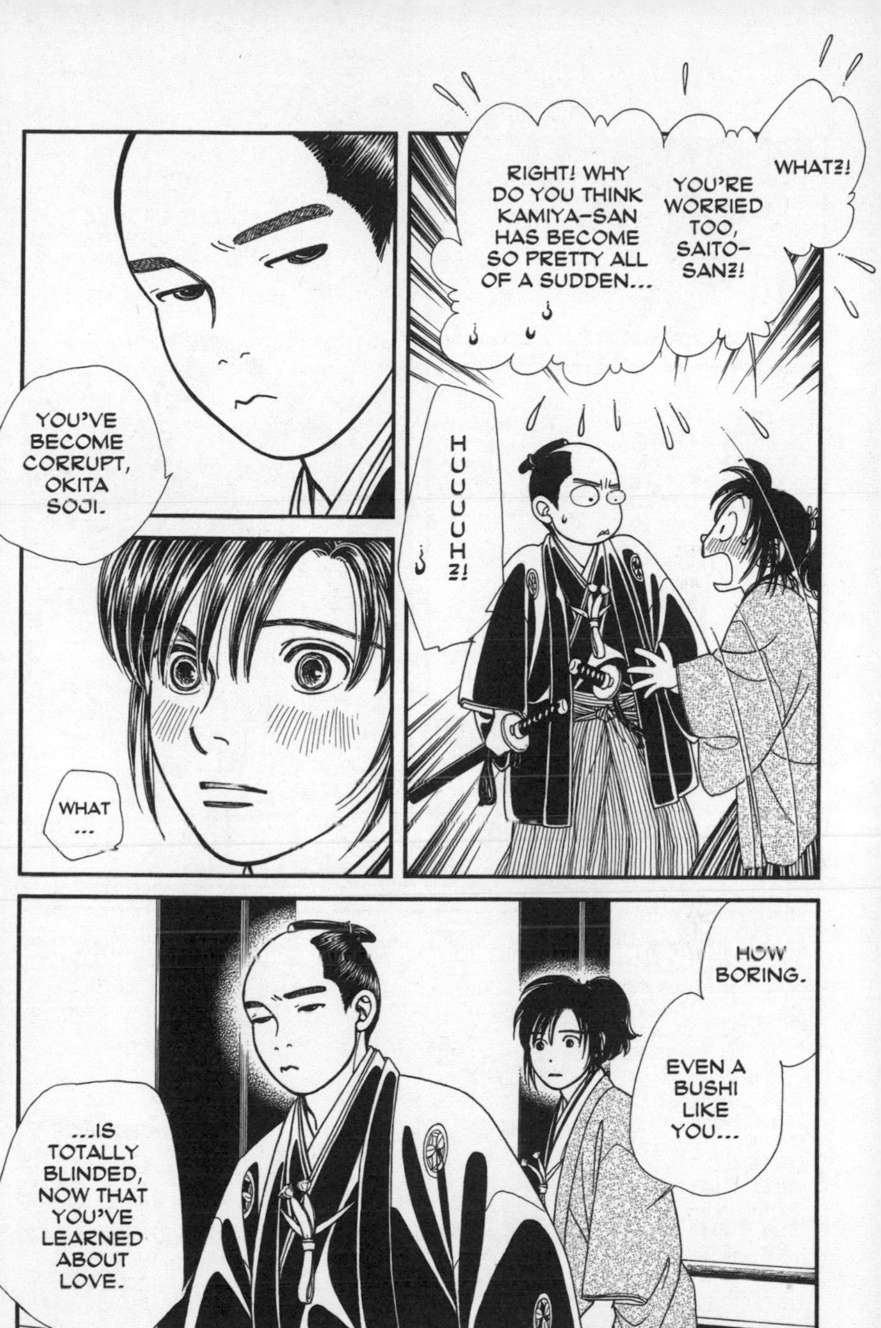
WHAT?!
YOU'RE WORRIED TOO, SAITO-SAN?!
RIGHT! WHY DO YOU THINK KAMIYA-SAN HAS BECOME SO PRETTY ALL OF A SUDDEN...
HUUUUUH?!
YOU'VE BECOME CORRUPT, OKITA SOJI.
WHAT...
HOW BORING.
EVEN A BUSHI LIKE YOU...
...IS TOTALLY BLINDED, NOW THAT YOU'VE LEARNED ABOUT LOVE.

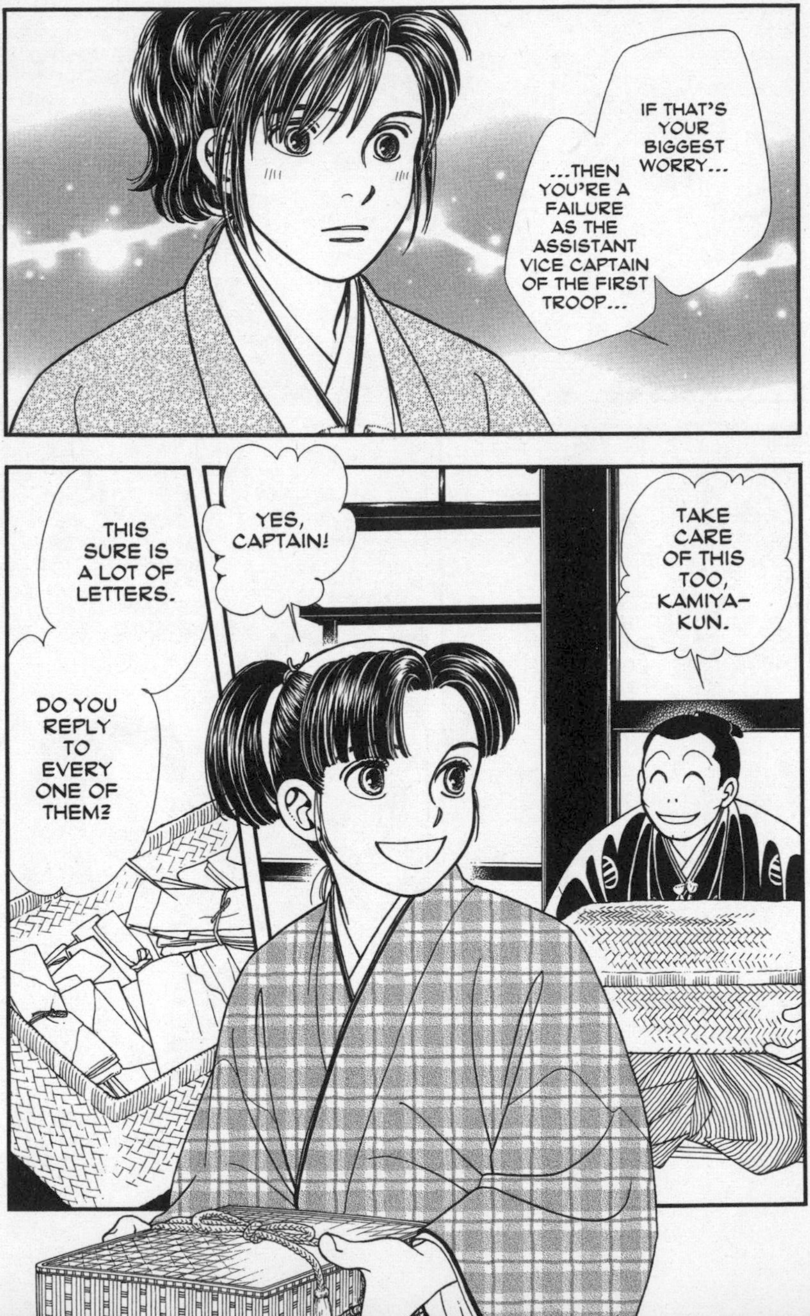
IF THAT'S YOUR BIGGEST WORRY...
...THEN YOU'RE A FAILURE AS THE ASSISTANT VICE CAPTAIN OF THE FIRST TROOP...
TAKE CARE OF THIS TOO, KAMIYA-KUN.
YES, CAPTAIN!
THIS SURE IS A LOT OF LETTERS.
DO YOU REPLY TO EVERY ONE OF THEM?

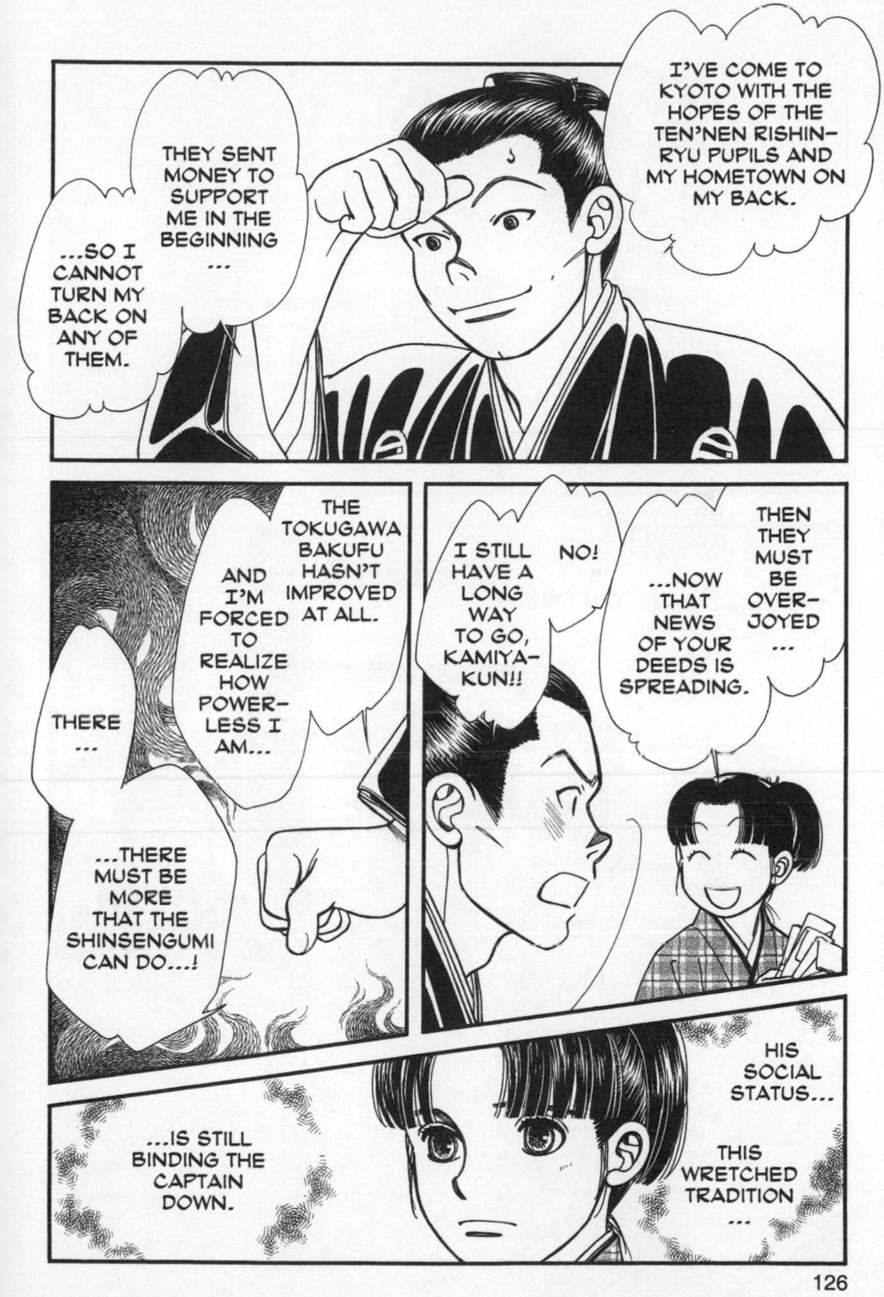
I'VE COME TO KYOTO WITH THE HOPES OF THE TEN'NEN RISHIN-RYU PUPILS AND MY HOMETOWN ON MY BACK.
THEY SENT MONEY TO SUPPORT ME IN THE BEGINNING...
...SO I CANNOT TURN MY BACK ON ANY OF THEM.
THEN THEY MUST BE OVER-JOYED...
...NOW THAT NEWS OF YOUR DEEDS IS SPREADING.
NO!
I STILL HAVE A LONG WAY TO GO, KAMIYA-KUN!!
THE TOKUGAWA BAKUFU HASN'T IMPROVED AT ALL.
AND I'M FORCED TO REALIZE HOW POWER-LESS I AM...
THERE...
...THERE MUST BE MORE THAT THE SHINSENGUMI CAN DO...!
HIS SOCIAL STATUS...
THIS WRETCHED TRADITION...
...IS STILL BINDING THE CAPTAIN DOWN.

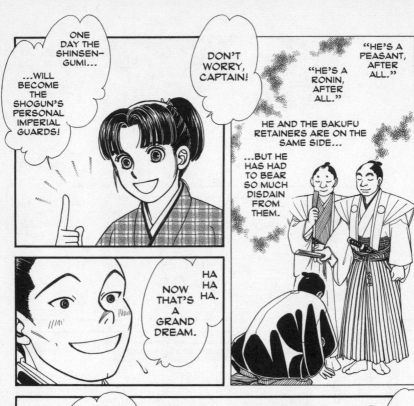

"HE'S A PEASANT, AFTER ALL."
"HE'S A RONIN, AFTER ALL."
HE AND THE BAKUFU RETAINERS ARE ON THE SAME SIDE...
...BUT HE HAS HAD TO BEAR SO MUCH DISDAIN FROM THEM.
DON'T WORRY, CAPTAIN!
ONE DAY THE SHINSEN-GUMI...
...WILL BECOME THE SHOGUN'S PERSONAL IMPERIAL GUARDS!
HA HA HA.
NOW THAT'S A GRAND DREAM.
AFTER ALL ...
...DREAMS FALL APART THE MOMENT YOU GIVE UP.
SO AS LONG AS YOU KEEP CHASING YOUR DREAM FOR THE REST OF YOUR LIFE...
...YOU NEVER HAVE TO GRIEVE OVER THE FACT THAT YOUR DREAM NEVER CAME TRUE.

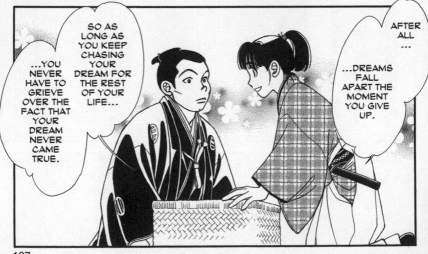

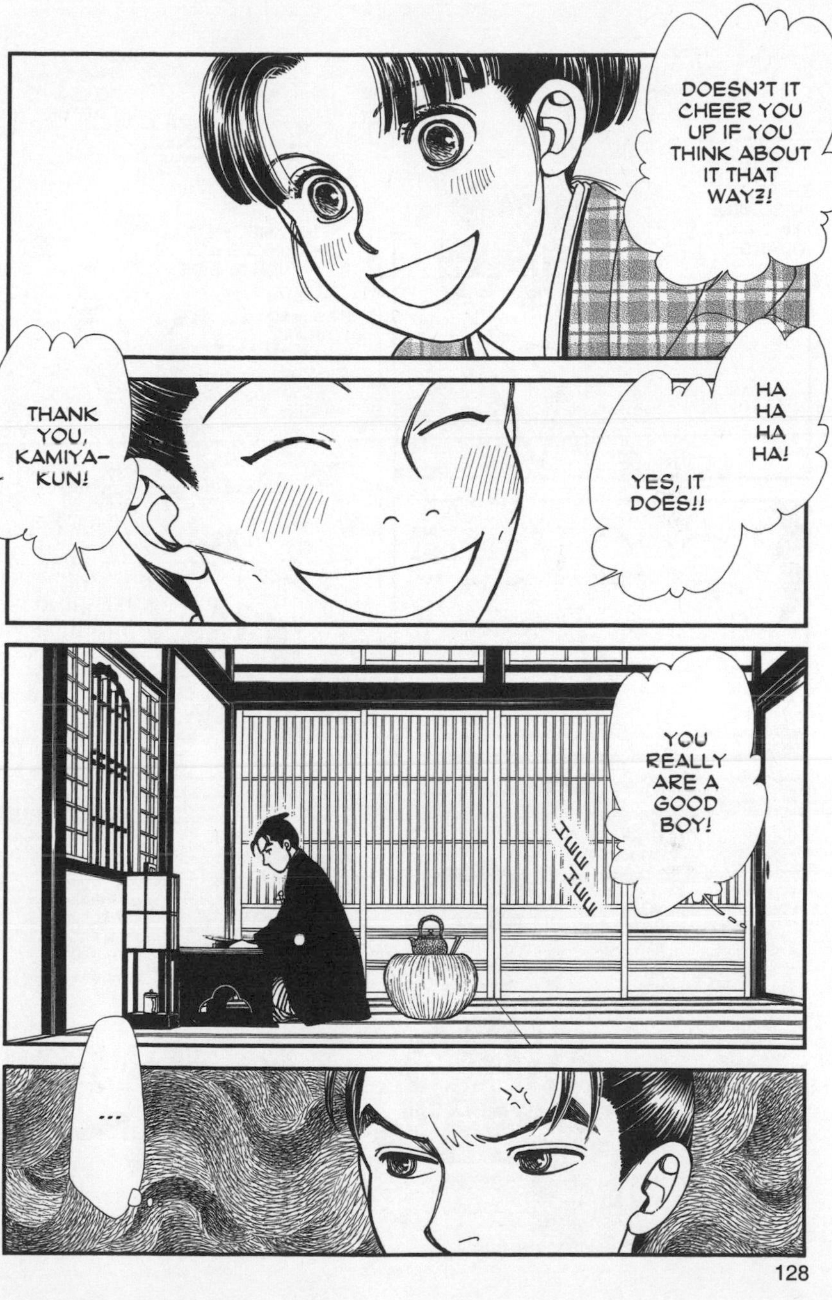

DOESN'T IT CHEER YOU UP IF YOU THINK ABOUT IT THAT WAY?!
HA HA HA HA!
YES, IT DOES!!
THANK YOU, KAMIYA-KUN!
YOU REALLY ARE A GOOD BOY!
HEEEH
...

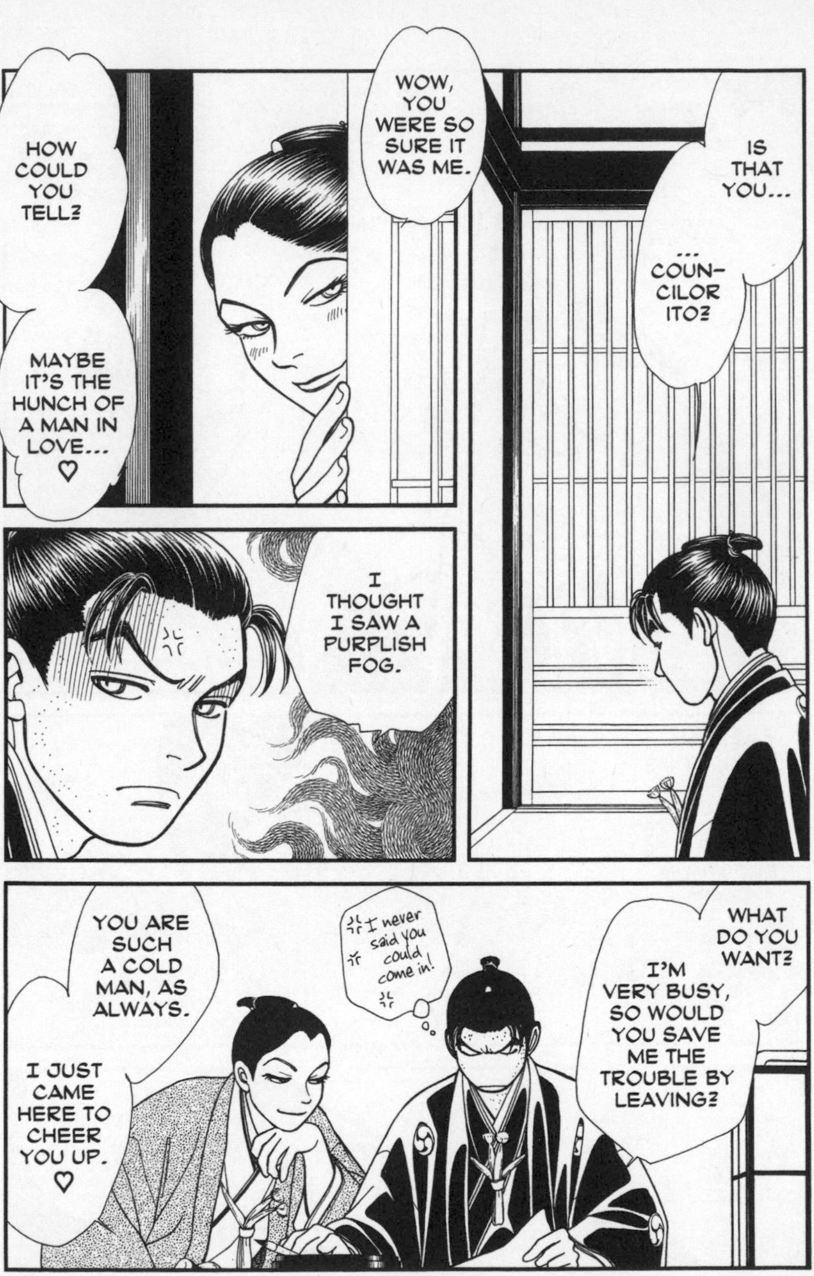
IS THAT YOU...
...COUNCILOR ITO?
WOW, YOU WERE SO SURE IT WAS ME.
HOW COULD YOU TELL?
MAYBE IT'S THE HUNCH OF A MAN IN LOVE... ♡
I THOUGHT I SAW A PURPLISH FOG.
WHAT DO YOU WANT?
I'M VERY BUSY, SO WOULD YOU SAVE ME THE TROUBLE BY LEAVING?
I never said you could come in!
YOU ARE SUCH A COLD MAN, AS ALWAYS.
I JUST CAME HERE TO CHEER YOU UP. ♡

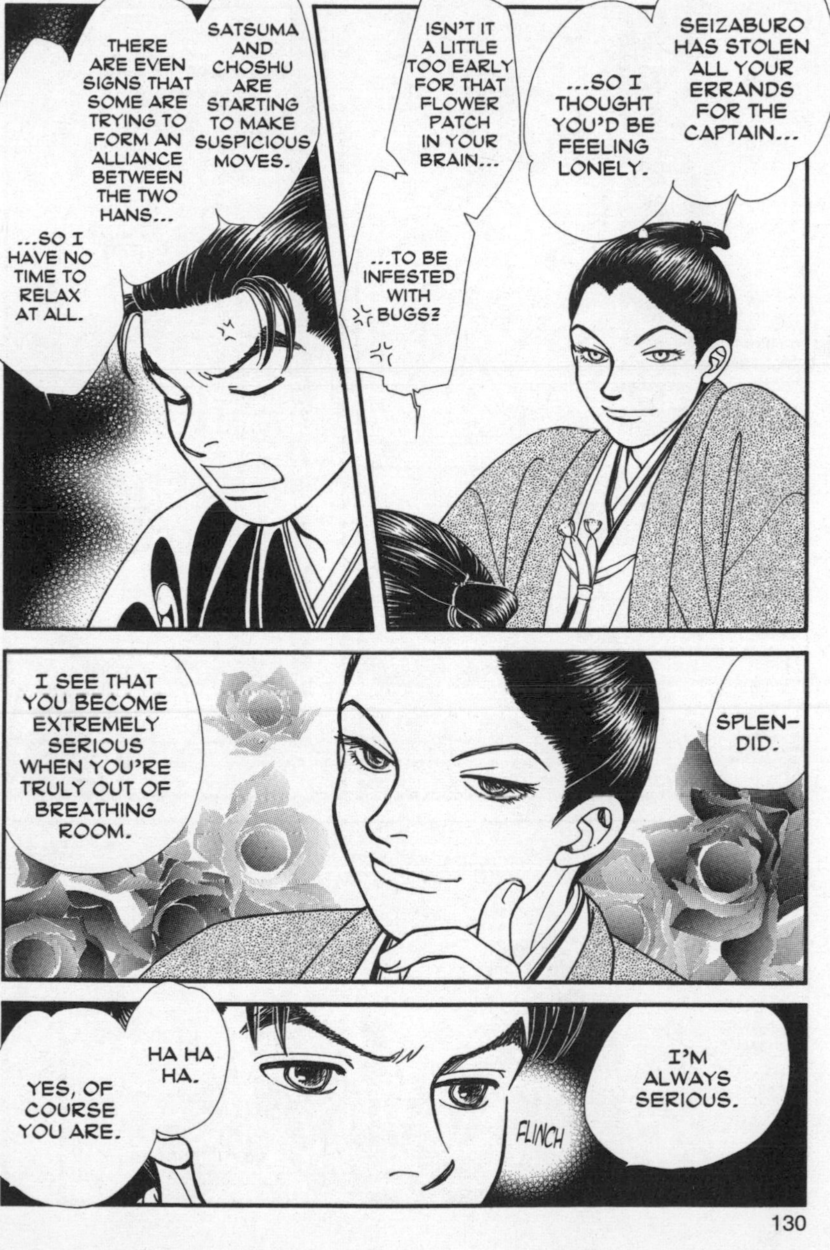
SEIZABURO HAS STOLEN ALL YOUR ERRANDS FOR THE CAPTAIN...
...SO I THOUGHT YOU'D BE FEELING LONELY.
ISN'T IT A LITTLE TOO EARLY FOR THAT FLOWER PATCH IN YOUR BRAIN...
...TO BE INFESTED WITH BUGS?
SATSUMA AND CHOSHU ARE STARTING TO MAKE SUSPICIOUS MOVES.
THERE ARE EVEN SIGNS THAT SOME ARE TRYING TO FORM AN ALLIANCE BETWEEN THE TWO HANS...
...SO I HAVE NO TIME TO RELAX AT ALL.
SPLEN-DID.
I SEE THAT YOU BECOME EXTREMELY SERIOUS WHEN YOU'RE TRULY OUT OF BREATHING ROOM.
I'M ALWAYS SERIOUS.
FLINCH
HA HA HA.
YES, OF COURSE YOU ARE.

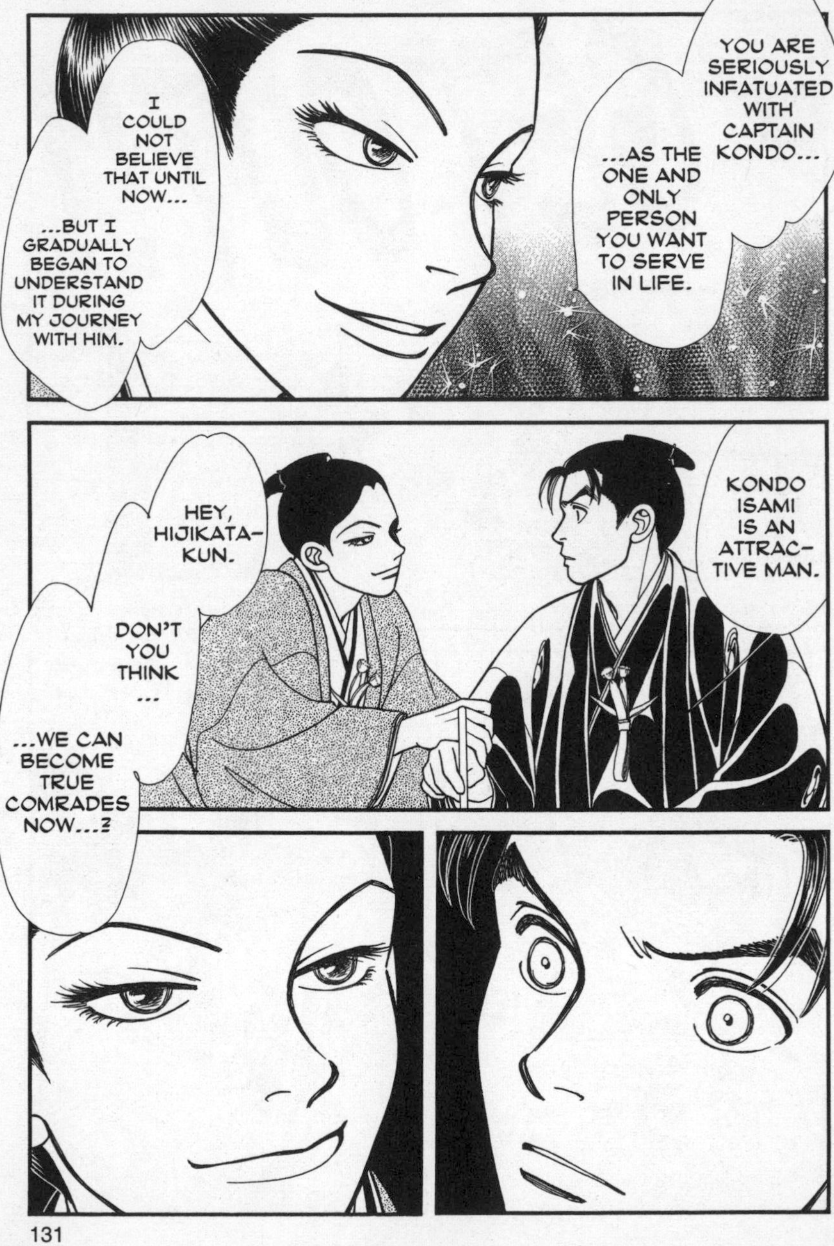
YOU ARE SERIOUSLY INFATUATED WITH CAPTAIN KONDO...
...AS THE ONE AND ONLY PERSON YOU WANT TO SERVE IN LIFE.
I COULD NOT BELIEVE THAT UNTIL NOW...
...BUT I GRADUALLY BEGAN TO UNDERSTAND IT DURING MY JOURNEY WITH HIM.
KONDO ISAMI IS AN ATTRACTIVE MAN.
HEY, HIJIKATA-KUN.
DON'T YOU THINK ...
...WE CAN BECOME TRUE COMRADES NOW...?

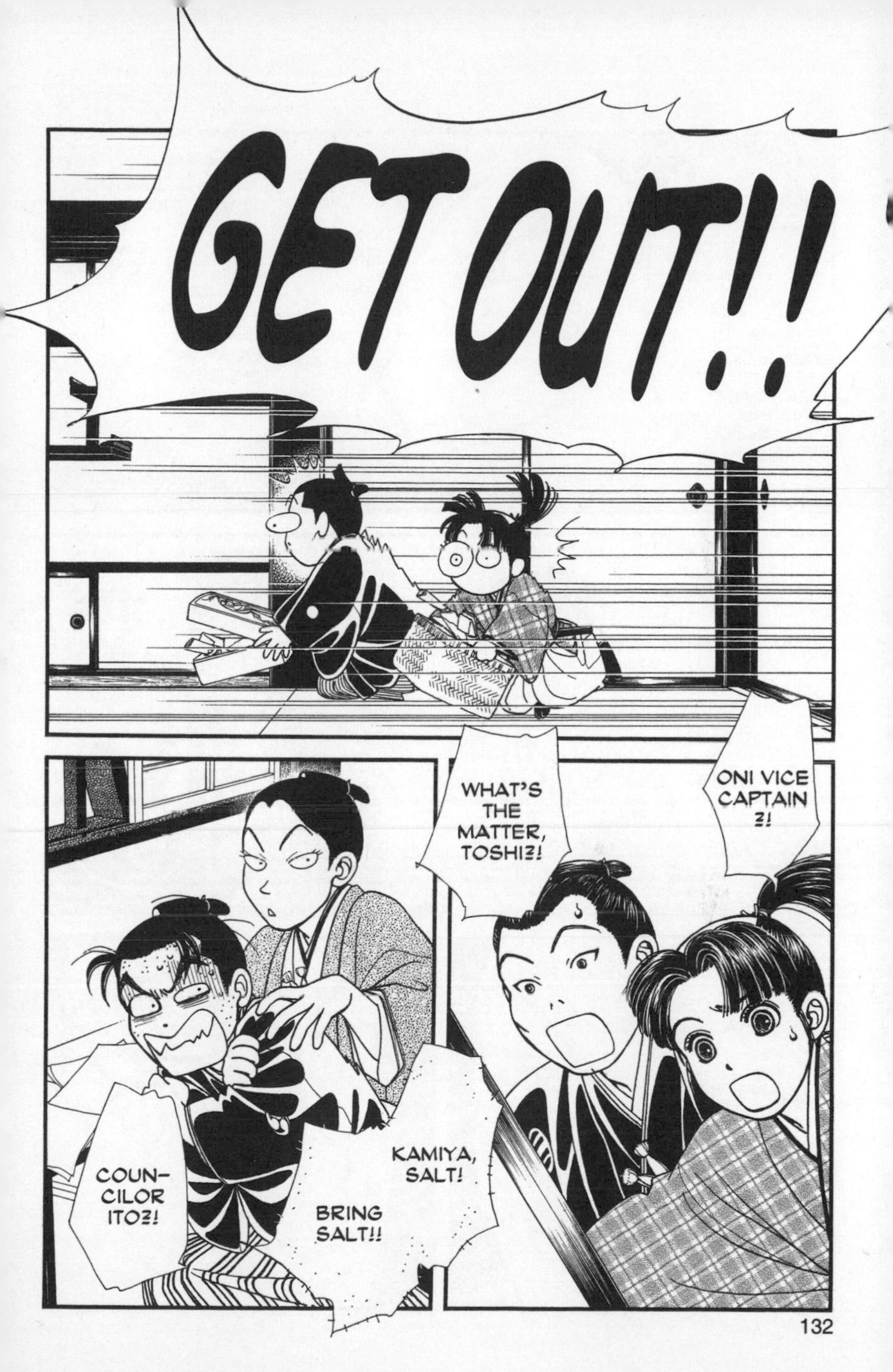
GET OUT!!
ONI VICE CAPTAIN?!
WHAT'S THE MATTER, TOSHI?!
KAMIYA, SALT!
BRING SALT!!
COUNCILOR ITO?!

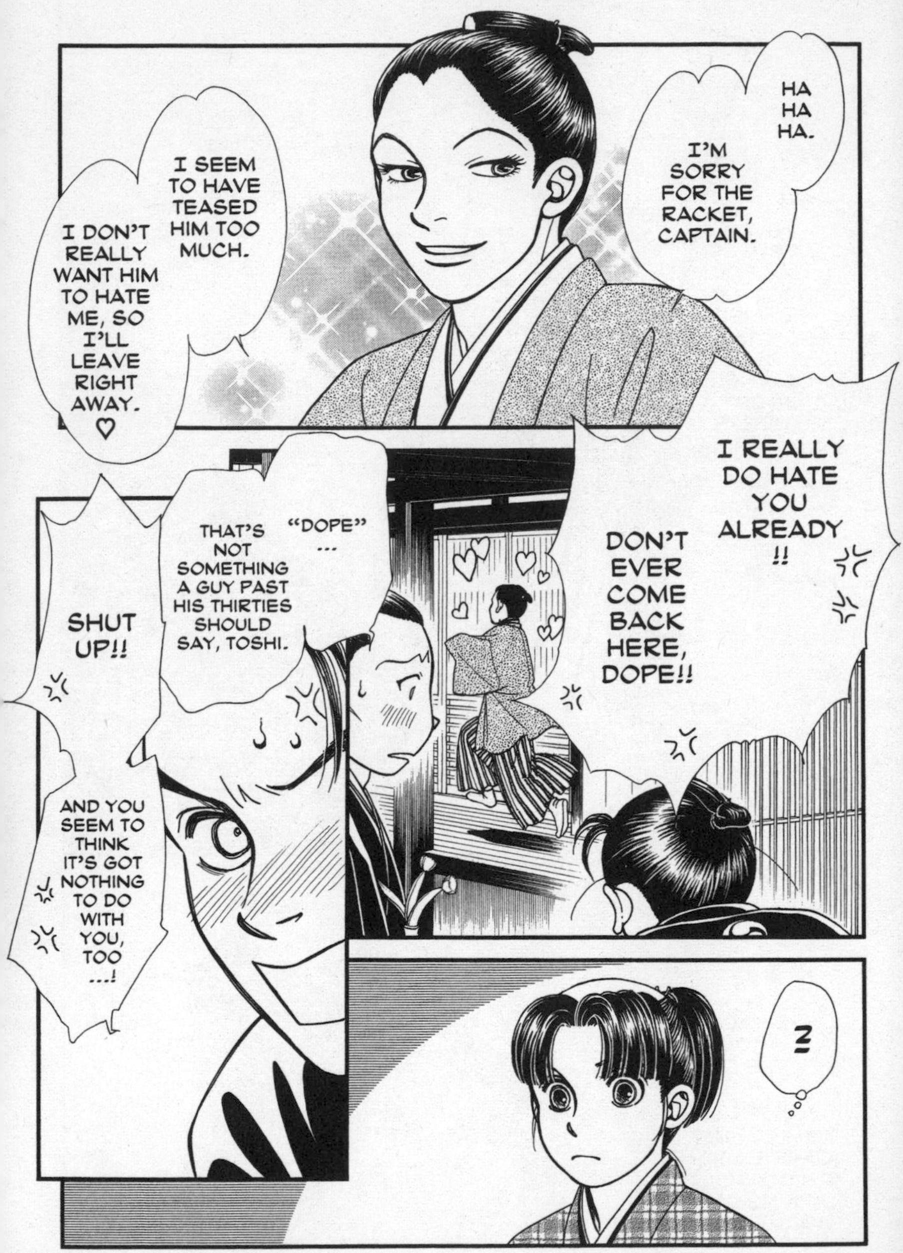
HA HA HA.
I'M SORRY FOR THE RACKET, CAPTAIN.
I SEEM TO HAVE TEASED HIM TOO MUCH.
I DON'T REALLY WANT HIM TO HATE ME, SO I'LL LEAVE RIGHT AWAY. ♡
I REALLY DO HATE YOU ALREADY!!
DON'T EVER COME BACK HERE, DOPE!!
"DOPE"...
THAT'S NOT SOMETHING A GUY PAST HIS THIRTIES SHOULD SAY, TOSHI.
SHUT UP!!
AND YOU SEEM TO THINK IT'S GOT NOTHING TO DO WITH YOU, TOO...!

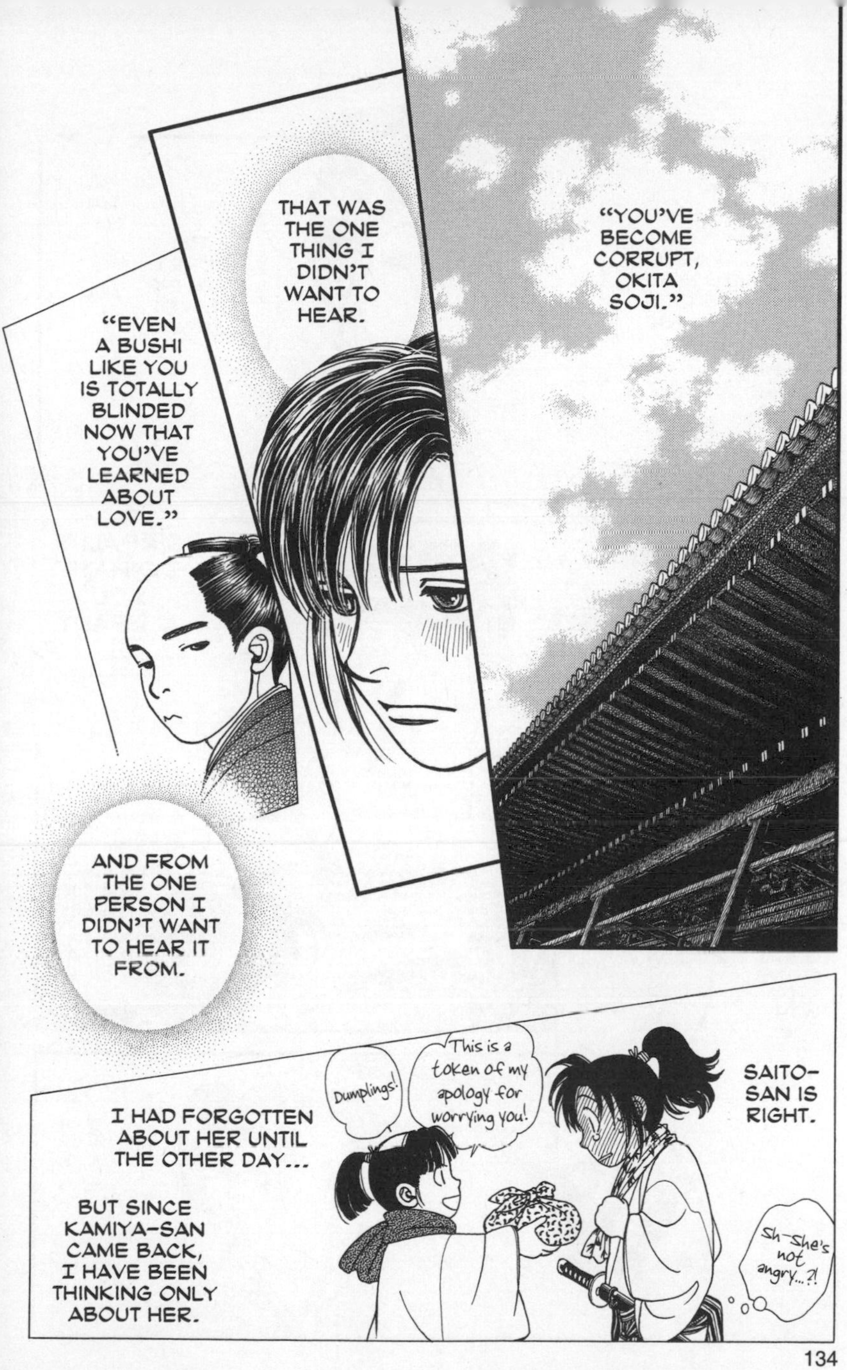
"YOU'VE BECOME CORRUPT, OKITA SOJI."
THAT WAS THE ONE THING I DIDN'T WANT TO HEAR.
"EVEN A BUSHI LIKE YOU IS TOTALLY BLINDED NOW THAT YOU'VE LEARNED ABOUT LOVE."
AND FROM THE ONE PERSON I DIDN'T WANT TO HEAR IT FROM.
SAITO-SAN IS RIGHT.
Sh-She's not angry...?!
This is a token of my apology for worrying you!
Dumplings!
I HAD FORGOTTEN ABOUT HER UNTIL THE OTHER DAY...
BUT SINCE KAMIYA-SAN CAME BACK, I HAVE BEEN THINKING ONLY ABOUT HER.

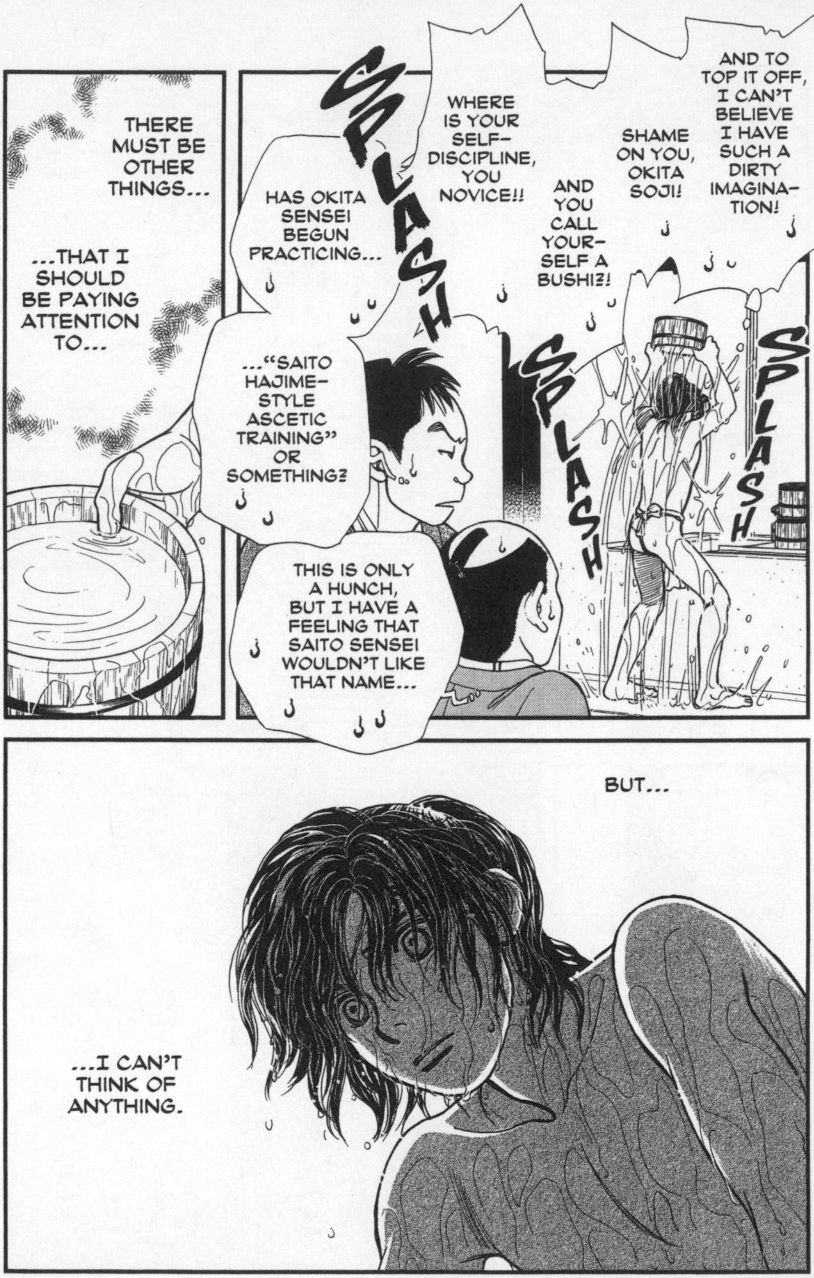
AND TO TOP IT OFF, I CAN'T BELIEVE I HAVE SUCH A DIRTY IMAGINATION!
SHAME ON YOU, OKITA SOJI!
AND YOU CALL YOURSELF A BUSHI?!
WHERE IS YOUR SELF-DISCIPLINE, YOU NOVICE!!
SPLASH
SPLASH
SPLASH
HAS OKITA SENSEI BEGUN PRACTICING...
..."SAITO HAJIME-STYLE ASCETIC TRAINING" OR SOMETHING?
THIS IS ONLY A HUNCH, BUT I HAVE A FEELING THAT SAITO SENSEI WOULDN'T LIKE THAT NAME...
THERE MUST BE OTHER THINGS...
...THAT I SHOULD BE PAYING ATTENTION TO...
BUT...
...I CAN'T THINK OF ANYTHING.

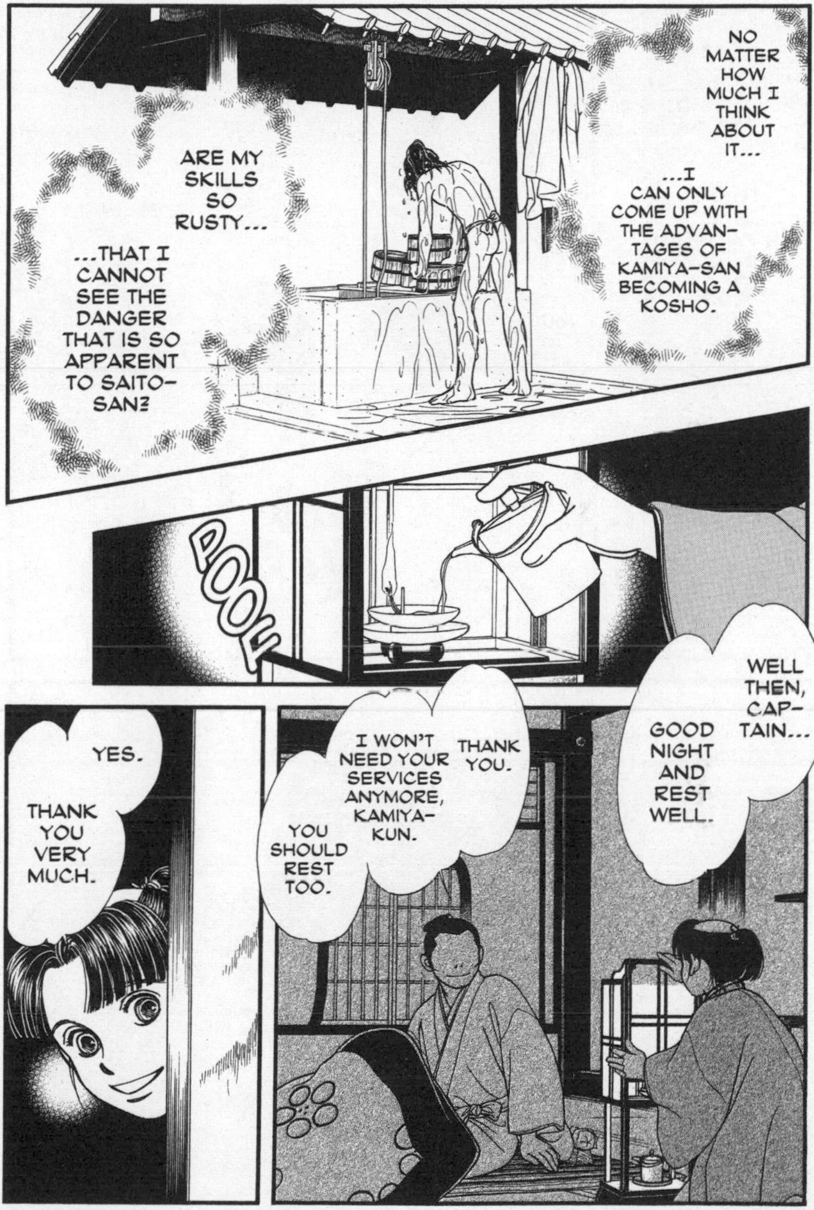
NO MATTER HOW MUCH I THINK ABOUT IT...
...I CAN ONLY COME UP WITH THE ADVANTAGES OF KAMIYA-SAN BECOMING A KOSHO.
ARE MY SKILLS SO RUSTY...
...THAT I CANNOT SEE THE DANGER THAT IS SO APPARENT TO SAITO-SAN?
POOF
WELL THEN, CAPTAIN...
GOOD NIGHT AND REST WELL.
THANK YOU.
I WON'T NEED YOUR SERVICES ANYMORE, KAMIYA-KUN.
YOU SHOULD REST TOO.
YES.
THANK YOU VERY MUCH.

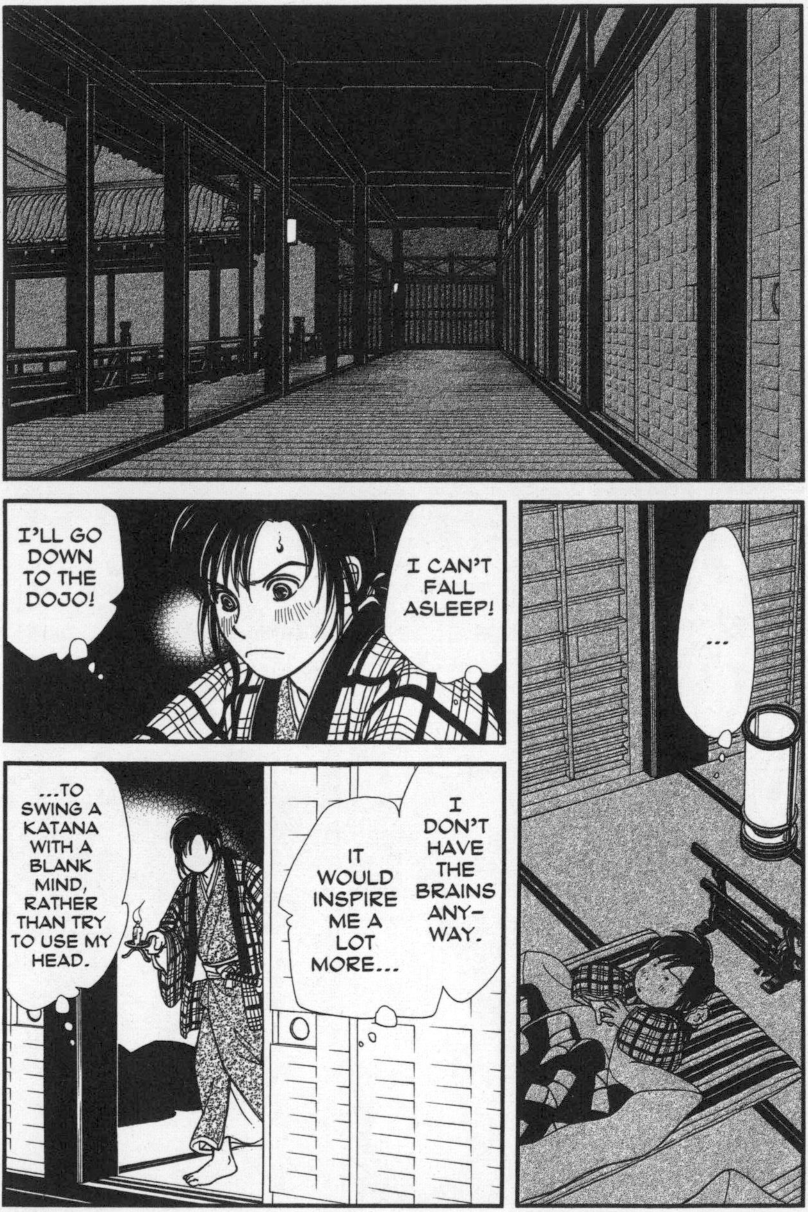
...
I CAN'T FALL ASLEEP!
I'LL GO DOWN TO THE DOJO!
I DON'T HAVE THE BRAINS ANY-WAY.
IT WOULD INSPIRE ME A LOT MORE...
...TO SWING A KATANA WITH A BLANK MIND, RATHER THAN TRY TO USE MY HEAD.

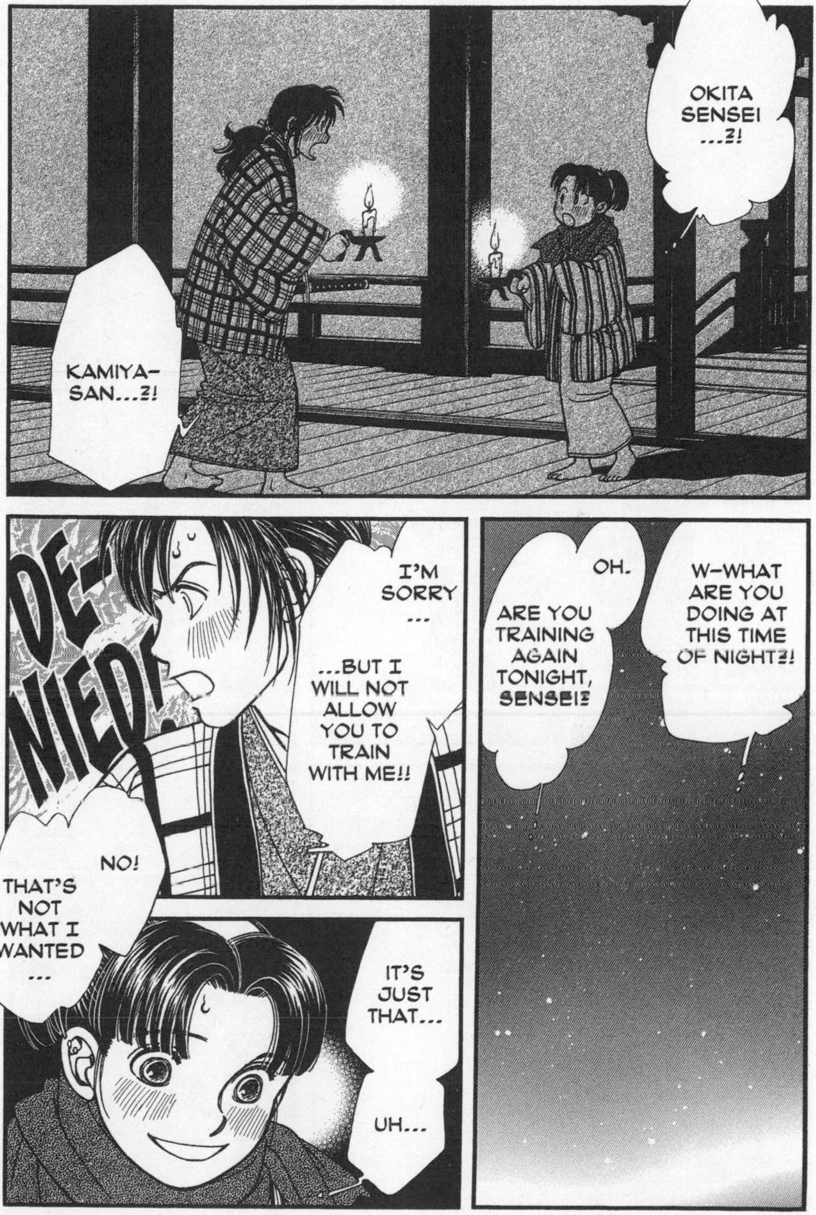
OKITA SENSEI ...?!
KAMIYA-SAN...?!
W-WHAT ARE YOU DOING AT THIS TIME OF NIGHT?!
OH. ARE YOU TRAINING AGAIN TONIGHT, SENSEI!?
I'M SORRY ...
...BUT I WILL NOT ALLOW YOU TO TRAIN WITH ME!!
DE-NIED!
IT'S JUST THAT...
UH...
NO! THAT'S NOT WHAT I WANTED ...

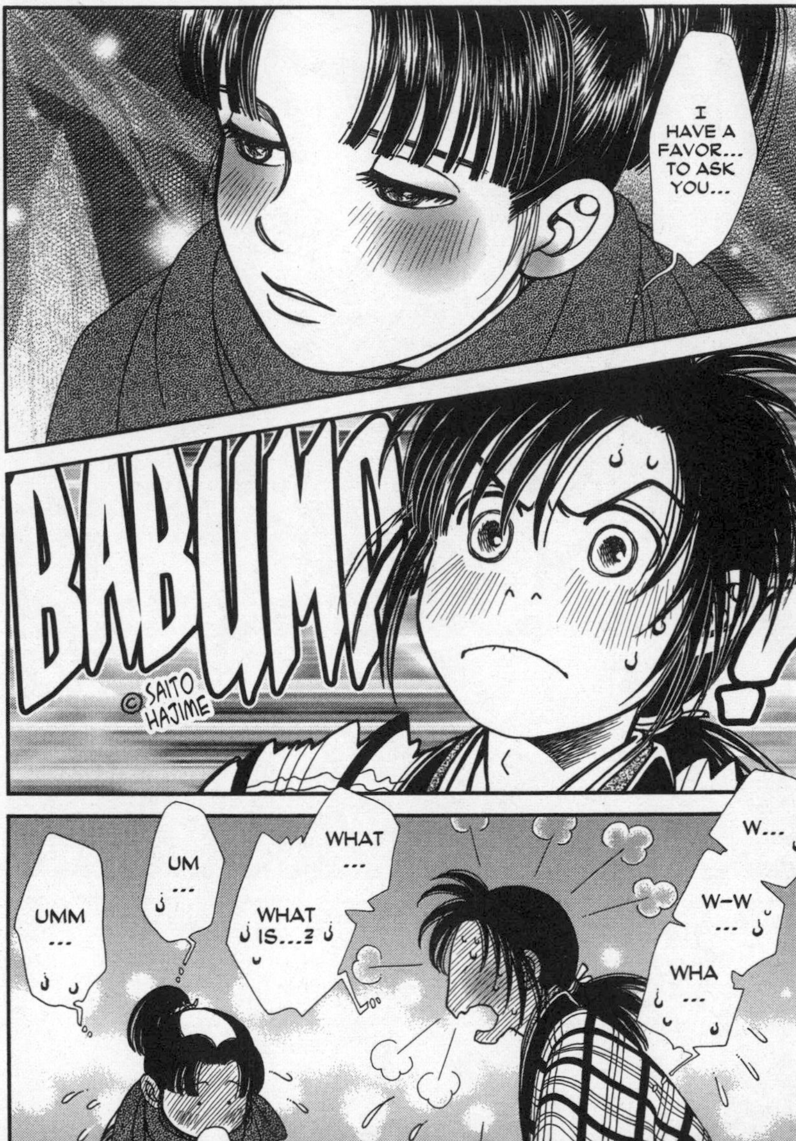

I HAVE A FAVOR... TO ASK YOU...
BABUM
!?
© SAITO HAJIME
W...
W-W ...
WHA ...
WHAT ...
WHAT IS...?
UM ...
UMM ...

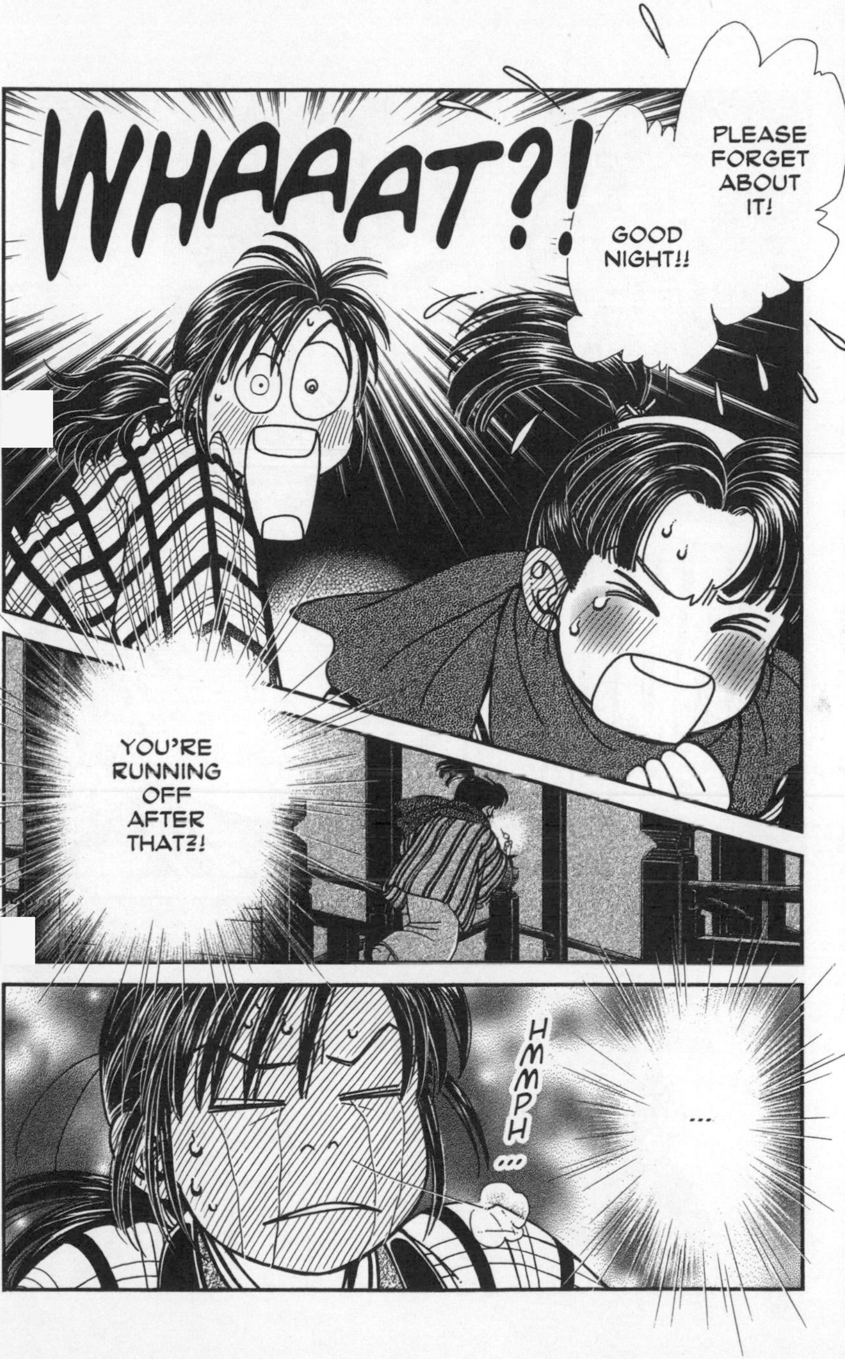
PLEASE FORGET ABOUT IT!
GOOD NIGHT!!
WHAAAT?!
YOU'RE RUNNING OFF AFTER THAT?!
...
HMMPH...

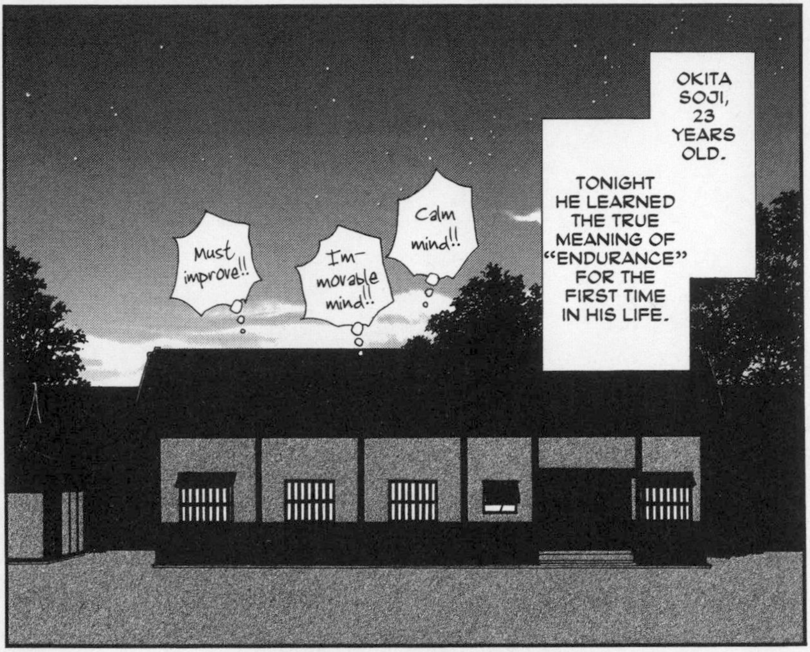
OKITA SOJI, 23 YEARS OLD.
TONIGHT HE LEARNED THE TRUE MEANING OF "ENDURANCE" FOR THE FIRST TIME IN HIS LIFE.
Calm mind!!
I'm-movable mind!!
Must improve!!

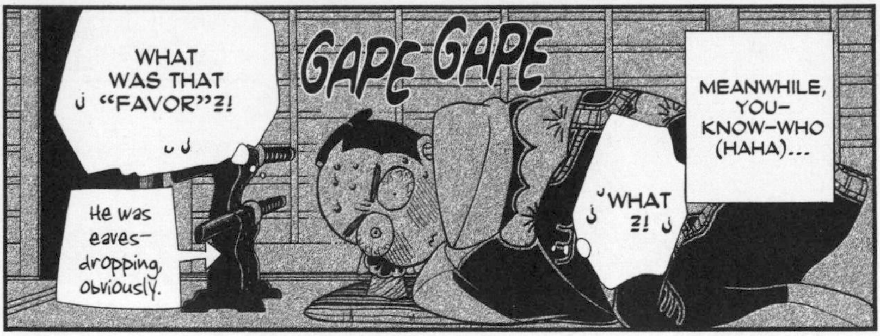
MEANWHILE, YOU-KNOW-WHO (HAHA)...
WHAT?!
GAPE GAPE
WHAT WAS THAT "FAVOR"?!
He was eaves-dropping, obviously.

TO BE CONTINUED!

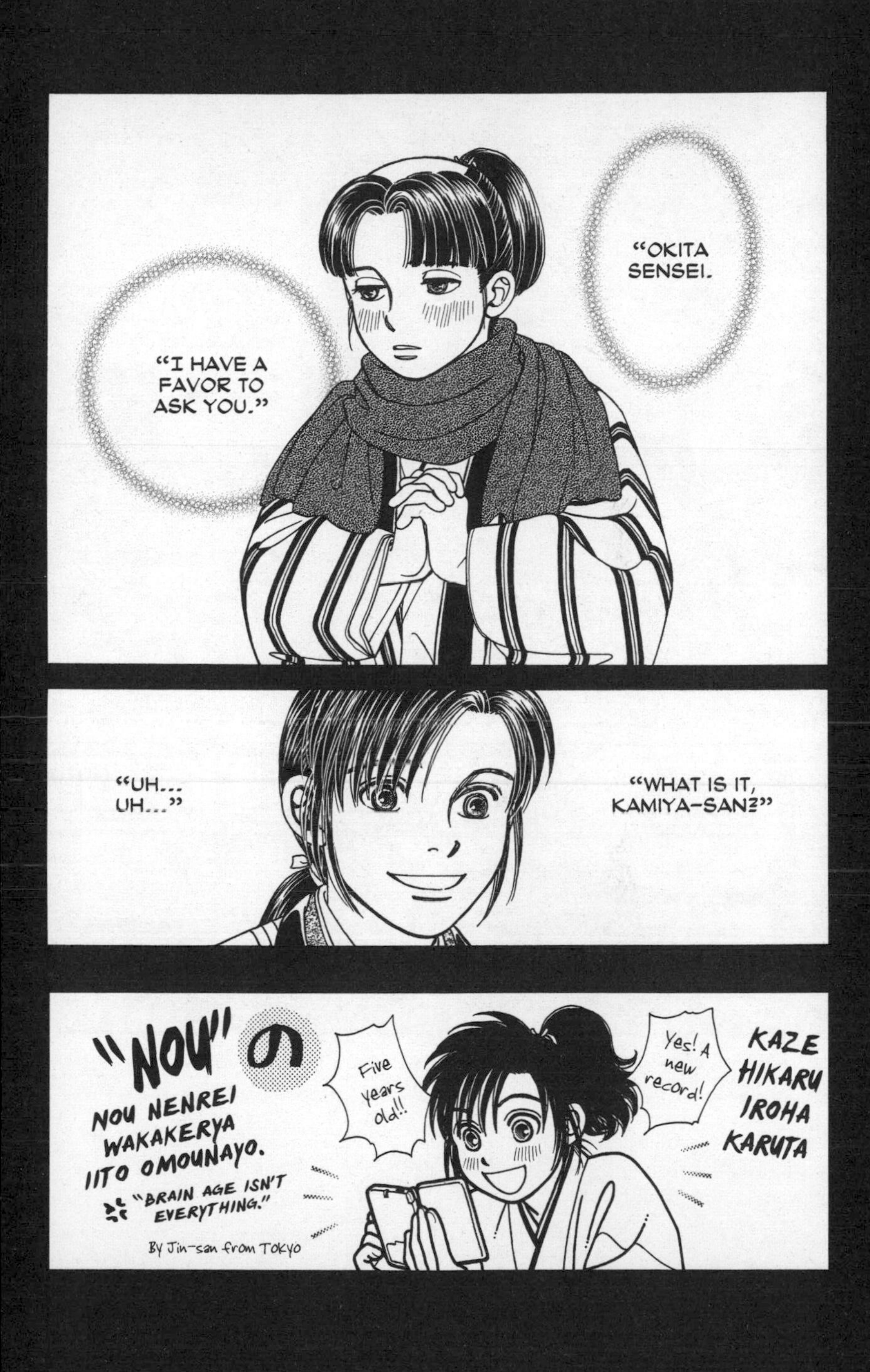
"OKITA SENSEI.
"I HAVE A FAVOR TO ASK YOU."
"WHAT IS IT, KAMIYA-SAN?"
"UH... UH..."
KAZE HIKARU IROHA KARUTA
Yes! A new record!
Five years old!!
"NOU" の
NOU NENREI WAKAKERYA IITO OMOUNAYO.
"BRAIN AGE ISN'T EVERYTHING."
By Jin-san from TOKYO

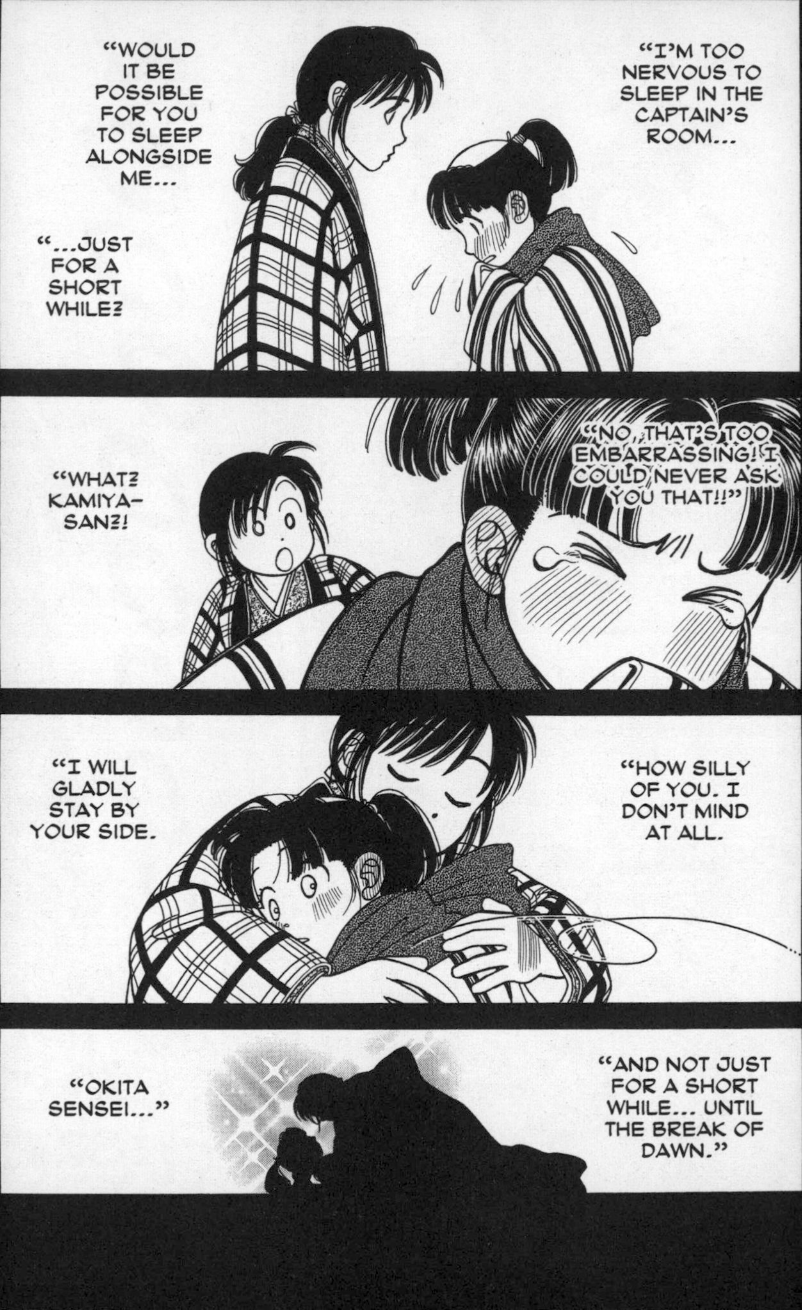
"I'M TOO NERVOUS TO SLEEP IN THE CAPTAIN'S ROOM...
"WOULD IT BE POSSIBLE FOR YOU TO SLEEP ALONGSIDE ME...
"...JUST FOR A SHORT WHILE?
"NO, THAT'S TOO EMBARRASSING! I COULD NEVER ASK YOU THAT!!"
"WHAT? KAMIYA-SAN?!
"HOW SILLY OF YOU. I DON'T MIND AT ALL.
"I WILL GLADLY STAY BY YOUR SIDE.
"AND NOT JUST FOR A SHORT WHILE... UNTIL THE BREAK OF DAWN."
"OKITA SENSEI..."

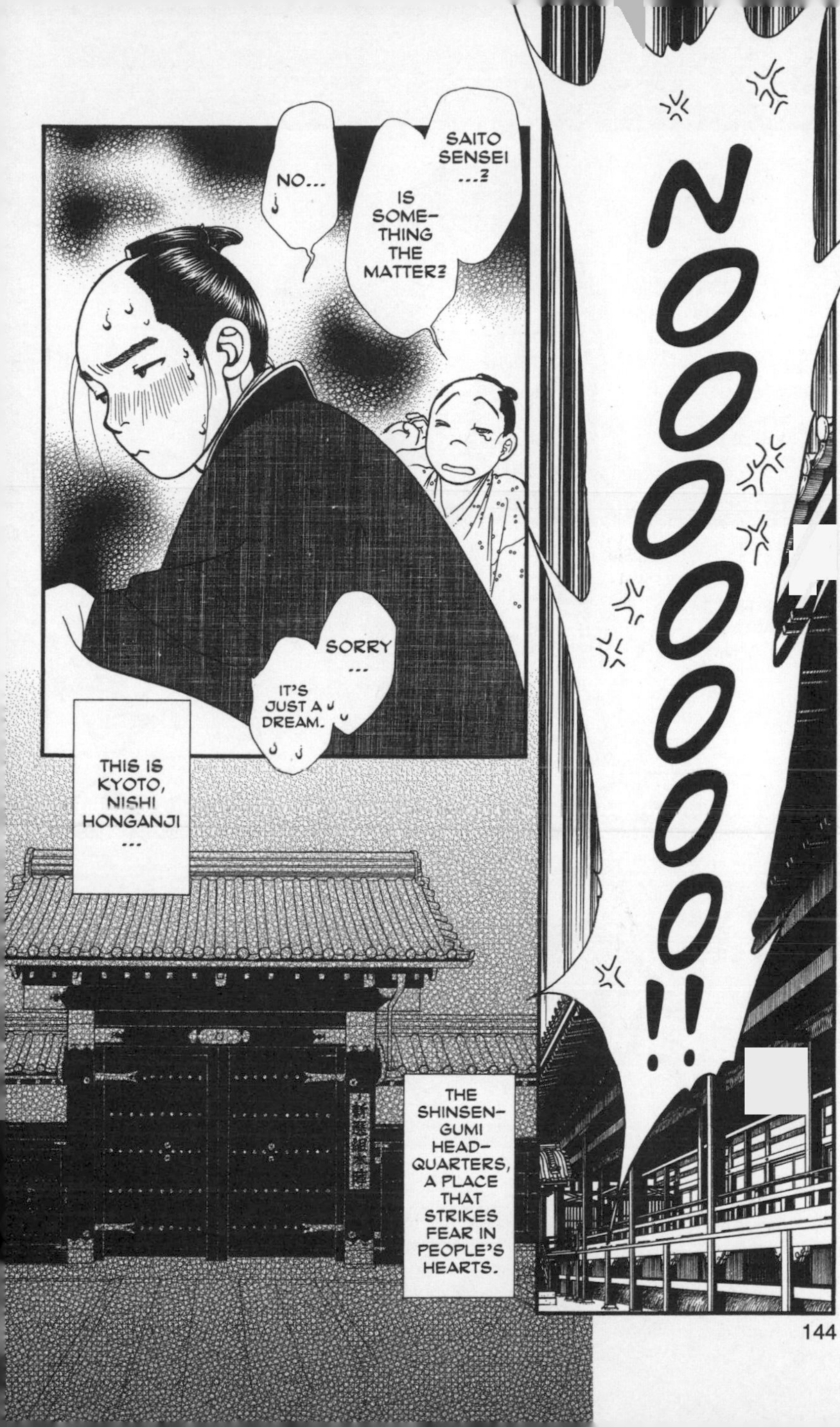
NOOOOOOOO!!
SAITO SENSEI...? IS SOMETHING THE MATTER?
NO...
SORRY... IT'S JUST A DREAM.
THIS IS KYOTO, NISHI HONGANJI...
THE SHINSENGUMI HEADQUARTERS, A PLACE THAT STRIKES FEAR IN PEOPLE'S HEARTS.

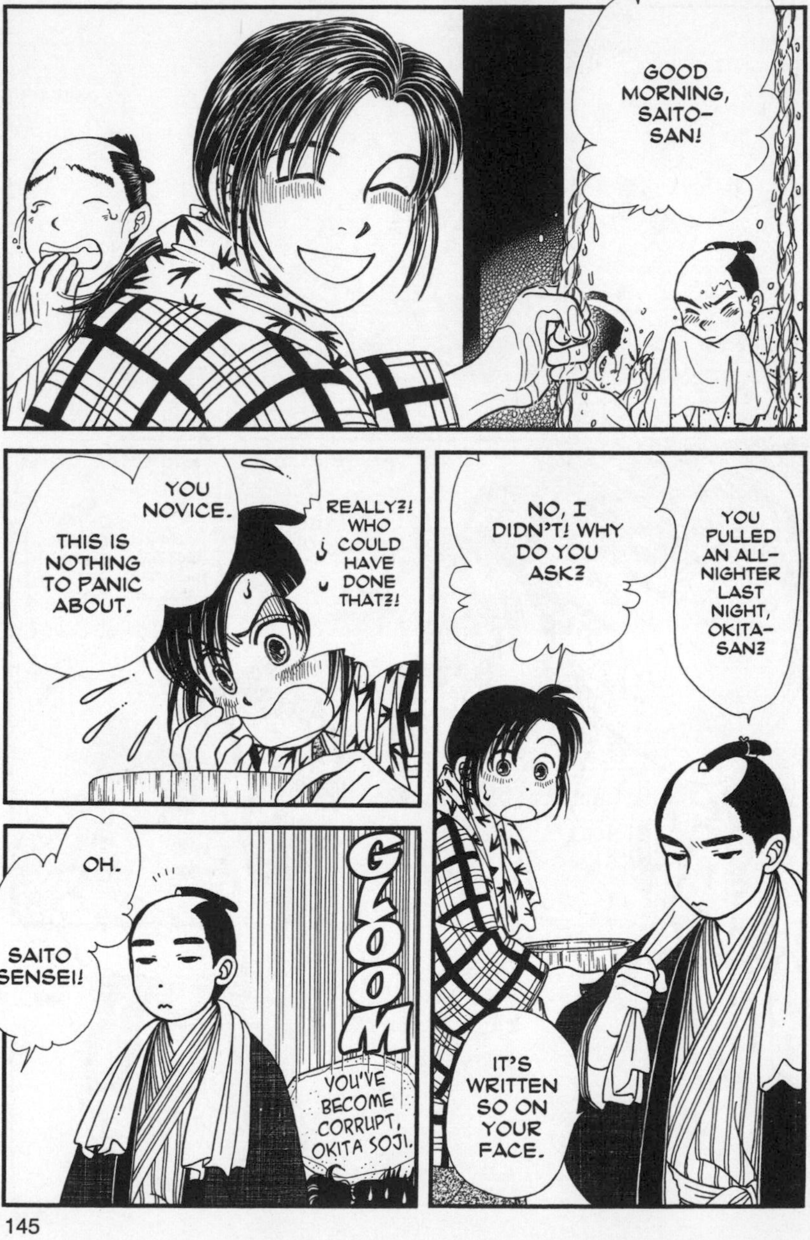
GOOD MORNING, SAITO-SAN!
YOU PULLED AN ALL-NIGHTER LAST NIGHT, OKITA-SAN?
NO, I DIDN'T! WHY DO YOU ASK?
IT'S WRITTEN SO ON YOUR FACE.
REALLY?! WHO COULD HAVE DONE THAT?!
YOU NOVICE.
THIS IS NOTHING TO PANIC ABOUT.
GLOOM
YOU'VE BECOME CORRUPT, OKITA SOJI.
OH.
SAITO SENSEI!

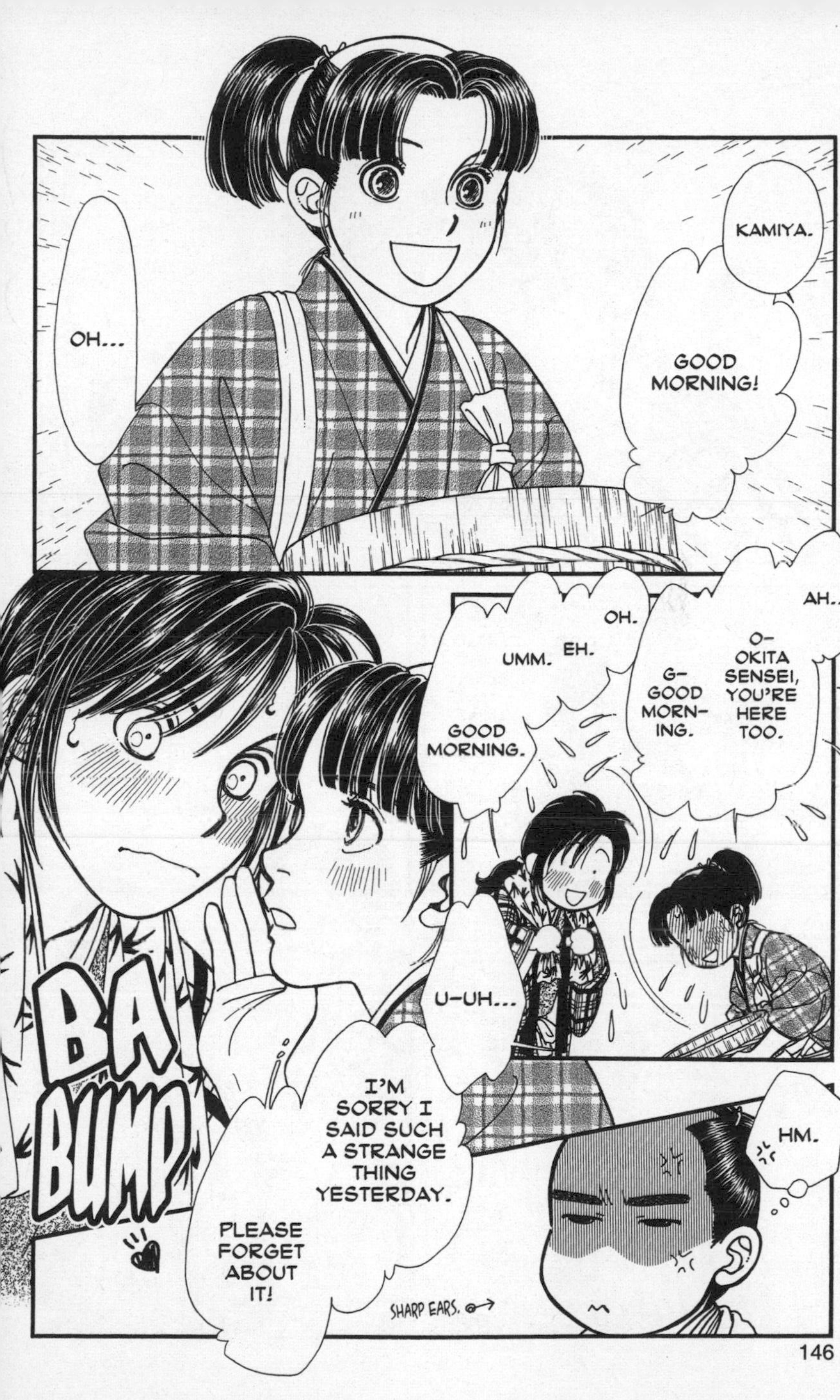
KAMIYA.
GOOD MORNING!
OH...
AH...
O-OKITA SENSEI, YOU'RE HERE TOO.
G-GOOD MORN-ING.
OH.
EH.
UMM.
GOOD MORNING.
U-UH...
HM.
I'M SORRY I SAID SUCH A STRANGE THING YESTERDAY.
PLEASE FORGET ABOUT IT!
SHARP EARS.
BA BUMP

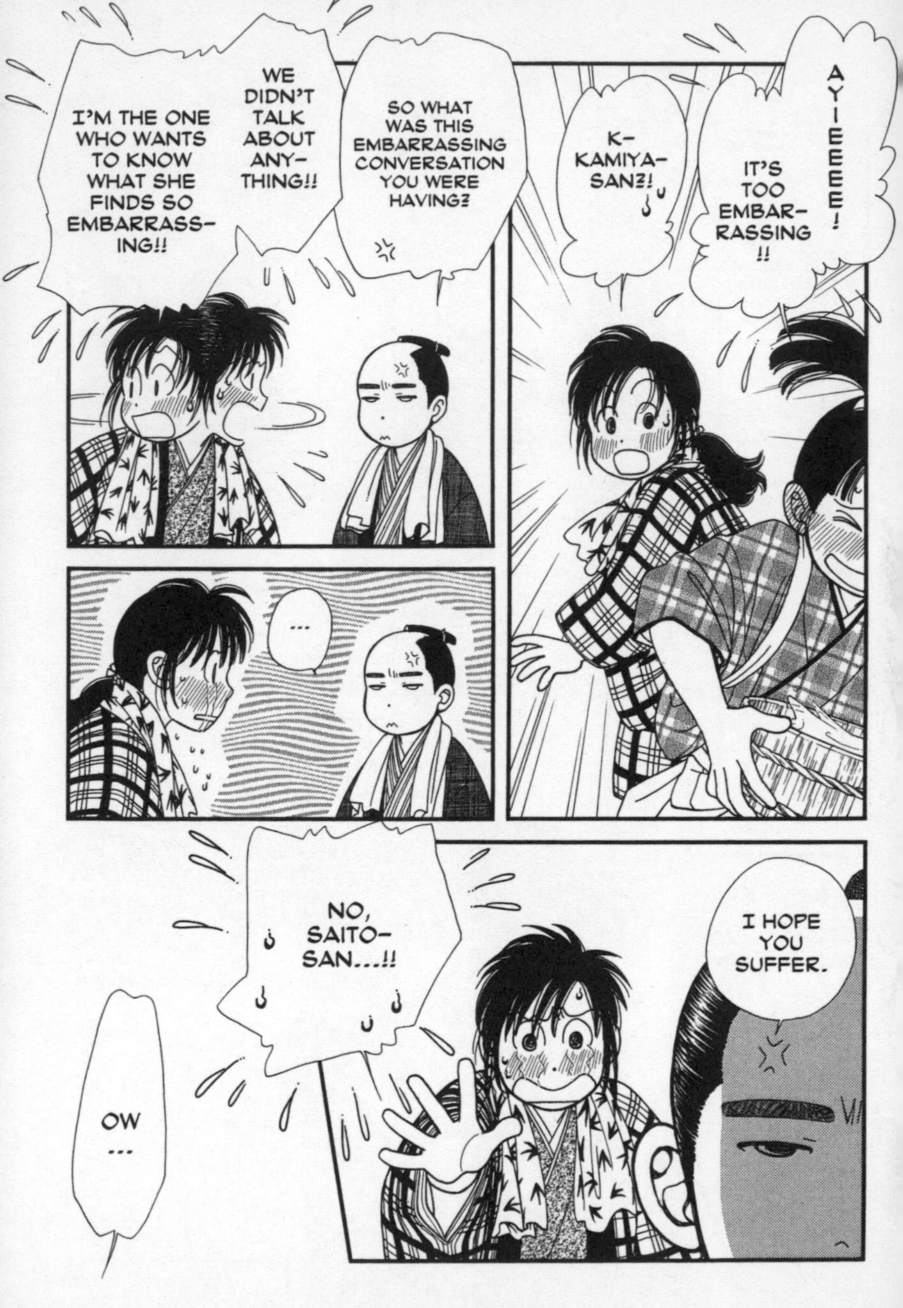
AYIEEEE!
IT'S TOO EMBARRASSING!!
K-KAMIYA-SAN?!
SO WHAT WAS THIS EMBARRASSING CONVERSATION YOU WERE HAVING?
WE DIDN'T TALK ABOUT ANYTHING!!
I'M THE ONE WHO WANTS TO KNOW WHAT SHE FINDS SO EMBARRASSING!!
...
I HOPE YOU SUFFER.
NO, SAITO-SAN...!!
OW...

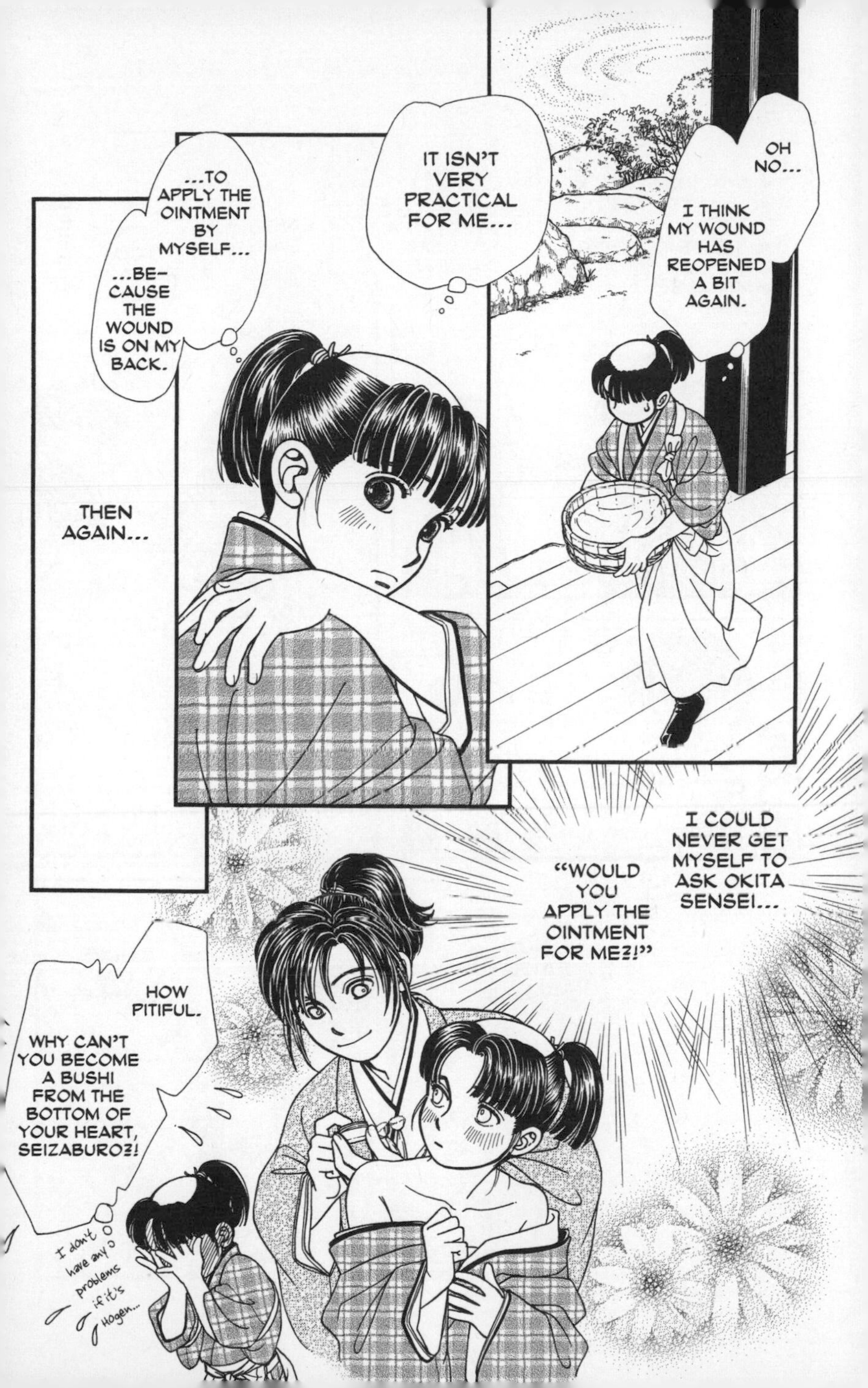
OH NO...
I THINK MY WOUND HAS REOPENED A BIT AGAIN.
IT ISN'T VERY PRACTICAL FOR ME...
...TO APPLY THE OINTMENT BY MYSELF...
...BE-CAUSE THE WOUND IS ON MY BACK.
THEN AGAIN...
I COULD NEVER GET MYSELF TO ASK OKITA SENSEI...
"WOULD YOU APPLY THE OINTMENT FOR ME?!"
HOW PITIFUL.
WHY CAN'T YOU BECOME A BUSHI FROM THE BOTTOM OF YOUR HEART, SEIZABURO?!
I don't have any problems if it's Hogen...

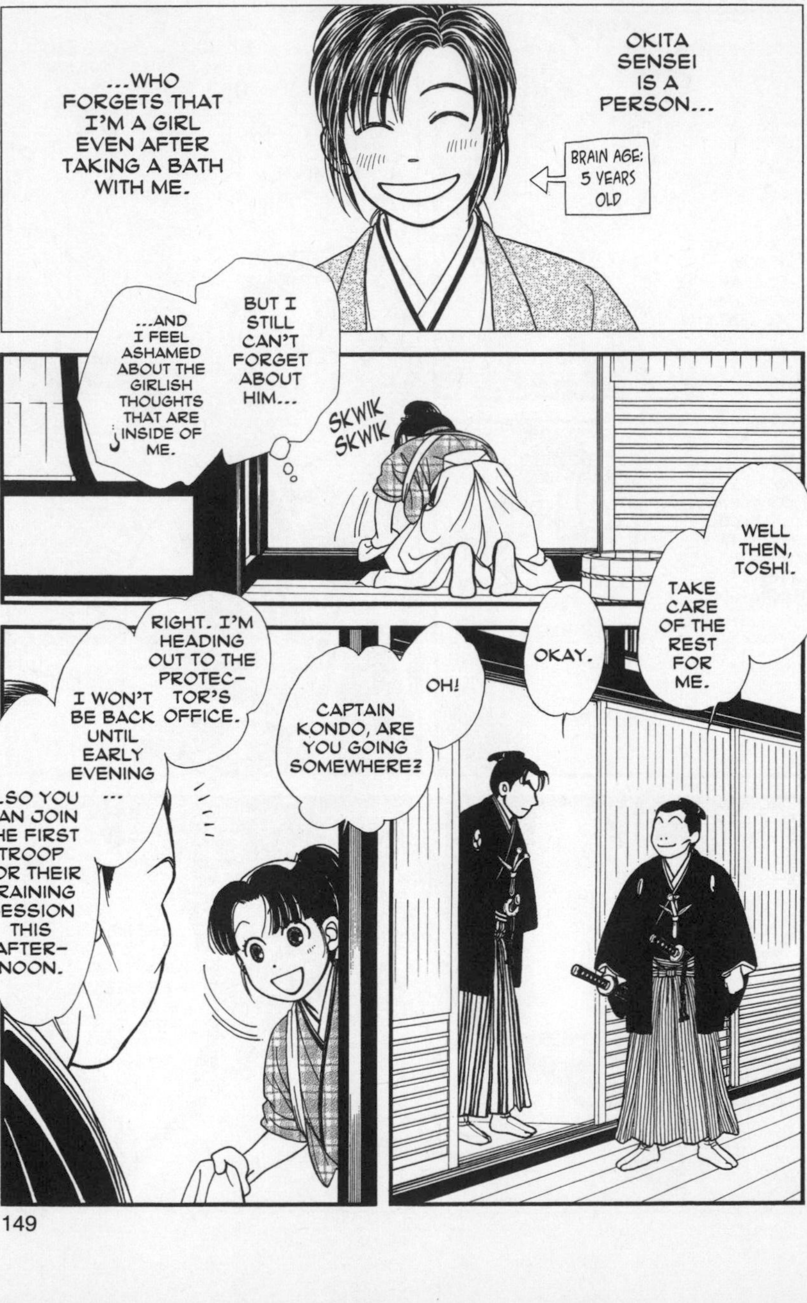
OKITA SENSEI IS A PERSON...
BRAIN AGE: 5 YEARS OLD
...WHO FORGETS THAT I'M A GIRL EVEN AFTER TAKING A BATH WITH ME.
BUT I STILL CAN'T FORGET ABOUT HIM...
...AND I FEEL ASHAMED ABOUT THE GIRLISH THOUGHTS THAT ARE INSIDE OF ME.
SKWIK SKWIK
WELL THEN, TOSHI.
TAKE CARE OF THE REST FOR ME.
OKAY.
OH!
CAPTAIN KONDO, ARE YOU GOING SOMEWHERE?
RIGHT. I'M HEADING OUT TO THE PROTECTOR'S OFFICE.
I WON'T BE BACK UNTIL EARLY EVENING...
...SO YOU CAN JOIN THE FIRST TROOP FOR THEIR TRAINING SESSION THIS AFTERNOON.

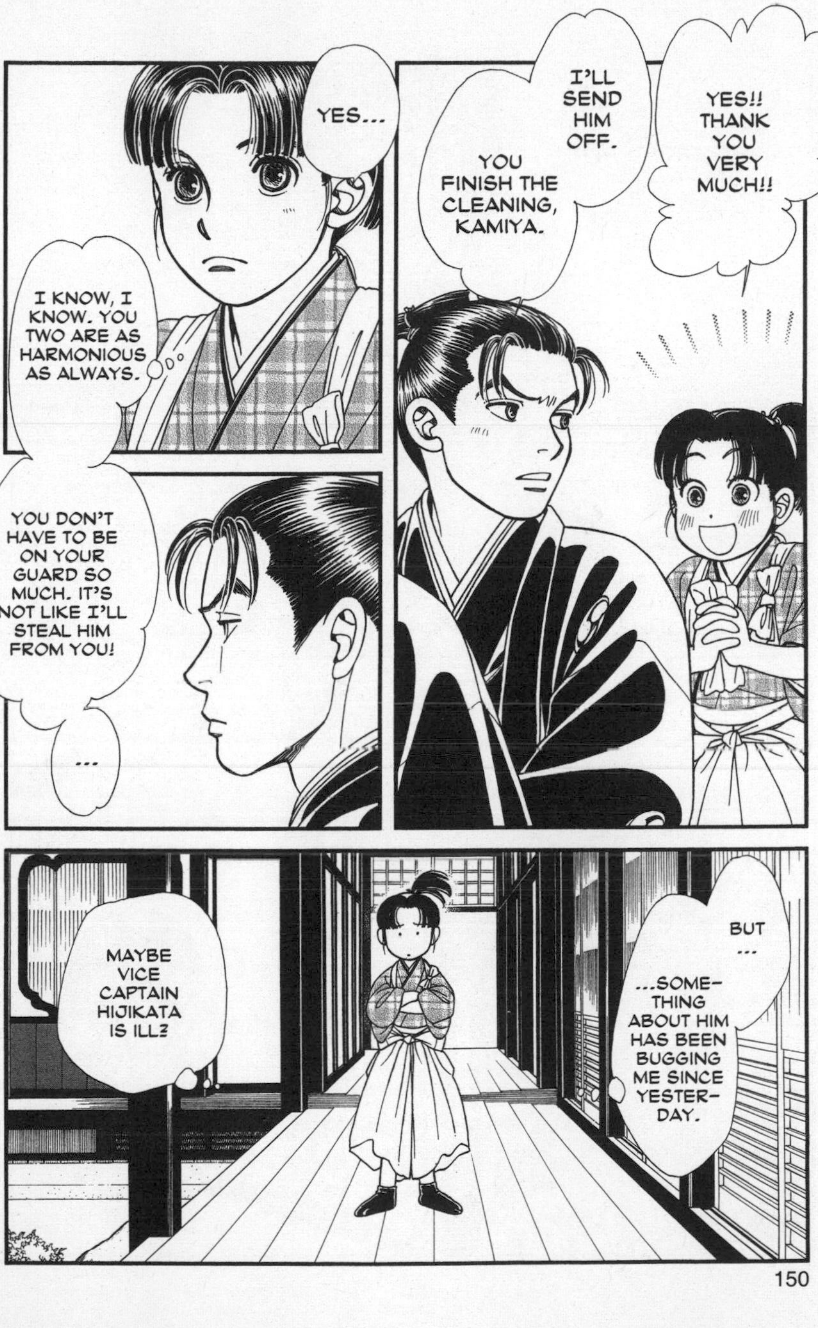
YES!! THANK YOU VERY MUCH!!
I'LL SEND HIM OFF.
YOU FINISH THE CLEANING, KAMIYA.
YES...
I KNOW, I KNOW. YOU TWO ARE AS HARMONIOUS AS ALWAYS.
YOU DON'T HAVE TO BE ON YOUR GUARD SO MUCH. IT'S NOT LIKE I'LL STEAL HIM FROM YOU!
...
BUT ...
...SOME-THING ABOUT HIM HAS BEEN BUGGING ME SINCE YESTER-DAY.
MAYBE VICE CAPTAIN HIJIKATA IS ILL?

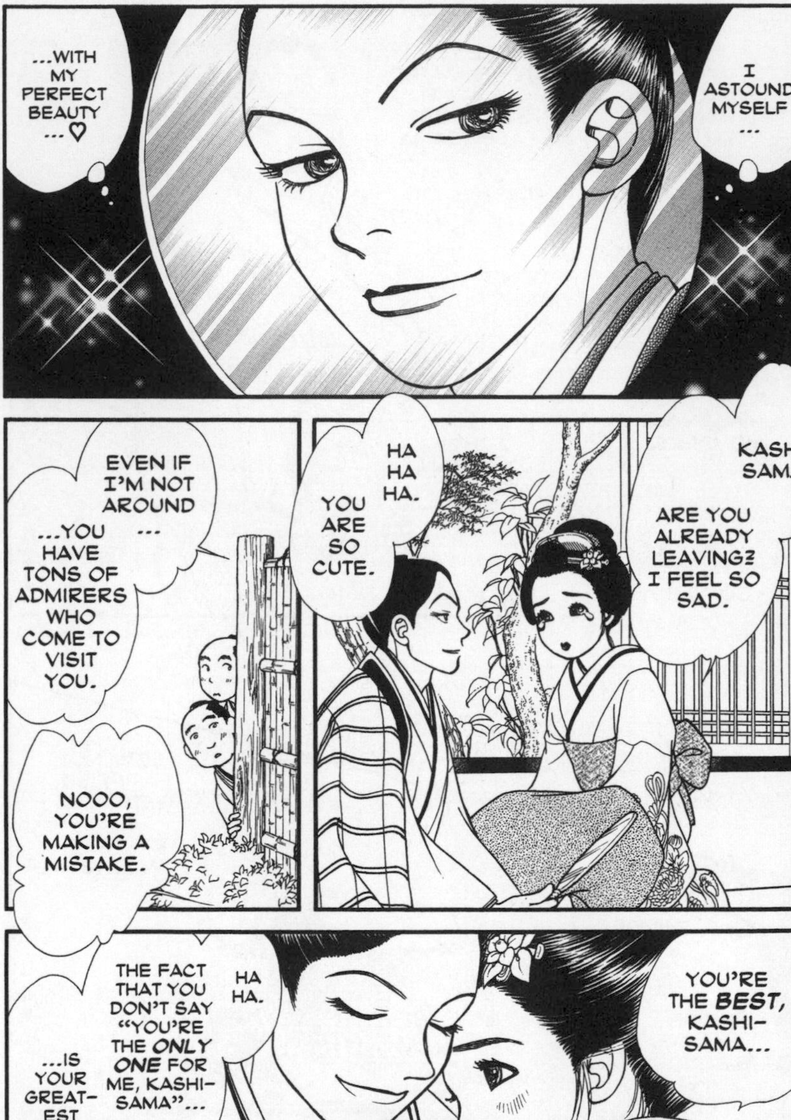
I ASTOUND MYSELF...
...WITH MY PERFECT BEAUTY...♡
KASHI-SAMA.
ARE YOU ALREADY LEAVING? I FEEL SO SAD.
HA HA HA.
YOU ARE SO CUTE.
EVEN IF I'M NOT AROUND...
...YOU HAVE TONS OF ADMIRERS WHO COME TO VISIT YOU.
NOOO, YOU'RE MAKING A MISTAKE.
YOU'RE THE *BEST*, KASHI-SAMA...
HA HA.
THE FACT THAT YOU DON'T SAY "YOU'RE THE *ONLY ONE* FOR ME, KASHI-SAMA"...
...IS YOUR GREATEST VIRTUE, HANAKA.

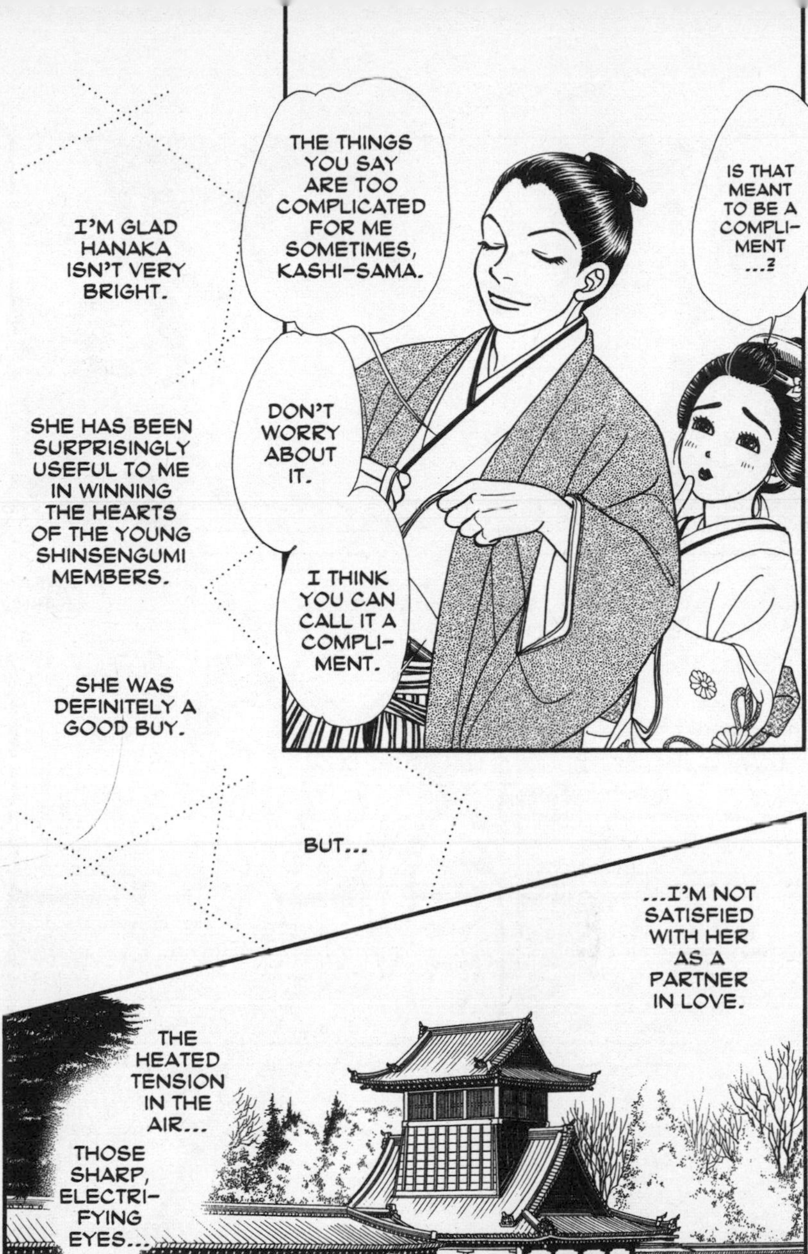
IS THAT MEANT TO BE A COMPLIMENT ...?
THE THINGS YOU SAY ARE TOO COMPLICATED FOR ME SOMETIMES, KASHI-SAMA.
DON'T WORRY ABOUT IT.
I THINK YOU CAN CALL IT A COMPLIMENT.
I'M GLAD HANAKA ISN'T VERY BRIGHT.
SHE HAS BEEN SURPRISINGLY USEFUL TO ME IN WINNING THE HEARTS OF THE YOUNG SHINSENGUMI MEMBERS.
SHE WAS DEFINITELY A GOOD BUY.
BUT...
...I'M NOT SATISFIED WITH HER AS A PARTNER IN LOVE.
THE HEATED TENSION IN THE AIR...
THOSE SHARP, ELECTRIFYING EYES...

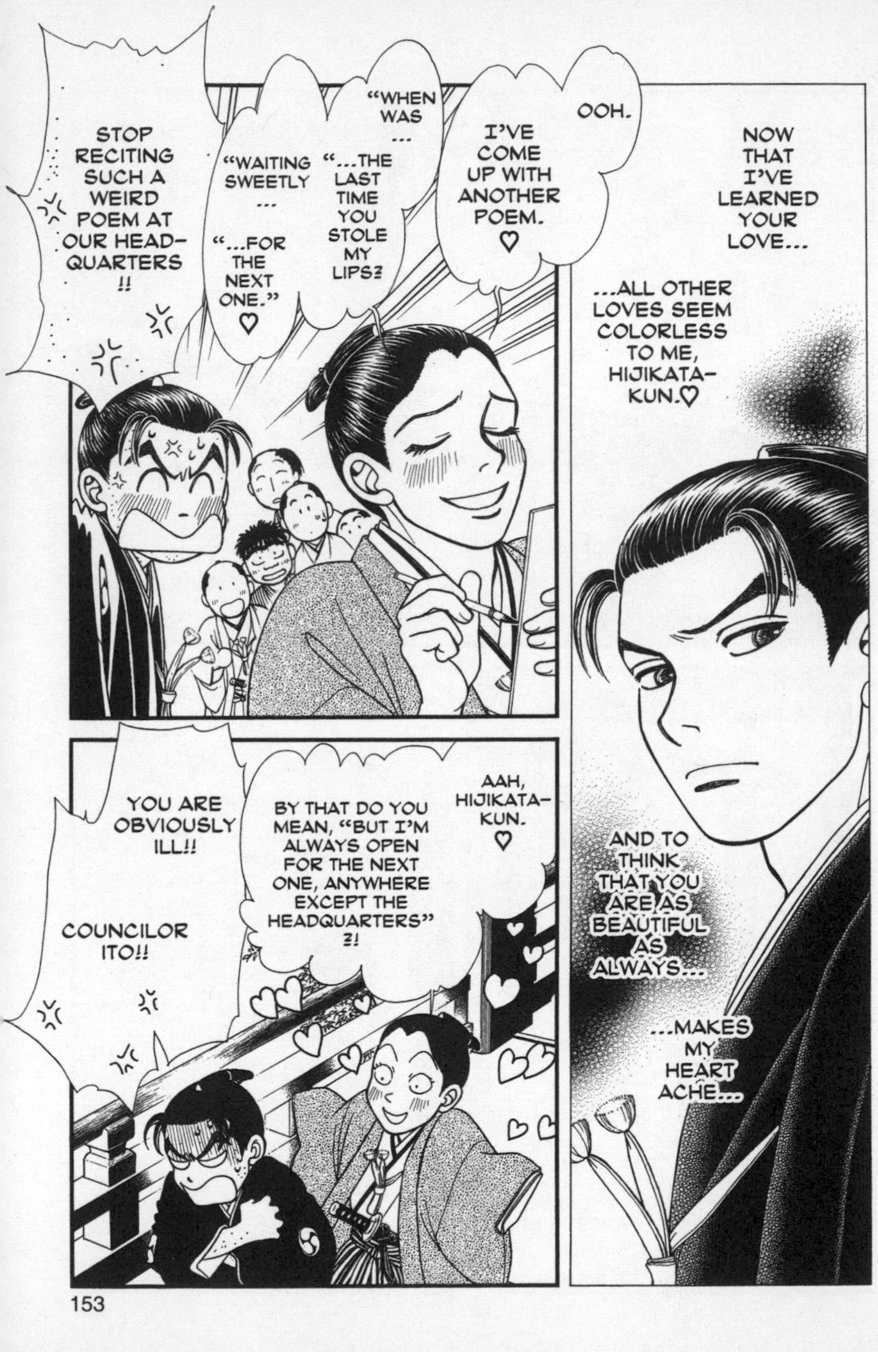
NOW THAT I'VE LEARNED YOUR LOVE...
...ALL OTHER LOVES SEEM COLORLESS TO ME, HIJIKATA-KUN.♡
AND TO THINK THAT YOU ARE AS BEAUTIFUL AS ALWAYS...
...MAKES MY HEART ACHE...
OOH.
I'VE COME UP WITH ANOTHER POEM. ♡
"WHEN WAS...
"...THE LAST TIME YOU STOLE MY LIPS?
"WAITING SWEETLY...
"...FOR THE NEXT ONE." ♡
STOP RECITING SUCH A WEIRD POEM AT OUR HEAD-QUARTERS!!
AAH, HIJIKATA-KUN. ♡
BY THAT DO YOU MEAN, "BUT I'M ALWAYS OPEN FOR THE NEXT ONE, ANYWHERE EXCEPT THE HEADQUARTERS"?!
YOU ARE OBVIOUSLY ILL!!
COUNCILOR ITO!!

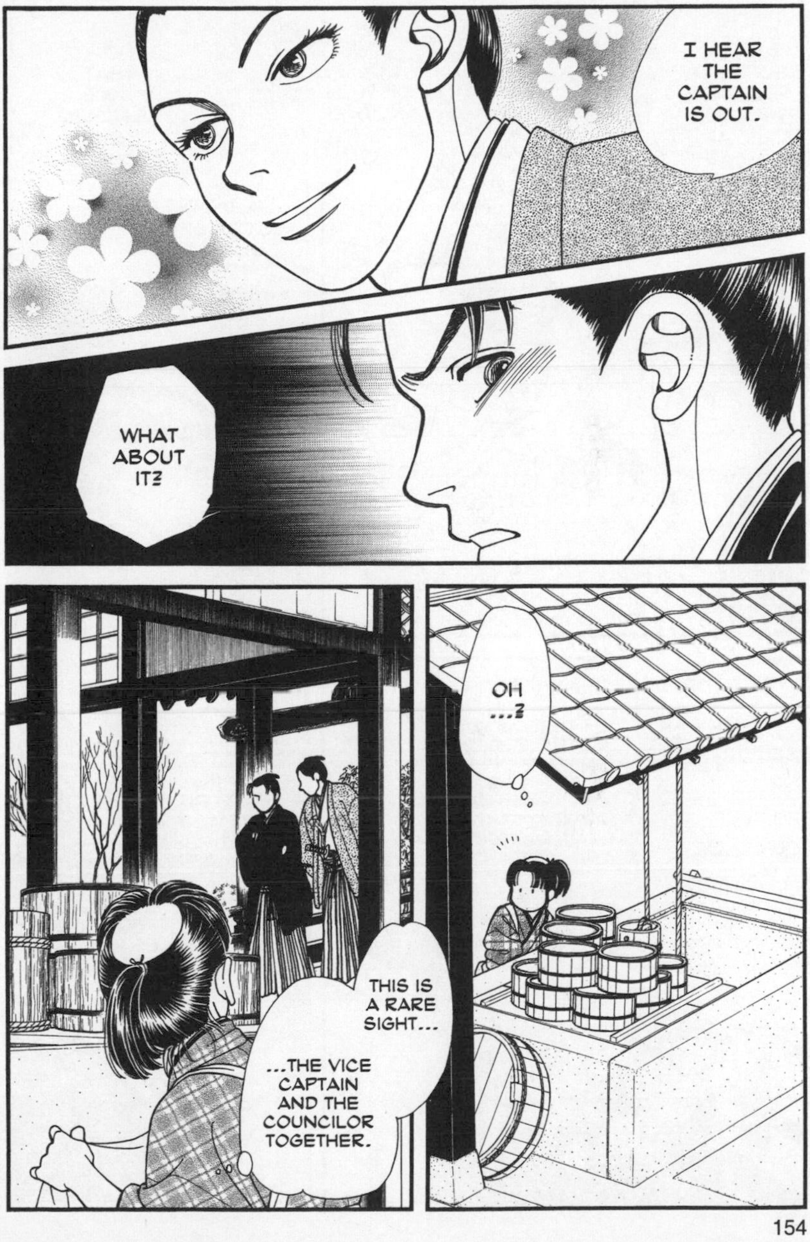
I HEAR THE CAPTAIN IS OUT.
WHAT ABOUT IT?
OH ...?
THIS IS A RARE SIGHT...
...THE VICE CAPTAIN AND THE COUNCILOR TOGETHER.

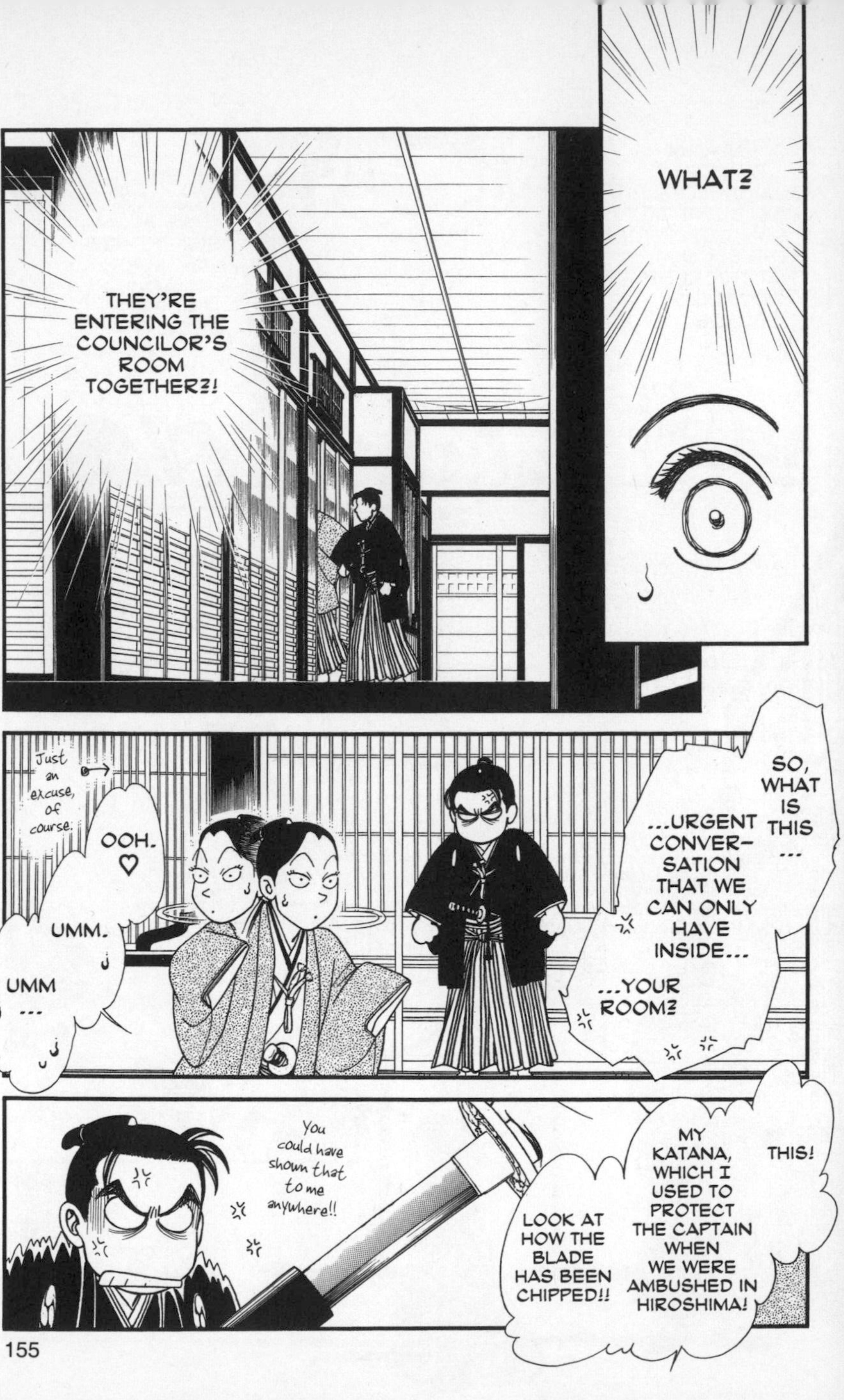
WHAT?
THEY'RE ENTERING THE COUNCILOR'S ROOM TOGETHER?!
SO, WHAT IS THIS ...
...URGENT CONVERSATION THAT WE CAN ONLY HAVE INSIDE...
...YOUR ROOM?
Just an excuse, of course.
OOH. ♡
UMM. UMM ...
THIS!
MY KATANA, WHICH I USED TO PROTECT THE CAPTAIN WHEN WE WERE AMBUSHED IN HIROSHIMA!
LOOK AT HOW THE BLADE HAS BEEN CHIPPED!!
You could have shown that to me anywhere!!

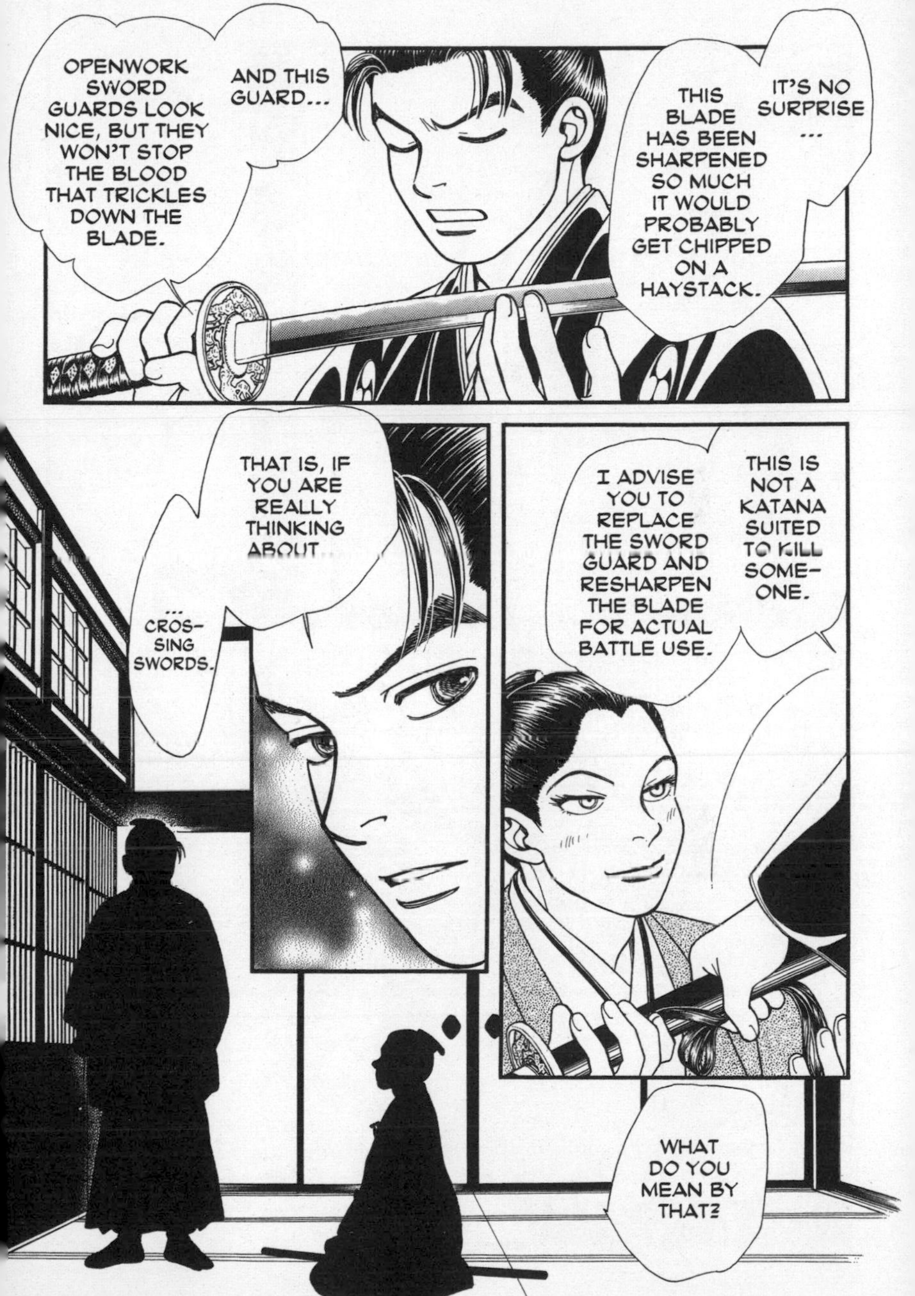
IT'S NO SURPRISE ...
THIS BLADE HAS BEEN SHARPENED SO MUCH IT WOULD PROBABLY GET CHIPPED ON A HAYSTACK.
AND THIS GUARD...
OPENWORK SWORD GUARDS LOOK NICE, BUT THEY WON'T STOP THE BLOOD THAT TRICKLES DOWN THE BLADE.
THIS IS NOT A KATANA SUITED TO KILL SOME-ONE.
I ADVISE YOU TO REPLACE THE SWORD GUARD AND RESHARPEN THE BLADE FOR ACTUAL BATTLE USE.
THAT IS, IF YOU ARE REALLY THINKING ABOUT...
... CROS-SING SWORDS.
WHAT DO YOU MEAN BY THAT?

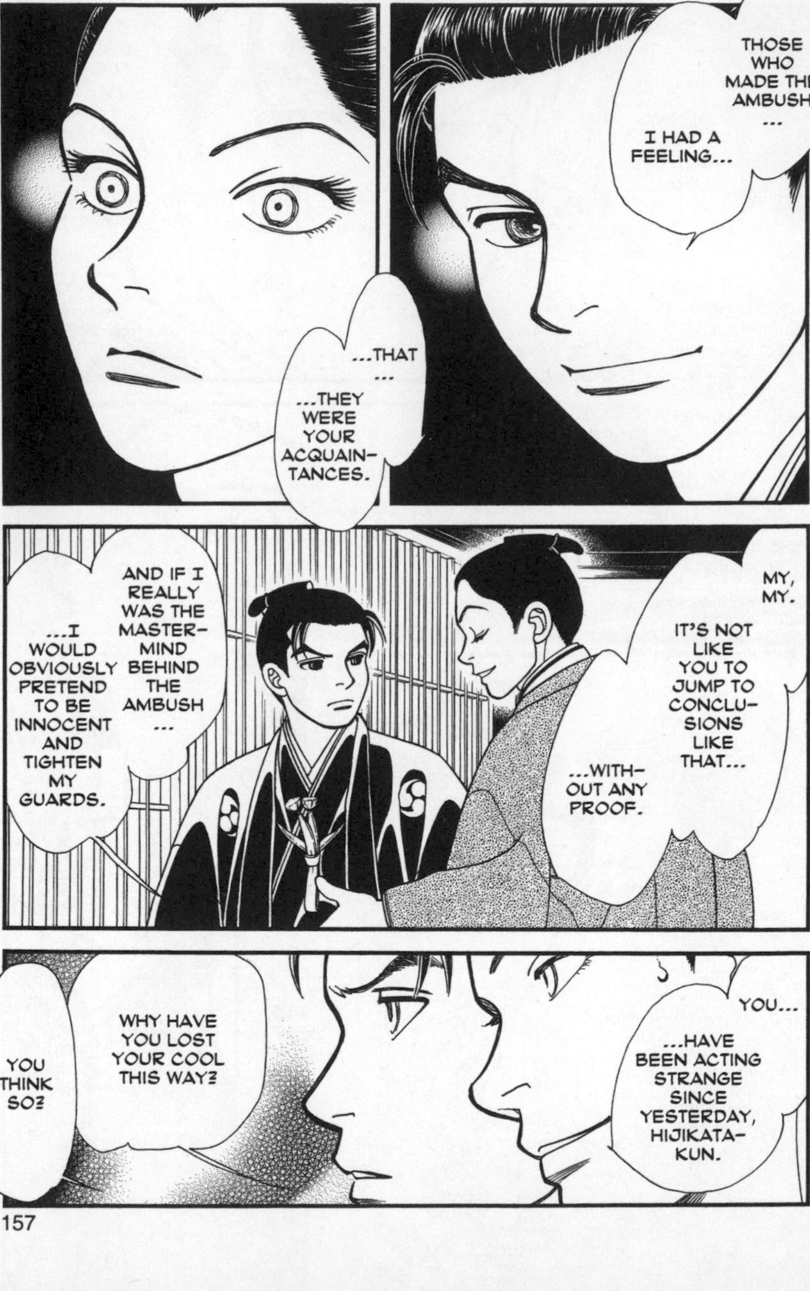
THOSE WHO MADE THE AMBUSH ...
I HAD A FEELING...
...THAT ...
...THEY WERE YOUR ACQUAINTANCES.
MY, MY.
IT'S NOT LIKE YOU TO JUMP TO CONCLUSIONS LIKE THAT...
...WITHOUT ANY PROOF.
AND IF I REALLY WAS THE MASTERMIND BEHIND THE AMBUSH ...
...I WOULD OBVIOUSLY PRETEND TO BE INNOCENT AND TIGHTEN MY GUARDS.
YOU...
...HAVE BEEN ACTING STRANGE SINCE YESTERDAY, HIJIKATA-KUN.
WHY HAVE YOU LOST YOUR COOL THIS WAY?
YOU THINK SO?

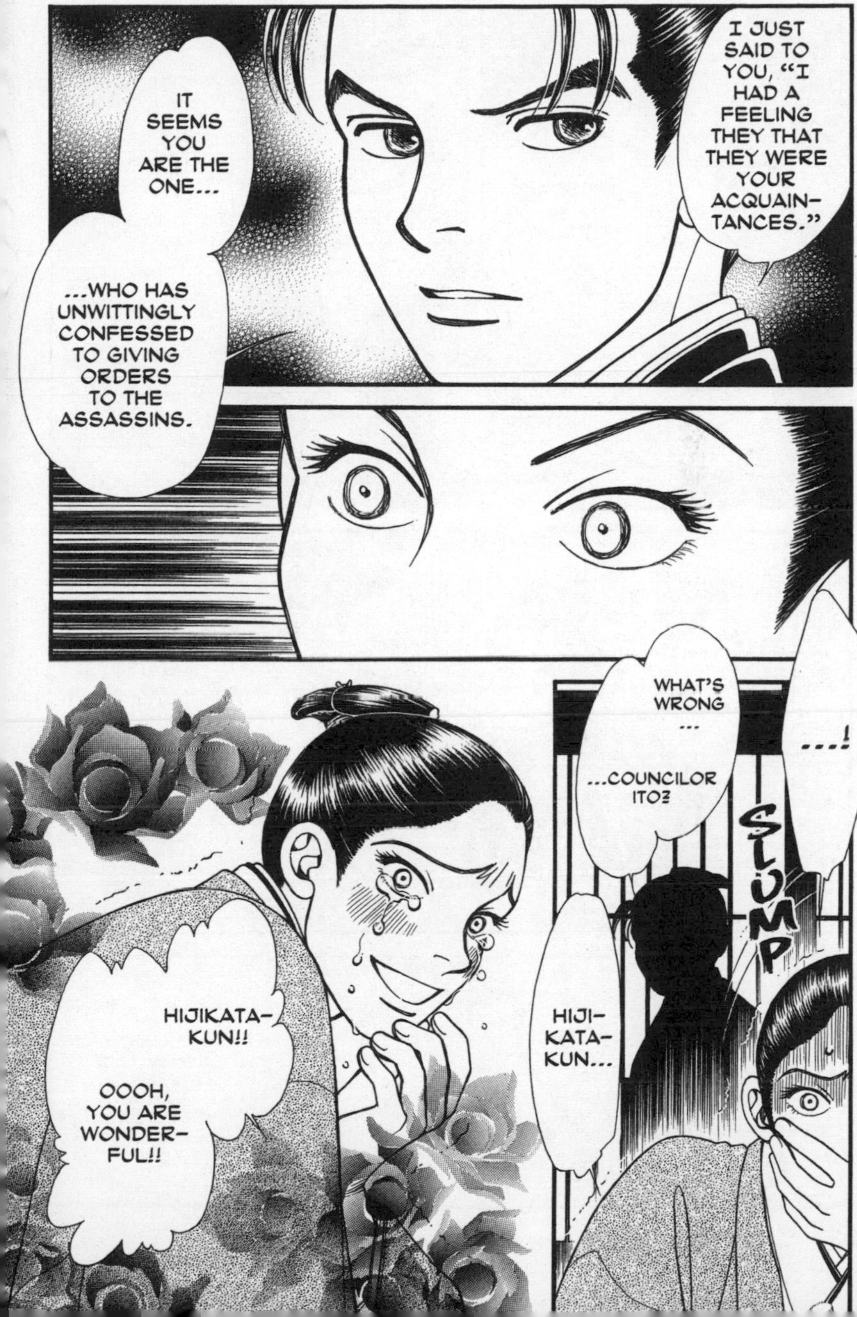
I JUST SAID TO YOU, "I HAD A FEELING THEY THAT THEY WERE YOUR ACQUAINTANCES."
IT SEEMS YOU ARE THE ONE...
...WHO HAS UNWITTINGLY CONFESSED TO GIVING ORDERS TO THE ASSASSINS.
...!
WHAT'S WRONG ...
...COUNCILOR ITO?
SLUMP
HIJI-KATA-KUN...
HIJIKATA-KUN!!
OOOH, YOU ARE WONDERFUL!!

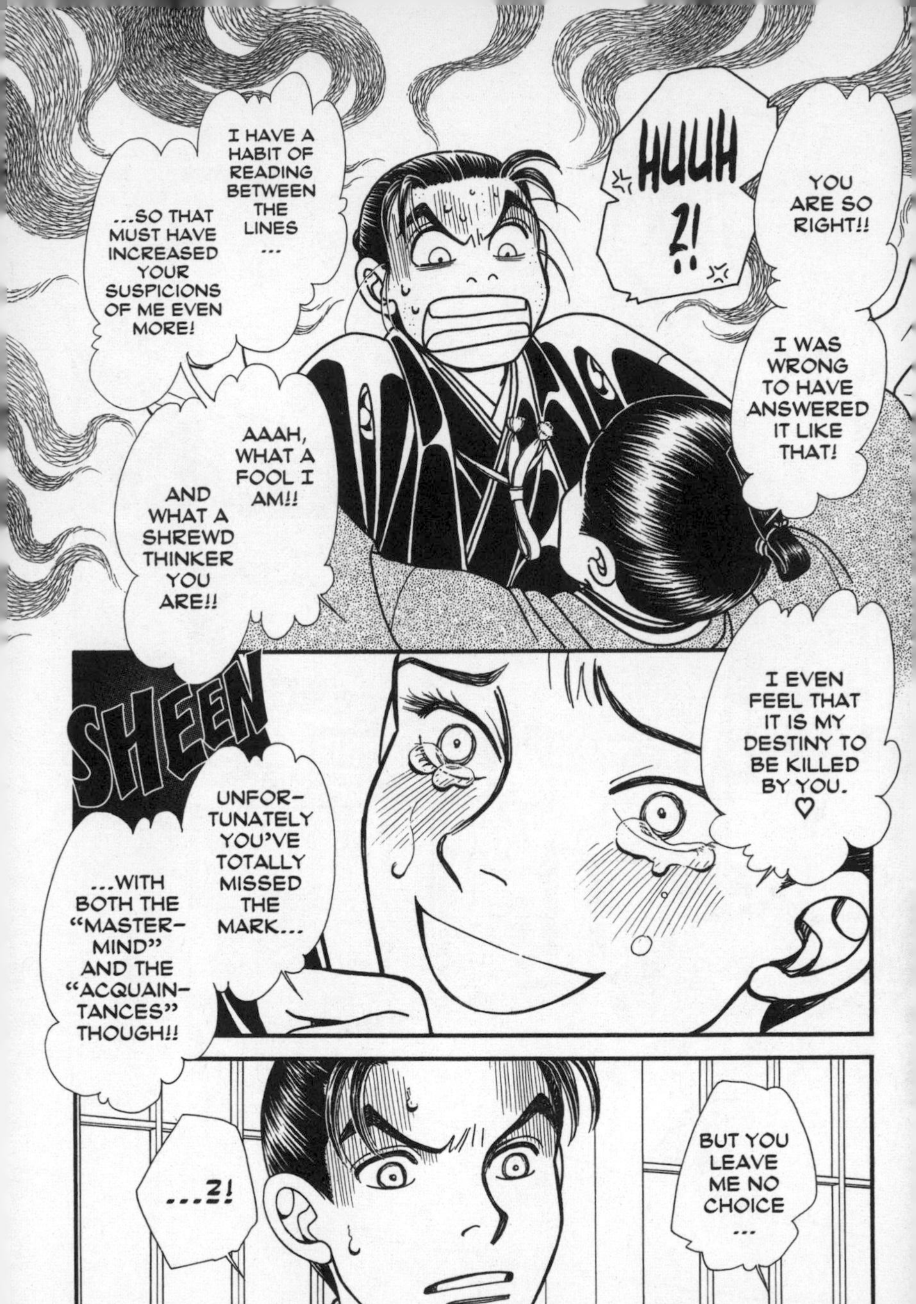
YOU ARE SO RIGHT!!
HUUH ?!
I WAS WRONG TO HAVE ANSWERED IT LIKE THAT!
I HAVE A HABIT OF READING BETWEEN THE LINES...
...SO THAT MUST HAVE INCREASED YOUR SUSPICIONS OF ME EVEN MORE!
AAAH, WHAT A FOOL I AM!!
AND WHAT A SHREWD THINKER YOU ARE!!
I EVEN FEEL THAT IT IS MY DESTINY TO BE KILLED BY YOU. ♥
SHEEN
UNFORTUNATELY YOU'VE TOTALLY MISSED THE MARK...
...WITH BOTH THE "MASTERMIND" AND THE "ACQUAINTANCES" THOUGH!!
BUT YOU LEAVE ME NO CHOICE...
...?!

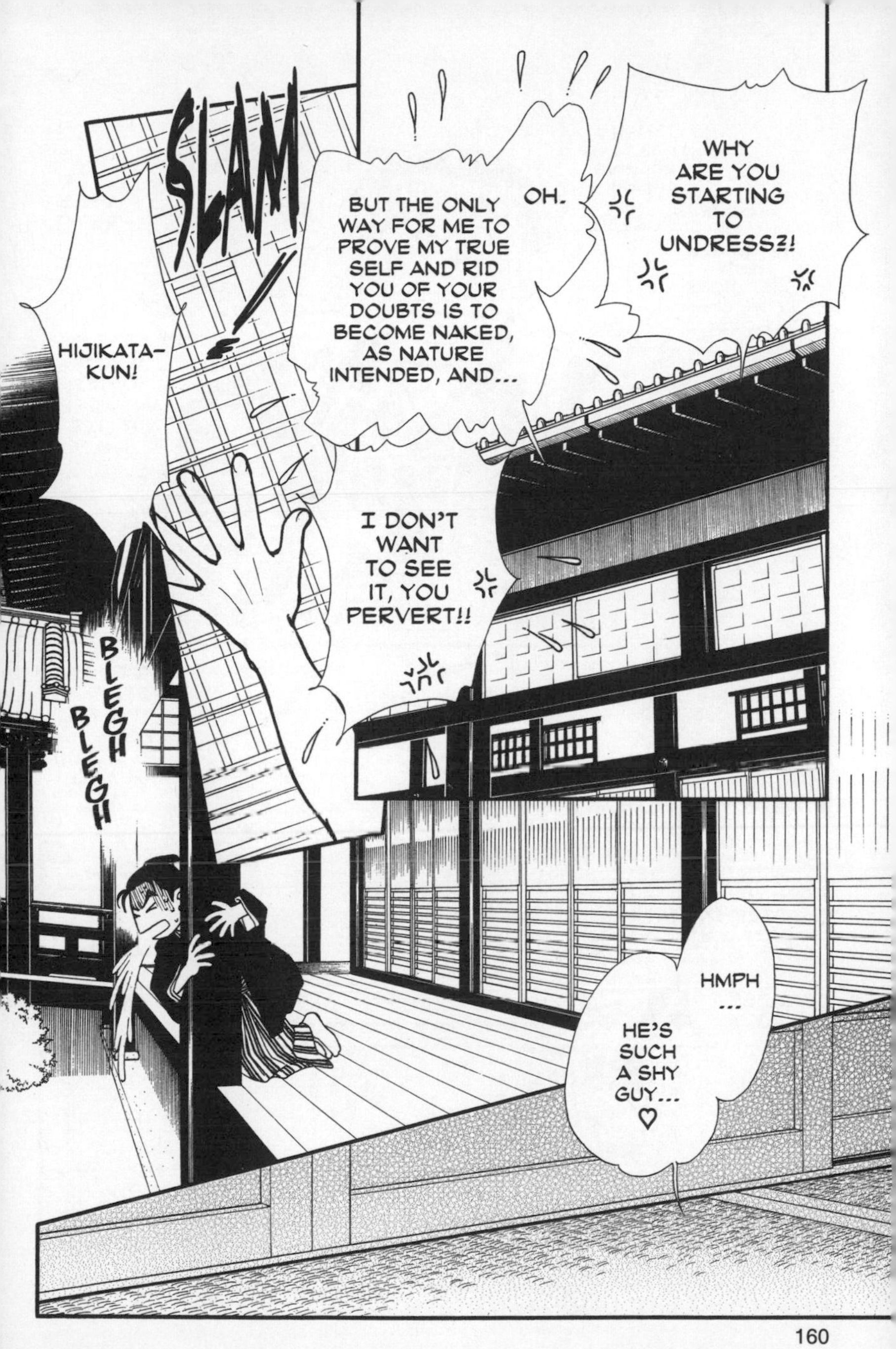
WHY ARE YOU STARTING TO UNDRESS?!
OH.
BUT THE ONLY WAY FOR ME TO PROVE MY TRUE SELF AND RID YOU OF YOUR DOUBTS IS TO BECOME NAKED, AS NATURE INTENDED, AND...
I DON'T WANT TO SEE IT, YOU PERVERT!!
SLAM
HIJIKATA-KUN!
BLEGH BLEGH
HMPH ... HE'S SUCH A SHY GUY... ♡

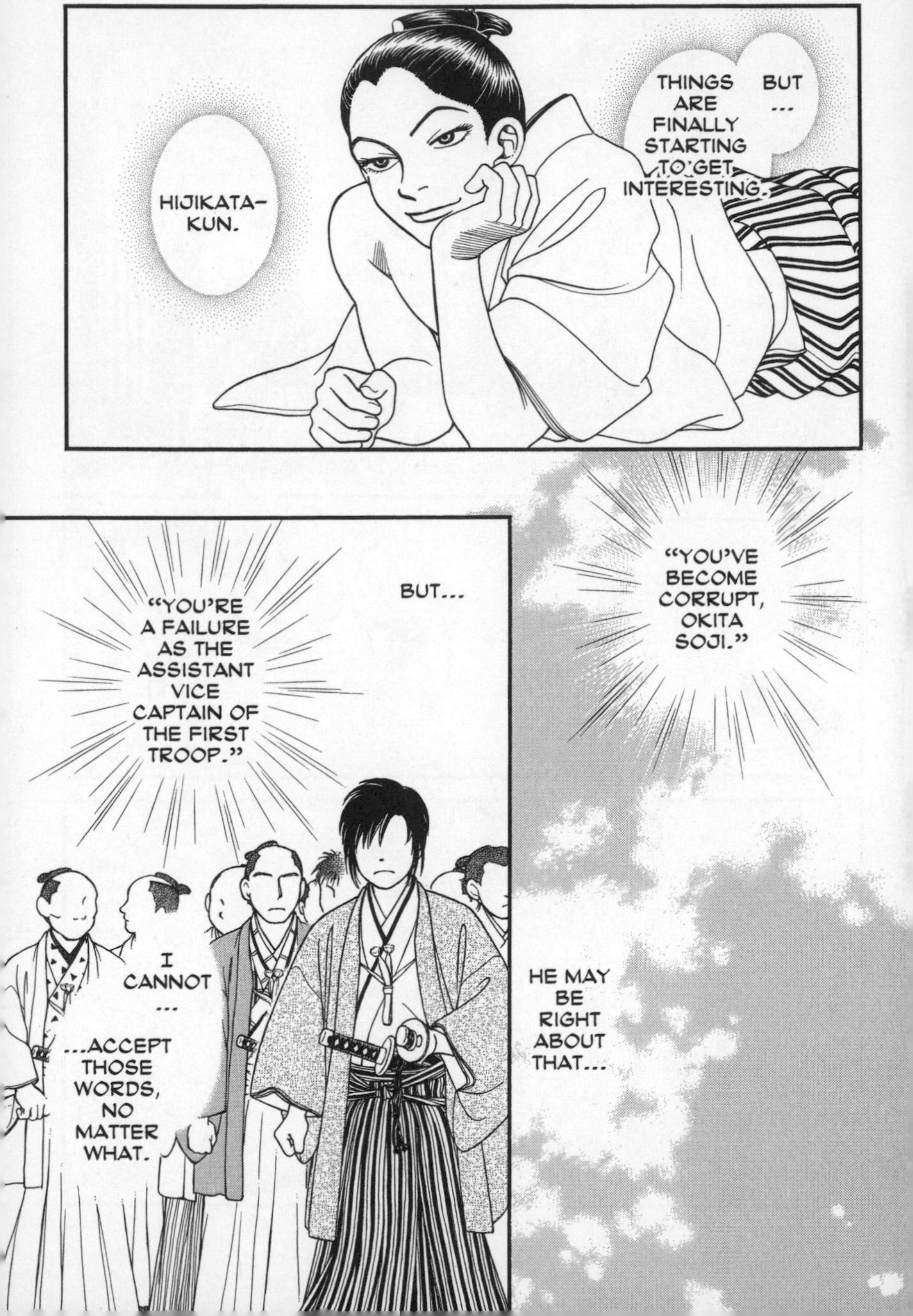
BUT ...
THINGS ARE FINALLY STARTING TO GET INTERESTING.
HIJIKATA-KUN.
"YOU'VE BECOME CORRUPT, OKITA SOJI."
HE MAY BE RIGHT ABOUT THAT...
BUT...
"YOU'RE A FAILURE AS THE ASSISTANT VICE CAPTAIN OF THE FIRST TROOP."
I CANNOT ...
...ACCEPT THOSE WORDS, NO MATTER WHAT.

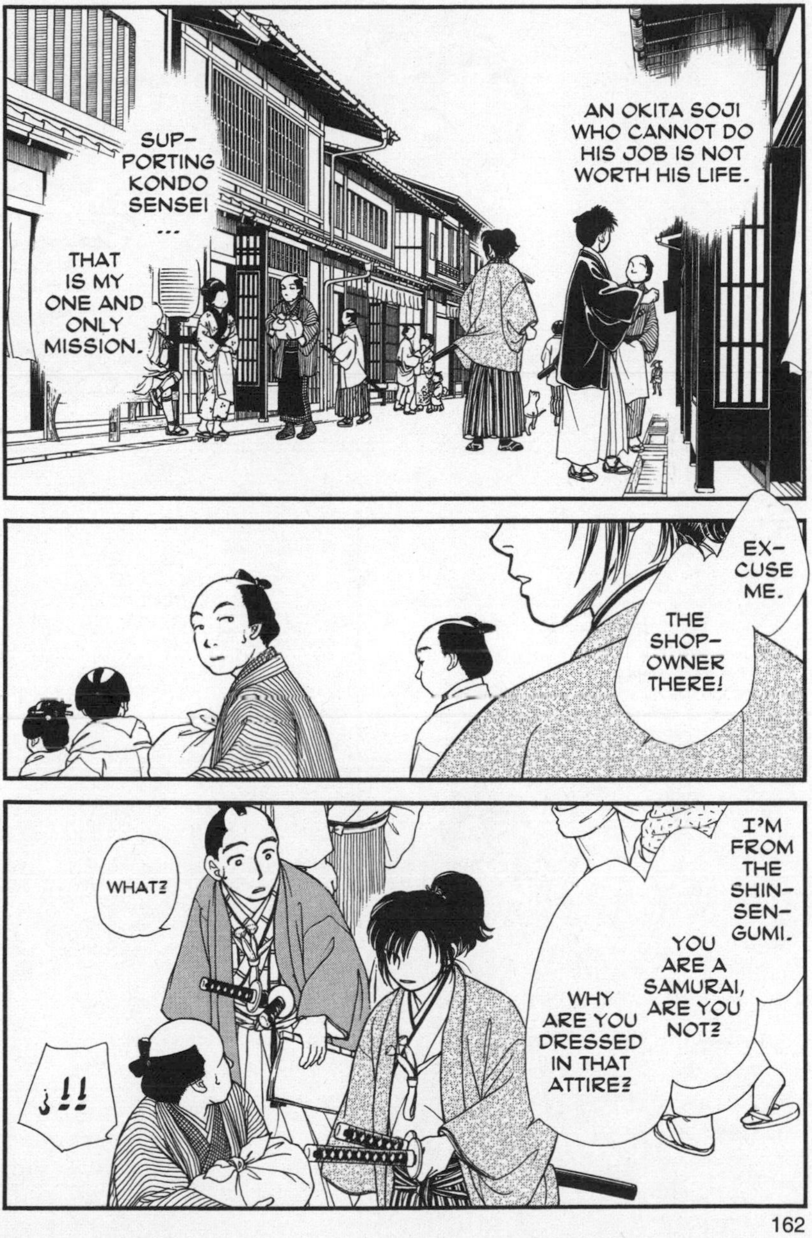
AN OKITA SOJI WHO CANNOT DO HIS JOB IS NOT WORTH HIS LIFE.
SUPPORTING KONDO SENSEI...
THAT IS MY ONE AND ONLY MISSION.
EXCUSE ME.
THE SHOPOWNER THERE!
I'M FROM THE SHINSENGUMI.
YOU ARE A SAMURAI, ARE YOU NOT?
WHY ARE YOU DRESSED IN THAT ATTIRE?
WHAT?
¿!!

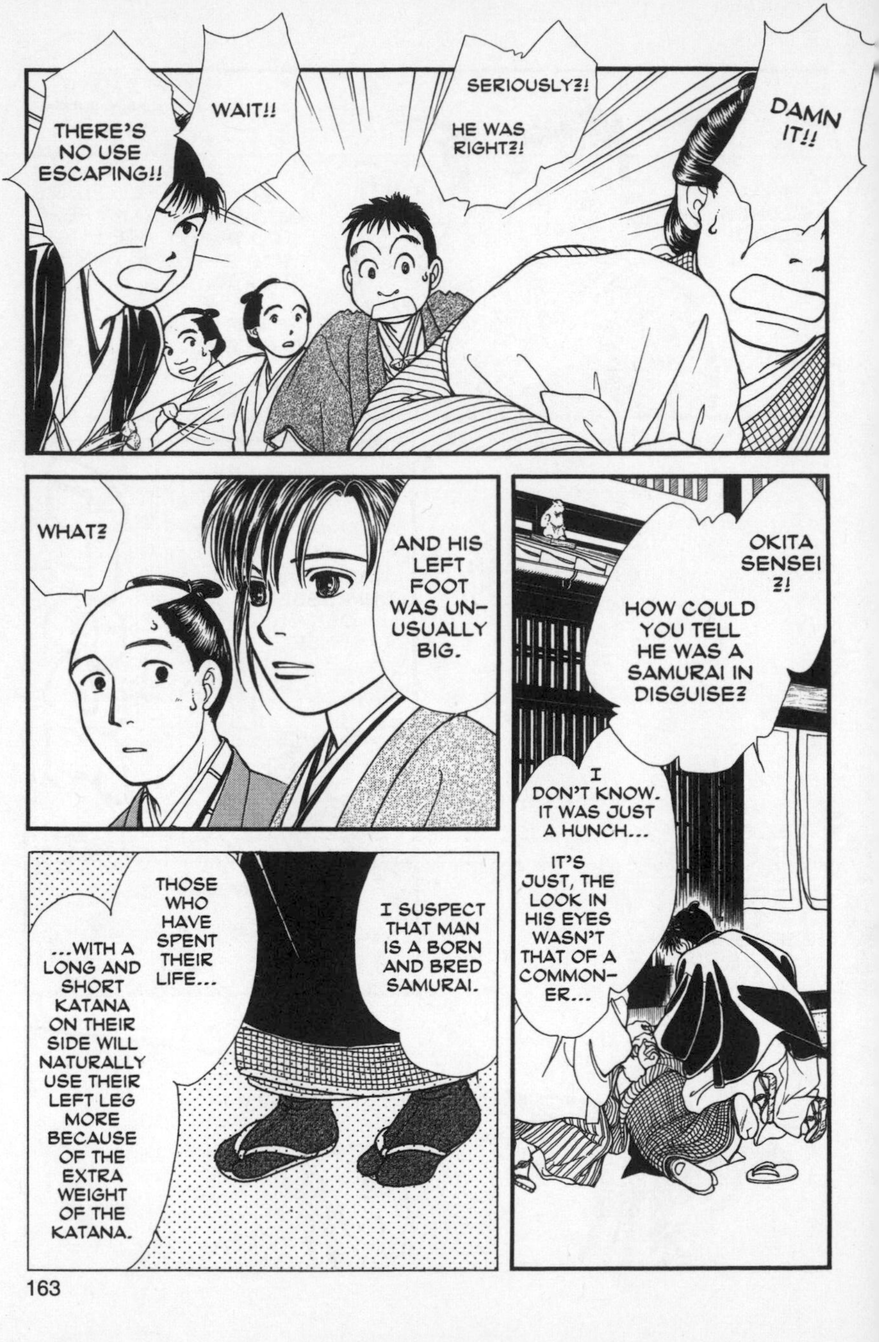
DAMN IT!!
SERIOUSLY?!
HE WAS RIGHT?!
WAIT!!
THERE'S NO USE ESCAPING!!
OKITA SENSEI?!
HOW COULD YOU TELL HE WAS A SAMURAI IN DISGUISE?
I DON'T KNOW. IT WAS JUST A HUNCH...
IT'S JUST, THE LOOK IN HIS EYES WASN'T THAT OF A COMMONER...
AND HIS LEFT FOOT WAS UNUSUALLY BIG.
WHAT?
I SUSPECT THAT MAN IS A BORN AND BRED SAMURAI.
THOSE WHO HAVE SPENT THEIR LIFE...
...WITH A LONG AND SHORT KATANA ON THEIR SIDE WILL NATURALLY USE THEIR LEFT LEG MORE BECAUSE OF THE EXTRA WEIGHT OF THE KATANA.

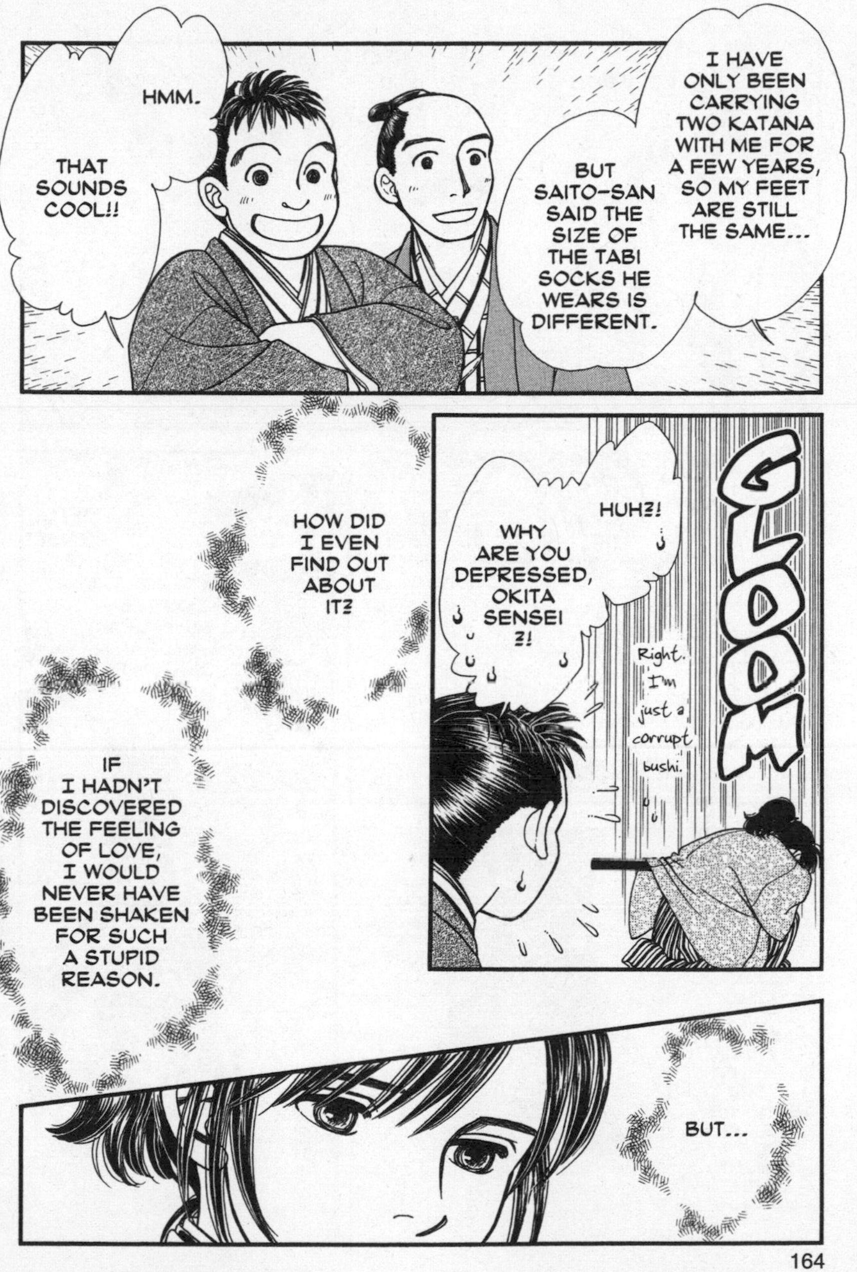
I HAVE ONLY BEEN CARRYING TWO KATANA WITH ME FOR A FEW YEARS, SO MY FEET ARE STILL THE SAME...
BUT SAITO-SAN SAID THE SIZE OF THE TABI SOCKS HE WEARS IS DIFFERENT.
HMM.
THAT SOUNDS COOL!!
GLOOM
Right. I'm just a corrupt bushi.
HUH?!
WHY ARE YOU DEPRESSED, OKITA SENSEI?!
HOW DID I EVEN FIND OUT ABOUT IT?
IF I HADN'T DISCOVERED THE FEELING OF LOVE, I WOULD NEVER HAVE BEEN SHAKEN FOR SUCH A STUPID REASON.
BUT...

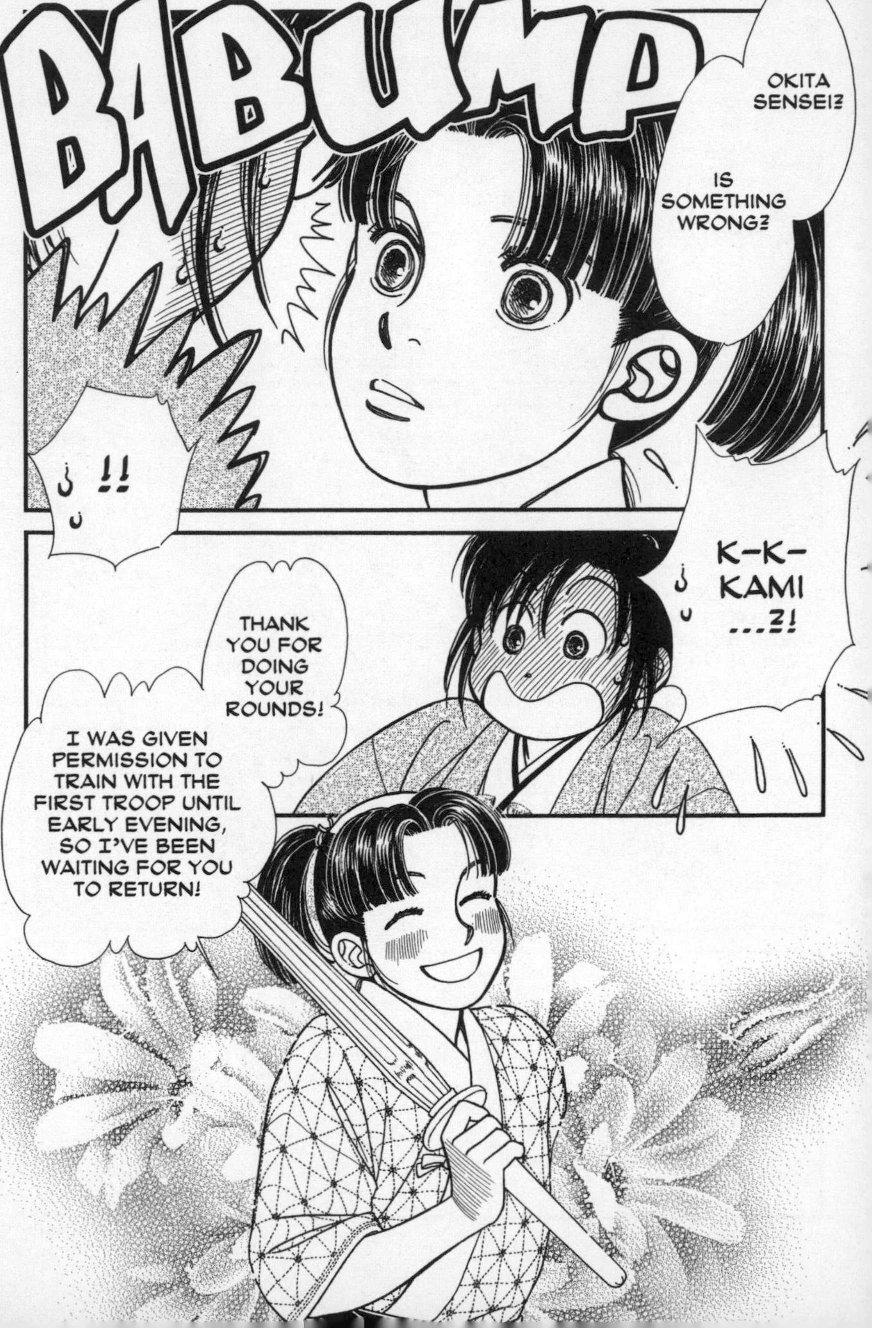
OKITA SENSEI?
IS SOMETHING WRONG?
BABUMP
!!
K-K-KAMI ...?!
THANK YOU FOR DOING YOUR ROUNDS!
I WAS GIVEN PERMISSION TO TRAIN WITH THE FIRST TROOP UNTIL EARLY EVENING, SO I'VE BEEN WAITING FOR YOU TO RETURN!

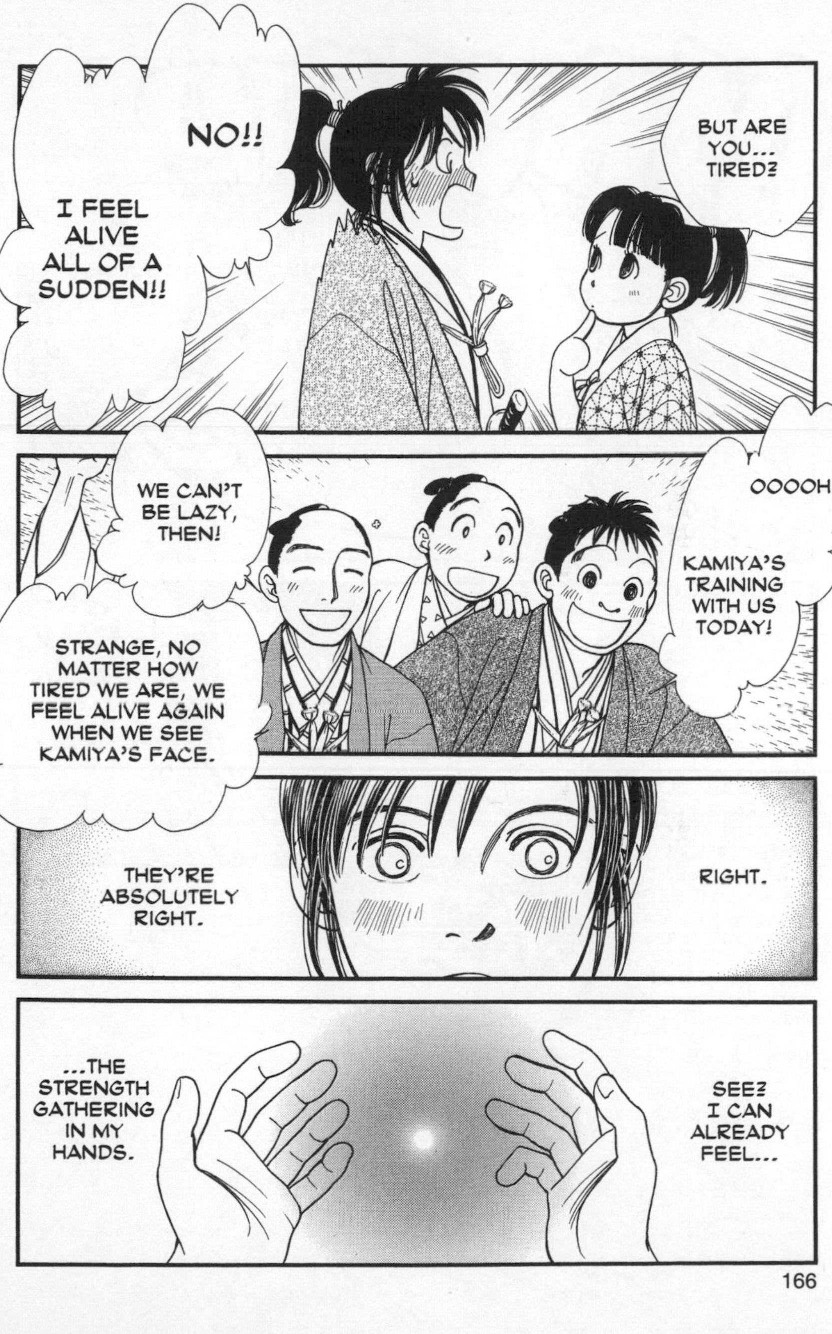
BUT ARE YOU... TIRED?
NO!!
I FEEL ALIVE ALL OF A SUDDEN!!
OOOOH.
KAMIYA'S TRAINING WITH US TODAY!
WE CAN'T BE LAZY, THEN!
STRANGE, NO MATTER HOW TIRED WE ARE, WE FEEL ALIVE AGAIN WHEN WE SEE KAMIYA'S FACE.
RIGHT.
THEY'RE ABSOLUTELY RIGHT.
SEE? I CAN ALREADY FEEL...
...THE STRENGTH GATHERING IN MY HANDS.

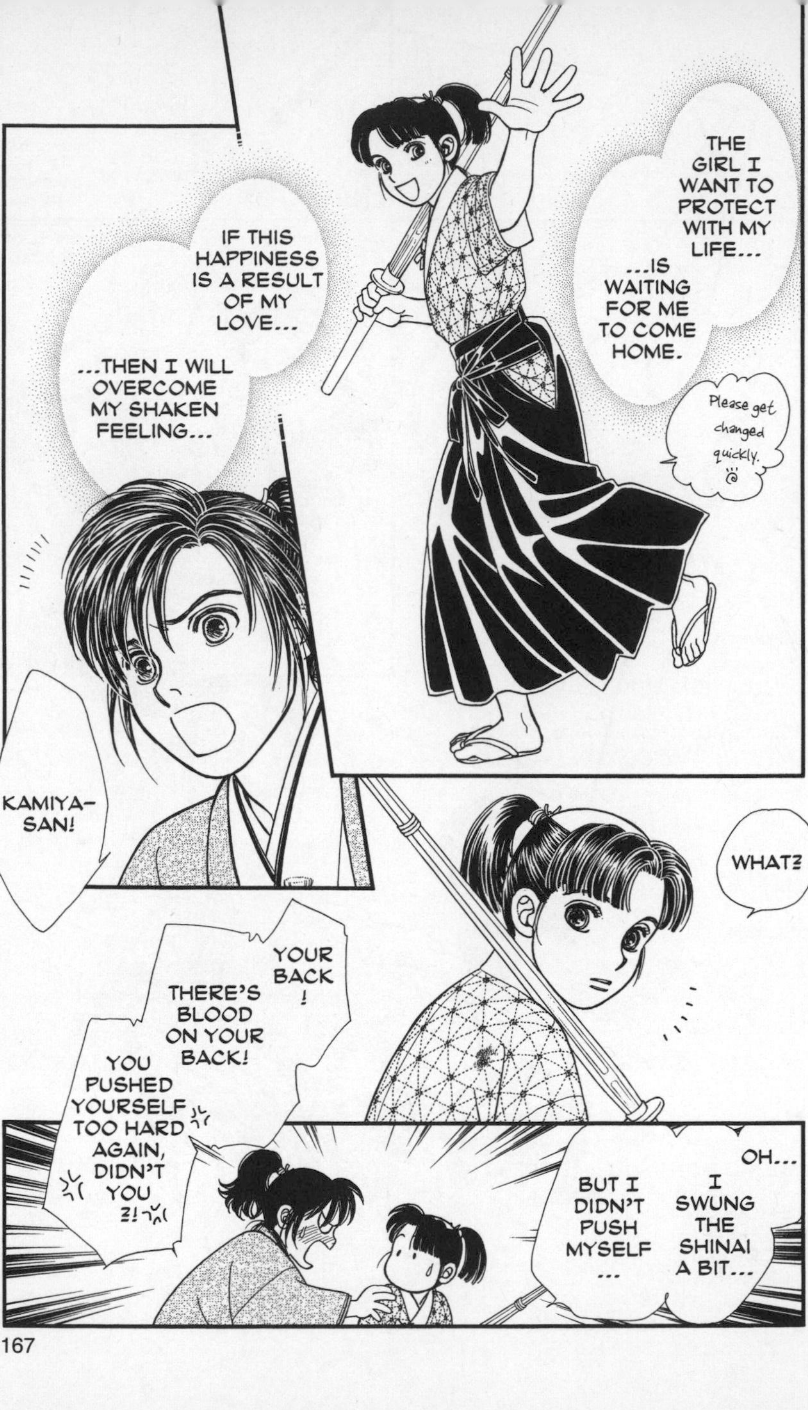
THE GIRL I WANT TO PROTECT WITH MY LIFE...
...IS WAITING FOR ME TO COME HOME.
Please get changed quickly.
IF THIS HAPPINESS IS A RESULT OF MY LOVE...
...THEN I WILL OVERCOME MY SHAKEN FEELING...
KAMIYA-SAN!
WHAT?
YOUR BACK!
THERE'S BLOOD ON YOUR BACK!
OH... I SWUNG THE SHINAI A BIT...
BUT I DIDN'T PUSH MYSELF...
YOU PUSHED YOURSELF TOO HARD AGAIN, DIDN'T YOU?!

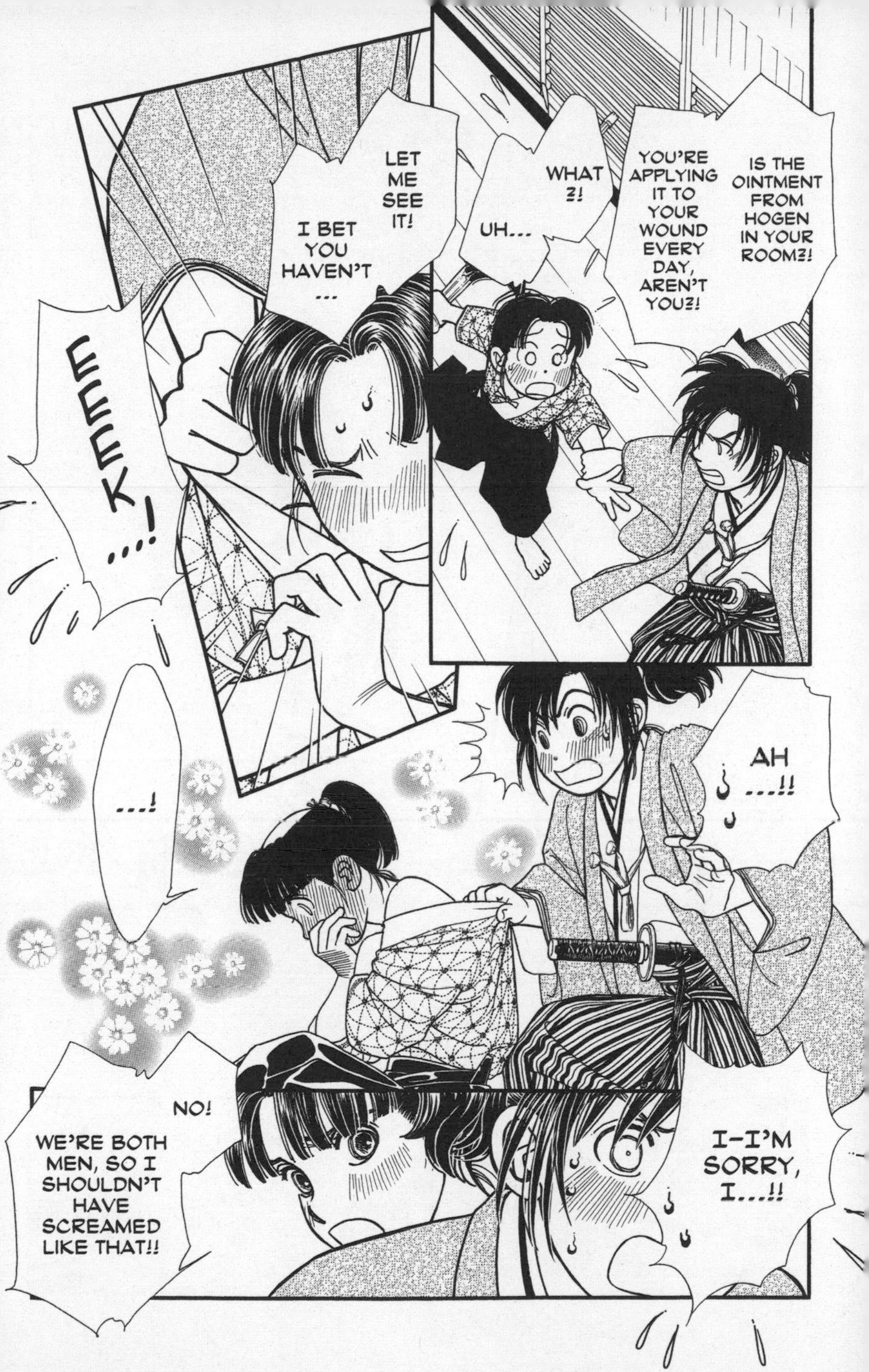
IS THE OINTMENT FROM HOGEN IN YOUR ROOM?!
YOU'RE APPLYING IT TO YOUR WOUND EVERY DAY, AREN'T YOU?!
WHAT?!
UH...
LET ME SEE IT!
I BET YOU HAVEN'T ...
EEEK...!
AH ...!!
...!
I-I'M SORRY, I...!!
NO!
WE'RE BOTH MEN, SO I SHOULDN'T HAVE SCREAMED LIKE THAT!!

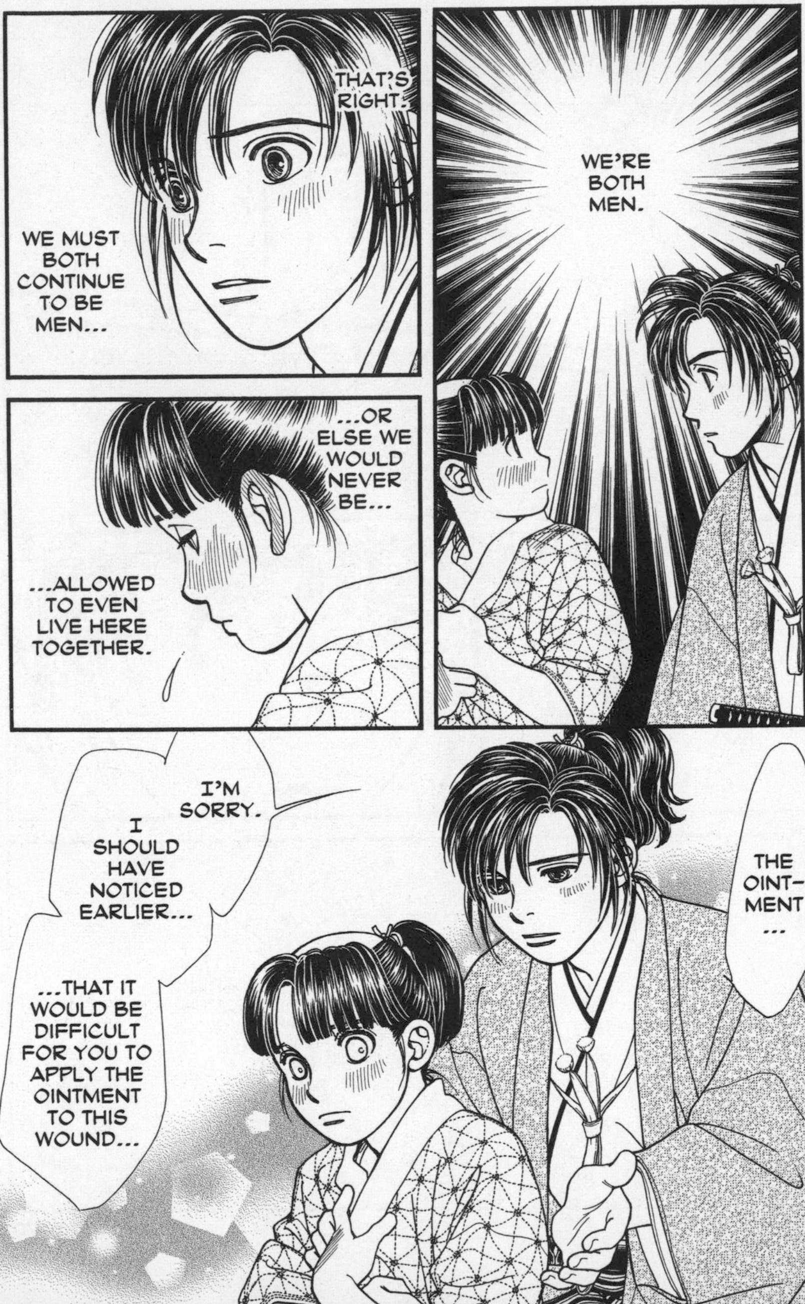
WE'RE BOTH MEN.
THAT'S RIGHT.
WE MUST BOTH CONTINUE TO BE MEN...
...OR ELSE WE WOULD NEVER BE...
...ALLOWED TO EVEN LIVE HERE TOGETHER.
THE OINT-MENT...
I'M SORRY.
I SHOULD HAVE NOTICED EARLIER...
...THAT IT WOULD BE DIFFICULT FOR YOU TO APPLY THE OINTMENT TO THIS WOUND...

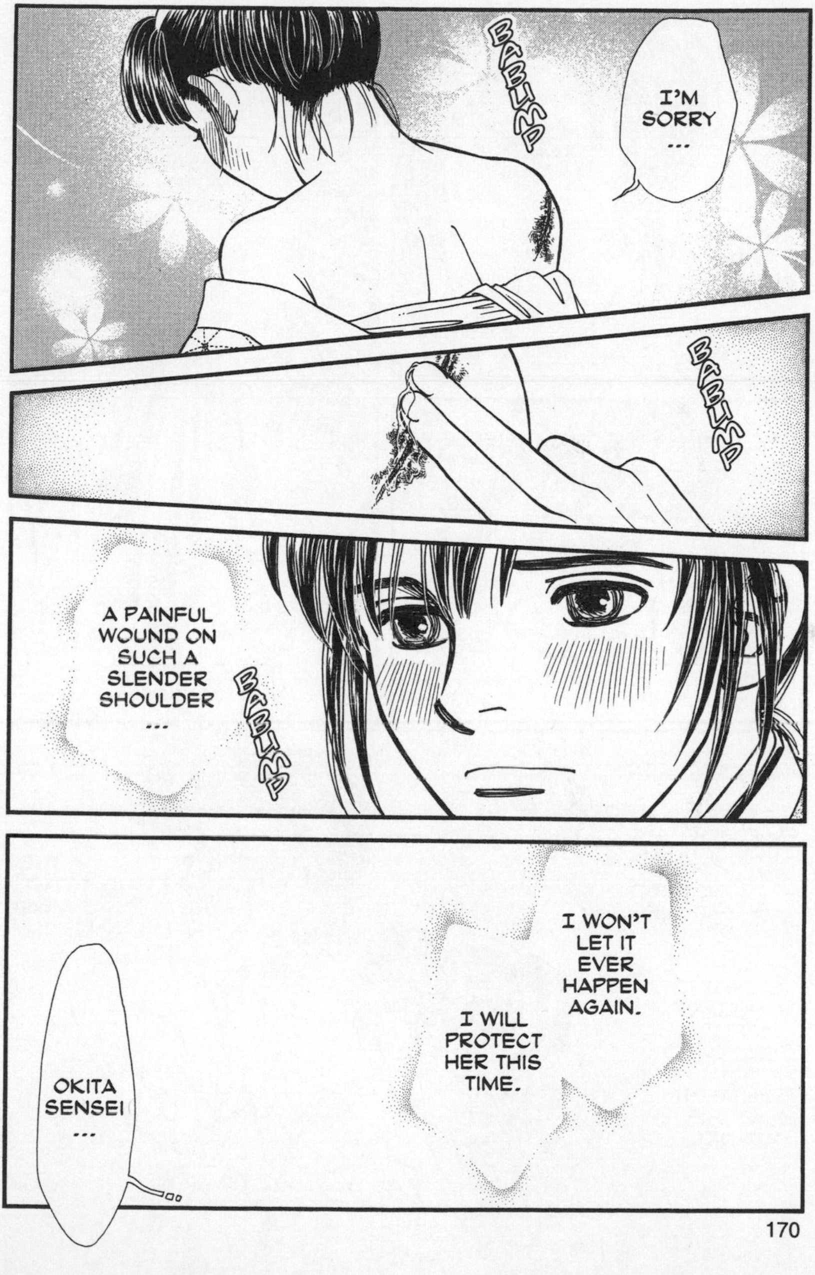

I'M SORRY ...
BABUMP
BABUMP
A PAINFUL WOUND ON SUCH A SLENDER SHOULDER ...
BABUMP
I WON'T LET IT EVER HAPPEN AGAIN.
I WILL PROTECT HER THIS TIME.
OKITA SENSEI ...

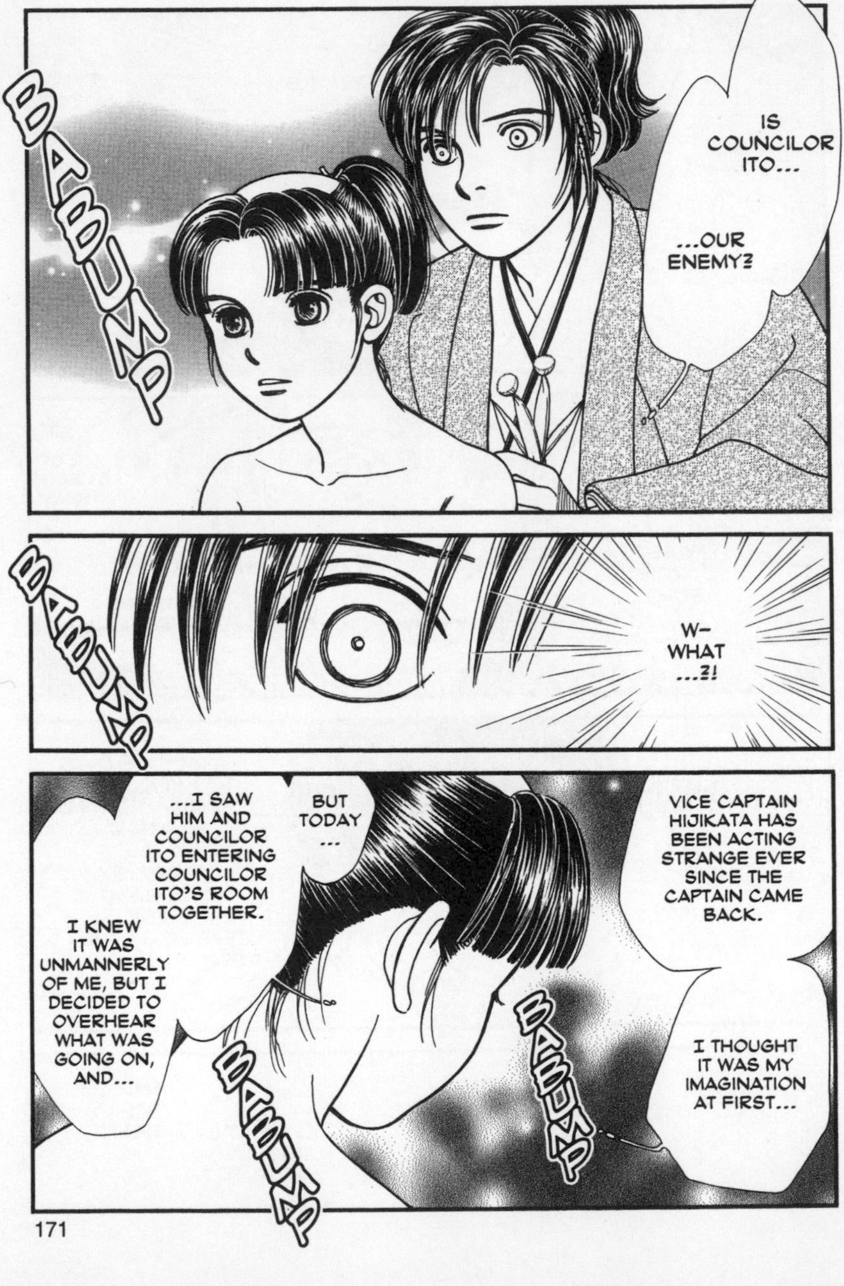
IS COUNCILOR ITO...
...OUR ENEMY?
BABUMP
W-WHAT ...?!
BABUMP
VICE CAPTAIN HIJIKATA HAS BEEN ACTING STRANGE EVER SINCE THE CAPTAIN CAME BACK.
I THOUGHT IT WAS MY IMAGINATION AT FIRST...
BABUMP
BUT TODAY ...
...I SAW HIM AND COUNCILOR ITO ENTERING COUNCILOR ITO'S ROOM TOGETHER.
I KNEW IT WAS UNMANNERLY OF ME, BUT I DECIDED TO OVERHEAR WHAT WAS GOING ON, AND...
BABUMP

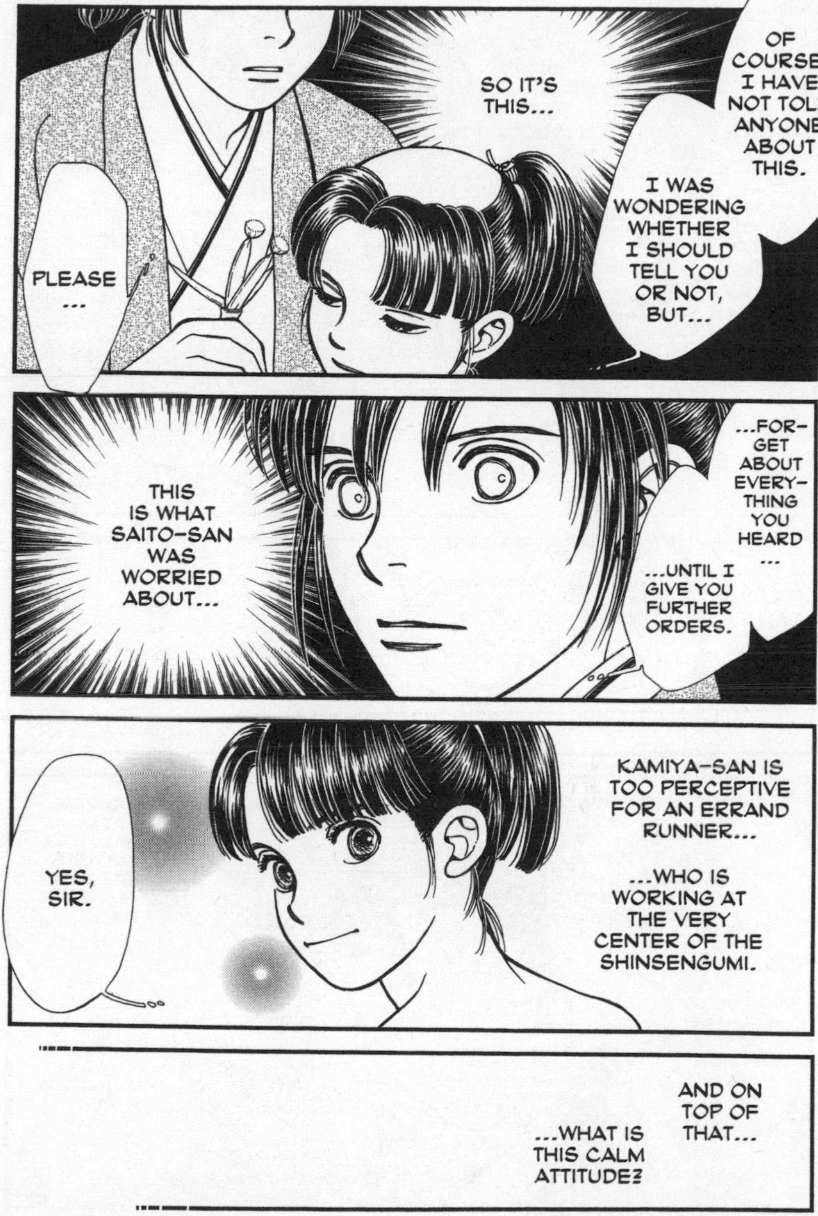
OF COURSE, I HAVE NOT TOLD ANYONE ABOUT THIS.
I WAS WONDERING WHETHER I SHOULD TELL YOU OR NOT, BUT...
SO IT'S THIS...
PLEASE ...
...FOR-GET ABOUT EVERY-THING YOU HEARD ...
...UNTIL I GIVE YOU FURTHER ORDERS.
THIS IS WHAT SAITO-SAN WAS WORRIED ABOUT...
KAMIYA-SAN IS TOO PERCEPTIVE FOR AN ERRAND RUNNER...
...WHO IS WORKING AT THE VERY CENTER OF THE SHINSENGUMI.
YES, SIR.
AND ON TOP OF THAT...
...WHAT IS THIS CALM ATTITUDE?

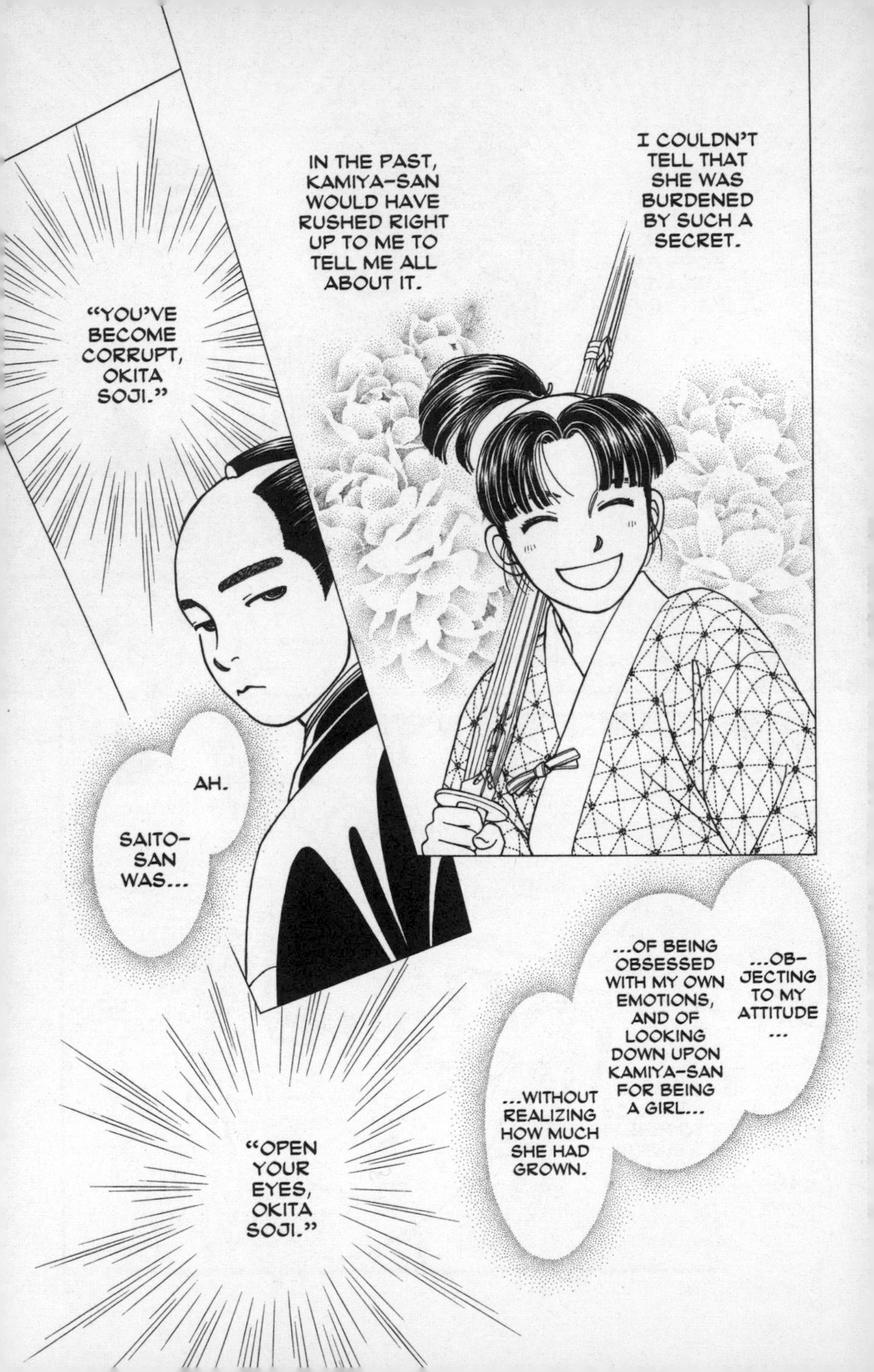
I COULDN'T TELL THAT SHE WAS BURDENED BY SUCH A SECRET.
IN THE PAST, KAMIYA-SAN WOULD HAVE RUSHED RIGHT UP TO ME TO TELL ME ALL ABOUT IT.
"YOU'VE BECOME CORRUPT, OKITA SOJI."
AH.
SAITO-SAN WAS...
...OB-JECTING TO MY ATTITUDE...
...OF BEING OBSESSED WITH MY OWN EMOTIONS, AND OF LOOKING DOWN UPON KAMIYA-SAN FOR BEING A GIRL...
...WITHOUT REALIZING HOW MUCH SHE HAD GROWN.
"OPEN YOUR EYES, OKITA SOJI."

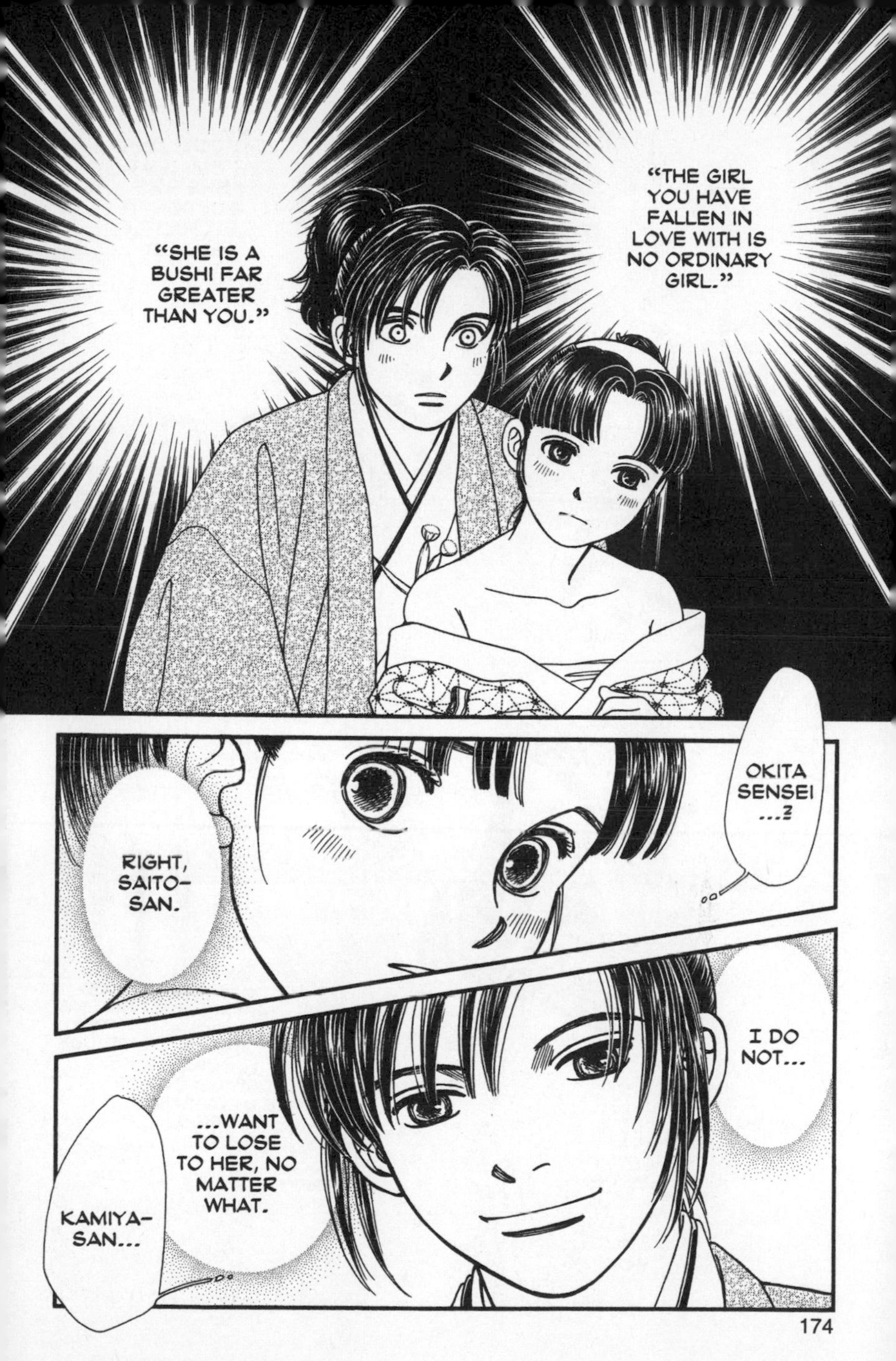
"THE GIRL YOU HAVE FALLEN IN LOVE WITH IS NO ORDINARY GIRL."
"SHE IS A BUSHI FAR GREATER THAN YOU."
OKITA SENSEI ...?
RIGHT, SAITO-SAN.
I DO NOT...
...WANT TO LOSE TO HER, NO MATTER WHAT.
KAMIYA-SAN...

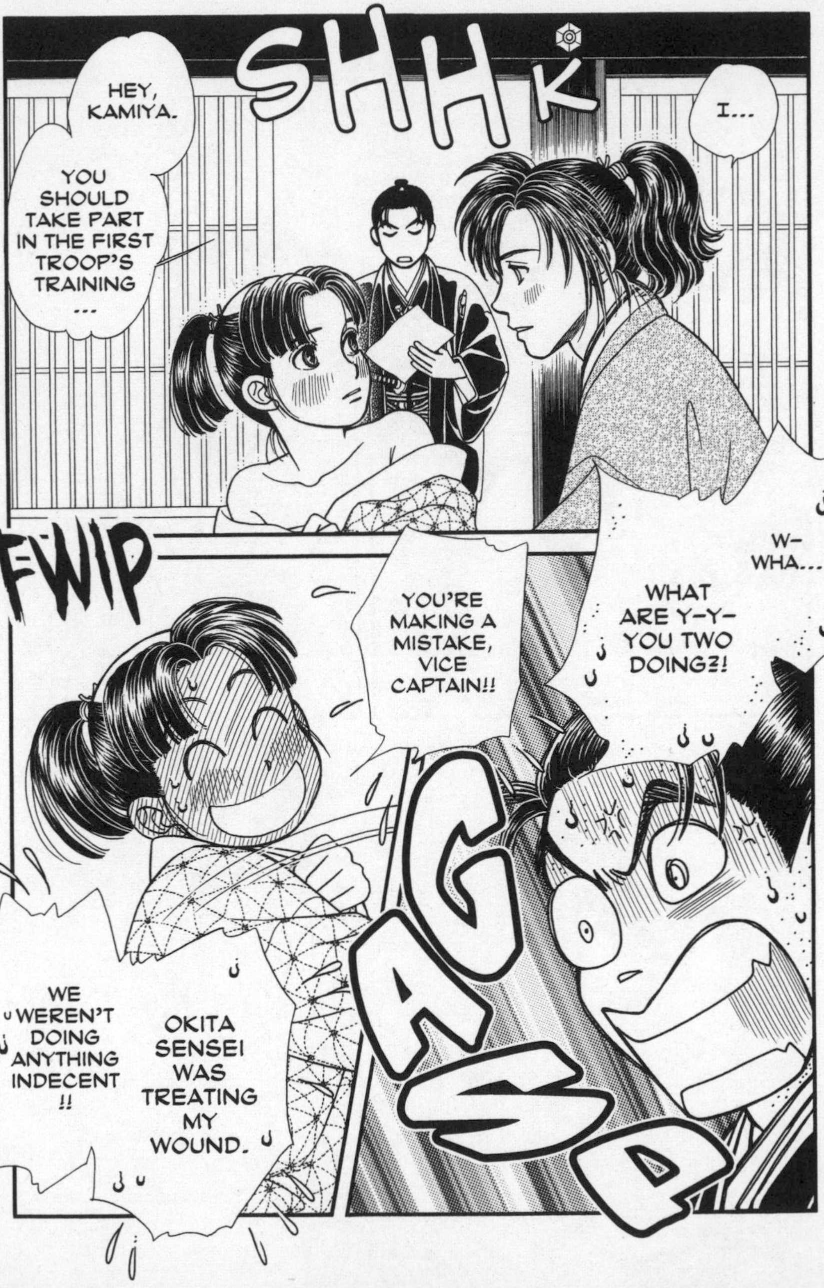
I...
SHHK
HEY, KAMIYA.
YOU SHOULD TAKE PART IN THE FIRST TROOP'S TRAINING...
W-WHA...
WHAT ARE Y-Y-YOU TWO DOING?!
YOU'RE MAKING A MISTAKE, VICE CAPTAIN!!
FWIP
GASP
OKITA SENSEI WAS TREATING MY WOUND.
WE WEREN'T DOING ANYTHING INDECENT!!

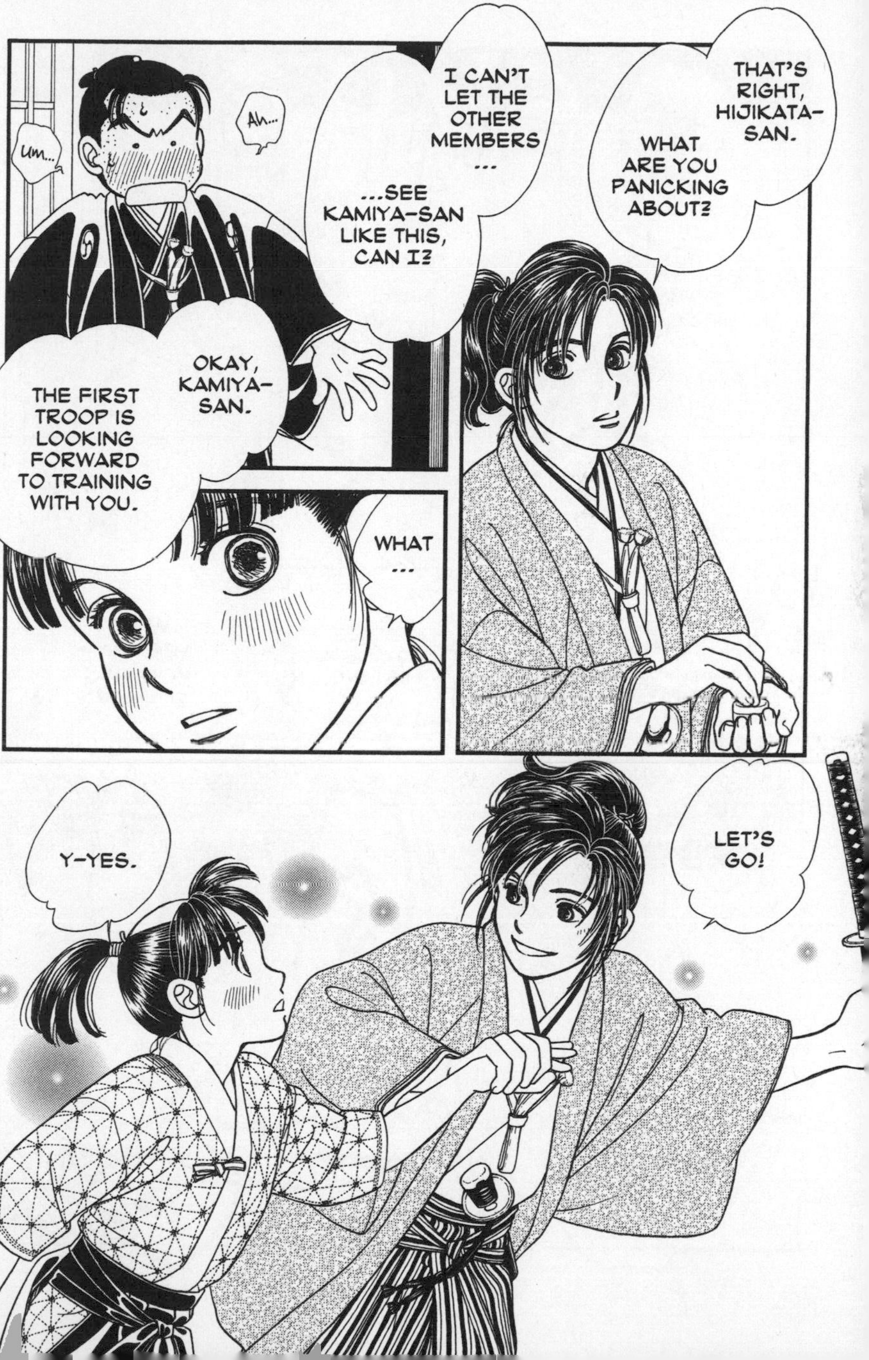
THAT'S RIGHT, HIJIKATA-SAN.
WHAT ARE YOU PANICKING ABOUT?
I CAN'T LET THE OTHER MEMBERS ...
...SEE KAMIYA-SAN LIKE THIS, CAN I?
Ah...
Um...
OKAY, KAMIYA-SAN.
THE FIRST TROOP IS LOOKING FORWARD TO TRAINING WITH YOU.
WHAT ...
LET'S GO!
Y-YES.

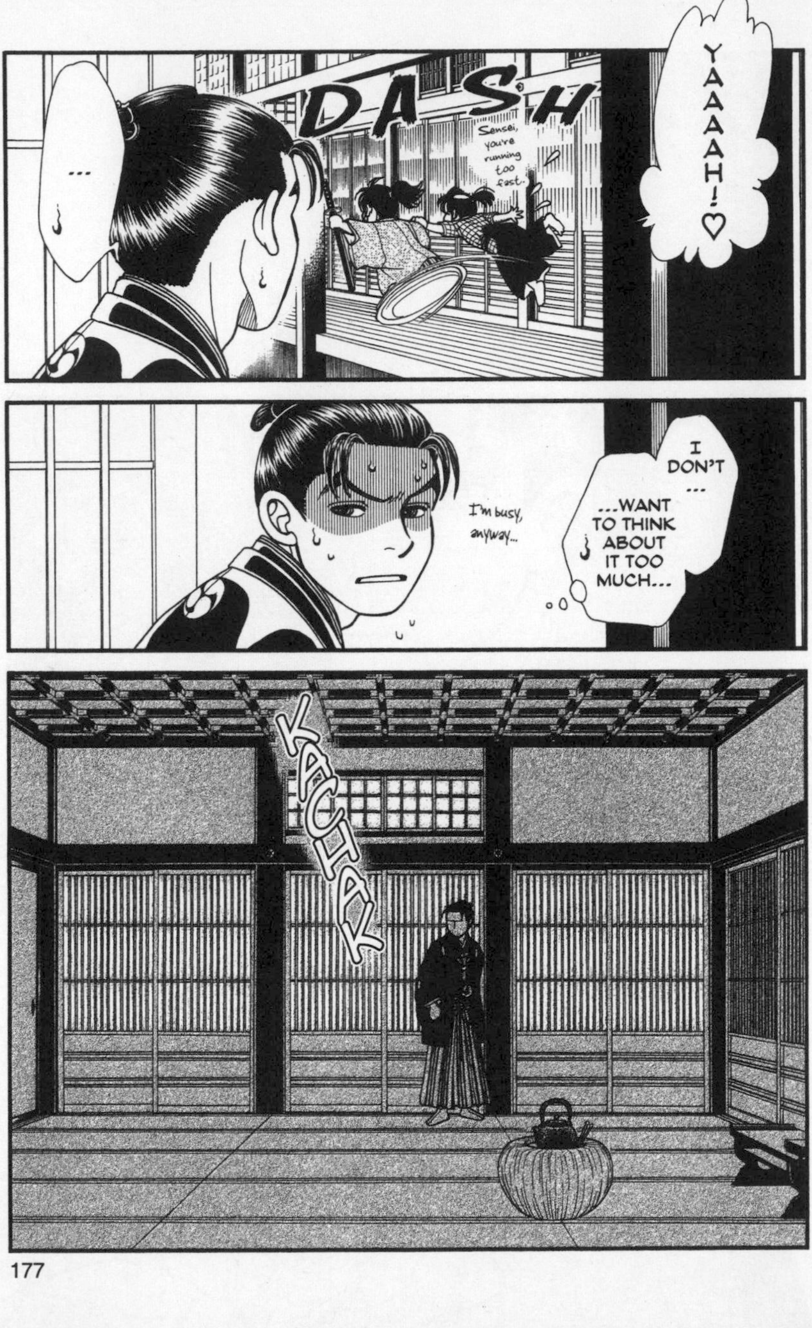
YAAAAH!♡
DASH
Sensei, you're running too fast.
...
I DON'T... ...WANT TO THINK ABOUT IT TOO MUCH...
I'm busy, anyway...
KACHAK

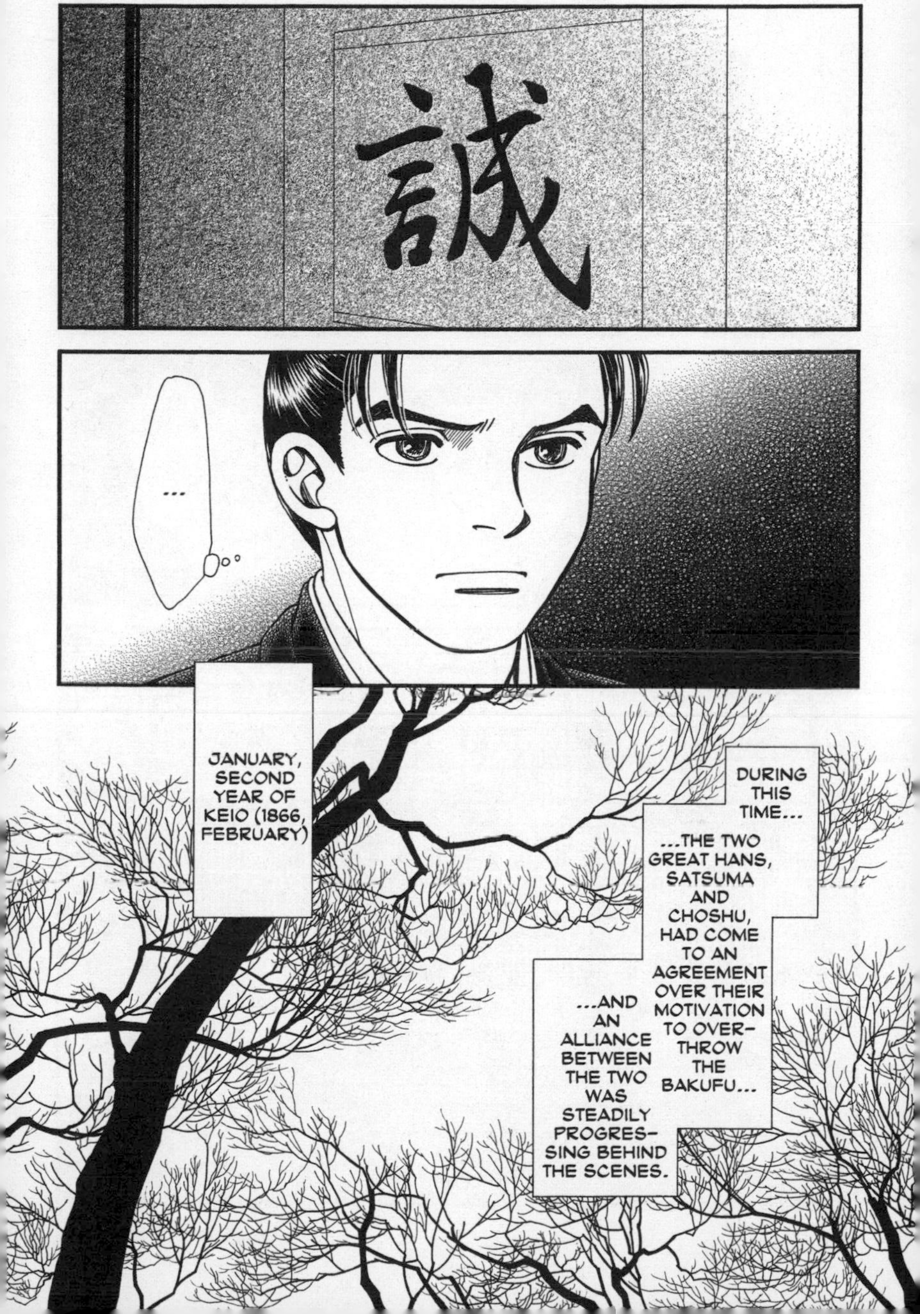
誠
...
JANUARY, SECOND YEAR OF KEIO (1866, FEBRUARY)
DURING THIS TIME...
...THE TWO GREAT HANS, SATSUMA AND CHOSHU, HAD COME TO AN AGREEMENT OVER THEIR MOTIVATION TO OVER-THROW THE BAKUFU...
...AND AN ALLIANCE BETWEEN THE TWO WAS STEADILY PROGRES-SING BEHIND THE SCENES.

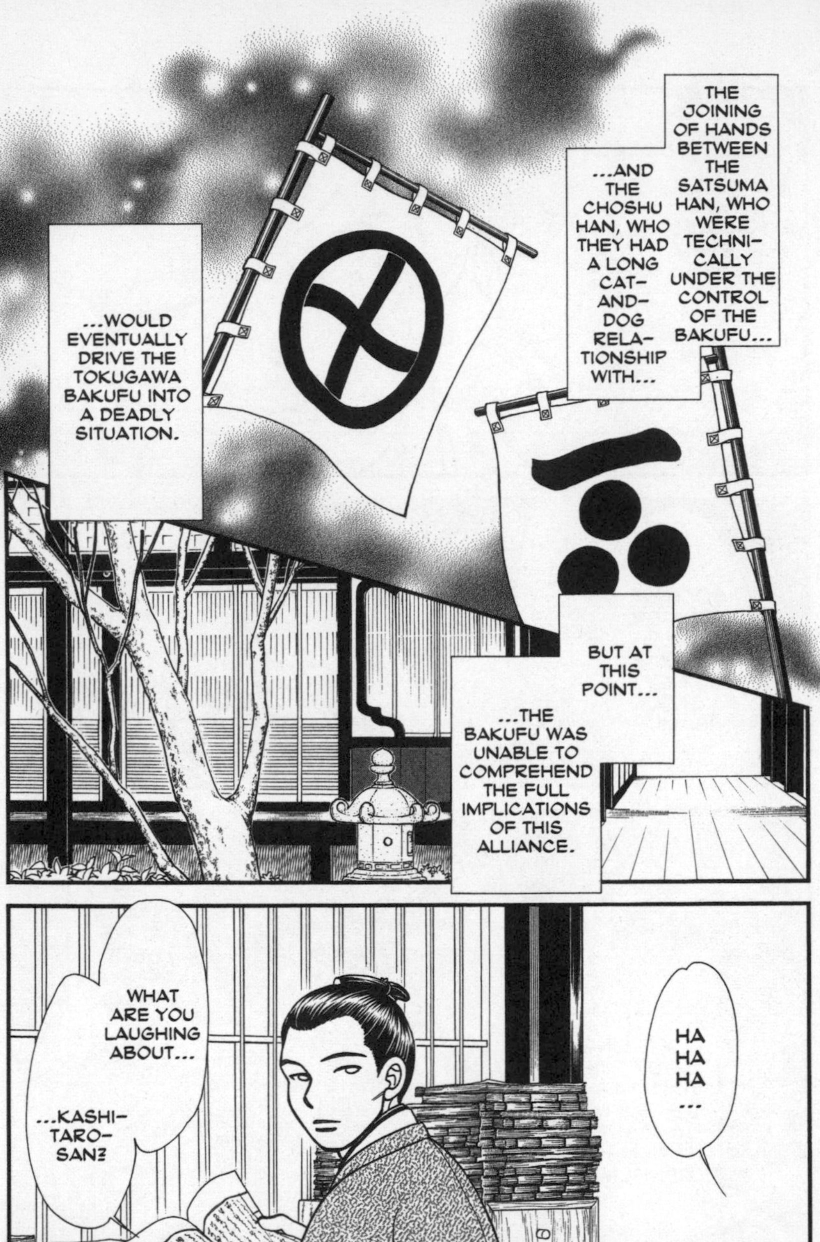
THE JOINING OF HANDS BETWEEN THE SATSUMA HAN, WHO WERE TECHNICALLY UNDER THE CONTROL OF THE BAKUFU...
...AND THE CHOSHU HAN, WHO THEY HAD A LONG CAT-AND-DOG RELATIONSHIP WITH...
...WOULD EVENTUALLY DRIVE THE TOKUGAWA BAKUFU INTO A DEADLY SITUATION.
BUT AT THIS POINT...
...THE BAKUFU WAS UNABLE TO COMPREHEND THE FULL IMPLICATIONS OF THIS ALLIANCE.
HA HA HA ...
WHAT ARE YOU LAUGHING ABOUT...
...KASHITARO-SAN?

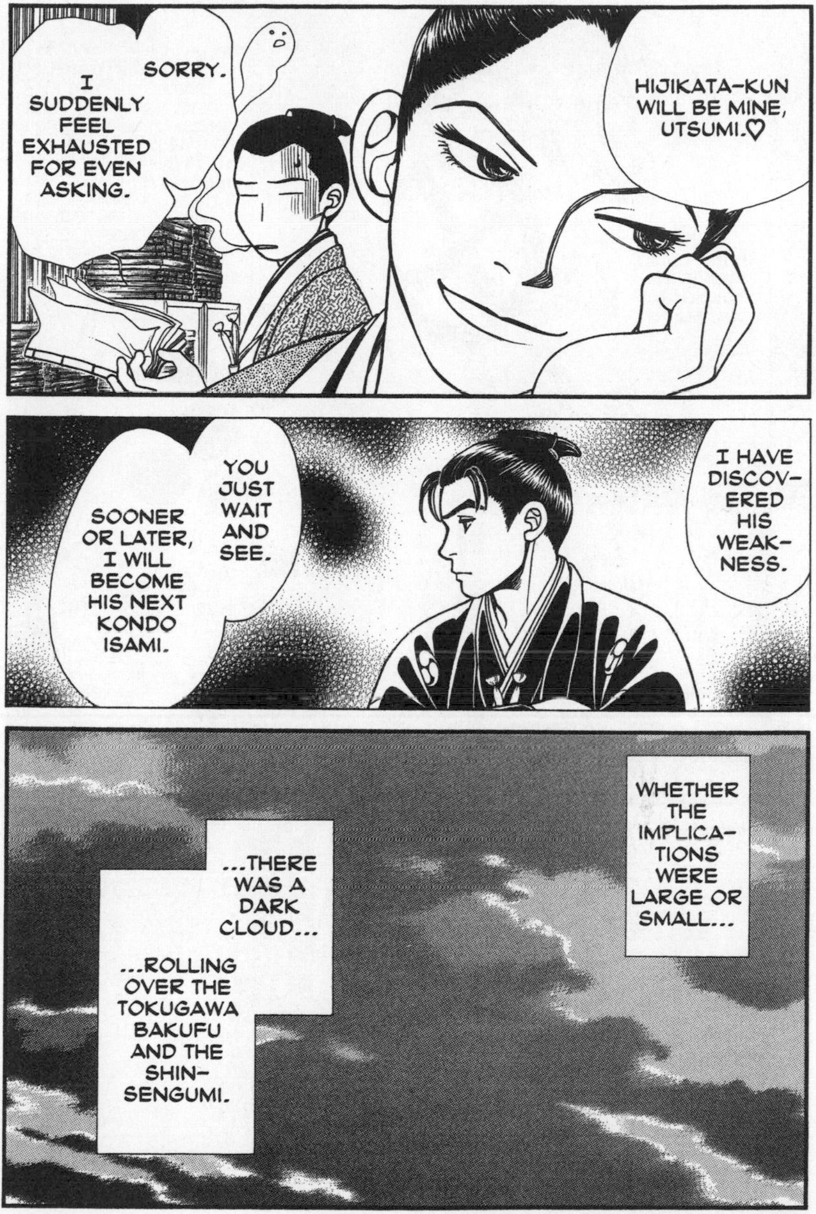
HIJIKATA-KUN WILL BE MINE, UTSUMI.♡
SORRY.
I SUDDENLY FEEL EXHAUSTED FOR EVEN ASKING.
I HAVE DISCOVERED HIS WEAKNESS.
YOU JUST WAIT AND SEE.
SOONER OR LATER, I WILL BECOME HIS NEXT KONDO ISAMI.
WHETHER THE IMPLICATIONS WERE LARGE OR SMALL...
...THERE WAS A DARK CLOUD...
...ROLLING OVER THE TOKUGAWA BAKUFU AND THE SHINSENGUMI.

TO BE CONTINUED!

TAEKO WATANABE PRESENTS

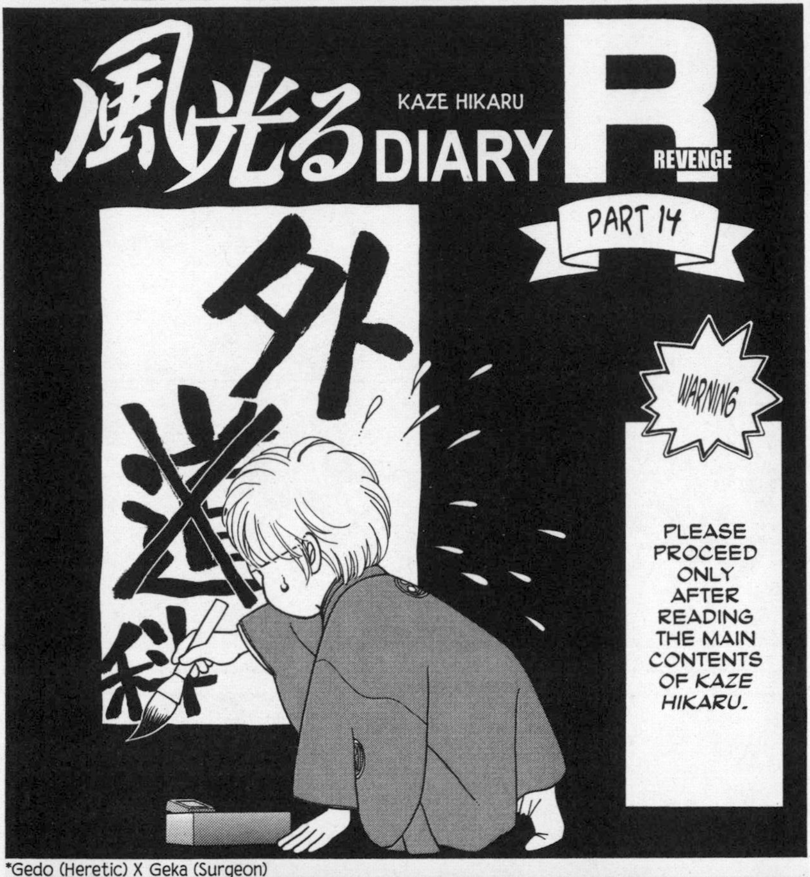
風光る
KAZE HIKARU
DIARY
R
REVENGE
PART 14
WARNING
PLEASE PROCEED ONLY AFTER READING THE MAIN CONTENTS OF *KAZE HIKARU*.

*Gedo (Heretic) X Geka (Surgeon)

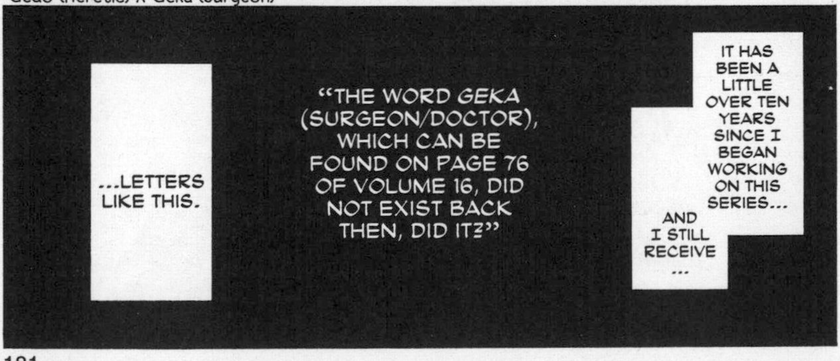
IT HAS BEEN A LITTLE OVER TEN YEARS SINCE I BEGAN WORKING ON THIS SERIES...
AND I STILL RECEIVE ...
"THE WORD *GEKA* (SURGEON/DOCTOR), WHICH CAN BE FOUND ON PAGE 76 OF VOLUME 16, DID NOT EXIST BACK THEN, DID IT?"
...LETTERS LIKE THIS.

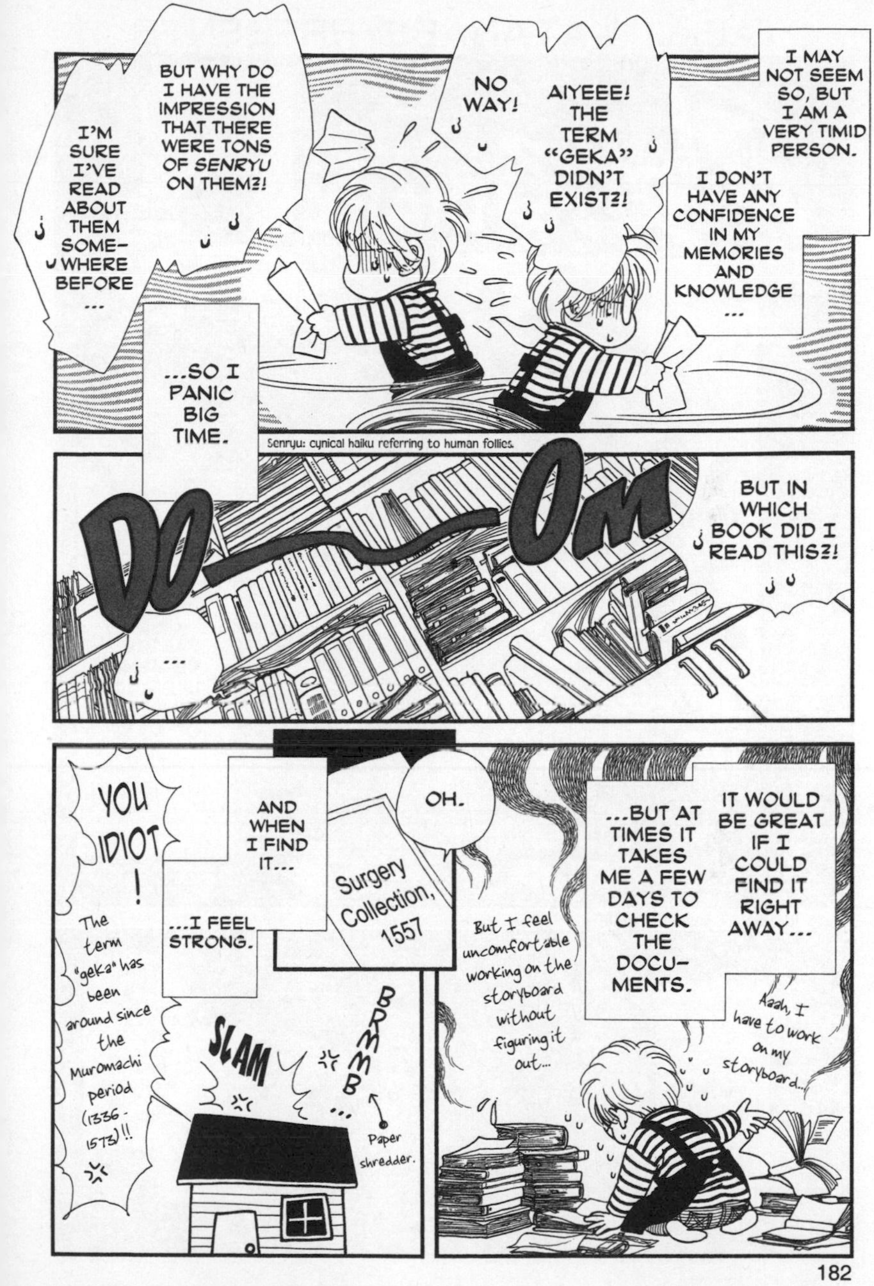
I MAY NOT SEEM SO, BUT I AM A VERY TIMID PERSON.
I DON'T HAVE ANY CONFIDENCE IN MY MEMORIES AND KNOWLEDGE...
AIYEEE! THE TERM "GEKA" DIDN'T EXIST?!
NO WAY!
BUT WHY DO I HAVE THE IMPRESSION THAT THERE WERE TONS OF *SENRYU* ON THEM?!
I'M SURE I'VE READ ABOUT THEM SOME-WHERE BEFORE...
...SO I PANIC BIG TIME.
Senryu: cynical haiku referring to human follies.
BUT IN WHICH BOOK DID I READ THIS?!
DO—OM
...
IT WOULD BE GREAT IF I COULD FIND IT RIGHT AWAY...
...BUT AT TIMES IT TAKES ME A FEW DAYS TO CHECK THE DOCU-MENTS.
Aaah, I have to work on my storyboard...
But I feel uncomfortable working on the storyboard without figuring it out...
OH.
Surgery Collection, 1557
AND WHEN I FIND IT...
...I FEEL STRONG.
BRMMB...
Paper shredder.
SLAM
YOU IDIOT!
The term "geka" has been around since the Muromachi period (1336-1573)!!

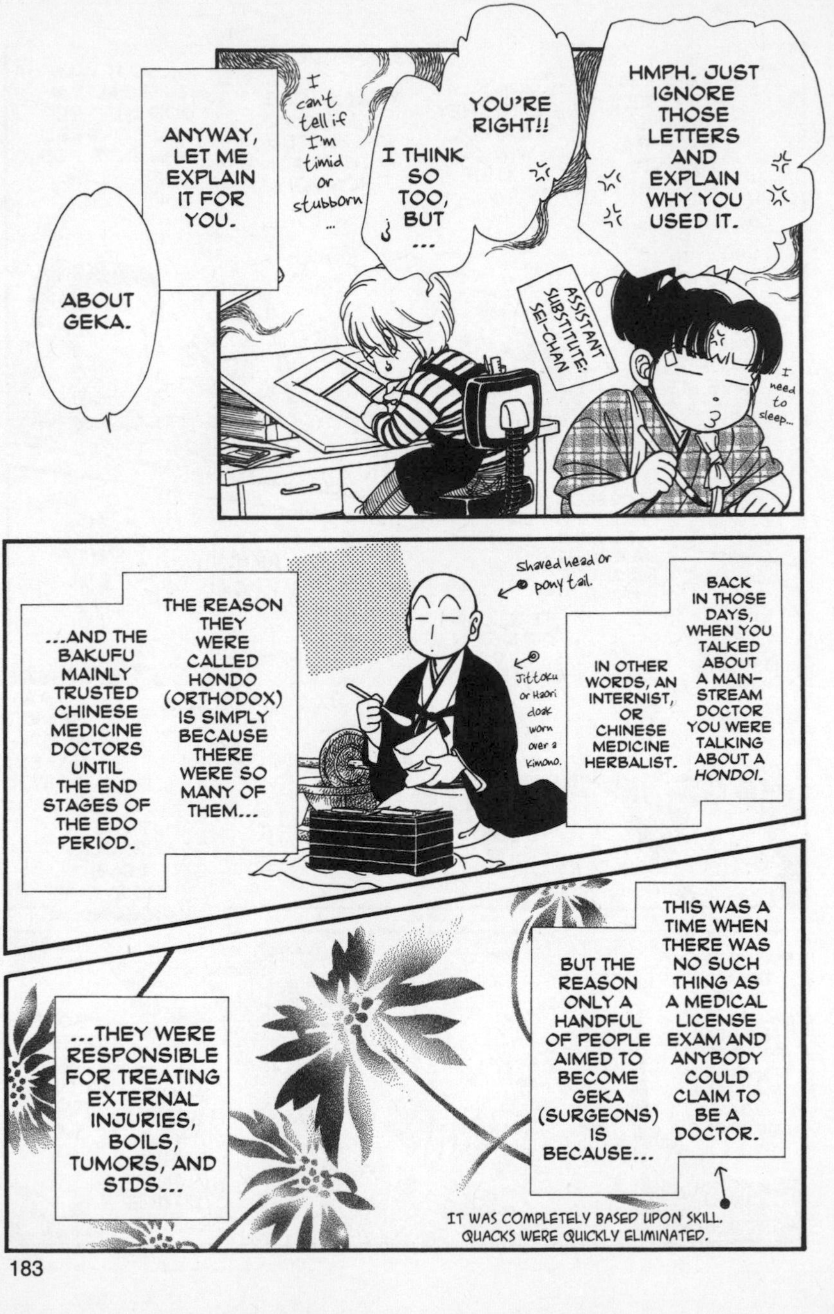
HMPH. JUST IGNORE THOSE LETTERS AND EXPLAIN WHY YOU USED IT.
I need to sleep...
ASSISTANT SUBSTITUTE: SEI-CHAN
YOU'RE RIGHT!!
I THINK SO TOO, BUT ...
I can't tell if I'm timid or stubborn ...
ANYWAY, LET ME EXPLAIN IT FOR YOU.
ABOUT GEKA.
BACK IN THOSE DAYS, WHEN YOU TALKED ABOUT A MAIN-STREAM DOCTOR YOU WERE TALKING ABOUT A *HONDOI.*
IN OTHER WORDS, AN INTERNIST, OR CHINESE MEDICINE HERBALIST.
Shaved head or pony tail.
Jittoku or Haori cloak worn over a kimono.
THE REASON THEY WERE CALLED HONDO (ORTHODOX) IS SIMPLY BECAUSE THERE WERE SO MANY OF THEM...
...AND THE BAKUFU MAINLY TRUSTED CHINESE MEDICINE DOCTORS UNTIL THE END STAGES OF THE EDO PERIOD.
THIS WAS A TIME WHEN THERE WAS NO SUCH THING AS A MEDICAL LICENSE EXAM AND ANYBODY COULD CLAIM TO BE A DOCTOR.
IT WAS COMPLETELY BASED UPON SKILL. QUACKS WERE QUICKLY ELIMINATED.
BUT THE REASON ONLY A HANDFUL OF PEOPLE AIMED TO BECOME GEKA (SURGEONS) IS BECAUSE...
...THEY WERE RESPONSIBLE FOR TREATING EXTERNAL INJURIES, BOILS, TUMORS, AND STDS...

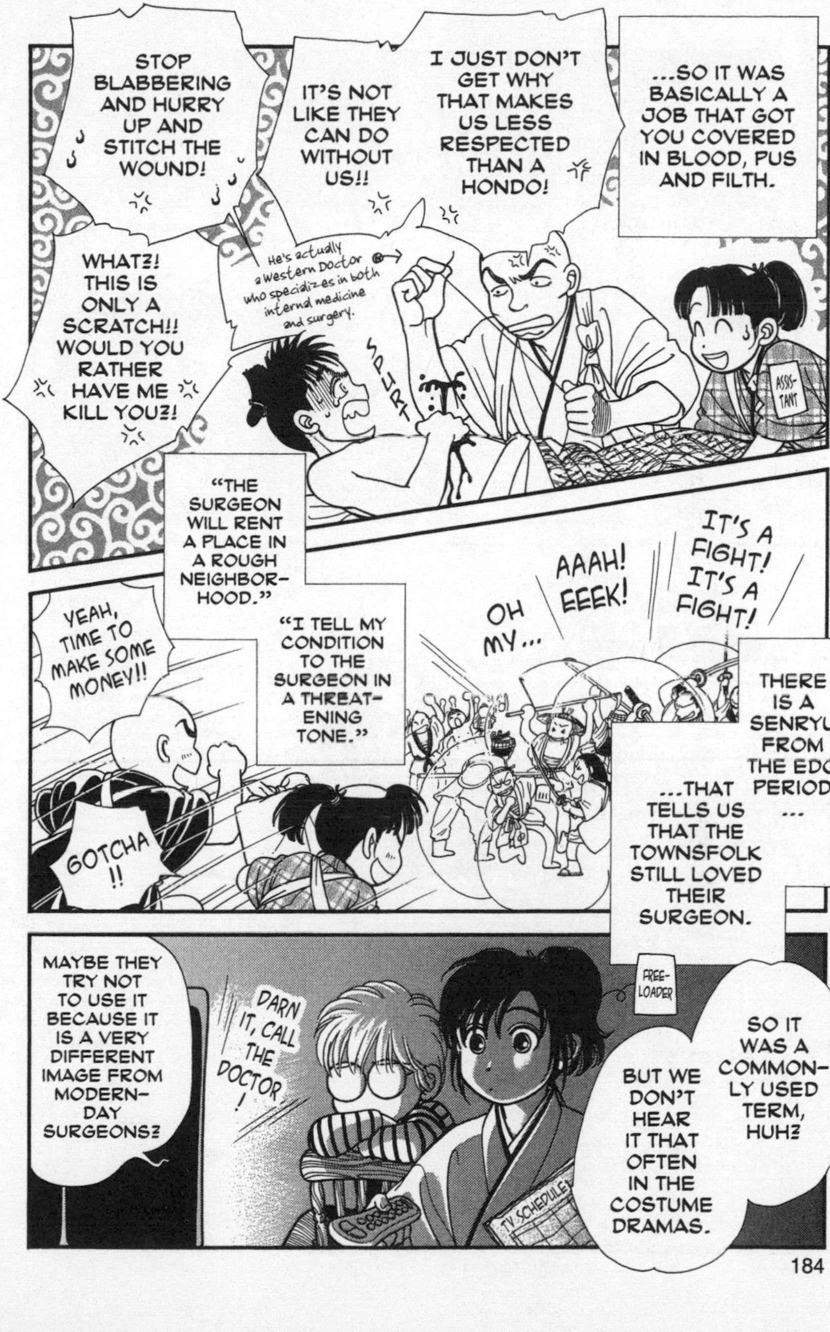
...SO IT WAS BASICALLY A JOB THAT GOT YOU COVERED IN BLOOD, PUS AND FILTH.
I JUST DON'T GET WHY THAT MAKES US LESS RESPECTED THAN A HONDO!
IT'S NOT LIKE THEY CAN DO WITHOUT US!!
STOP BLABBERING AND HURRY UP AND STITCH THE WOUND!
ASSISTANT
He's actually a Western Doctor who specializes in both internal medicine and surgery.
SPURT
WHAT?! THIS IS ONLY A SCRATCH!! WOULD YOU RATHER HAVE ME KILL YOU?!
THERE IS A SENRYU FROM THE EDO PERIOD...
...THAT TELLS US THAT THE TOWNSFOLK STILL LOVED THEIR SURGEON.
IT'S A FIGHT! IT'S A FIGHT!
AAAH! EEEK!
OH MY...
"THE SURGEON WILL RENT A PLACE IN A ROUGH NEIGHBORHOOD."
"I TELL MY CONDITION TO THE SURGEON IN A THREATENING TONE."
YEAH, TIME TO MAKE SOME MONEY!!
GOTCHA!!
SO IT WAS A COMMONLY USED TERM, HUH?
BUT WE DON'T HEAR IT THAT OFTEN IN THE COSTUME DRAMAS.
FREE-LOADER
T.V. SCHEDULE
DARN IT, CALL THE DOCTOR!
MAYBE THEY TRY NOT TO USE IT BECAUSE IT IS A VERY DIFFERENT IMAGE FROM MODERN-DAY SURGEONS?

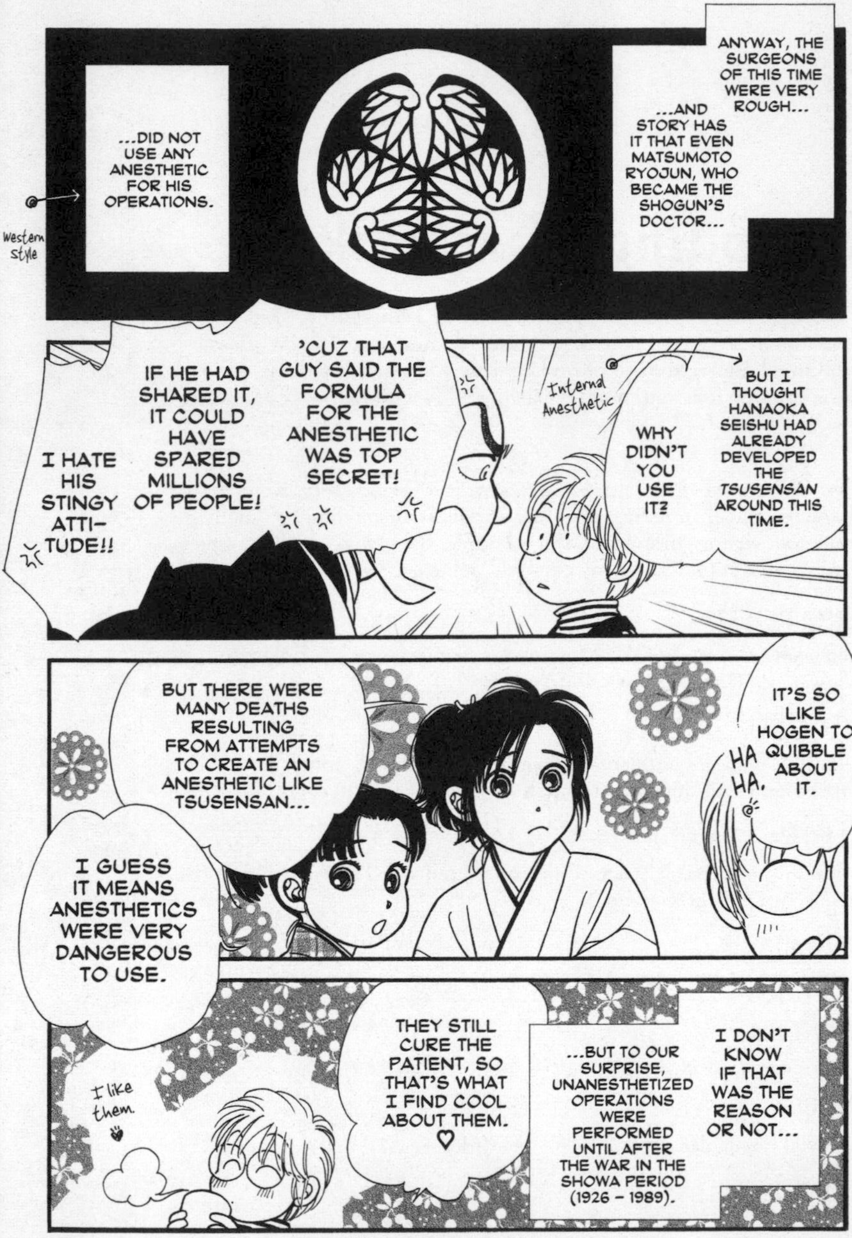
ANYWAY, THE SURGEONS OF THIS TIME WERE VERY ROUGH...
...AND STORY HAS IT THAT EVEN MATSUMOTO RYOJUN, WHO BECAME THE SHOGUN'S DOCTOR...
...DID NOT USE ANY ANESTHETIC FOR HIS OPERATIONS.
Western style
BUT I THOUGHT HANAOKA SEISHU HAD ALREADY DEVELOPED THE *TSUSENSAN* AROUND THIS TIME.
Internal Anesthetic
WHY DIDN'T YOU USE IT?
'CUZ THAT GUY SAID THE FORMULA FOR THE ANESTHETIC WAS TOP SECRET!
IF HE HAD SHARED IT, IT COULD HAVE SPARED MILLIONS OF PEOPLE!
I HATE HIS STINGY ATTI-TUDE!!
IT'S SO LIKE HOGEN TO QUIBBLE ABOUT IT.
HA HA.
BUT THERE WERE MANY DEATHS RESULTING FROM ATTEMPTS TO CREATE AN ANESTHETIC LIKE TSUSENSAN...
I GUESS IT MEANS ANESTHETICS WERE VERY DANGEROUS TO USE.
I DON'T KNOW IF THAT WAS THE REASON OR NOT...
...BUT TO OUR SURPRISE, UNANESTHETIZED OPERATIONS WERE PERFORMED UNTIL AFTER THE WAR IN THE SHOWA PERIOD (1926 - 1989).
THEY STILL CURE THE PATIENT, SO THAT'S WHAT I FIND COOL ABOUT THEM. ♡
I like them.

Decoding Kaze Hikaru

Kaze Hikaru is a historical drama based in 19th century Japan and thus contains some fairly mystifying terminology. In this glossary we'll break down archaic phrases, terms and other linguistic curiosities for you so that you can move through life with the smug assurance that you are indeed a know-it-all.

First and foremost, because *Kaze Hikaru* is a period story, we kept all character names in their traditional Japanese form—that is, family name followed by first name. For example, the character Okita Soji's family name is Okita and his personal name is Soji.

AKO-ROSHI:
The *ronin* (samurai) of Ako; featured in the immortal Kabuki play *Chushingura* (Loyalty), aka *47 Samurai*.

BAKUFU:
Literally, "tent government." Shogunate; the feudal, military government that dominated Japan for more than 200 years.

BUSHI:
A samurai or warrior (part of the compound word *bushido*, which means "way of the warrior").

CHAN:
A diminutive suffix that conveys endearment.

DONO:
An honorific suffix that implies "Lord" or "Master."

HAN:
A feudal domain of Japan during the Edo period.

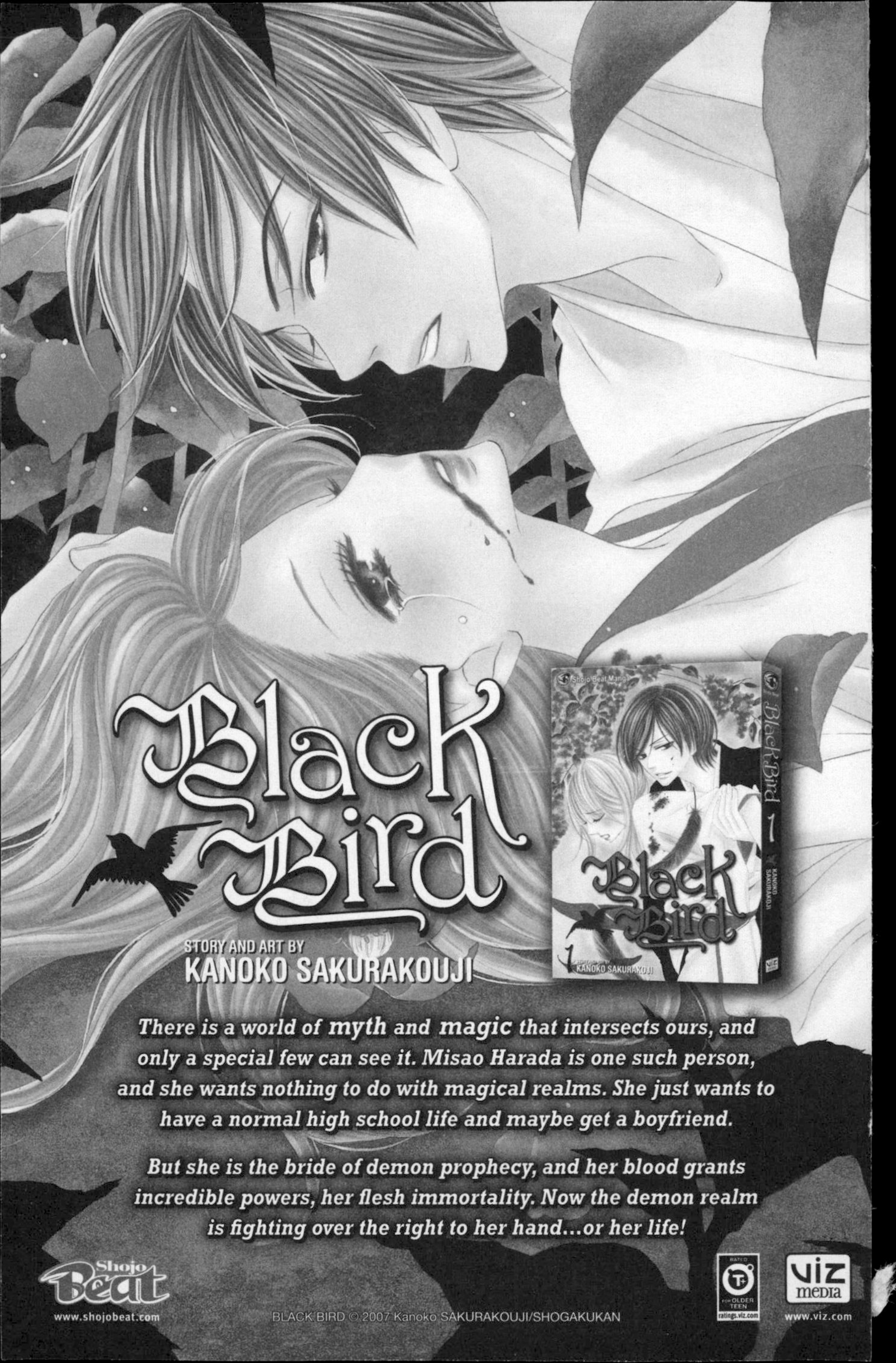
Black Bird
STORY AND ART BY
KANOKO SAKURAKOUJI
Shojo Beat Manga
Black Bird
1
KANOKO SAKURAKOUJI
There is a world of myth and magic that intersects ours, and only a special few can see it. Misao Harada is one such person, and she wants nothing to do with magical realms. She just wants to have a normal high school life and maybe get a boyfriend.
But she is the bride of demon prophecy, and her blood grants incredible powers, her flesh immortality. Now the demon realm is fighting over the right to her hand...or her life!
Shojo Beat
www.shojobeat.com
BLACK BIRD © 2007 Kanoko SAKURAKOUJI/SHOGAKUKAN
RATED T+ FOR OLDER TEEN
ratings.viz.com
VIZ media
www.viz.com

SURPRISE!

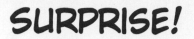

You may be reading the wrong way!

It's true: In keeping with the original Japanese comic format, this book reads from right to left—so action, sound effects, and word balloons are completely reversed. This preserves the orientation of the original artwork—plus, it's fun! Check out the diagram shown here to get the hang of things, and then turn to the other side of the book to get started!

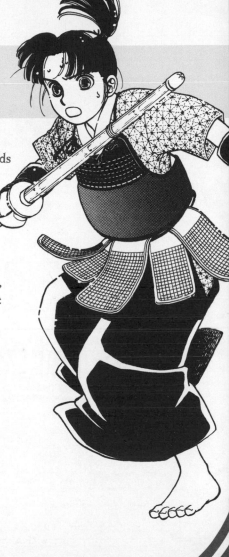

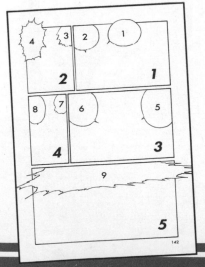

-HAN:

The same as the honorific -*san*, pronounced in the dialect of southern Japan.

KENDO:

A Japanese fencing sport that uses bamboo swords.

-KUN:

An honorific suffix that indicates a difference in rank and title. The use of -*kun* is also a way of indicating familiarity and friendliness between students or compatriots.

MIBU-ROSHI:

A group of warriors that supports the Bakufu.

MON:

The smallest unit of currency at the time; 4,000 *mon* equaled one *ryo*.

ONE'E-CHAN or NE'E-CHAN: "Sister" or "Lady." This is a familiar way of addressing a female.

ONI'I-CHAN or NI'I-CHAN: "Brother" or "Mister." This is a familiar way of addressing a male.

ONI:

Literally "ogre," this is Sei's nickname for Vice Captain Hijikata.

RANPO:

Medical science derived from the Dutch.

RONIN:

Masterless samurai.

RYO:

At the time, one *ryo* and two *bu* (four *bu* equaled roughly one *ryo*) were enough currency to support a family of five for an entire month.

-SAMA:

An honorific suffix used for one of higher rank; a more respectful version of *-san*.

-SAN:

An honorific suffix that carries the meaning of "Mr." or "Ms."

SENSEI:

A teacher, master or instructor.

SEPPUKU:

A ritualistic suicide that was considered a privilege of the nobility and samurai elite.

SHINAI:

The bamboo rod used to represent a sword in the practice of *kendo*.

SONJO-HA:

Those loyal to the emperor and dedicated to the expulsion of foreigners from the country.

TEN'NEN RISHIN-RYU:

The school of martial art practiced by members of the Shinsengumi.

TOKUGAWA BAKUFU:

The last feudal military government of Japan's pre-modern period, directed by hereditary leaders—shoguns—of the Tokugawa clan.

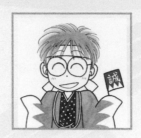

Part three of the secret theme. I'm sure this time there are those who are slapping their knees, saying, "Aah, now I get it!"... Right? Anyway, the seasonal phrase for this volume is the Milky Way... But am I the only one who feels like that's a summer phrase?

It's probably because I'm thinking of the Tanabata Festival. But July 7 in the old calendar was considered part of autumn, so Tanabata is actually a seasonal word for autumn. I was born and grew up in Tokyo, and when I saw a sky full of stars in Canada twenty years ago, I asked the stupidest question: "How come that part of the sky has a lighter color?" I remember being deeply moved after hearing that it was the Milky Way. "Wow, it really does look like someone spilled milk in the sky!" But I've never had an opportunity to see the Milky Way since then. So I at least want these two to enjoy it.

Taeko Watanabe debuted as a manga artist in 1979 with her story *Waka-chan no Netsuai Jidai* (Love Struck Days of Waka). *Kaze Hikaru* is her longest-running series, but she has created a number of other popular series. Watanabe is a two-time winner of the prestigious Shogakukan Manga Award in the girls' category—her manga *Hajime-chan ga Ichiban!* (Hajime-chan Is Number One!) claimed the award in 1991, and *Kaze Hikaru* took it in 2003.

Watanabe read hundreds of historical sources to create *Kaze Hikaru*. She is from Tokyo.

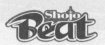

KAZE HIKARU
VOL. 23
Shojo Beat Edition

STORY AND ART BY
TAEKO WATANABE

KAZE HIKARU Vol. 23
by Taeko WATANABE
© 1997 Taeko WATANABE
All rights reserved.
Original Japanese edition published by SHOGAKUKAN.
English translation rights in the United States of America and Canada arranged with
SHOGAKUKAN.

Translation & English Adaptation/Tetsuichiro Miyaki
Touch-up Art & Lettering/Rina Mapa
Design/Veronica Casson
Editor/Megan Bates

Printed in the U.S.A.

Published by VIZ Media, LLC
P.O. Box 77010
San Francisco, CA 94107

10 9 8 7 6 5 4 3 2 1
First printing, August 2015

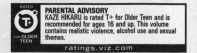

www.viz.com

www.shojobeat.com